The Suicidal State

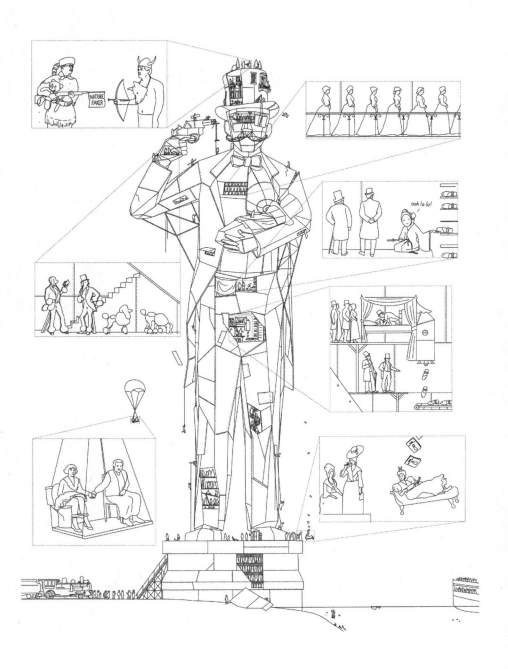

The Suicidal State

*Race Suicide, Biopower, and the
Sexuality of Population*

MADOKA KISHI

OXFORD
UNIVERSITY PRESS

Oxford University Press is a department of the University of Oxford. It furthers the University's objective of excellence in research, scholarship, and education by publishing worldwide. Oxford is a registered trade mark of Oxford University Press in the UK and in certain other countries.

Published in the United States of America by Oxford University Press
198 Madison Avenue, New York, NY 10016, United States of America.

© Oxford University Press 2024

All rights reserved. No part of this publication may be reproduced, stored in a retrieval system, or transmitted, in any form or by any means, without the prior permission in writing of Oxford University Press, or as expressly permitted by law, by license or under terms agreed with the appropriate reprographics rights organization. Inquiries concerning reproduction outside the scope of the above should be sent to the Rights Department, Oxford University Press, at the address above.

You must not circulate this work in any other form
and you must impose this same condition on any acquirer

Library of Congress Cataloging-in-Publication Data
Names: Kishi, Madoka, author.
Title: The suicidal state : race suicide, biopower, and the sexuality of population / Madoka Kishi.
Description: New York, NY : Oxford University Press, [2024] | Includes bibliographical references and index.
Identifiers: LCCN 2024017966 (print) | LCCN 2024017967 (ebook) | ISBN 9780197690079 (hardback) | ISBN 9780197690093 (epub)
Subjects: LCSH: American literature—19th century—History and criticism. | American literature—20th century—History and criticism. | Race in literature. | Population in literature. | Sex in literature. | Suicide in literature. | Biopolitics in literature.
Classification: LCC PN56.R16 K57 2024 (print) | LCC PN56.R16 (ebook) | DDC 810.9/352996073—dc23/eng/20240629
LC record available at https://lccn.loc.gov/2024017966
LC ebook record available at https://lccn.loc.gov/2024017967

DOI: 10.1093/9780197690109.001.0001

Printed by Integrated Books International, United States of America

Frontispiece by Adam Douglas Thompson.

For Benjy, my everything

Contents

Introduction	1
1. Sacrificial Ecstasy: *The Bostonians*, Neurasthenia, and the "Obscure Hurt"	41
2. Flirting with Death: *The Awakening*'s Liberal Erotic Economy and the Consuming Desire of New Women	69
3. The Spectral Lineage: Jack London, Teutonism, and Interspecies Kinship	98
4. Gertrude Stein's Melting Pot: Jewishness and the Excretory Pleasure of *The Making of Americans*	129
Coda: Hindsight 20/20, or Asiatic Im-Personality	161
Acknowledgments	183
Notes	189
Bibliography	225
Index	243

Introduction

The Race That Kills Itself

Paul's case has been closed too soon. Not that we don't know the cause of his death; it was a clear case of suicide. The young dandy in Willa Cather's 1905 short story threw himself in front of a fast-approaching locomotive after his nine-day stay at the Waldorf-Astoria. The extravagant sojourn was paid for with funds that he stole from his workplace in Pittsburgh. But this case of theft has been resolved as well. As Paul learns from the newspaper, his father refunded the full amount to the company, rushing to New York to bring him back to Cordelia Street. So Paul leaps, in order to flee from "the flavourless, colourless mass of every-day existence" on Cordelia Street, escaping into the lavishly illumed "blue of Adriatic water, the yellow of Algerian sands" that flash through his brain as his body floats in the air.[1] Much like Fred Herko's self-defenestration performed to Mozart's "Coronation Mass in C Major"— the grand jeté that José Esteban Muñoz calls a "death art"—Paul's fatal jump marks the culminative performance of his queer excess.[2] For Paul is, without a doubt, extra: his infatuation with theater, his "hysterically defiant manner," his constant lies, his flamboyant attire, and that "scandalous red carnation" in his buttonhole.[3] Every symptom of his deviance is, in turn, anchored by the abundance of physiological signs—his delicate frame, his "white, blue-veined face," his "abnormally large" pupils with "a glassy glitter," his ever-nervously twitching lips and eyebrows, his trembling fingers—marking him as a clinical case of some sort, even though nobody knows what exactly those signs signify.[4] Perhaps it is a case of degeneration, that mysterious fin-de-siècle epidemic that scandalized the United States, especially after the publication of Max Nordau's eponymous book (which Cather vehemently hated).[5] Even though this catchall diagnosis—for enervation, nervous disorder, and sexual perversion—does not offer much of an insight, it should still relieve those who knew Paul from the hermeneutic burden that his singularity imposes. The news of his self-inflicted death would only gild the lily, prompting them to repeat their original conclusion with a shrug or two: "Paul's was a bad case."[6]

The Suicidal State. Madoka Kishi, Oxford University Press. © Oxford University Press 2024.
DOI: 10.1093/9780197690109.003.0001

2   THE SUICIDAL STATE

Such is the normalizing impulse inherent in the logic of the case, according to Lauren Berlant. The case secures the biopolitical order by "folding the singular into the general": it manages singularities by transforming them into exemplars, incorporating them into a statistical entity called the population.[7] As Paul becomes a "case," he is enmeshed into "the immense design of things," the abstracted pattern of regularity and probability that structures the life of the population.[8]

But I would like to hold open Paul's case for the moment, not so much to retrieve Paul's singularity per se as to linger on the affordances of its very exemplarity as a case of suicide. That is, to consider what his self-inflicted death exemplifies in the biopolitical order of things, and what kind of generality and collectivity his solitary death would engender. For one, the duality of criminality and clinicality of Paul's "case" marks the discursive confluence of suicide itself at the turn of the twentieth -century. As we will discuss later, the decades known as the Progressive Era were a transfer point in which the definition of suicide, once known as *felo de se* ("felon of him- or herself") and understood as self-murder, came fully under the domain of medicine and psychiatry. Further, "Paul's Case" is exemplary in that it furnishes one of numerous cases of literary suicide during the period, both enacted and attempted. Hyacinth Robinson in *Princess Casamassima* (1886) shoots himself; Cho-Cho-San in "Madame Butterfly" (1898) cuts her throat; Dave in Charles Chesnutt's "Dave's Neckliss" (1899) hangs himself; both Edna Pontellier in *The Awakening* (1899) and the eponymous hero of *Martin Eden* (1909) drown themselves in the ocean; George Hurstwood in *Sister Carrie* (1900) and Godfrey St. Peter in *The Professor's House* (1925) asphyxiate themselves by gas (though only the former follows through); Lily Bart in *The House of Mirth* (1905) overdoses most likely on purpose; Marion Lenoir in *The Clansman* (1905) jumps off a cliff; and David Hersland in *The Making of Americans* (1925) starves himself to death. These mounting cases suggest that it is time for a new investigation, one that suggests a consideration of not individual but mass suicide, and even the nature of the possible criminality of their deaths; for these suicidal figures constitute no ordinary criminals in the eyes of the power that established its dominion over life—the one that Michel Foucault called biopower.

Suicide confounds and frustrates biopower. In contrast to its sovereign predecessor, which wields the "right to take life or let live," biopower is said to manifest its power through "the right to make live and to let die."[9] That is, the alleged aim of biopower is to "make live," to manage, optimize, and secure

INTRODUCTION   3

the life of the population, sometimes by systemic neglect, or "letting die" a part deemed deleterious to the collective life. Crucially, then, as Foucault notes in an underattended passage of *The History of Sexuality Vol. 1*, death foments anxiety for biopower: it marks "the moment when the individual escapes all power."[10] Suicide is, Foucault further notes, the most scandalous of all deaths for biopower, because the individual's determination to kill oneself "testifie[s] to the individual and private right to die."[11] Suicide thus became "one of the first astonishments of a society in which political power had assigned itself the task of administering life."[12]

Epitomized by the rise of Taylorism, domestic sciences, and eugenics, the Progressive Era embodies the managerial ethos of biopower through and through, conceptualizing human life as reproducible and optimizable.[13] As such, the Progressive Era brims also with biopower's anxiety over self-inflicted death. Turn-of-the-century newspapers extensively covered suicides on a near-daily basis, and the nationwide increase of suicide was cyclically reported with detailed statistics. An 1886 article feverishly noted in a tone of alarm: "Suicide, or self-murder is becoming an event of startling frequency in our country. At no time since the people came to these valleys has there been so many suicides in proportion to the population as of late."[14] *The Saint Paul Daily Globe* reported in 1895 that "in the last five years the number of suicides had more than doubled, which is out of all proportion to the gain in population."[15] Such an uptick did not stop with the dawn of the new century, as reported in 1904: "The last few years shows a marvelous increase. There were only about one-third as many cases of self-destruction in 1891 as in 1903."[16] The beginning of the following decade saw this increase continue at an unprecedented rate, leading a reporter to conclude: "Suicides are, indeed, becoming so common that they no longer startle."[17]

These suicides' refusal of life would make them kin to those who were designated as "criminal[s] against the race" by Theodore Roosevelt, one of the most infamous icons of Progressivism. They are liable for, or at least complicit in, what Roosevelt saw as the gravest problem that the nation faces: namely, "race suicide, complete or partial."[18] *Race suicide*, the quirky trope Roosevelt favored and deployed repeatedly in his writings and speeches, gained wide currency amidst the shifting racial landscape of the turn-of-the-century United States. Not that Roosevelt was much concerned with the rising suicide rate in the country itself, nor with the self-inflicted deaths of literary figures (though, as we will see in Chapter 3, Roosevelt was no stranger to weighing in on literary controversies). Rather, the phenomenon that vexed

4   THE SUICIDAL STATE

him was the dropping birthrate of so-called "old-stock" Americans: native-born whites with Anglo-Saxon (or other northern European) origins. In Roosevelt's imaginary, independent-minded New Women and pleasure-loving dandies increasingly eschewed procreation in their egoistic pursuit of self-interest. Their apathy toward the collective survival and the preservation of the white race were, so to speak, suicidal: "The man or woman who deliberately avoids marriage, and has a heart so cold as to know no passion and a brain so shallow and selfish as to dislike having children, is in effect a criminal against the race, and should be an object of contemptuous abhorrence by all healthy people."[19]

The term *race suicide* became wildly popular as Roosevelt repeatedly used it to support his pro-natal agenda.[20] The phrase itself, though, was originally coined by Edward Alsworth Ross, one of the founders of American sociology and an ardent advocate of restrictions against the entry of the so-called "new immigrants." In "The Causes of Race Superiority" (1901), Ross refurbished Francis Amasa Walker's argument published ten years earlier, which had connected the fertility decline of native-born Americans to the rapidly increasing immigrants and their offspring.[21] Yet Ross's poetic genius was to recast old-stock Americans' waning reproductive capacity as a sign of their self-restraint, or even of their stoic self-relinquishment—in other words, the ultimate sign of their self-governing subjectivities. Native-born white Americans were being outbred, Ross argues, by races capable of "multiply[ing] on a lower [economic] plane"; for the old-stock Americans' proud racial traits of self-reliance and self-denial "overrule[d] [their] strongest instincts."[22] Refusing to beget offspring in erratic economic conditions, it seems, old-stock Americans preferred to choose the path to extinction. Ross ventures: "For a case like this I can find no words so apt as 'race suicide.' There is no bloodshed, no violence, no assault of the race that waxes upon the race that wanes. The higher race quietly and unmurmuringly eliminates itself."[23]

Ross's uncanny lyricism, which prematurely mourned the passing of the white race, rendered race suicide the shibboleth of Progressive Era nativism. The specter of the noble race killing itself made frequent appearances in newspapers and journals throughout the Progressive Era, finding its apotheosis in Madison Grant's white supremacist gospel, *The Passing of the Great Race* (1916).[24] The apocalyptic scenario, of course, did not materialize. Old-stock Americans did not die out, and the concept of race suicide has largely sunk beneath our contemporary critical radar, though one can scarcely

INTRODUCTION 5

encounter a book of period American studies that does not flickeringly mention it as a ludicrous signifier of Progressive Era racial hysteria.

Absurd as its extinction narrative is, I argue, the compelling metaphoricity of the phrase *race suicide*—italicized henceforth when referring to figuration, rather than discourse—offers a rich field for investigating how the concept of race was materialized in relation to self-inflicted death. To belabor the obvious, a race cannot literally commit suicide. If we were to follow the definitional lights of another fin-de-siècle sociologist, Émile Durkheim, suicide constitutes a *"case of death resulting directly or indirectly from a positive or negative act, carried out by the victim himself, which he was aware would produce this result."*[25] A race cannot knowingly and voluntarily kill itself, since "it" neither knows itself nor has the agency to terminate "its" life. Put simply, under the elegiac cadence of the term *race suicide*, the collectivity of the concept of race jarringly annexes the singularity of a suicidal individual—an individual, say, like Paul, who wastes his precious whiteness in his fatal jump, enacting his "loathing of respectable beds" and short-circuiting the heteronormative telos of reproduction.[26] Like a fractal in which each part represents the structure of the whole, the literary suicides under examination in this book synecdochically embody the race that kills itself in miniature.

The Suicidal State theorizes and historicizes the jointure between the national discourse of race suicide and the literary craze for individual suicide. In so doing, my project seeks to understand the rhetoric of *race suicide* as marking the tropological fusion between the individual and the collective body, suturing two distant poles of biopower: an *"anatomo-politics of the human body"* that disciplines the individual body and a *"biopolitics of the population"* that massifies individual bodies into a statistical entity to be calculated, monitored, and regulated.[27] In particular, this book sees self-inflicted death, both in the figuration of *race suicide* and in literary suicides, as colliding with the node forged between social and individual bodies, thereby offering a fertile space for reconceptualizing biopower.

In so doing, *The Suicidal State* argues that race suicide provides a powerful heuristic for understanding the amalgamation of race, sexuality, and the social body—in short, the population. As we will see in the following sections, the figuration of the race that kills itself stands as the prototypical example of biopolitical rhetoric in at least the following four senses. First, deploying the image of the dying social body, the figuration of *race suicide* mournfully animated a "race"—specifically, the old-stock American. To use Judith Butler's phrasing, "grievability is a condition of a life's emergence

6 THE SUICIDAL STATE

and sustenance": "Precisely because a living being may die, it is necessary to care for that being so that it may live. Only under conditions in which the loss would matter does the value of the life appear."[28] In the figuration of *race suicide*, the "race" attains the height of liveliness, enlivened through images of death. It constitutes a precarious subjecthood whose potential loss of life should be grieved and therefore must be prevented. Second, the creation of the "race" as the eminently grievable is, as Butler further argues, predicated on the production of "others whose loss is no loss, and who remain ungrievable."[29] The discourse of race suicide thus orchestrated the schemes by which the grievable would survive the ungrievable: the successive enactments of immigration restrictions starting with the 1875 Page Law and culminating in the Johnson-Reed Act of 1924, the intensification of lynching against the backdrop of Jim Crow's codification, the coerced assimilation policies against Native Americans, and the state-sanctioned involuntary sterilization of the "unfit" deemed constitutional by *Buck v. Bell* in 1927. These white supremacist and eugenicist politics were legitimized by a necropolitical dictum: "Eradicate the sub-race; or *you* shall die."

Third, though coming into being in the age when biologized race began to gain discursive dominance, the discourse of race suicide availed itself of the mutability of the term *race*. While race suicide specifically referred to the dropping birthrate of a certain racial group, namely, old-stock white Americans, in effect it became the problem of "the race," whose proliferation was equated with the life of the nation. Thus, the bodies of old-stock Americans were amassed and regimented by the state as *the* social body. Fourth, by designating old-stock Americans who refused to breed self-murderers of the social body, the discourse of race suicide reinforced the chiasmic relation between race and sex. While it forged and materialized race as something that could be reproduced only through procreative sex, it calcified procreative sex as essential for the survival of "the race," strengthening disciplinary control over the bodies of old-stock Americans. In so doing, the rhetoric of race suicide fused the individual life into the life of "the race," so much so that the two are indistinguishable. In essence, race suicide urged individual old-stock Americans: "Procreate; otherwise *you* shall die."

By examining the co-construction of race and sexuality encapsulated in the discourse and the figuration of race suicide through their reflections in Progressive Era literature, *The Suicidal State* explores suicide's relation to the biopolitical logics of preservation, survival, and reproduction. On the one

INTRODUCTION 7

hand, race suicide as an alarmist, pro-natal discourse exemplifies what Lee Edelman influentially calls "reproductive futurism": a constitutive fantasy of the social in which biological reproduction—figured by "the Child"—is understood to be the *sine qua non* for the continuation of social life, while providing an alibi for the violent abjection of those placed outside the politics of reproduction. On the other hand, however, the suicidal impetus presupposed in *race suicide* as a figuration constitutes what Edelman calls "the social order's death drive," putting in question the fundamental "presupposition that the body politic must survive."[30] That is, by symptomatically endowing the social body with suicidality, *race suicide* hints at a biopolitical anxiety that biopower's administration over life might have a fissure: subjects under the control of its life-administering power could choose to do away with their lives.

Literature of this period, I argue, seized on this possibility in its proliferation of suicidal characters, portraying their struggle to disarticulate their imagined singularity from the collective entity, population. In examining suicide's aspiration to sidestep the imperative to live and reproduce, *The Suicidal State* ultimately seeks to theorize a biopolitics of suicide. It asks: What does suicide's undoing of the self mean for biopolitics? How does it reconfigure subjectivity, relationalities, intimacies, bodies and pleasures? What kind of agency—if any at all—does it forge, when it approaches the zero degree of subjectivity? Could such an agency *sous rature* mobilize a politics—say, what Heather Love terms the "politics of refusal"—in its attempt to elude, withdraw from, and frustrate biopolitics, or are their deaths co-opted into the biopolitical order of things?[31]

Before delving into these questions surrounding suicide's queer affordances in individual chapters, I will map the ways in which the deployment of race suicide discourse in the Progressive Era United States ultimately points to what Foucault formulates as biopolitics' fundamental suicidality in his remarks on the Nazi regime: "We have an absolutely racist State, an absolutely murderous State, and an absolutely suicidal State. A racist State, a murderous State, and a suicidal State."[32] First, I will chart how the anthropomorphizing trope of the *social body*—the rhetoric that undergirds *race suicide*—came to life under biopower's regime, superseding its sovereign counterpart, the *body politic*. The following two sections will elaborate how the US social body was discursively enfleshed as a biologically vulnerable entity facing death, a precarious life that needs protection from two enemies: the external threat of immigrants as well as the internal threat of

8   THE SUICIDAL STATE

degeneration. In the fourth section, I will turn to the shifting discourse on suicide from the late nineteenth century to the first decades of the twentieth century, charting the ways in which the psychoanalytic concept of the death drive was invented as a double perversion of the life instinct: namely, a negation both of self-preservation and of procreation. The last section will inquire how the literary—especially the aesthetic mode known as naturalism—provides a rich field of exploration for suicide's queer affordances as it is placed at the intersection between individual and populational lives.

Animating the Social Body

A portrait of the race contemplating killing itself would be definitionally grotesque; upon closer investigation, its melancholic visage proves to be composed of myriad human bodies mashed together à la Giuseppe Arcimboldo's portraits. In one way, this grotesquerie illustrates the intersection between Foucault's two "poles" of biopower, one individualizing and the other massifying. On the one hand, the anatomo-politics of discipline trains the body into docility, molding individual subjectivity through institutional surveillance at schools, asylums, and prisons, as well as through its internalized form, self-surveillance. On the other hand, biopolitics amasses and manages the population by targeting its biological processes such as "the birth rate, the mortality rate, various biological disabilities, and the effects of the environment."[33] As such, unlike anatomo-politics, biopolitics pays no heed to individuals, however anomalous they are. Rather than disciplining, biopolitics regulates and manages, seeking to "establish an equilibrium, maintain an average, establish a sort of homeostasis, and compensate for variations within this general population and its aleatory field."[34] Through the use of a calculus of probabilities, biopower seeks to manage the risks of otherwise random events, sometimes by intervening into them and sometimes by counteracting their effects. Thus, biopolitics seeks to install a "security mechanism" to ensure the preservation of collective life itself.[35] Race suicide, with its anthropomorphizing of the population, laminates the anatomo-politics of the human body onto the biopolitics of the population.

But what exactly is this corpus called the "population," and what does it mean for bodies, subjectivized through disciplinary power, to be massified into this entity and governed to protect the "security" of its life? According to Foucault's genealogy of governmentality—his term for an assemblage

INTRODUCTION 9

of techniques, institutions, and mentalities that enables the modern (read, liberal) form of governing—the population was not the simple sum of individuals residing in a certain territory; as it was "discovered" in the eighteenth century, population was understood to be a "natural phenomenon," a statistical datum of the human species at large.[36] This so-called "'naturalness' of the population" was conceived as such alongside the conceptualization of the market as *laissez-faire*: both phenomena presuppose their own rhythm and internal regularities—rates of birth, death, morbidity, even accidents, in the case of population—which are, by and large, intractable.[37] Much like its role in classical liberal economy, the state's responsibility vis-à-vis the population is to "respect these natural processes, or at any rate to take them into account, get them to work, or to work with them."[38] That is to say, state intervention is only called for when a threat to the supposed homeostasis emerges: Foucauldian "security" refers to this ensuring of the internal regularities. Thus, in its calculation of the "cost" of probable events, the apparatus of security operates *not* according to "a binary division between the permitted and the prohibited" but according to "a bandwidth of the acceptable that must not be exceeded," which surrounds an optimal average.[39] As Foucault's example of smallpox inoculation makes clear, this "bandwidth" of securitization often involves letting a certain number of deaths happen in the name of optimizing collective life.

Despite Foucault's overall emphasis on governmentality's *laissez-faire* mode of operation (a point to which we will return in Chapter 2), interventional techniques are still regularly called for in this biopolitical framework. Defined as a "natural phenomenon," the life of the population is subject to countless contingencies and constantly exposed to risks, thereby inviting administrative interventions to sustain its supposed homeostasis. In one sense, however, this threat to security is integral to the mechanism of liberal governmentality and its biopolitics: in Foucault's pithy phrasing, "There is no liberalism without a culture of danger."[40] As Thomas Lemke glosses this, "the striving for security and the danger of insecurity are complementary aspects of liberal governmentality," since fear of danger cultivates the subjectivity optimized for capitalist economy.[41] In other words, there is no security in the biopolitical regime, but only the incessant effort of securitization. For this securitization to function, the so-called naturalness of the population must be "penetrable": it has to have "a surface on which authoritarian . . . transformations can get a hold."[42] In order to manage the population and maintain its equilibrium, biopolitical agents—whether the state or other institutions—must find a penetrable surface to adjust the population from within. That is why, in the context of population management, "discipline was never more important or more valued," for anatomo-politics provides access to the population, which cannot be directly controlled.[43] The biopolitics of population thus incorporates an anatomo-politics of discipline.

Sex, for Foucault, constitutes one such penetrable surface, pointing to "the juncture of the 'body' and the 'population.' "[44] Sex's "procreative effects" locate it within the sphere of population, inviting various biopolitical interventions including public health measures, eugenic programs, and advertising campaigns. At the same time, conceived as the deepest reservoir of the truth of the self, sexuality's subjectivizing force and its "eminently corporeal mode of behavior" render the individual body the ideal site of discipline and surveillance.[45] Foucault's emphasis on sexuality as a suture between the individual body and the population, however, has been left strangely underattended by sexuality studies. The neglect of the "Malthusian couple"— to use Foucault's term for one of the four problematics of sexuality—might stem in part from what Penelope Deutscher incisively terms the "repudiation of a procreative hypothesis."[46] That is, Foucault's nimble-footed sidestepping of the repressive hypothesis has resulted in an overhasty dismissal of the role of procreative sex and its populational impacts on the construction of sexuality.[47]

Like Deutscher, a number of theorists of biopolitics chart sites of interdigitation between anatomo- and biopolitics in the vicinity of sexuality and reproduction.[48] As Ann Stoler argues in *Race and the Education of Desire*, race—a thematic implicit but left largely underdeveloped in Foucault's conceptualization of sexuality—has proved an especially rich locus to rethink biopower and its governmentality. Stoler understands the interlocking of sexuality and colonialism (one of the critical oversights of Foucault's Eurocentric narrative) as a matrix of disciplinary formations of desire. This colonialist play of desire forges the notion of self-governing European selves that are simultaneously exposed to the risk of degeneracy transmitted from the colonies, thereby producing and reproducing "the colonial order of things" that sanctions the domination of racialized human lives in the name of security.[49] The domain of the sexual is not only inseparable from racialization but also, as Kyla Schuller argues in *The Biopolitics of Feeling*, interlocked with the discourse of heredity. Especially in the context of the nineteenth-century United States, the neo-Lamarckian notion of a mutable, impressible body—referring both to the sentimental impressibility

INTRODUCTION 11

to be affected by its surroundings and to the nervous system that accumulates impressions and transmit them to offspring—constitutes a "somatic interface" that sutures the individual body and the population.[50] Through hereditary transmissions, bodies that are constantly open to erotic and sensorial interpellation become responsible for the national and racial integrity.

This sex-race-heredity complex, as we will see in more in detail in the next section, continues to be crucial to the discourse of race suicide and its pronatal nativism in the Progressive Era. Yet as the biopolitical state continued to consolidate during the Progressive Era, the hereditary capacities of individual bodies were no longer the only "somatic interface" of governmentality. If *biopolitics* is the name for the "politicization of biology" (exemplified here by the political control over the procreative aspects of sex), we might think of its reversal as another venue of governmentality's access to the soma of the population.[51] That is, with what can be called a "biologization of politics," biologizing rhetoric and figurations enflesh the polity and start to incorporate the anatomo-political technique of discipline—the one usually reserved for individuals—to manage the population.

The somatization of the social in the phrase the *social body*—the rhetorical ground for the race that kills itself—records a profound historical shift in power's modality. Though often conflated with the *body politic*, the *social body* has a much shorter history than its sovereign counterpart. As Ernst Kantorowicz's classic *The King's Two Bodies* shows, the *body politic* was a concept most animated in the Middle Ages, conceived as the king's immortal "superbody": it articulates the abstract kingship that is incarnated in the king's *body natural* and transmitted through to ensuing generations after his death.[52] In contrast, the phrase *social body* emerged at the end of the eighteenth century and became popular in the nineteenth century, the period largely overlapping with the solidification of liberal governmentality and its biopolitics.[53] Though seldom noted, its earliest English usage is found in a translation of *The Declaration of the Rights of Man and of the Citizen*, dramatically marking biopower's deposing of sovereign power.[54] That is, the beheading of the king gave birth to a new subject called the social body, a supposedly more democratic, decentered model of the polity that represents the "population."

When the biopolitics of the population finds its corporeal medium in the social body, it starts to answer a question often posed about Foucault's seemingly decentered microphysics of power: "How is it that this headless body often behaves *as if* it indeed had a head"?[55] Born in the regime of

12 THE SUICIDAL STATE

securitization and its corollary fomentation of insecurity, the life of the social body is always deemed precarious. Such precarity paradoxically naturalizes and substantiates the social body, endowing it with what Eric Santner calls "the strange materiality of the 'flesh.'"[56] Just as the abstract kingship of the body politic was in fact underwritten by the monarch's body natural—his simultaneously mortal and "sublime flesh"—biopolitics requires a corporeal underpinning, seeking to incorporate sovereignty's afterlife, "the royal remains," into its structure.[57] Thus, reversing the transubstantiation of the king's natural body into the body politic, biopower personifies the abstract subject "population" in the mold of a sovereign "I" through the trope of the *social body*, assuming the vulnerable naturalness of its predecessor.

Crucially, this vulnerability of the social body becomes the precondition of biopower's omnipresent management of life, for biopolitical intervention into the population is sanctioned only by the danger against which it is said to defend life. Simply put, the social body's precariousness justifies the anonymous, urgent call for its securitization—"society must be defended"— thereby furnishing biopolitics an alibi for its existence. This precarity, furthermore, sanctions the social body's inheritance of the sovereign right to kill in the form of self-defense. As Foucault notes, biopower exercises the "old sovereign right to kill" only in the name of defense against "biological threat," whether coming from within or without.[58] In this sense, biopower and biopolitics are inseparable from what Achille Mbembe calls necropower and necropolitics, "the power and the capacity to dictate who may live and who must die," distributing death according to its murderous calculus of life.[59]

In a striking moment, Foucault gives voice to this necropolitical operation of biopower by ventriloquizing the eerily animated social body: "The more inferior species die out, the more abnormal individuals are eliminated, the fewer degenerates there will be in the species as a whole, and the more I—as species rather than individual—can live, the stronger I will be, the more vigorous I will be. I will be able to proliferate."[60] Biopolitics forges the alleged biological threat from which it protects the social body by hierarchizing human lives according to putative biological difference. The existence of a biological threat that endangers the life of the social body sanctions biopolitical interventions into the population; in turn, it seeks to eliminate the pathogenic other it created according to a eugenic calculus, wherein the "my life" of "I—as species" becomes more livable through their death, whether such killing takes the form of slow death by systemic neglect or more overtly violent forms of exploitation.[61]

INTRODUCTION 13

Immigration Restrictions and the
Biologization of the Social Body

Race suicide, with its alarmist imaginary of a social body at risk, tropologically enacts the biopolitical deployment of insecurity. By imagining the native-born white race as endangered by pathogenic others—exemplified primarily by the phantasm of over-fertile immigrants—the figuration of *race suicide* transfers the monarch's sublime flesh into the population of old-stock Americans. In his description of race suicide, Madison Grant's *The Passing of the Great Race* illustrates such a bestowal of vulnerable sublimity:

> These immigrants adopt the language of the native[-born white] American; they wear his clothes; they steal his name; and they are beginning to take his women, but they seldom adopt his religion or understand his ideals, and while he is being elbowed out of his own home the American looks calmly abroad and urges on others the suicidal ethics which are exterminating his own race.[62]

While being stripped of "his clothes," "his name," and "his women" by immigrants, the proverbial native-born American still stands imperially (even "look[ing] calmly abroad," pointing to Pacific aspirations). His body, now denuded, reveals its ethereal whiteness and its resemblance to the royal remains of sovereignty—the whiteness that is all the more precious as it is now imbued with a "suicidal ethics," rendering the right to kill into self-governing asceticism. Through the invocation of insecurity, this population—now transformed into "the American"—is crucially naturalized as *the* social body.

Grant's conflation of a particular race—native-born white Americans—with the nation and the national population as a whole is representative of a much wider body of race suicide discourse. This slippage was ingrained from the beginning of race suicide's popularization when Theodore Roosevelt introduced the phrase race suicide as "fundamentally infinitely more important than any other question in this country."[63] Roosevelt continued this transposition of whiteness into nation at his 1906 State of the Union Address:

> There are regions in our land, and classes of our population, where the birth rate has sunk below the death rate. Surely it should need no demonstration to show that willful sterility is, from the standpoint of the nation,

14   THE SUICIDAL STATE

from the standpoint of the human race, the one sin for which the penalty is
national death, race death; a sin for which there is no atonement.[64]

In a deft slight of hand, Roosevelt glides from understanding whites as a class
of the population enacting a "willful sterility" (that is, race suicide) to rendering them into the totality of the population in the appositional melding
of "national death" and "race death." Roosevelt here draws on the multiva-
lence of the term *race*. Originally referring to stocks of animals or varieties of
plants in the sixteenth century, *race* gradually began to refer to humans, becoming interchangeable with *people, nation, kind, type, variety, stock*, and so
forth.[65] As such, according to given periods and contexts, *race* carried a range
of reference, encompassing meanings that were occupational (the "race
of bishops"), genealogical (the "race of Abraham"), gendered (the "softer
race"), religious (the "Hindu race"), linguistic (the "English-speaking race"),
geographical (the "European race"), national (the "American race"), tribal
(the "Teutonic race"), phenotypical (the "white race"), and/or references to a
species (the "human race"). While definitions of *race* increasingly coagulated
around the senses of species, nation, tribe, and phenotype by the second half
of the nineteenth century, all four of these denotations stood on equal footing
at the time of Roosevelt's address.[66]

The polysemous slipperiness of race enabled Roosevelt and other race-
suicide advocates to construct the population (and its embodiment, the social body) as a singular, white entity. That is, while its primary referent is
tribal (Anglo-Saxon/Teutonic) or phenotypical (white), *race* in *race suicide*
holds onto its reference to the nation ("the American race") and even the
species ("the human race"), equating whiteness with the nation and, by extension, humanity. In Foucauldian terms, then, race suicide stipulates and
constructs the population as having its own "homeostasis." When race suicide threatens a crisis that demands the state's "rare" intervention, the
biopolitical state seizes the opportunity to maximize its regulatory power in
the name of ensuring the security of the population: that is, to maintain the
supposed homeostasis by protecting the whiteness of the nation.

Crucially, the synecdochic substitution of whiteness for nation reveals the
mystical, headless body of Foucauldian power to be guided, at bottom, by a
project of state racism. Rather than limited to that of the turn-of-the-century
United States, such racism pervades the Foucauldian understanding of
populational homeostasis across contexts. Insofar as securitization requires
the maintenance of homeostasis, the mechanisms to ensure this homeostasis

INTRODUCTION 15

are themselves techniques of racial enforcement. Put simply, biopolitical securitization is, by definition, a mechanism to ensure the structure of dominance by maintaining the status quo, even if it means the exercise of the sovereign right to kill.

From its inception, race suicide was eugenic in its differential valuation of lives and in its effort to increase a part of the population. However, the failure of this positive eugenic project, when combined with the rise of genetic science, led its proponents—including Roosevelt, Ross, and Grant—to negative eugenics. Grant, for example, called on the state to "eliminate the worst by segregation or sterilization," and the state answered this demand.[67] Immigration restrictions became the primary instrument of such securitization. Coinciding with the rise of modern immunology and hereditary science, Progressive Era immigration regulations reified the social body as a white biological entity to be protected. As Kyla Schuller argues, the rediscovery of Mendelian genetics in 1900 all but terminated the neo-Lamarckian conception of heredity that sees the body as transformable through discipline and social reform. In its calculation of genetic probabilities and risks, hereditary science "helped instantiate what Foucault names the 'instrument of security,'" which seeks to "optimize the biopotential of the population."[68] This increasing biological determinism, as Ed Cohen forcibly argues, coincided historically with immunology's imagination of the body as a fortress to be defended. By conceptualizing self-defense at the cellular level, immunology forged "a peculiar hybrid of military, political, and biological thinking" and created an antagonistic relation between the self and the pathogenic other.[69] Together these discourses marked a shift within individual bodies from what Benjamin Kahan terms "the open (environmental) body [to] the closed (biological) body."[70]

Progressive Era immigration restrictions transpose this closedness onto the national social body: the social body is biologized as an entity that has its own immunological system and hereditary makeup to be protected against foreign incursion. Race suicide initially mobilized an immunological rhetoric of self-defense in its advocacy for immigration restrictions against Asians. Notably, as I argue in the Coda, Edward Ross originally came up with the concept of race suicide in his argument for Asian exclusion, as his vision of white reproductive weakness was contrasted with the "heavy influx of a prolific race from the Orient."[71] Fears of race suicide fueled the growth of federal restrictions on Asian immigration that had started in the 1870s. These laws primarily imagined Chinese and other Asian immigrants

16 THE SUICIDAL STATE

as forced laborers—"coolies" in the case of men and "sex slaves" in the case of women—whose non-agential foreign bodies were invading the liberal labor market and normative white marriage. The first restrictive federal immigration law, the Page Act of 1875, barred the entry of Chinese women (while allegedly targeting prospective prostitutes in general).[72] Along with antimiscegenation state laws, the Page Act functioned as a *de facto* negative eugenic policy against Chinese immigrants, who, as a result, formed bachelor communities in which women comprised less than 10 percent of the population.[73] Even after the enactment of the Chinese Exclusion Act of 1882, the fear of the "silent replacement of Americans by Asiatics" endured.[74] The Immigration Act of 1917 extended the exclusion to most Asians by creating "the barred Asiatic zone," and the five-decade project of Asian exclusion was completed by the Immigration Act of 1924, which categorically prohibited the immigration of aliens ineligible for naturalization. As stated in *Chae Chan Ping v. United States* (1889), Asian immigrants were cast as paradigmatically unassimilable and yet rapidly infesting aliens who threatened the nation's "right of self-preservation."[75]

Significantly, Chinese immigrants were understood biomedically as disease agents. Coinciding with the popularization of germ theory and modern immunology, Chinese exclusion happened largely under the rubric of public health, as Chinese bodies were imagined to transmit syphilis and leprosy (Hansen's disease) to white populations.[76] While the Page Act conceived Chinese women as syphilitic prostitutes, Chinese male immigrants coming through Angel Island were also subjected to rigorous physical examinations, including strip searches seeking "'abnormalities' below the waist."[77] Because syphilis and leprosy were purportedly caused and disseminated by physical proximity and heredity, Chinese prostitutes and male domestic servants incited fears of Chinese racial degeneration infiltrating white families and marriages.

The bioregulation of Asian immigration provided a blueprint for similar efforts targeting other groups of immigrants, culminating in the end of open immigration from Europe by the Immigration Act of 1924. Legally classified as white and therefore eligible for citizenship, southern and eastern European immigrants were racially marked as different from old-stock Americans. As Chapter 3 and Chapter 4 will detail, they were categorized as "Alpine," "Mediterranean," "Slavic," or "Hebrew," while old-stock Americans were now designated "Teutonic," as characterized by the influential racial

INTRODUCTION   17

taxonomy of William Z. Ripley's *The Races of Europe* (1899).[78] Arguments against southern and eastern European immigration often deployed the language of race suicide and its evocation of biological threat against old-stock Americans. Leading education reformer Ellwood Cubberley argued that the influx of southern and eastern European immigrants "served to dilute tremendously our national stock, and to corrupt our civic life," characterizing these immigrants as "illiterate, docile, lacking in self-reliance and initiative and not possessing Anglo-Teutonic conceptions of law, order and government."[79] Prescott Hall, one of the cofounders of Immigration Restriction League, argued more explicitly that "the native children are murdered by never being allowed to come into existence."[80]

Such discourses, along with actual legislation against immigration, were directly shaped by the burgeoning science of eugenics. Coined by Francis Galton in 1883, eugenics rapidly developed after the aforementioned rediscovery of Mendelian genetics in 1900. In the United States, the development of eugenics was headquartered at the Eugenics Record Office (ERO) in Cold Spring Harbor, New York, under the direction of Charles B. Davenport with Harry H. Laughlin serving as superintendent. Research from the ERO provided the intellectual framework for the central immigration laws of the early twentieth century.[81] At Davenport's suggestion, Henry Herbert Goddard administered the first IQ test in the United States at Ellis Island to passengers coming steerage with the result that "over 80 percent of all Jewish, Polish, Italian, Hungarian, and Russian immigrants were [deemed] 'feeble-minded defectives,'" leading to the introduction of a literacy test with the Immigration Act of 1917.[82] While the 1917 Act was influenced by eugenic thought and rhetoric, the Immigration Act of 1924 was more actively framed by the eugenicists themselves. The national quota system introduced in 1924 cemented this restriction by setting an annual ceiling on the number of immigrants from each country, admitting up to two percent of each group that had already been present in 1890. Crucially, the idea to use the 1890 census—which was conducted before large-scale immigration from southern and eastern Europe—as a tool for exclusion began in Madison Grant's Sub-Committee on Selective Immigration of the Eugenic Committee. Laughlin, along with the author of the wildly popular *The Rising Tide of Color Against White-World-Supremacy* (1922), Lothrop Stoddard, gave critical testimony to Congress on immigration and "held regular sessions with the bill's cosponsor, Representative Johnson . . . [who] was a member of the American Eugenics Society."[83]

18   THE SUICIDAL STATE

The Sexuality of Population

While the discourse of race suicide deployed immigration restrictions to protect the social body from foreigners (understood to be a biological threat coming from outside), it also increasingly began to focus on threats from within. Robert DeCourcey Ward, one of the founders of the Immigration Restriction League, articulates this dual conceptualization of eugenic securitization in his aptly titled "Eugenic Immigration" (1913): "National eugenics for us . . . means the prevention of the breeding of the unfit native as well as the prevention of the immigration, and of the breeding after admission of the unfit alien."[84] Evangelists of race suicide progressively turned to compulsory sterilization.[85] As Madison Grant puts it, when "efforts to avert race suicide" by promoting old-stock Americans' natality fail and "the undesirables" proliferate, there is only one option left for "race improvement": "The state through sterilization must see to it that his [the undesirable's] line stops with him."[86] The first law to legalize compulsory sterilization passed in Indiana in 1907, leading to the nationwide spread of state-sanctioned negative eugenics. As Elaine Tyler May explains: "Within the next two decades, . . . 23 states had compulsory sterilization laws on the books, 17 had active programs, and 6,244 people had been sterilized."[87]

If, as I have been arguing, the discourse of race suicide and its promotion of immigration restrictions animated the social body as a biological entity with its own immunological system and hereditary makeup, compulsory sterilization helped conceptualize the social body as a reproductive one. Oliver Wendell Holmes's infamous Supreme Court decision in *Buck v. Bell* (1927), which upheld the constitutionality of state-led compulsory sterilization of the "unfit," exemplifies this biopolitical rhetoric:

> It is better for all the world, if instead of waiting to execute degenerate offspring for crime, or to let them starve for their imbecility, society can prevent those who are manifestly unfit from continuing their kind. The principle that sustains compulsory vaccination is broad enough to cover cutting the Fallopian tubes.[88]

Holmes here analogizes the involuntary sterilization of Carrie Buck, an eighteen-year-old Virginian woman deemed hereditarily "feebleminded," to a 1905 precedent which granted the state of Massachusetts the power of "compulsory vaccination." In so doing, he intertwines two discourses, Mendelian

INTRODUCTION 19

genetics and modern immunology, to securitize the social body. That is, by invoking Buck's "Fallopian tubes" as an agent threatening "society"—or "all the world," in his grandiose rhetoric—Holmes's opinion arrogates her reproductive organs to the domain of public health. The Fallopian tubes no longer belong to Buck's body; they belong to the social body. The social body has now become a reproductive one.

But if indeed the social body is reproductive, what does that body reproduce? To entertain this question, it might be helpful to examine the logic of the term *reproduction* itself. Prior to the eighteenth century, the word *reproduction* primarily denoted "duplication," not species reproduction; this latter biological and sexual valence emerged only in the late eighteenth century and became pervasive in the nineteenth century, overlapping with the rise of biopolitics (OED).[89] The simultaneous emergence of *biological reproduction* and biopolitics represents a recasting of procreation within the logic of population. In contrast to the previously dominant vocabulary of *procreation,* which etymologically summons a "bringing forth," the *re* prefix of *reproduction* imagines childbirth as a repetition—a production of similitude or even identicality. This identicality embodies the homeostatic ideal of the population, answering the question of what the social body's reproductive organs produce: identicality itself.

Understanding this biopolitical logic of reproduction in the context of what Alys Eve Weinbaum brilliantly terms "the race/reproduction bind" enables us to see that this identicality is another name for white racial purity, at least in the turn-of-the-century United States.[90] Weinbaum's term designates the entwined formation of nationalist, racist, and imperialist ideologies rooted in the inextricability of race and reproduction, or what she describes as "the notion that race can be *reproduced.*"[91] Pushing this crucial insight further, *The Suicidal State* contends that race, in its allegedly biologized, immutable, and hereditary sense, was conceptualized as an entity that *could only be reproduced* via heterosexuality. While the many valences of the term *race* persisted, *race* as a marker of physiological differences began to predominate under a new genetic regime of scientific racism in the post-Mendelian era. In this new model, which was crystalized in *Plessy v. Ferguson* (1896) (discussed further in Chapter 2), *race* was no longer controlled solely through an optical regime, but instead was moored by the invisible structures of genes and heredity. In this newly constructed biologized model, race was imagined as a prototype to be copied and an essence that was to be transmitted. This reproducing (in the sense of the copy

20 THE SUICIDAL STATE

and the transmission) of race could only be realized through procreation, leading to a period reimagining of procreative sex as *the* means for the reproduction of race.

This genetic model of race was materialized through the reinforcement of anti-miscegenation laws, operating according to a very different logic from that under slavery. Prior to Reconstruction, sexual relations between white men and Black women had been read under the sign of what Brian Connolly calls "the rapacious process of capital accumulation that abolitionists referred to as slave breeding."[92] In a way only heightened by the passage of the Act Prohibiting Importation of Slaves in 1807, the so-called slave breeding brutally framed interracial procreation in a quantifying register as the reproduction of labor and capital. However, Reconstruction witnessed an enormous change in the meaning of Black-white sexual relations. As indexed by the coinage of the term *miscegenation* in 1864—which emerged from the polygenist idea of Blacks and whites being different species—the product of cross-racial breeding was increasingly regarded as a hereditary threat.[93] Even as the popularization of Darwinism outmoded such a conceptualization, miscegenation as a hereditary threat continued to haunt race relations, leading to the intensification of anti-miscegenation laws and their enforcement. While regulation of intermarriage between whites and Blacks dates as far back as the mid-seventeenth century, the late nineteenth and early twentieth century gradually extended these prohibitions to unions between whites and Asians, as well as between whites and Native Americans, indicative of the new concerns with white racial purity. As a result, toward the end of the Progressive Era, twenty-eight states and territories enacted new anti-miscegenation legislation.[94]

The text of Virginia's Racial Integrity Act of 1924—the act that most explicitly codified the so-called "one-drop rule" through its ban on intermarriage—exemplifies the new genetic regime of racial reproduction: "It shall hereafter be unlawful for any white person in this state to marry any save a white person, or a person with no other admixture of blood than white and American Indian. For the purpose of this act, the term 'white person' shall apply only to the person who has no trace whatsoever of any blood other than Caucasian."[95] As evidenced by its lexical deployment of the vocabularies of "mixture" and "generation," the law's true target is to regulate procreation rather than to prohibit interracial marriage per se.[96] The law was initially conceptualized and lobbied for by three prominent eugenicists in Virginia, who founded the Anglo-Saxon Clubs of America and convinced the legislature to adopt the law. We can understand the law's eugenic under-pinning to reimagine sexual relations between whites and non-whites as a biological problem, striving to eliminate the perceived degenerative effects of cross-racial reproduction.[97] Tellingly, the most fervent of the advocates, Walter Plecker, repeatedly referred to the danger of " 'hybrids', 'inbreeding', 'reversion', and 'race suicide', " as he supported the passage of the Act.[98]

Furthermore, in defining "white person[s]" as having "no trace whatso-ever of any blood other than Caucasian," the law posited whiteness as an un-tainted sameness that could be transmitted across generations. This focus on the bloodlines of offspring suggests that race is, as Ladelle McWhorter puts it in her remarks about species, "all about sex—all about who has sex with whom."[99] The bloody record of lynching, which reached its apex in the 1890s, represented the extra-legal complement to these anti-miscegenation laws that regulated "who has sex with whom." Lynching, as many scholars have pointed out, was often meted out in the name of protecting white women from the imagined threat of Black male hypersexuality. As Melissa Stein documents, spectacles of lynching increasingly involved genital mu-tilation of its victims, even featuring "the victims' genitals as postmortem souvenirs."[100] Such mutilation mirrored contemporary medical discourse that pathologized Black male sexuality as *furor sexualis* and counseled cas-tration as an alternative remedy with "the added eugenic benefit of 'race improvement.' "[101] The conceptualization of Black castration as a means of (white) "race improvement" epitomized the logic of biologized race, where sex is definitionally built into race and cannot be conceptualized apart from it. Marion Lenoir's suicide in Thomas Dixon's *The Clansman* (1905), in which she jumps off a cliff after being raped by a former slave, emblematizes the way in which race suicide's securitizing logic and its binding of race and sex brutally sanctioned the white social body's right to kill Black subjects. In Dixon's historical fantasy, it is the white girl's dead body with a smile on her lips—"Death is sweet now," the fifteen-year-old girl says as she takes her own life—that gave rise to the original Ku Klux Klan.[102] When held by D. W. Griffith's 1915 filmic gaze, the girl's corpse gave birth to a nation, an anony-mous white horde embodied not only by the climactic Klan ride, but also by its enthusiastic audience who was, to use Richard Dyer's phrase, awash with "the radiation of the light reflected off the screen" as the white Klan sheets swirled around and engulfed the frame.[103]

This welding of race, sex, and reproduction has crucial implications for the history of heterosexuality as well. As Jonathan Ned Katz illuminates in

22   THE SUICIDAL STATE

The Invention of Heterosexuality, the term *heterosexuality* was initially coined as a clinical term for pathologically excessive different-sex sexual desire, contrasted with procreative sex. In *Dorland's Medical Dictionary* (1901), heterosexuality was still defined as an "abnormal or perverted appetite toward the opposite sex."[104] It was only in the late 1920s that the term *heterosexuality* was normalized through its potential—if unrealized—relation to procreation, as it was understood to express "heteroerotic emotions" and thereby potentially enhanced the "reproductive capacity" of the dwindling white middle class.[105] This shift suggests the strangely contiguous histories of the two terms: *race* as a biologized entity and *heterosexuality* as the normative form of sexuality, both coagulated in the first decades of the twentieth century. The synchronicity seems to indicate the two terms' joint-construction with its conceptual dependency on procreative sex, or what Henry Abelove memorably calls "sexual intercourse so-called": "penis in vagina, vagina around penis, with seminal emission uninterrupted."[106] Simply put, race was conceptualized as produced through heterosexual procreative sex; heterosexuality was constructed as the means of racial reproduction.

The Suicidal State argues that the race suicide discourse records—and even catalyzed—the formulation of this chiasmatic relation between race and sex, consolidating biologized race as an entity reproduced by procreative sex. The discourse of race suicide imagines a white social body that, with its waning sexual capacity, fails to reproduce its whiteness. If, as I have been arguing, reproduction is mimetic, this failure takes two dominant shapes: an unwillingness or inability to produce a copy, or a damaged replication of the original. In the first instance, as we will see in Chapter 1 and Chapter 2, race suicide locates its problem in nonreproductive "fit" whites exemplified by the New England suffragist and the New Woman (contrasted with "overfertile" immigrants), thereby fomenting antifeminist and anti-immigrant discourses.[107] The second case—the problem of a faulty copy—points not only to miscegenation but also to procreation by "unfit" whites, as evidenced by race-suicide advocates' turn toward compulsory sterilization.

This biopolitical turn, as Holmes' reference to "degenerate offspring" in *Buck v. Bell* shows, is supported by degeneration theory. In degeneration theory disseminated from B. A. Morel's *Treatise on the Physical, Intellectual, and Moral Degeneration of the Human Species* (1857), degeneration was conceptualized as a problem of faulty reproduction, defined as "a morbid deviation from an original type." In the context of the Progressive Era, degeneration primarily connotes racial devolution, where the "higher race"

INTRODUCTION   23

regresses and sheds its racial merits, becoming closer to the "lower race," or non-whites who were often overdetermined as "degenerate races." This condition was understood to be passed from generation to generation, eventuating in insanity, congenital idiocy, and, over the course of several generations, ultimately leading to sterility. As eugenicists' interest in female promiscuity as a form of "feeblemindedness" attests, degeneration was also understood to spread throughout the population through reckless procreation. Degeneration theory, then, imagined "unfit" whites' reproduction to produce a series of defective copies that paradoxically would bring about the extinction of the white race.

As is well-known, the word "degenerate" was also associated with so-called sexual perversion, which took the form not only of female promiscuity, but also of homosexuality and gender deviance. Because the "higher race" was associated with greater anatomical and gender differentiation, gender deviance such as female masculinity and male effeminacy were conceptualized as closer to the "lower races" and the product of racial degeneration.[108] As Melissa Stein argues, degeneration theorists placed homosexuals and inverts in a double bind, accusing them of race suicide both for not procreating and, if they did, for tainting the race.[109] In *The Female-Impersonators* (1922), Jennie June (also known under the names Ralph Werther and Earl Lind) defends congenital gender inversion, writing: "The chief charge against androgynes is that they are guilty of 'the awful crime of race suicide.' But it is the fault of Nature alone that the ultra-androgyne is incapable of doing his part in the perpetuation of the race."[110] Later in the text, the "awful crime" is described as being "as heinous as murder, because it strikes at the very existence of the race."[111] Twenty years after Roosevelt's accusation that non-procreative whites are "criminal[s] against the race," the relay between criminality and race suicide here encompasses queer and trans subjects. Just as heterosexuality was naturalized as a means of racial reproduction, queerness was conceptualized as an existential threat to the race.[112]

While my project thus understands the twinned birth of biologized race and sexuality as manifested and mediated by the discourse of race suicide, it argues that the process of co-construction was much messier and more winding than how it has been narrated. Though such works as Siobhan Somerville's *Queering the Color Line* and Roderick Ferguson's *Aberrations in Black* make foundational arguments about the racialized nature of heteronormativity, these studies revolve predominantly around the two axes of Black and white, homo- and heterosexuality. In emphasizing the

24   THE SUICIDAL STATE

co-constitution of Blackness and homosexuality around the turn of the century, their works leave much of the rich terrain of the sexuo-racial spectrum uncharted. One of my contentions is that the high-contrast binaries of Black/white and homo/heterosexuality operated to eclipse amorphous otherness, thereby constructing the Black and/or homosexual body as the tangible counterpoint to the white, heterosexualized social body. Yet as the following chapters will demonstrate, the Progressive Era was not only the height of anti-Black violence (Chapter 2); it was also a period marked by the exclusion of eastern and southern European immigrants (Chapter 4) and Asian immigrants (Coda), as well as by the coercive assimilation policies taken against Native Americans (Chapter 3). All of these, in addition to the logics of Jim Crow, facilitated the biological engineering of the reproductive social body as white and heterosexual.

Accordingly, instead of taking the a priori categories of homo/hetero and Black/white as its starting point, *The Suicidal State* inquires into the very process of the sexuo-racial construction of the US social body, focusing on the penumbrae of white heteronormativity. If, as David Halperin contends in *How to Do the History of Homosexuality*, "homosexuality" was invented as an umbrella term that absorbs "a number of different notions about same-sex sexual attraction"—namely, a psychological condition (gender orientation), an erotic desire (sexual object-choice), and a sexual practice (sexual behavior)—a similar process occurred in the realm of race.[113] That is, "whiteness" as a racial category slowly developed in the Progressive Era United States, combining different models of the "dominant race." As an umbrella concept, whiteness subsumes overlapping yet different organizing logics of racial dominance: Anglo-Saxons, Teutons, Caucasians, or Aryans. Each of these categories, as we will see in the following chapters, has its particular logic for legitimizing the structure of dominance. As Reginald Horsman summarizes, the white Americans at the turn of the century

> had evidence plain before them that they were a chosen people; from the English they had learned that the Anglo-Saxons had always been peculiarly gifted in the arts of government; from the scientists and ethnologists they were learning that they were of a distinct Caucasian race, innately endowed with abilities that placed them above other races; from the philologists, often through literary sources, they were learning that they were the descendants of those Aryans who followed the sun to carry civilization to the whole world.[114]

INTRODUCTION   25

Each of these racial categories was deployed, according to a given time and place, to exclude certain groups from the center of racial dominance. The fuzzy contours of what we know today as "whiteness" were gradually drawn through a negotiation of the uneasy coexistence of competing categorizations, as well as against the polychromatic background of racial others. Building on the insights of critics of whiteness studies, *The Suicidal State* tries to capture "whiteness not as monolithic but as variegated," visualizing the ways in which it has come to represent the normality mediated through heterosexuality.[115] In so doing, it offers a new account of the relationship between race and sexuality at the crucial moment of their development.

Suicide, a Biopolitical Scandal

Put simply, race suicide molds a social body in the image of an individual body that is white, degenerated, and becoming sterile. This degenerated social body appears strangely animate in the works of G. Frank Lydston, one of the founders of American sexology. Best known as the first physician to implant a whole testicle into a male body (an experiment he reportedly performed on his own body), Lydston was deeply concerned with issues of white male sterility, commenting on such topics as the dangers of miscegenation, venereal disease, and the use of Black castration, as well as race suicide.[116] In *The Disease of the Society* (1904), Lydston postulates a simultaneously homologous and correspondent relationship between the individual body and the social body, where the individual body is both a component and a mirror image of the body social. In Lydston's organismic view, conditions such as "crime, prostitution, pauperism, insanity in its sociologic relations, [and] anarchy" constitute "patholog[ies] of the social body," which are often caused by "actual physical disease in offenders against society."[117] This anthropomorphization of the social body leads Lydston to a diagnosis: "The body social is growing more and more neuropathic," since "America has for many years furnished conditions peculiarly favorable to degeneracy."[118]

This vision of the neuropathic social body—imagined as brimming with degenerate individuals—redoubles the rhetorical force of *race suicide* by tapping into both its figurative and literal meanings. That is, while *race suicide* figures decreasing white fertility as "suicide," degeneration was understood to cause actual suicidal desire, thereby imagining a literal suicide of the social body. The degenerate social body is not only becoming sterile and failing to

26 THE SUICIDAL STATE

reproduce its whiteness; it is also trying to kill itself. Pointing to the steady increase of suicides in the United States, Lydston argues: "Suicide is perhaps more intimately associated with insanity than is any other antisocial act. Its prevalence is one of the most convincing proofs of the fact that under present conditions a certain rather constant percentage of degeneracy is to be counted on in every social system."[119] For American medical practitioners, degeneracy was understood in the same register as what was known as the "distinctly American condition"—neurasthenia, nervous enervation caused by overcivilization (a point to which we will return in Chapter 1). Summarizing a paper titled "Racial Deterioration: Increase of Suicide," an 1897 newspaper article reports: "The increase of suicide, the paper attributed to heredity and to the fertility of the degenerated portion of the community. It is a product of civilization, [and] depends chiefly on some constitutional depravity, as is shown by the emanation from bad stock."[120] Degenerate individuals—if they procreate—disseminate the germ of death in the social body through the hereditary transmission of suicidal tendencies.

This hereditarization of suicidal tendencies marks a distinct moment in the US conceptual history of suicide. Though the term *suicide* was coined in the seventeenth century England "to replace the more overtly condemnatory vocabulary of homicide, slaughter, and murder ('self-slaughter,' self-murder,' 'self-homicide')," it was still heavily stigmatized as a moral sin in the US colonial period, often regarded as "the worst kind of Murder."[121] Although the willful suicide was criminalized as a *felo de se* ("a felon of himself") and punished heavily until the mid-eighteenth century, it became less prosecuted circa the 1776 Independence, as juries increasingly attributed it to "mental derangement (*non compos mentis*)."[122] This shift from crime to pathology, as Foucault briefly mentions, indexes the transition of power from sovereign to nascent biopower.[123] The medicalization of suicide accelerated at the beginning of the nineteenth century, when humane societies, the precursors to asylums, emerged to prevent suicide and offer "moral treatment" to cure the ill.[124] This disciplinary control intensified throughout the century as asylums proliferated, and suicide became a central object for the embryonic discipline of psychiatry.

While this disciplinary model regarded suicidal desire as "curable," the rise of neurological psychiatry at the end of the century increasingly understood it in relation to degeneracy, framing suicide in hereditary terms. S. A. K. Strahan exemplifies this deterministic view, understanding suicide to result from degeneracy, marked by what he calls "the suicidal instinct," or an "absence of th[e] fundamental instinct for self-preservation."[125] As Ian Marsh argues, while this model of "diseased instincts" might be traced as far back as James Cowles Prichard's *A Treatise on Insanity and Other Disorders Affecting the Mind* (1835), the linkage between suicide and instinct became far more prominent in relation to degeneracy, where "the instinct for life itself" was understood to be "diseased or perverted," thereby resulting in suicide.[126] This perversion of self-preservatory instinct, Strahan argues, expands intergenerationally: "The family degeneracy, of which suicide is one of the ordinary signs, deteriorates rapidly to sterility, impotent idiocy, and extinction of the family."[127] Crucially, on their way to suicidal extinction, these degenerates "contaminate the race by the propagation of their unfitness."[128] Thus, the hereditary model understood suicide as an individuated pathology that threatened the race and the population. In this sense, *race suicide*, in its figuration of willful sterility as a self-inflicted death, effected a double perversion of "two fundamental instincts, those of procreation and of self-preservation."[129]

The Suicidal State takes this degeneracy model of suicide as our historical starting point, tracing the gradual shift to a more psychoanalytic understanding that emerged by the second decade of the twentieth century. In doing so, this project charts how death came to be privatized and eroticized, imagined as an escape from the biopolitics of population. Both as a discourse and a figuration, "race suicide" doubly exemplifies this yoking of sex and death: while the pro-natal discourse of race suicide propagates the reproductive imperative to preserve the social body and protect it from a potential death, *race suicide* as a figuration signals the repudiation of such a biopolitical mandate, testifying to the death drive of the social body. If suicide's—and by extension, *race suicide*'s—renunciation of the imperative to live, to procreate, and to reproduce the (social) body was understood as a perversion both of life-preserving and procreative instincts, such a perversion was an erotically charged one as well, particularly in the burgeoning discourse of psychoanalysis.

This eroticization of death is exemplified by the conceptualization of the "death instinct" in Freud's *Beyond the Pleasure Principle* (1920). Whereas neurological psychiatry postulated the "suicidal instinct" as a congenital and hereditary pathology of the degenerate subject, Freudian psychoanalysis universalizes it as one that exists in all subjects.[130] Through this universalization of suicidality, as Marsh argues, psychoanalysis and psychological therapies constructed a suicidal subjectivity optimized for

28   THE SUICIDAL STATE

disciplinary control, wherein "the suicidal patient was no longer just to be confined, contained and restrained, but was now ... required to confess."[131] At the same time, this universalization "rigorously opposed the political and institutional effects of the perversion-heredity-degenerescence system," to use Foucault's uncharacteristically warm description of psychoanalysis as he describes Freud's theorization of universal bisexuality and polymorphous perversity. Foucault here means that psychoanalysis' universalizing impulse prevented the delimitation of perversion, degeneracy, and pathologized heredity to minoritized and marginalized bodies. If, as Sander Gilman argues, Freudian psychoanalysis aims at "a universalization of human experience and an active exclusion of the importance of race from its theoretical framework" (particularly because of its Jewish origin, a racial category heavily associated with degeneration in Europe, a point to which I will return in Chapter 4), its departure from the degeneracy model might bespeak its opposition to biopolitical techniques of racialization.

In *Beyond the Pleasure Principle,* Freud hypothesizes that the fundamental pleasure of being lies in the elimination of external sensations, designating the organism's tendency to pursue this state of equilibrium the *pleasure principle.* This theorization of pleasure builds on his *Three Essays on the Theory of Sexuality* (1905), where he argues that, *contra* sexological consensus, sexual aim consists not in procreation and the preservation of the species but in "replacing the projected sensation of stimulation in the erotogenic zone."[132] However, while *Three Essays* holds onto the developmental narrative in which heterosexual intercourse becomes the primary means to remove sexual tension, *Beyond the Pleasure Principle* offers a new theory of pleasure. In this later text, sex is understood to serve the *reality principle,* which preserves life and operates against the pleasure principle to deter its fulfilment. The pleasure principle, which Freud also refers to as the "Nirvana principle," attempts "to return to the quiescence of the inorganic world" that supposedly existed before the inception of life; as Freud succinctly puts it, the pleasure principle ultimately "seems actually to serve the death instincts."[133] The reality principle, on the other hand, serves the *life instinct,* which subsumes the self-preservatory instinct and the sexual instinct, demanding the temporary postponement of the pleasure principle's satisfaction—the "return to the inanimate state"—prolonging the course toward death.

What is at stake here is *not* whether the death drive actually exists. Rather, what I am pointing at here is that Freud's theorization of the death instinct

INTRODUCTION 29

and the pleasure principle counteracts the turn-of-the-century biopolitical deployment of sex. In defining pleasure as the elimination of excitement, *Beyond the Pleasure Principle* broke with the populational underpinning of sexuality, wherein the "sexual instinct" had primarily been understood to be, to use sexologist Richard von Krafft-Ebing's words, "indispensable for the preservation of the race."[134] In one sense, Freud's theorization of pleasure as the elimination of tension that consummates in death defies the logic of preservation itself. That is, inasmuch as sex is a means for obtaining this pleasure, its goal is no longer the preservation of the race, but rather overcoming the instinct of self-preservation. Simply put, the death instinct counters the logic of biopolitics that aims at preservation, security, and reproduction.

The suicidal social body imagined by the figuration, *race suicide*, I argue, restages the death instinct in the collective rather than individual body, exemplifying what Lee Edelman calls "the social order's death drive."[135] That is, while the alarmist discourse of race suicide constitutes a paradigmatic example of Edelman's reproductive futurism in its equation of sterility with futurity's dead end, *race suicide*, as a figuration, envisions a social body driven by the pleasure principle, pursuing self-shattering jouissance. Crucially, in its death-laden animation of the white social body—as a precarious life to be protected on the discursive level, and as a psychic structure irresistibly drawn to death on the figural level—race suicide stages the racializing logic inherent in reproductive futurism. Edelman's *No Future* has been critiqued, most famously by José Esteban Muñoz, for its apparent indifference to race and its concomitant reproduction of the "monolithic figure of the child that is indeed always already white."[136] Race suicide's deployment of reproductive futurism illustrates that the Child, in its capitalized figuration of both futurity and reproduction, is *in fact*—at least figuratively—white. That is, the Child represents not only biological reproduction but also the logic of *re*production itself, where the current social order is imagined to be replicated, preserved, and secured. In the turn-of-the-century US context, the color of that biopolitical order was overdeterminedly white, although (as we will see in the following chapters) its whiteness was perpetually in contention.

The social order's death drive—of which *race suicide* provides one historical instantiation—threatens to rupture this reproductive logic itself. Crucially, as Edelman emphasizes, this death drive is "internal to the social," for it marks "the hole in the Symbolic" where the Real peeks through.[137] That is, the drive to shatter the social order emanates from the fissure that was inevitably left in the process of social signification in the very construction of the social order itself. For the biopolitical state, this cleft consists of, at least partly, the unnamable and un-grievable lives that are being neglected, exploited, and disposed in the name of the population's security. Or rather, they constitute non-lives in the eyes of biopower, and as such, they become the living-death in the social body.

This living-death underpins biopower's right to kill, which, according to Foucault, ultimately turns against itself. In his explanation of state racism's "vital importance" to the operation of biopower, he invokes the Nazi regime as a prime example of the biopolitical state, pointing to its suicidality: "We have an absolutely racist State, an absolutely murderous State, and an absolutely suicidal State. A racist State, a murderous State, and a suicidal State."[138] As we have seen, biopower structurally requires a biological threat to its population, for it provides the only pretext for the interventionist approach to the population, endowing biopower, in that process, the right to kill. For the Nazi regime, however, the extermination of other races was not the sole means to protect the Aryan race. Rather, its racial purity and regeneration were ultimately understood to be achieved by "expos[ing] its own race to the absolute and universal threat of death," as exemplified by Hitler's Telegram 71 ordering the destruction of the nation upon the loss of the war.[139] Despite Nazism's incommensurable terror, Foucault sees biopower's simultaneously murderous and suicidal operation in the case of the Third Reich as generalizable to the modern state writ large: "The final solution for the other races, and the absolute suicide of the . . . race. That is where this mechanism inscribed in the working of the modern State leads."[140]

What does it mean, then, that the biopolitical state is intrinsically suicidal, that every social order under biopower's life-administration possesses—or is possessed by—the death drive? Robert Esposito provides one entryway into this paradox, explaining that biopower's investment in life makes death itself its ultimate threat. While the Jewish people constituted for Nazis the agent of living-death that must be eradicated, "the only way for an individual or collective organism to save itself definitively from the risk of death is to die."[141] Esposito likens this protective self-killing to an autoimmune illness of the social body, where "the protective apparatus becomes so aggressive that it turns against its own body (which is what it should protect), leading to its death."[142]

Esposito shares this biomedical metaphor with Jacques Derrida, who argues, in his texts written in the wake of the suicidal attack of 9/11, that "suicidal autoimmunity" is constitutive to democracy: democracy, in its attempt to protect itself, undoes itself.[143] On the one hand, the democratic polity attempts "to immunize itself, to protect itself against the aggressor (whether from within or without)," and thereby "secrete[s] its enemies on both sides . . . so that its only apparent options remained murder and suicide."[144] By disavowing, suppressing, or expelling the "enemies of democracy" that might as well be bred by and within its own system, democracy undoes itself: it compromises itself and becomes a semblance of its putative enemy.[145] On the other hand, Derrida argues, such an autoimmune undoing constitutes "at the same time . . . chance and threat, threat as chance."[146] For ultimately what autoimmunity threatens to destroy is "the I [*moi*] or the self [*soi*], the *ego* or the *autos*, ipseity itself."[147] In other words, suicidal autoimmunity undermines the sovereignty of the self by undoing the boundary between the self and the non-self. In so doing, it pries open and exposes itself to all those who it has previously excluded. Hence Derrida calls autoimmunity "this poisoned medicine, this *pharmakon* . . . that is sometimes called 'the death drive.'"[148]

Derrida's suicidal autoimmunity thus vividly portrays the social order's death drive in an even more pronouncedly corporeal way by using biopower's privileged metaphor, immunity, and thereby enables us to think of race suicide's—and by extension, suicide's—relation to biopolitics. As we have seen, the simultaneous rise of modern immunology and the discourse of race suicide constructed the US social body as a vulnerable biological entity, authorizing the forceful disposal of the undesirable in the name of its defense. In this sense, autoimmunity—a phenomenon first observed at precisely the moment of Ross's invention of *race suicide*—provides an apt figuration for the irony of such a biopolitical defense mechanism, which now turns against itself and exposes itself to the other that it has excluded—be it Blacks, immigrants, or queers. In this framework, the suicidal state—of which *race suicide* becomes a historical manifestation—invites democracy's simultaneous undoing and becoming through its autoimmune disorder.

Much as autoimmunity's democratic undoing of the sovereign self is alluring, however, its biomedical metaphoricity seems indicative of our profound enmeshment in the figuration of the *social body*. To put it differently, if the biopolitics of population deployed the image of the precarious (white) body to massify individual bodies into its life-administration process, and if we are to defy its massifying eugenic calculus, perhaps we must step outside of this biologizing rhetoric itself. In other words: how can we

32   THE SUICIDAL STATE

articulate autoimmunity's suicidal undoing of the self without reinforcing the biologization of the social order—the logic that underwrites the murderous operation of biopower? Is it possible for us to escape biopower at all—to retrieve the individual body from enmeshment in the biopolitical social body?

Literary Counter-Conduct

Suicide is loaded with these questions for Foucault himself. Ever critical of "the promise of a 'liberation'" given by biopower in exchange for the participation in the discourse of sexuality, Foucault's view on death is uncharacteristically romantic.[149] While the discourse of sexuality exploits sex "as *the* secret" to be confessed and thus subjectivizes individuals, Foucault says, death has become "the most secret aspect of existence, the most 'private.'"[150] Foucault here seems to suggest that whereas sexuality—situated at the node of reproductive biopolitics and disciplinary anatomo-politics—conjoins the individual body into the social body, the singularity of death cordons off the fantastical realm unmediated by biopower: the most private, the most intimate, and the most unknowable.

Suicide, among other deaths, occupies a privileged place in Foucault's thought, signaling the potential to short-circuit biopower and exemplifying, therefore, what he designates as *counter-conduct*. If biopolitical governmentality—like its precursor, pastoral power—seeks to shepherd its subjects and direct, manage, or choreograph their conduct (hence governmentality's moniker, "conduct of conduct"), counter-conduct expresses the desire to "be conducted differently," or to "escape direction by others and to define the way for each to conduct himself."[151] It is not revolt (for it is more decentered and subdued), nor dissidence (for it lacks heroism); it is a struggle, a web of conducts by which one refuses, nullifies, or parries its obligatory relation to the matrix of power, while forging new forms of subjectivities, relationalities, and ways of being in the world. As Arnold Davidson explains, counter-conduct for Foucault is an ethical and political cornerstone for "becoming other than what we are."[152] One such counter-conduct that fascinated Foucault in the contemporary sphere is the "homosexual way of life" (rather than homosexuality as a sexual identity, or even as same-sex sexual acts); another, what Davidson calls "[one] of Foucault's most disquieting acclamations of counter-conduct," is suicide.[153]

INTRODUCTION   33

Indeed, Foucault sees suicide as a conduct that enables new configurations of lifeways and aesthetics: as he puts it, "there is no conduct more beautiful . . . than suicide."[154] Albeit tongue-in-cheek, Foucault rapturously talks about suicide on multiple occasions—eroticizing it, even, as he fantasizes about "suicide festivals or orgies," and calling suicide "a fathomless pleasure whose patient and relentless preparation will enlighten all of your life."[155] For Foucault, just as two men in an intense friendship open up "the formation of new alliances" as they "invent, from A to Z, a relationship that is still formless," conducting oneself toward suicide breaks open a richly unstructured field of relations outside biopolitics' encaging lockstep. While Foucault's theorization of friendship has long provided a locus for imagining possibilities for life outside state-sanctioned forms of intimacy, suicide's erotic potential has been left underattended in queer studies. However, if suicide constitutes "the simplest of pleasures" for Foucault—as he dubs it in the title of an essay on suicide—such pleasure might bring forth what he famously envisages as a "different economy of bodies and pleasure": an extraterritorial realm lying beside biopower's deployment of sexuality, where the individual body is loosened from the social body's clutches and structured otherwise.

The Suicidal State amplifies Foucault's muted suggestion and explores suicide's queer potential as a counter-conduct, especially as it was imagined at the dawn of modern sexuo-racial regimes. Suicidal figures in Progressive Era literature, I argue, literalize and enact *race suicide* on the level of individual bodies, short-circuiting the biopolitical imperatives of racial preservation and self-preservation. Their suicides, in other words, constitute double perversions of the life-instincts, both procreative and self-preservative. As such, their suicides gesture toward new erotic relationalities and pleasures that fall outside of the bio- and anatomo-political discourse of sexuality, even as they liquidate their subjectivity in the very act.

Literature became a privileged site for exploring such elusive possibilities because, as Heather Love beautifully puts it, it "accounts for experience at the juncture of the psychic and the social."[156] What this means is that literature and sexuality are situated alike at the node between the individual and the social, between anatomo- and biopolitics. The Progressive Era texts that we examine here belong loosely to a genre called naturalism—a transient aesthetic movement situated between realism and modernism, often characterized by its deterministic world view, clinical detachment, and infatuation with hereditary and evolutionary discourses, as well as its will to describe, to classify, and to massify.[157] If, as D. A. Miller argues, the

34 THE SUICIDAL STATE

nineteenth-century realist novel is a dispositif of disciplinary power that trains the reader into a depth-model subject, my contention is that naturalist fiction registers an aesthetic shift of governmentality, exemplifying the ethos of a biopolitics of population (a point to which I will return in Chapter 2).[158] That is, what Georg Lukács characterizes in "Narrate or Describe?" (1936) as the "levelling" effect of naturalism's descriptive method, which "debases characters to the level of inanimate objects," is in tandem not only with the development of capitalism, but more broadly with biopolitics and its liberal governmentality, the power that aims to manage the population with no heed to individuals.[159] In this sense, as Emily Steinlight argues in the context of the Victorian novel in *Populating the Novel*, naturalist fiction of the Progressive Era United States marks the flourishing of "the biopolitical imagination," where "mass life rather than individuals ... had become fiction's main concern."[160]

Naturalism's departure from liberal subjectivity, to be sure, has become something of a critical cliché, ever since earlier works of New Historicist criticism—most notably Walter Benn Michaels's *The Gold Standard and the Logic of Naturalism* and Mark Seltzer's *Bodies and Machines*—resuscitated naturalism from critical neglect by dazzlingly showcasing the genre's denaturalization of personhood. Be it the rise of corporate personhood (Michaels) or the mechanical reproduction of statistical persons (Seltzer), naturalist fiction in their accounts works to radically evacuate the agency endowed to the liberal subject.[161] Still, the rise of the de-individuating imaginary in naturalism that was to be further intensified in modernism (we will discuss this aesthetic shift in Chapter 4) does not mean that the literary so easily dispensed with the private self. The Progressive Era literature we examine here more or less presupposes the operation of liberal personhood, and it is this hardwired mechanism's breakdown with the growing awareness of its own fungibility that these texts capture through the portrayal of suicide. The biopolitics of population cannot operate without an anatomo-politics of discipline; for, in order to secure its population, biopolitics presupposes the successful work of disciplinary power, whereby its populational elements are trained to behave more or less predictably according to the norms of the liberal subject. The individual self that is forged for the smooth operation of the collective entity, in turn, necessarily creates turbulent and yet rich system errors of pursuing and believing in its singularity, and the literary has remained a domain suited to record such errant but vital beliefs, which we sometimes call love, desire, or hope.

INTRODUCTION   35

Naturalist fiction, with its nervous awareness of the individual's subsumption into the larger order of things, records this double bind in which the biopolitical subject lives. As Jennifer Fleissner argues in her brilliant reconsideration of naturalism as an aesthetic mode of compulsion, naturalist fiction records "instead of either the social determining the natural or the simple opposite . . . the ongoing negotiations between the two," and, in so doing, it reconfigures what we usually think of agency, will, or freedom.[162] Like Fleissner's compulsion, I argue, suicide in naturalist fiction becomes a rich site of inquiry into what it means to conduct oneself in the otherwise of disciplinary subjectivity, or what can be called the litotic agency of suicide. In exploring the literary affordance of suicide's undoing of the self as a counter-conduct, a form of agency flickering in double-negative, my project aligns with a growing body of work about literary suicide.[163] This scholarship posits suicide as a paradox which is, as Andrew Bennett describes, uniquely agential in its destruction of agency: "a profound unfathomable denial, destruction, or negation of the self, and simultaneously . . . an ultimate assertion of identity and agency."[164] In particular, my project shares an interest in the erotic force of self-annihilation with queer work by Dana Seitler and Benjamin Bateman. Seitler's important essay on queer narratology sees suicide as "a particularly queer form of resistance to the constraining narratives of life itself."[165] Suicidal fantasies of the self's undoing, Seitler argues, sidestep "existing understandings of the plot that square off the patterns for living" and create an alternative space for being. Similarly, in *The Modernist Art of Queer Survival*, Benjamin Bateman sees suicide as a paradoxical form of "survival in which the self expands by losing and lives by dying." That is, by relinquishing, surrendering, abandoning the self's sovereignty, suicide radically puts pressure on "national, racial, sexual, and creaturely limits on what counts as (my and our) life."[166]

While my project echoes Bateman's urgent call for the reconfiguration of survival—under whose name, as we continue to witness, too many lives are trampled—*The Suicidal State* argues that suicide is a mode of and problem for governmentality where the biopolitical calculus of life is put into question. That is, this book theorizes a biopolitics of suicide, especially as it focuses on the racializing force of biopolitics in the Progressive Era United States. Characters under examination in this project are, by and large, situated at the center of the white social body: Olive Chancellor, Henry James's New England Brahmin heroine; Edna Pontellier, Kate Chopin's bourgeois wife, from Roosevelt's favorite "old Kentucky race"; Martin Eden, Jack London's

36 THE SUICIDAL STATE

self-made author, herald of the new white manhood; and David Hersland, Gertrude Stein's representative man of the generic, rising American middle class. In their own ways, these characters, as well as their creators, are hailed by—and, in varying degrees, enmeshed into—the discourse of race suicide. Their use of the allegedly most private thing, sex, never is their own. The fastening between the two bodies—individual and social—is so tight that only through death, it seems, can they claim their private selfhood and their desire. They not only, as the popularizers of race suicide admonished, betray the nation's reproductive imperative by endangering the life of the social body, but they also become traitors to the power that makes life and disallows death by their prodigal wasting of their lives.

The book opens with a chapter tracing the prehistory of race suicide discourse. Chapter 1, "Sacrificial Ecstasy: *The Bostonians*, Neurasthenia, and the 'Obscure Hurt,'" begins in New England in the 1880s, as the region was both the historical center of American Anglo-Saxonism and the place where the drop in the white birthrate was first reported with alarm. The diminishing fertility of New England Anglo-Saxons was often associated with neurasthenia, a disease that designated the debilitation of nerves caused by overcivilization. Though the disease was associated with infertility and suicidality, as was the case with degeneracy, its prevalence among elite New Englanders made neurasthenia—dubbed "Americanitis"—a dual emblem of the old-stock American's racial vulnerability and superiority, prefiguring race suicide's securitizing rhetoric of whiteness. Reading Henry James's queer heroine Olive Chancellor—a dedicated Boston feminist who desires to sacrifice her life to the cause of women—under the sign of such a diagnosis, I argue that *The Bostonians* theorizes how a neurasthenic subject forges queer intimacy with the social body, circumventing the twin Rooseveltian imperatives of reproduction and self-preservation. In particular, I contend that Olive Chancellor's self-sacrificial, suicidal eroticism is effectuated through a quasi-religious desire for wounding, which furnishes a site of pleasure and communal identification as it promises to suture her into the social body on the model of Christ's stigmata.

Chapter 2, "Flirting with Death: *The Awakening*'s Liberal Erotic Economy and the Consuming Desire of New Women," portrays the fin-de-siècle life and death of the "[arch-]criminal against the race": the New Woman, who turned away from motherhood to pursue her own pleasure. This chapter charts the construction of whiteness under Jim Crow in the 1890s, understanding race as formed at the intersection between biological reproduction and property reproduction. Examining the landmark Supreme Court decision *Plessy v. Ferguson* (1896) and the plaintiff Homer Plessy's status as a Creole of color, this chapter recasts Cheryl Harris' foundational reading of the case as designating whiteness as "status property," arguing that whiteness was rather constructed as "family property" that could only be reproduced through heterosexual reproduction. Attending to the complex racialization of white Creoles and Creoles of color in New Orleans, this chapter investigates how the grammar of liberalism—especially its *laissez-faire* articulation—organizes the narrative structure and the erotic economy of Kate Chopin's *The Awakening* (1899). In this reading, the New Woman heroine Edna Pontellier's suicide—by which she evades the clutches of motherhood, which she calls "the soul's slavery"—becomes an act where she squanders whiteness as family property by reclaiming it as her own to dispose of, embodying the narcissistic pleasure of turn-of-the-century cultures of consumption. The liberal logic of self-ownership that structures Edna's suicide is, I argue, established through the material and aesthetic consumption of Black deaths, appropriating the slave suicides represented in William Wells Brown's *Clotel* (1853) and Charles Chesnutt's "Dave's Neckliss" (1889).

Chapter 3, "The Spectral Lineage: Jack London, Teutonism, and Interspecies Kinship," moves from the previous chapters' focus on women to center the crisis of white manhood that race suicide fomented, tracking its manifestation in the rise of US Teutonism in the first decades of the twentieth century. Even though Teutonism is often conflated with its sibling discourse, Anglo-Saxonism, I argue that US Teutonism—later repackaged as Nordicism in Madison Grant's *Passing of the Great Race*—was constructed as whiteness's atavistic return to a Viking-age northern European origin, aiming to disidentify from neurasthenic Anglo-Saxon heritage. Jack London's works set in Alaska and the Yukon stage this phantasmal revivification of the primordial virile tribe, superimposing the image of Viking Age Scandinavia onto the American Northland as the symbolic homeland of the Teutons. Crucially, in London's settler-colonist imagination, this transmutation of whiteness is effectuated through contact with and the massacre of Alaska Natives, paralleling the exterminationist violence of Progressive Era assimilation policies enacted on Native Americans. While the appropriation of the Native practice of totemic kinship opens up a queer space of interspecies intimacy for London, the murderousness of forceful assimilation haunts his work, culminating in the suicide of the eponymous hero of his autobiographical novel, *Martin Eden* (1909).

38 THE SUICIDAL STATE

Chapter 4, "Gertrude Stein's Melting Pot: Jewishness and the Excretory Pleasure of *The Making of Americans*," charts the way in which eastern and southern European new immigrants—whose fertility had precipitated fears of race suicide—were gradually assimilated into the US social body, gaining access to unmarked whiteness. Period discussion over the assimilability of new immigrants often deployed a range of alimentary metaphors—"racial indigestion," "alien indigestion," and the "melting pot"—to imagine the process as their digestive assimilation into the US social body. In her three-generation saga of two immigrant families, *The Making of Americans* (1925), Gertrude Stein takes up this alimentary imaginary but from the other end of the gastrointestinal tract, rescripting the assimilative production of Americans as the social body's excremental process. Reading Stein's text across three versions in relation to her own Jewishness, this chapter maps how the completed 1925 version fossilizes each of the version's aesthetic modes: namely, a realist narrative revolving around individuals, a naturalist compulsion to classify character types, and ultimately a modernist impersonality that manifests human fungibility in a populational calculus. I argue that this trajectory accompanies Stein's increasing abstraction of Jewishness, where she replaces heterosexual racial reproduction with queer coprophilic poetics. David Hersland's suicidal self-starvation, in this reading, erases his own (and Stein's) Jewishness through an anal erotics, transforming himself and other descendants of immigrants into the disembodied white American race, the very exemplification of the ethos of race suicide.

The book closes with the Coda, "Hindsight 20/20, or Asiatic Impersonality," which revisits Edward Ross's initial inspiration for the discourse of race suicide, Asian immigration. By overlaying the rhetoric of Asian exclusion at the turn of the century onto the scenes of anti-Asian violence during the COVID-19 pandemic, the Coda inquires into the association between Asians and death as expressing the absence of their agency in the American imaginary. Taking as its starting point the curious slogan aiming to fight against anti-Asian violence, "I am not a virus," the Coda situates the discourse of Asian virality within Progressive Era immigration histories that linked Asian bodies to leprosy and syphilis. In particular, I trace how fears of fungible, proliferating Asian bodies infecting the US social body—epitomized by "coolies"—gave rise to the discourse of race suicide. In this rhetoric, the figure of the submissive, efficient, and impersonal Asian immigrant emerged as the antipode of the liberal subject, and yet tailor-made for the coming age of standardization and automation. I term this model of subjectivity "Asiatic im-personality" and read it in relation to a number of Madame Butterfly texts, focusing especially on David Belasco's dramatic adaptation, which is the first to feature Cho-Cho-San's death by suicide. In so doing, I historicize a model of Asian subjectivity that maps its contours in relation to the white liberal subject's construction of Blackness as "anti-Human," theorizing the populational imaginary underpinning Asiatic im-personality.

Forged in the biopolitical matrix as fungibles, we still believe in our lives' uniqueness and singularity, because otherwise we can't quite live on, can't quite keep the system going on. At bottom, the discourse of race suicide was precipitated by the fearful awareness of human fungibility—that the "white race" might be replaced by immigrants—and this existential fear is, as I will discuss at the end of Chapter 4, inherited by the white supremacist terrorism of replacement theory in the twenty-first century.[167] Instead of negating one's fungibility through rendering others into unindividuated corpses, the suicides under examination in this book pursue their singularity through what Eve Sedgwick calls "being and learning to unbe a self," letting go of the attachments that enabled their very beings.[168]

But such conceptualizations of the self's voiding itself might well also be a self-indulgent, self-aggrandizing fantasy. We all know that suicide often takes forms other than the paradoxically agential act that annihilates agency that this book tends to portray through its readings of Progressive Era texts. In many cases, we don't quite kill ourselves; *it* happens to us when the self has already been attenuated after the long and slow debilitation from depression, from poverty, from illness, from injury, from rejections, from abuse, from life's foreclosure. *It* also happens to us when the self suddenly collapses under an excess of feeling, pain, or pressure that has accumulated over time. In short, suicide often feels either too lymphatic or too impulsive (or the combination of both) to be framed with such grandiose words as refusal, negation, or even counter-conduct—even though, as every failed suicide knows, to make *it* happen and bring *it* forth requires either extreme levels of diligence and determination or the complete lack thereof, both of which often feel overwhelming for what little self is still left there. Suicide requires commitment, and those who have committed themselves to it at the very least should not be stigmatized.

If the realization of unbeing only visits us, occurs to us, or materializes for and in us, and we cannot quite find it even as we ardently court it, did such a realization visit those Progressive Era suicides at the moment of their deaths? Perhaps, albeit flickeringly—at least, so it seems at the final

40 THE SUICIDAL STATE

moment of Martin Eden's life as Jack London imagines his suicidal dive into the ocean: "And somewhere at the bottom he fell into darkness. That much he knew. He had fallen into darkness. And at the instant he knew, he ceased to know."[169] The realization is evanescent, with its form not the flash of enlightenment but pitch darkness. Their self-inflicted deaths, of course, did not even leave a scratch on the American social body or its continuous reproduction of whiteness. But because of that stroke of otherwise irrealizable learning and its contents foreclosed to us, these suicides seem to occupy the place of the subject supposed to know. As empty placeholders, they teach us nothing, just as they died for nothing. But still, what if this "nothing" is exactly what we need to learn?[170]

Because of their dying-for-nothingness, the Progressive Era suicides seem to beckon us into the pedagogy of unbeing, especially when it has become, at last, painfully evident that the biopolitics of security, preservation, and reproduction is built on and fueled by the state apparatus's daily production of ungrievable corpses. We adhere to this system partly because we believe our lives are produced and sustained by it; our enmeshment in this matrix makes our animacy, both as the collective-singular and as the incommensurable singularity, feel so real. Yet we also know that this "we" or "I" is but a biopolitical illusion that is always disproportionally structured. Some of us have already been dead—been let die, been killed—in the name of the optimization of collective life. Then again, this crisis is not suicidal, since the idea that "we" are all implicated in the single inescapable system is at the core of the biopolitical calculus of population; its systemic neglect is simply genocidal, and its executor is the biopolitical "we." If such a reflection in the mirror is petrifying enough, it might, perhaps, facilitate the pedagogy of unbeing, of being-nobody, of learning to inhabit the void that is left after the self is emptied out, even if it means that we will then have to learn how to live on in this suicidal state.

1
Sacrificial Ecstasy

The Bostonians, Neurasthenia, and the "Obscure Hurt"

"Poodle Henry James"

On October 19, 1884, the *New York Times* reported that a "self-invited guest" filled the room with loud applause as he mounted the platform of the Brooklyn Young Republican Club's inaugural meeting.[1] The return of the twenty-five-year-old Theodore Roosevelt from Dakota was dramatic enough; after losing his wife and his mother on the same day earlier the same year, the young assemblyman of New York had refused renomination and left his home state to seek solace in hunting in the West, leaving his political career indefinitely suspended. Upon his abrupt return to New York, Roosevelt surprised the audience by declaring his support of James Blaine's presidential nomination despite his undisguised abhorrence of this scandal-tainted candidate. In supporting Blaine, Roosevelt confronted his former allies, Republican reformists known as "mugwumps," who were now backing the Democratic candidate Grover Cleveland against party politics. In his fervent speech denouncing the mugwumps, seemingly out of nowhere, Roosevelt referred to a prominent novelist. The *Times* reported:

> Mr. Roosevelt said that his hearers had read to their sorrow the works of Henry James. He bore the same relation to other literary men that a poodle did to other dogs. The poodle had his hair combed and was somewhat ornamental, but never useful. He was invariably ashamed to imitate the British lion. In Mr. Roosevelt's opinion there were many traits in the "Poodle Henry James" that the independents of the Henry James order of intellect had in common. These men formed quite a number of the bolters this year. They were possessed of refinement and culture to see what was wrong, but possessed none of the robuster virtues that would enable them to come out and do the right.[2]

The Suicidal State. Madoka Kishi, Oxford University Press. © Oxford University Press 2024.
DOI: 10.1093/9780197690109.003.0002

42 THE SUICIDAL STATE

As Philip Horne documents, Roosevelt had seen Henry James only once before the speech. Their first meeting was in Boston in January 1883, of which Roosevelt wrote: "The Bostonians were awfully kind to us . . . I was introduced to James, the novelist, and had a most pleasant time."[3] Their encounter seemed agreeable enough. As Horne wonders, therefore, "just why James strayed into Roosevelt's line of fire" in his speech against mugwumps requires some parsing.[4]

To solve the mystery, it might be helpful to begin by understanding how the sex/gender system was mapped onto the Progressive political landscape, particularly in relation to the reformist mugwumps, a group of politicians who opposed corruption and the spoils system even if it meant working across party lines. As Kevin Murphy argues, opponents of the mugwumps denounced their disavowal of party loyalty as "a threat not only to the binary structure of the two-party system but also to essentialist distinctions between men and women."[5] Attacking the implausibility of the mugwumps' agenda, party politicians derided the elite, college-bred Northeastern reformers for their lack of virility, calling them "political hermaphrodites," "political epicenes," and "third sex reformer[s]."[6] In one striking instance in March 1886, the Republican Senator John J. Ingalls stated:

> The neuter gender is not popular either in nature or society. "Male and female He created them." But there is a third sex, if that can sex be called which sex has none, resulting sometimes from a cruel caprice of nature, at others from accident or malevolent design, possessing the vices of both and the virtues of neither; effeminate without being masculine or feminine; unable either to beget or to bear; possessing neither fecundity nor virility; endowed with the contempt of men and the derision of women, and doomed to sterility, isolation, and extinction. . . . These political epicenes, without pride of ancestry or hope of posterity, chant in shrill falsetto their songs of praise of non-partisanship and civil-service reform.[7]

As Murphy argues, party politicians criticized the fruitlessness of mugwump politics with the sexological rhetoric that heterosexualized the American social body, presaging the extinction narrative of race suicide. The third-sex reformers were, they claimed, unable to "beget or bear" the political future and "doomed to sterility, isolation, and extinction," the very picture of political degeneration.

SACRIFICIAL ECSTASY   43

In this context, Roosevelt's speech at the Brooklyn Young Republican Club emerges as a performance of distancing himself from his former allies in order to avoid the charge of impotence. For Roosevelt, the figure of an artificially bred, ornamented "poodle" served to capture his former allies' flaccidness, especially when combined with the name of the well-known celibate novelist whom Roosevelt reportedly dubbed a "little emasculated mass of inanity" elsewhere.[8] It is important to note, though, that the young politician who rode roughshod over the "Poodle Henry James" in his 1884 speech was not yet the fearless Rough Rider that he would be known to be thirteen years later. Rather, Roosevelt's vexation at James and the mugwumps bespeaks his anxiety over his own gender identity in the increasingly heterosexualized American political landscape. Born in the highest circle of New York aristocracy to a Southern belle and a descendant of the earliest Dutch settlers, Theodore "Teddy" Roosevelt was stricken from a young age by congenital nervous diarrhea and asthma, along with numerous minor ailments. Even after the bookish boy made over his physique during his Harvard days and started to climb the political ladder, Roosevelt was anything but the symbol of turn-of-the-century American masculinity. In fact, in his early political career, newspapers "lampooned Roosevelt as the quintessence of effeminacy," heaping scorn on his "high voice, tight pants, and fancy clothing": "Weakling," "Punkin-Lily," and "Jane-Dandy" were some of the epithets attached to Roosevelt during his first term as a Republican assemblyman of New York in 1882.[9] On the day he made his debut at the Assembly, the young politician, clad in "trousers . . . as tight as a tailor could make them," was even dubbed the Legislature's "Oscar Wilde."[10]

In short, "Poodle Henry James" presented an abject mirror image for the young Roosevelt from which he needed to break away: bookishness, European aristocratic sensibility, and decadent effeminacy with a hint of homosexuality. Cliché as it is, his fabled first killing of the grizzly during the 1884 expedition functioned as a rite of passage, one that symbolized his coming into political virility. As he stated in an interview with the *New York Tribune* in July 1884, those who "have accused [him] of representing the kidglove element in politics" would be "electrif[ied]" "if they could see [him] galloping over the plains, day in and day out, clad in a buckskin shirt and leather chaparajos, with a big sombrero on [his] head."[11] To the young politician who would soon call himself the "Cowboy of the Dakotas" upon running for mayor of New York, the celibate novelist's delicate sensibility

44 THE SUICIDAL STATE

nurtured in European high culture offered a handy doormat with which to wipe off the smear of effeminacy.[12]

James did hear the rumor of Roosevelt's jeering and wrote to his friend from London in November 1884: "What was Roosevelt's allusion to, or attack upon, me, in his speech?"[13] Yet in 1884, little did he expect that Roosevelt would keep lambasting him for over a decade. On February 15, 1887, Roosevelt wrote in a letter to Henry Cabot Lodge: "Thank Heaven Henry James is now an avowedly British novelist."[14] In a letter to Brander Matthews on June 29, 1894, he wrote, "What a miserable little snob Henry James is. His polished, pointless, uninteresting stories about the upper social classes of England make one blush to think that he was once an American."[15] A little earlier that same year, Roosevelt had even publicly denounced the cosmopolitan novelist in a thinly veiled attack:

> The undersized man of letters, who flees his country because he, with his delicate, effeminate sensitiveness, finds the conditions of life on this side of the water crude and raw; in other words, because he finds that he cannot play a man's part among men, and so goes where he will be sheltered from the winds that harden stouter souls. This *emigre* may write graceful and pretty verses, essays, novels; but he will never do work to compare with that of his brother, who is strong enough to stand on his own feet, and do his work as an American.[16]

In short, Roosevelt concluded, "He is a silly and undesirable citizen. He is as emphatically a noxious element in our body politic as is the man who comes here from abroad and remains a foreigner."[17] Even before it finds the vehicle of *race suicide* with the influx of so-called new immigrants, Roosevelt's message was consistent: the celibate novelist is as un-American as an immigrant, and there is no place for either of them in the American body social.

But Henry James was an American no less—even as he left the country in 1883 without returning for more than two decades—and he was about to prove as much. The same year Roosevelt mocked him as "Poodle," James was writing a novel in which he aspired to make "the whole thing as local, as American, as possible," in an attempt to "show that [he] *can* write an American story."[18] His 1886 novel *The Bostonians*, which he designed as "a very *American* tale, a tale very characteristic of our social conditions," found a perfect outlet: it was serialized in the *Century Illustrated Monthly Magazine*, which promoted American cultural nationalism in the post-Reconstruction period under the editorship of a prominent mugwump, Richard Watson Gilder.[19] As James wrote in "Anthony Trollope," an essay he had also published in the *Century* in July 1883, no English writers had yet discovered the way to portray "the American heart"; what is more, "we ourselves have not yet learned to represent our types very finely—are not apparently even very sure what our types are."[20]

James's own answer to what defined "our types," the subject he chose for his "very national, very typical" novel, was "one of those friendships between women which are so common in New England."[21] The heroine of *The Bostonians* indeed reifies a distinct American type, one that prefigured Roosevelt's nightmare: the old-stock American's moribund future of race suicide. Bereaved of her parents and her brothers, Olive Chancellor is the sole name bearer of the Chancellors, a family that "belonged to the *bourgeoisie*— the oldest and best."[22] Yet the proud Boston Brahmin lineage is destined to vanish with her, for Olive Chancellor is a "signal old maid. That was her quality, her destiny . . . She was so essentially a celibate" (816). The perpetuation of her family name and the old American stock is neither her destiny nor desire. She is "a female Jacobin," a suffragist who is ready to "reform the solar system if she could get hold of it," and she finds her ideal mate in Verena Tarrant, a celebrated séance medium, who becomes her feminist protégé (805, 806). Like her fellow third-sex reformists, the mugwumps, Olive Chancellor is a figure of sterility, extinction, and even death itself, for ultimately, her "most secret, . . . most sacred hope" is to "be a martyr and die" for the feminist cause (811). Upon their first meeting, her Mississippian cousin Basil Ransom immediately senses that Olive Chancellor is possessed by death: "This pale girl, with her light-green eyes, her pointed features and nervous manner, was visibly morbid; it was as plain as day that she was morbid" (810). Yet the moment Basil is thrilled with this "great discovery," the narrator intervenes: "It proves nothing of any importance, with regard to Miss Chancellor, to say that she was morbid: any sufficient account of her would lie very much to the rear of it. Why was she morbid, and why was her morbidness typical?" (810).

Olive Chancellor's morbidness is typical, I argue, because her willful sterility and death wish heralds the suicidality of old-stock Americans. Though the term *race suicide* itself was still awaiting its 1901 debut, the last few decades of the nineteenth century already saw the signs of racial anxiety over what Roosevelt later called "the diminishing birth rate among the old native American stock."[23] The epicenter of this population shift was New England,

46   THE SUICIDAL STATE

the region that Roosevelt referred to as the place "where the English stock was purest," thus designating it as old-stock Americans' glorious site of origin.[24] New England—Boston in particular—was witnessing the heyday of Anglo-Saxonism in the 1880s. Particularly influential in this development were Henry Adams's lectures at Harvard from 1873 to 1874, which resulted in *Essays in Anglo-Saxon Law* (1876), a volume cowritten with his students. Among Adams's students was Henry Cabot Lodge, whose belief in Anglo-Saxon superiority later made him a leading anti-immigration advocate, as well as other New England intellectuals—Barrett Wendell, Herbert Baxter Adams, and John Fiske, among others—who helped popularize Anglo-Saxonism, often idealizing New England's town meetings as direct heirs to the Anglo-Saxon tribal council.[25]

It is no surprise, then, that the beginning of Roosevelt's battle against race suicide coincided with his discovery of the dropping fertility rate in New England in the 1890 census.[26] Over a decade prior to Roosevelt's realization, however, New England intellectuals were already seeing the shadow of race suicide; or rather, the high tide of Anglo-Saxonism acquired its force precisely because of the fear of waning Anglo-Saxon dominance in the region. Nathan Allen, in "Changes in New England Population" (1883), referred to the 1880 census and warned of the ongoing displacement of the native-born American population by immigrants in New England. Because the foreign-born population was increasingly replacing old-stock Americans as agricultural workers, the native-born population increasingly worked indoors. As a result, native-born Americans were understood to suffer a "loss of physical vigor and character," which led them to a "physical degeneracy" that prevented the procreation of healthy offspring.[27] As historian Barbara Solomon writes, "a steady increase in divorces and suicides as well as a lowering birth rate" led numerous New England intellectuals to elegize the collapse of the region and the atrophy of the old American stock.[28] So much so that Barrett Wendell wrote in his diary in May 1884: "I wonder if anybody ever reached thirty-five in New England without wanting to kill himself."[29]

Chronicling the prehistory of the race suicide panic, this chapter explores the way in which the novelist "Poodle Henry James" rewrites the Rooseveltian narrative of reproductive Americanism through the portrayal of a celibate New England heroine enchanted by sacrificial death. In creating an old-stock heroine marked by neurasthenia—a catchall "nervous disease" that was often associated with sexual debilitation and suicidal depression—and presenting her as a representative "American type," *The Bostonians* foretells the story of race suicide through degenerating Anglo-Saxonism in New England. In doing so, James presents a reproductively sterile yet erotically fecund relationship between two women as a counternarrative to the increasingly heterosexualized rhetoric of post-Reconstruction nationalism. By superimposing Olive Chancellor's nonparticipation in the Civil War onto his own, I will argue, Henry James imagines a way that their social stigma becomes a wound, one that is open for relationality and identification, suturing the individual bodies of the third-sex reformers to the wounded body social. The neurasthenic American heroine's suicidal ideation, in this reading, marks her desire for a sacrificial ecstasy that constitutes her quasi-religious, metaphysical eros. While this pleasure is ultimately not granted to Olive Chancellor within the narrative, as we will see at the end of this chapter, it is to be conferred on the protagonist of the novel that James wrote and published immediately after *The Bostonians*: *The Princess Casamassima* (1886).

The Neurasthenic Race

Upon his first encounter with our heroine, what strikes Basil Ransom is his Yankee cousin's intense nervousness. Olive Chancellor is "peculiarly . . . constituted" by her "nervous and serious" nature; her nervousness subjects her to "fits of tragic shyness, during which she was unable to meet even her own eyes in the mirror" or, even worse, to "tears, headaches, a day or two in bed, acute emotion" (872, 809, 813). Accordingly, as we have seen, Basil concludes that this pathetically nervous "pale girl" is "morbid"; but the narrator derides Basil's obtuseness the moment he makes this "great discovery." Olive's morbidness is writ large; in itself, it is no secret. Again, at issue here is why her morbid nervousness is "typical" and how it constitutes her as an American "type."

Olive Chancellor's nervousness indeed epitomizes a famous fin-de-siècle American type, especially in the context of the medical discourse of the time. As Wendy Graham incisively argues, "Olive Chancellor markedly resembles the congenital degenerates, moral perverts, and constitutional neurotics populating contemporary medical journals."[30] Many physicians argued that both the decline of the fertility rate and the desire for death rampant among elite New Englanders were caused by the same factor: neurasthenia, a disease roughly translated as "lack of nerve energy."[31] In 1884, for instance, John Ellis

48 THE SUICIDAL STATE

published *Deterioration of the Puritan Stock and Its Causes*, deploring the decay of New England, which was, he claimed, brought forth by the "degeneracy of the native stock."[32] The "moribund condition of the puritan stock" was frequently ascribed to the rise of the suffrage movement, which allegedly led native-born New England women—including our heroine—"into a fatuous struggle to compete with man in masculine pursuits, overtasking her powers of endurance and debilitating her nervous system."[33]

First coined in 1869 and initially imagined as endemic to Northern industrial cities, neurasthenia became a common diagnosis nationwide by the 1880s, popularized by New York nerve specialist George Beard. Neurasthenia understood those symptoms that formerly had no name—depression, insomnia, indigestion, anxiety, headaches, loss of sexual appetite, and sexual impotence, to name a few—to be caused by the debilitation of the nervous system. Designating the effects of modernization as the primary cause of nervous exhaustion, neurasthenia was first and foremost understood as a disease of civilization; more specifically, it was conceived as a disease unique to American civilization. In his *American Nervousness* (1881), Beard claimed that neurasthenia was caused by overstimulation of the nerves by such factors as "steam power, the periodical press, the telegraph, the sciences, and the intellectual activities of women" —all of which, he asserts, paradoxically made modern America distinct from civilizations of the past: "All this is modern, and originally American: no age, no country, and no form of civilization, not Greece, nor Rome, nor Spain, nor the Netherlands, in the days of their glory, possessed such maladies."[34]

In his explication of the causes of the illness, David Schuster argues, "Beard infused his discussion of neurasthenia with a powerful nationalist sentiment that supported the idea that America was an exceptional country in the history of nations."[35] As a national malady, neurasthenia created complex interactions between individual bodies and America's social body. As Schuster and Julian Carter contend, neurasthenia not only inscribed the national ethos into individual bodies, but implicitly racialized the national body, for this supposedly national disease was imagined as endemic primarily to the old American stock. When Beard catalogues the physiognomic features of the average nervous invalid, the archetypal patient he envisions is clearly an upper-class white: "The fine organization is distinguished from the coarse by fine, soft hair, delicate skin, nicely chiseled features, small bones, tapering extremities, and frequently by a muscular system comparatively small and feeble . . . It is the organization of the civilized, refined, and

SACRIFICIAL ECSTASY 49

educated, rather than of the barbarous and low-born and untrained."[36] As Schuster points out, Beard claims that "Catholics, southerners, Indians, blacks" are not susceptible to neurasthenia, thus framing the disease as "a white, Anglo-Saxon, Protestant, Yankee condition."[37]

As susceptibility to neurasthenia was believed to be hereditarily transmitted, the neurasthenic proclivity forged what Carter calls a "natural American aristocracy of nerves."[38] As such, the nervous disorder became an emblem of the dilemma that the old American stock faced, prefiguring race suicide's construction of whiteness as "both precious and vulnerable."[39] That is, while neurasthenia supposedly marked its sufferers' upper-class old-stock lineage, it also bespoke their inability to continue their racial stock, for one of its chief manifestations was sexual exhaustion, as epitomized by the title of Beard's last book, *Sexual Neurasthenia* (1884).[40] The neurasthenic social body was as gendered as it was racialized, for the loss of nerve energy was understood to be caused, at least partially, by deviations from traditional gender roles: increases in men's indoor (read: feminine) overwork and women's intellectual (read: masculine) activities. Its cure, therefore, was to return the patients to their respective gender spheres: Silas Weir Mitchell's infamous "rest cure" for neurasthenic women had its lesser-known male counterpart, dubbed the "West cure," in which his male patients were advised to head westward to hunt and work on ranches, just as Theodore Roosevelt successfully did in Dakota.[41] In short, if the neurasthenic social body was racially constructed as white, its imagined gender was neuter: it was—like the "third-sex" reformers—"doomed to sterility, isolation, and extinction."

What we see in Olive Chancellor—about whom Basil Ransom wonders "what sex" she belongs to—is the portrait of a neurasthenic (1108). Her tightly drawn white skin, colorless hair, cold hands, and painfully angular yet exquisitely delicate frame—everything about her constitutes "a nervous organization," while at the same time representing "something very modern and highly developed" (817).[42] Henry James was most likely familiar with the medical language surrounding neurasthenia, for the Jameses were notorious for their line of weak nervous systems. Ruth Bernard Yeazell documents: "Neurasthenia, like intelligence, seems to have run in the family. Medical reports and advice fill their letters to one another: insomnia, digestive disorders, backaches, and headaches came and went among them in rapid succession."[43] The James family history is colored by frequent nervous breakdowns: Henry Senior in 1844, Alice (who also suffered numerous minor "attacks") in 1868 and 1878, William in 1870, Robertson in 1881, and

50 THE SUICIDAL STATE

Henry Junior in 1910. Many family members underwent either Mitchell's rest cure or Beard's galvanic treatments. William consulted Beard for medical advice from 1879 to 1883, immediately before Henry Junior wrote *The Bostonians*, and later famously dubbed the disease "Americanitis."[44]

Particularly germane to Henry James's characterization of the morbidly nervous heroine of his American tale would be the case of the only daughter of the Jameses, Alice James, with whom Henry was living in a small house in Boston for a while after both of their parents died in 1882.[45] From her youth, Alice was bedridden, diagnosed with various "nervous diseases"—nervous hyperaesthesia, spinal neurosis, and hysteria—until she died of breast cancer at the age of forty-four in 1892. Yeazell argues that unlike William's and Henry's neurasthenia, which ultimately became a source of their intellectual productivity, "hers was not a case with any obvious compensations"; instead, "dying had become Alice James's chief vocation," as she constantly inscribed her contemplation of death in her diary.[46] Alice's breakdown in 1877, in particular, became a clear manifestation of her fascination with death, as her father Henry James Senior wrote in a letter to Robertson: "Alice is half the time, indeed much more than half, on the verge of insanity and suicide."[47] Despite her father's pathologization of her suicidality, however, Alice envisioned suicide as an act that would prove her own agency. When Alice asked her father for permission to kill herself and he granted it, she told him that now that "she could perceive it to be her *right* to dispose of her own body when life had become intolerable . . . she was more than content to stay by [his] side."[48] What Alice herself called her "mortuary inclinations" were, however, subdued when she met Katherine Peabody Loring.[49] This Boston social reformer became Alice's lifelong companion, declaring to Henry that it was her desire "quite as strongly as Alice's, to be with her to the end."[50] Henry witnessed Alice and Katherine's strong bond first-hand when the three of them spent time together in both Boston and London between 1881 and 1884, the period immediately preceding the composition of *The Bostonians*.

As Graham notes, the "parallels between Alice James and Olive Chancellor" are evident, especially in light of "their shared sexual nonconformity."[51] Like Alice James, who called herself a "flaccid virgin" and remained unmarried all her life, Olive Chancellor is "essentially a celibate"; like Alice, Olive is involved in a long-term, intense, passionate relationship with her feminist companion (816).[52] Graham rightly contends that in order to bring out "the specter of a not-yet-articulated female homosexuality," James drew on two cultural linkages: feminism and neurasthenia on the one hand,

SACRIFICIAL ECSTASY 51

feminism and gender nonconformity on the other.[53] Deploying feminism as its jointure, James created a new cultural type—the "hysterical lesbian suffragist"—who then became the prototype for what Theodore Roosevelt called "a criminal against the race . . . an object of contemptuous abhorrence by all healthy people."[54] In the early twentieth century, articles even started to designate the feminists associated with women's clubs as "commit[ting] race suicide and encourag[ing] other women to do likewise."[55]

However, while Graham explains Olive Chancellor's and, by extension, Alice James's nervous affliction as a consequence of sexual repression—in particular, their "repudiation of lesbian possibility"—this chapter will understand the nature of the sexual nonconformity shared by Alice and Olive in a different key.[56] As Hugh Stevens notes, the novel's insistence on Olive's "feverish cult of virginity" indeed seems to indicate that "James wants his reader to understand both that Olive Chancellor is passionately—and *erotically*—attracted to Verena, but that there is no sexual relationship between the women."[57] The absence of their physical relationship, however, becomes a sign of the repression of lesbianism only if we take sexual gratification as the sole parameter of erotic fulfillment. Rather than being a sign of repression, as Benjamin Kahan argues, "Olive's celibacy glows with eroticism, exemplifying a sexuality without a normative aspiration to sexual acts."[58] The shape of Olive Chancellor's erotic economy is not readily decipherable, but that is not because the author and the protagonist fail to find a proper articulation for her sexuality. Rather, I will argue, it is because such nonphysicality is central to the aim of Olive's erotic passion. That is, Olive's passional economy is *meta*physical, centering on a quasi-religious ecstasy of self-dispossession through sacrifice. Through this metaphysical desire for sacrificial death, Olive's neurasthenic suicidality demands the reconfiguration of the heterosexualized social body, cleaving open a place for the third-sex reformers.

The Wounded Body Social

To locate the definitional core of Olive Chancellor's sacrificial eroticism as one divorced from the physicality of sex, it would be helpful to return to the scene in which Basil Ransom first perceives her morbid nervousness. Her neurasthenic morbidity stares Basil in the face; it is no secret, and "any sufficient account of her would lie very much to the rear of that" (810). Were

52 THE SUICIDAL STATE

he to "explain that mystery," the narrator enigmatically says, Basil Ransom should have "gone back far enough" (810). Leaving Basil shrouded in his ignorance, the narrator indeed takes the reader to the "rear" of Olive's morbidness by "going back" to Basil's place of origin. For "the blighted South" from which Basil has come is in fact associated with Olive's own past (810): her "vivid remembrance" of the "blood and tears" of the Civil War, in which she lost her two brothers (811). Instead of loathing her brothers' former foe, however, Olive unexpectedly finds herself trembling with "a kind of tenderness of envy" upon her realization that Basil, as an ex-Confederate veteran, had once "offered his own life, even if it had not been taken" (811). Her tender envy discloses the secret lurking in the rear of her undisguised morbidness: "The most secret, the most sacred hope of her nature was that she might some day have such a chance, that she might be a martyr and die for something" (811). Before Olive and Basil meet Verena Tarrant, who mediates and visualizes their erotic rivalry, Olive already envies her cousin, designating him as her competitor. The prize at stake between them is, for Olive, the privilege to die as a sacred offering to the altar, which would compensate for her failure to offer her life during the War. Captivated by sacrificial death, Olive Chancellor is, in the word's primordial sense, morbid: she is held by *mori*.[59]

Olive's enchantment with sacrificial death figured by her envy for the Confederate veteran points to the thematic centrality of the Civil War in James's American tale. For, as scholars have pointed out, *The Bostonians* is a metaphorical Civil War narrative that revolves around a house once-again-divided between two cousins, a battle between a Confederate veteran and his New-England-bred feminist cousin. The novel's preoccupation with the Civil War should be understood in relation to the heightened nationalist desire for sectional reconciliation in the 1880s and 1890s, when the South's revisionist Lost Cause narrative was gradually gaining national popularity, albeit in a more depoliticized form. Mass-circulated magazines, targeting primarily Northern readers, helped create a nostalgic portrayal of the antebellum South through publications of local color sketches, while also promoting reinterpretations of the War that "celebrate[d] the valor and sacrifice of the men on both sides" through printing war memoirs.[60] *The Bostonians*' original venue of publication, the *Century*, was instrumental in shaping the era's post-Reconstruction nationalism, gaining its popularity through the publication of the massive Civil War memoir series *Battles and Leaders of the Civil War*, serialized from 1884 to 1887.[61] Tellingly, the first installment of

The Bostonians was followed by seven articles of *Battles and Leaders*, including Ulysses Grant's "The Battle of Shiloh."

As has often been argued, *The Bostonians* enacts what Nina Silber has famously called the "romance of reunion"—the popular marriage plot between a Northern hero and a Southern heroine, symbolizing national reconciliation—with an amply ironic twist.[62] The reversed gender assignments of the regions—the Southern man with a slaveholding past "liberating" a Northern woman from nerve-debilitating suffrage—and the sinister overtone of the final "union" between Verena and Basil demonstrate the cynicism of James's oblique deployment of the romance-of-reunion plot. As Ann Brigham argues, Verena and Basil forge their erotic bond at Harvard Memorial Hall, a "temple to youth, manhood, generosity," where deceased student soldiers are consecrated for their "sacrifice" (*Bostonians*, 1024); in this crucial scene, as Basil experiences an affective communion with the Union dead, he is inducted into their patriotic nationhood through his past of "shared personal manly sacrifice."[63] In this way, the novel highlights the way in which the era's national identity was shaped by the tacit acceptance of the Lost Cause's obliteration of racial subjugation—the process whereby nationhood was conflated with whiteness and manhood, while its fraught structure was bolstered by the narrative of heterosexual reunion and sacrifice.

Yet what seems to be left unexamined is how Olive and Verena's same-sex bond figures in James's critique of this popular national narrative—and how their relationship, rather than the allegory of heterosexual marriage, "typifies" the American social body. Olive Chancellor's exclusion from the heterosexualized social body likely echoed the novelist's own foreclosure, for James's peculiar sense of distance from nationhood was constituted, at least in part, by his nonparticipation not only in the racial reproduction of the old American stock but also in the Civil War. Like Olive, who has lost two brothers in the War, James remained a civilian while witnessing his two younger brothers, Wilky and Robertson, enlist. Wilky, whom James describes as "vastly attached to the negro-soldier cause," served in the 54th Massachusetts, "the first body of coloured soldiers raised in the North."[64] Severely wounded in the attack on Fort Wagner and without ever fully recovering from the permanent damage of the injury, Wilky died in 1884, immediately before James composed *The Bostonians*. Much like the morbid heroine of his oblique Civil War narrative, the novelist himself was haunted by his nonparticipation in the war and the bloody sacrifices that he could ill afford to make.

54 THE SUICIDAL STATE

James's account of his experience of the War—or the lack thereof—in his second autobiography, *Notes of a Son and Brother* (1914), is characteristically vague but marked singularly by "a horrid even if an obscure hurt" (240). The nature of the much-discussed wound—which allegedly disqualified him from participating in the War, caused his neurasthenic backache, and rendered him celibate for life—is deliberately obfuscated in James's dense narrative. What exactly happened to the eighteen-year-old James is never made entirely clear in his autobiography. All we know from his account is that what he calls "a private catastrophe or difficulty, bristling with embarrassments," reportedly occurred at the outbreak of the War, "during the soft spring of '61 by the firing on Fort Sumter, [and] Mr. Lincoln's instant first call for volunteers" (239). In "twenty odious minutes" in the midst of "a shabby conflagration," he was "jammed into the acute angle between two high fences, where the rhythmic play of [his] arms, in tune with that of several other pair, but at a dire disadvantage of position," trying to operate "a rural, a rusty, a quasi-extemporised old engine to work and a saving stream to flow" (240).

What probably happened was, as many commentators have speculated, that James injured his back while working as a volunteer at a Newport fire, crushed against fences in an attempt to run a rusty water pump. When exactly the accident happened is, however, still a subject of debate. Some argue, as James himself hints, that he was involved in the fire on the night of April 17, 1861; many more—including Leon Edel, Paul John Eakin, and John Halperin among others—suspect that his injury happened *not* in April but on the night of October 28, 1861, six months after Lincoln recruited initial volunteers.[65] Equally obscure is the severity of the hurt. That James's health was deemed not strong enough for enlistment was most likely true, for James's exemption due to physical disability was recorded in the local paper on September 5, 1863.[66] But whether the exemption was due to the injury at the site of the fire is not entirely clear. While James amply dramatizes the injury as catastrophic, he also narrates how he concealed it from everybody for as long as "three or four months" without causing any suspicion. When he eventually told his father about the injury, the Boston surgeon to whom his father took him treated his injury as if it were "a comparative pooh-pooh," refusing "either to warn, to comfort, or to command" (242).

Thus, whether the injury from a Newport fire actually was *the* cause of James's nonparticipation in the War or not is still a mystery, and "the obscure hurt remain[s] obscure," perhaps as James intended it to be.[67] Precisely because of its obscurity, however, the obscure hurt has become a potent metaphor for his non-normative manhood, sexual impotence, and queerness in James criticism. Regardless of when, how, and what exactly happened, this incident has been singled out as the defining moment of James's life, as that which "disqualified him not only from participation in the Civil war but also, forever, from the normal physical exertions of life, including sexual exertions, and rendered him a sort of invalid, permanent spectator of life, passive and celibate."[68] James's apologia for his nonparticipation in the War, brimming with shame and self-deprecation, seems to endorse the reading that the obscure hurt constituted a failure in "the trials of masculinity" for him—that is, a figurative, if not literal, castration.[69] When read this way, the language narrating the accident itself begins to seem distortedly phallic, a failed masturbatory effort: forced into a "dire disadvantageous position," he attempts to activate "a rusty . . . old engine" with the "rhythmic play" of his hands in order to pump out "a saving stream to flow," but all in vain (240).

The cosmopolitan youth missed the single most important event for the future of his homeland, which would have enabled him to bolster his fraught claim to national identity. His nonparticipation in the War, particularly at the side of "the stretcher on which [his] young brother was to lie for so many days," felt to him "a sore and troubled, a mixed and oppressive thing" (196). His injury was an "infinitely small affair in comparison" to Wilky's wounds (239). Amongst "the willing youths, all round, [who] were mostly starting to their feet," for James "to have trumped up a lameness at such a juncture could be made to pass in no light for graceful" (240). He was painfully aware that he could lay no claim to the "common Americanism" extended to his younger brothers when he unenthusiastically entered Harvard Law School in search of what he calls "any particular thing I might meanwhile 'do'" during the War (236).

Yet at the same time, the obscure hurt did constitute what the novelist would call "at the risk of any apparent fatuity . . . my 'relation to' the War" (236). That relation is, for sure, of a nature that can only exist in scare quotes; it is too tenuous to be straightforwardly called a relation. Still, in the very pain of the awareness of his nonrelation to the War and the pettiness of his own wound, James "flushed with emotions . . . with peculiar sharpness in the generalized pang of participation, that were all but touched in themselves as with the full experience" (197). Paradoxically enough, his nonparticipation in the War and the pang of shame it inflicts on him comprise something akin to the "full experience" of the War, forging "a relation to everything occurring

56 THE SUICIDAL STATE

round [him] not only for the next four years but for long afterward—that was at once extraordinary intimate and quite awkwardly irrelevant" (240).

As such, the obscure hurt offered James, through what he calls a "queer fusion or confusion," an access point of vexed identification with the American social body (239). The obscure hurt of his individual body, with the gnawing shame that its comparative smallness inflicts, opens a conduit for James to establish a chimerical relation to the "huge comprehensible ache" of the "enclosing social body, a body rent with a thousand wounds" (240). Such attachments catalyzed by imaginarily shared wounds "thus treated [him] to the honour of a sort of tragic fellowship" (240). The Civil War and the stinging sense of inadequacy from his nonparticipation paradoxically provided James with a sense of belonging: "He was now for the first time in presence of matters normally, entirely, consistently American," being able to "rinse [his] mouth of the European after taste" (244, 246). In short, the obscure hurt functions doubly as a stigma. The castratory wound surely marks James's disgrace for his nonparticipation in the War; at the same time, its shame splices his individual body into the lacerated social body like *stigmata*—holy wounds that are divinely impressed on mortals for redemptive identification with the savior's lacerated body in crucifixion.

The obscure hurt as stigmata, with the wound's crucial role in identity formation, reminds us of Wendy Brown's classic critique of identity politics in "Wounded Attachments."[70] When minoritarian subjects deploy their wounds of exclusion as leverage for their inclusion in the state, Brown argues, such wounded attachment to the state keeps the subject invested in "its own impotence," reifying and perpetuating "the humanist ideal—and a specific white, middle-class, masculinist expression of this ideal" against which it measures its injury.[71] Obvious are James's investments in the castratory wound, his attachment to his own impotence, and his staged claim for inclusion in the American body social that would exclude the celibate, cosmopolitan, neurasthenic novelist. And yet James's wounded attachment lacks the Nietzschean *ressentiment* and its debilitating vengefulness and rancor that are associated with Brown's model, instead radiating with pleasure. If the minoritarian identity that Brown postulates "posits a sovereign and unified 'I' that is disenfranchised by an exclusive 'we,'" James's castratory wound rather unsettles such a "language of 'I am'—with its defensive closure on identity," almost to the extent that his selfhood becomes shattered by the *jouissance* of shame.[72]

SACRIFICIAL ECSTASY   57

James's obscure hurt, in other words, seems to point to an alternative mode of relationality between the individual and the social body, as the eroticism of painful shame enables him to conjure up a relation "at once extraordinarily intimate and quite awkwardly irrelevant" (240). As Eve Sedgwick argues, Henry James was one of those for whom "shame is simply the first, and remains a permanent, structuring fact of identity."[73] Shame, Sedgwick says, both disrupts and constitutes identity at the same time. Even while a subject is flooded with shame when one's narcissism is broken as it is unreciprocated by the other, shame keeps us uncontrollably open to relationality; it is partly because of our helpless desire to reconstitute the broken circuit of identification with others and partly because of its highly contagious, transferential nature. James's shame of nonparticipation disrupts his already fraught American identity; but by that very shame, the obscure hurt is reconfigured as a site that is gaping open to relationality. That is, the wound generates erotic pleasure, a "romance of a more confused kind," oozing with painful shame and the unrequited desire for identification with "the American soldier in his multitude . . . in his depression, his wasted melancholy almost," who constitutes for the writer the "most attaching and affecting withal the most amusing figure of romance conceivable" (252). In other words, James embraces his castratory wound, an open site of identification where he can fantastically submerge himself in the collective pain of the social body without participating in the masculinized narrative of nationalism.

"The Ecstasy of the Martyr"

Olive Chancellor's erotic economy is, like her creator's, constituted by the obscure hurt as stigmata. Yet her hurt is even more obscure than that of the novelist, for she is, from the outset, foreclosed from making any "sacrifice" for the nation. If Olive Chancellor were to be admitted to the American body social without participating in the narrative of heterosexual union and the perpetuation of the old American stock, she would need a new wound that would splice her body to that of the nation. For that purpose, she starts what Leland Person aptly calls "a civil war of the sexes,"[74] where "the sacrifices, the blood, the tears, the terrors" would become "theirs" instead of men's (*The Bostonians*, 970). She is devoted to the feminist cause, body and soul, "asking no better fate than to die for it," even though it is "not clear to this

58   THE SUICIDAL STATE

interesting girl in what manner such a sacrifice (as this last) would be required of her" (835).

As epitomized in her use of "priesthood" as a trope for her feminism, Olive's enchantment with sacrifice is "so religious as never to be wanting in ecstasy" (927, 948). If "to be ec-static means, literally, to be outside oneself . . . to be transported beyond oneself by a passion,"[75] Olive's ecstatic attachment to feminism carries her away from herself, approaching the eroticism of religious sacrifice that Georges Bataille theorizes: "In sacrifice . . . [a] violent death disrupts the creature's discontinuity; what remains, what the tense onlookers experience in the succeeding silence, is the continuity of all existence with which the victim is now one."[76] When Olive Chancellor says, "I want to give myself up to others. . . . I want to enter into the lives of women who are lonely, who are piteous," what she longs for is such an eroticism of violent dispossession, which would enable her to lose herself in the common sisterhood through sacrificial death (*The Bostonians*, 833). Put differently, the erotic potential of the "ecstasy of the martyr" urges the passional subject to identify with the object at the cost of losing subjectivity through sacrificial death (935).

Much like Henry James, who was enchanted by the "romance of a more confused kind," Olive Chancellor is preoccupied with an equally, if not more, confused kind of "romance of the people": "She had an immense desire to know intimately some *very* poor girl" (832). In her desire to fraternize with working-class young women, Olive becomes a distinct type of what Scott Herring portrays as "the philanthropic Progressive slummer": middle-class Progressive female reformers who "often championed temperance, suffrage, and corporate reform while ministering financial and emotional aid to immigrants from a new form of cohabitation—the settlement house."[77] Against the backdrop of the increasing visibility of and surveillance over lesbianism, Herring argues, the same-sex, cross-class, and often international cohabitation at the settlement house provided Progressive female reformers with a safe haven of queer domesticity. As in the prototypical case of Hull House and Jane Addams—who, like Olive, was neurasthenic, remained unmarried, and engaged in long-lasting same-sex intimate relations— Progressive reformers could practice same-sex intimacy incognito, "melding into a 'mass' of undifferentiated social strangeness."[78]

Olive Chancellor, who has "scoured dirty children, and in squalid lodging houses, ha[s] gone into rooms where the domestic situation was strained and the noises made the neighbors turn pale," is one such queer Progressive

SACRIFICIAL ECSTASY 59

slummer (968). She is intoxicated with the idea of sacrificing herself for the oppressed working-class women and becoming one with them; her sensitive nerves are enraptured by the mere thought of "feminine anguish" as her visionary eyes daydream the procession of "all the bullied wives, the stricken mothers, dishonored, deserted maidens" passing in front of her and "stretch[ing] out ... myriad hands to her" (969). At the beginning of the novel, however, Olive finds herself unable to give herself up for sacrifice, precisely because of her bourgeois neurasthenic sensitivity. Ironically, her "most poignant suffering" does not come from her heroic feminist battle but "from the injury of her taste," and however much she "trie[s] to kill her nerve ... her susceptibility [is] constantly blooming afresh" (827). Standing next to Miss Birdseye, a legendary transcendental abolitionist and feminist who has "never had a penny in her life"—for she has given away everything for her causes—Olive Chancellor's bourgeois guilt and injured taste throb like Henry James's obscure hurt as he kneels at the side of Wilky's stretcher. She is too attached to her life to give it up, too propertied to meld into the mass.

Instead, Olive's sacrificial eroticism finds its channel when she meets Verena Tarrant. Olive trembles with "a nervous ecstasy of anticipation" at her first private meeting with this celebrated spiritualist medium. Growing up in the Cayuga community (a fictionalized name for John Humphrey Noyes's Oneida community), where there is no notion of private property based on monogamous family relations, Verena thoroughly lacks the concept of possession: she is, by birth, dispossessed of her privacy, the cornerstone of liberal selfhood. What defines Verena's character is this mode of dispossession, or what the novel terms her "singular hollowness" of self (857). In a tragicomical manner, the narrator confesses the impossibility of describing her consciousness:

> It was so singular on Verena's part, in particular, that I despair of presenting it to the reader with the air of reality. To understand it, one must bear in mind her peculiar frankness, natural and acquired, her habit of discussing questions, sentiments, moralities, her education, in the atmosphere of lecture-rooms, of *séances*, her familiarity with the vocabulary of emotion, the mystery of 'the spiritual life.' ... Her essence was the extraordinary generosity with which she could expose herself, give herself away, turn herself inside out, for the satisfaction of a person who made demands of her. (1153; italics original)

60   THE SUICIDAL STATE

In one sense, Verena represents disciplinary power's dream that turns into a nightmare: she is so well trained to confess that there is no secret left inside her to constitute a liberal self. Yet it is precisely because of this void of her interiority, in which everything has already been generously given away and nothing is left for the narrator to describe, that she successfully functions as a medium for Olive's feminism. She is an empty vessel: her eloquence comes from "some power outside—it seemed to flow through her. . . . It wasn't her—she had nothing to do with it" (851). Because she is so hollow, her body becomes a perfect chamber reverberating with the voices of others.

Verena's "unlimited generosity" (874), her talent as a medium to give herself away for sympathetic identification with others, is repeatedly referred to as a "gift": a thing simply granted outside the logic of exchange. For Olive, Verena is "the very type and model of the 'gifted being;' her qualities had not been bought and paid for" (908). As Verena herself describes the mesmeric trance as "giv[ing] out," the whole purpose of her being is to be given out to others like "some brilliant birthday-present, left at the door by an unknown messenger, to be delightful for ever as an inexhaustible legacy, and amusing for ever from the obscurity of its source" (908). Nothing about her is private; she is a gift given to the public.

Such a marker of dispossession, "giftedness," makes Verena—for Olive—a model sacrificial offering submitted to the altar (964). When Mrs. Burrage insinuates at the nature of Olive's suspicious intimacy with Verena, Olive says: "I am surprised at your not perceiving how little it is in my interest to deliver my—my victim up to you" (1088). Olive's peculiar diction, "my victim" (preceded by the hesitant stammer), takes on a particular significance, especially since it emerges at the moment when Olive attempts to define their relationship against Mrs. Burrage's sexual knowingness. If "victim"—a living creature killed and offered as a sacrifice (OED)—is the name that Olive gives to her partner, the act of sacrifice seems to suggest a way to interpret the passion that marks their singular relationship: that is, their relation is *passional* in the word's original sense, replete with the suffering of martyrdom. From the moment of their first interaction, Verena is susceptible to Olive's own ecstatic desire for sacrifice, ready to offer her life: "[Verena] flushed a little at this appeal, and the deeper glow of her eyes was the first sign of exaltation she had offered. 'Oh yes—I want to give my life!' she exclaimed, with a vibrating voice" (879).

For Olive, who has "so little of" the "giftedness" (964), Verena's generous selflessness seems to enable her to "los[e] herself" (873), since Verena's void

SACRIFICIAL ECSTASY 61

swallows and assimilates Olive into "the 'people'" that Olive imagines Verena to represent (873). Verena becomes one with Olive by identifying with Olive's feminist philosophy, which she memorizes as if it were "part of a catechism" (936). Olive is now ecstatic—beside herself—as she dislodges herself and inhabits Verena. Olive's quaint epistolary metaphor exemplifies the absorptive, identificatory logic of their relation: "I should like to be able to say that you are my form—my envelope. But you are too beautiful for that!" (946). Like a letter folded in a beautiful envelope, Olive is incorporated into Verena. When Verena confesses to Olive that without her she wouldn't be able to feel the suffering of women so intensely, Olive replies, "You have never yet said anything to me which expressed so clearly the closeness and sanctity of our union" (946). For Olive, the total correspondence of their feelings—or more precisely, her absorption into Verena—attests to the consummation of their "union of soul," the ultimate form of the consummation of Olive's metaphysical erotics (873). As Verena is stunned to realize, Olive is completely "wrapped up in her," and she would "suffer from the least deviation" (1069).

That deviation, however, becomes inevitable. What threatens their union is Verena's growing possession of her own interiority. Her envelope-like hollowness, which is crucial to Olive's identificatory eroticism, dissolves when it is occupied by its own "secret." Verena's excursion to the Harvard Memorial Hall with Basil begins to bear an erotic meaning precisely when Basil asks her to keep it just between them. When confronted by Olive, Verena realizes that it is "the only secret she ha[s] in the world—the only thing that [is] all her own" (1067). For Verena, who has been trained in Cayuga to expose herself so thoroughly that there is no boundary between the private and the public, her little secret becomes her first private property. The sweetness of this private possession makes her conscious that "the moment her secret [is] threatened it [becomes] dearer to her" (1067). It is easy to be generous when one owns nothing; it is quite another thing when one possesses something, albeit trivial as it is. Olive's presentiment of the loss of Verena's generosity, by which the spiritualist's daughter enthusiastically promises to give her life, is to be proven valid: "I wonder if you know what it means, young and lovely as you are—giving your life!" (879). Knowing finally what it means to give up something she possesses, Verena starts to wonder "how far it was necessary to go in the path of self-sacrifice" (1158). Verena is now ready to dispossess Olive of the gift she has given to her, the life of her own: "She had lent herself, given herself, utterly, and she ought to have known better if she didn't mean to abide by it" (1158).

62 THE SUICIDAL STATE

The language of the heated conversation between the two women embodies the way in which Verena reclaims her gift from Olive:

> She said to her again and again that she had utterly changed since that hour she came to her, in New York, after her morning with Mr. Ransom, and sobbed out that they must hurry away. Then she had been wounded, outraged, sickened, and in the interval nothing had happened, nothing but that one exchange of letters, which she knew about, to bring her round to shameless tolerance. Shameless, Verena admitted it to be; she assented over and over to this proposition, and explained, as eagerly each time as if it were the first, what it was that had come to pass, what it was that had brought her round. It had simply come over her that she liked him, that this was the true point of view, the only one from which one could consider the situation in a way that would lead to what she called a *real* solution—a permanent rest. On this particular point Verena never responded, in the liberal way I have mentioned, without asseverating at the same time that what she desired most in the world was to prove (the picture Olive had held up from the first), that a woman *could* live on persistently, clinging to a great, vivifying, redemptory idea, without the help of a man. (1153–1154)

The obliqueness of the passage that narrates the tête-à-tête between the two women stands out in the overall language of a novel that has little resemblance to the serpentine complexity of James's later works. The passage becomes dense precisely because both Verena and Olive are referred to with the same personal pronouns, "she" and "her," because of the sameness of their gender. Read contextually, many of the referents seem to be settled. For instance, the first sentence should be read as "[Olive] said to [Verena] again and again that [Verena] had utterly changed since that hour [Verena] came to [Olive], in New York, after [Verena's] morning with Mr. Ransom, and sobbed out that they must hurry away." Yet, in terms of syntax, there is no clear distinction between the two women: they are one and the same, "she" and "her." In this sense, Olive's identificatory erotic is consummated in the verbal intercourse with Verena as she was becoming one with her. However, the two women are soon to find themselves separated by proper nouns, when Olive proposes "what she called a *real* solution—a permanent rest"; to "this particular point"—double suicide as a solution—Verena cannot concede, insisting instead that they have to "live on persistently, clinging to a great, vivifying, redemptory idea" (1154).

Still Waiting, *Princess Casamassima*

Basil takes Verena away from the Boston Music Hall, where she was supposed to give her feminist speech; Verena utters, "Ah, now I am glad," though in tears (1218). Robbed of Verena, Olive stands alone in the Music Hall. Olive can no longer dream of that impossible, transcendental ecstasy of sacrifice that Verena's victimhood seemed to promise her. Yet her sacrificial desire—"the ecstasy of the martyr"—is not to be consummated until she is dispossessed of the gift with which he has been endowed (935). She has begged Verena once: "Don't fail me—don't fail me, or I shall die!" (929). Verena has now failed her, and Olive is finally ready to offer herself to the altar instead. As Basil runs off with Verena, he casts a backward glance at his cousin. The morbidity he saw in the "pale girl, with her light-green eyes" at the moment of their first encounter now bears a clearer meaning to him (835): "Her pale, glittering eyes [were] straining forward, as if they were looking for death" (1226). Olive walks toward the platform to expose herself "to the thousands she had disappointed and deceived"; like the "sacrificial figure of Hypatia, whirled through the furious mob of Alexandria," she is waiting to be "trampled to death and torn to pieces," to "find the fierce expiation" that "she sought" from the beginning of the narrative (1217).[79]

The coveted sacrificial death, however, is not to be granted. As Basil observes, "even when exasperated, a Boston audience is not ungenerous" (1218). When Olive stands alone on the stage, "every sound instantly dropped, the hush was respectful, the great public waited. . . . It was not apparent that they were likely to hurl the benches at her" (1218). Unlike the mob that lacerated Hypatia, the ever-civil crowd of Boston does not desire Olive's sacrifice. Like her creator, she is too morbid, too signal, too singular to become one with the "mighty multitude," only allowed to hanker after that impossible identification (1210). Her mergence into the social body is thus denied, but it marks, perhaps, what Benjamin Kahan calls "the decisive beginning of Olive's feminist speaking career" instead.[80] Standing in for Verena, Olive now has to speak on her own. Earlier in the novel, Verena has pointed out to Olive: "Why, Olive, you are quite a speaker yourself! . . . You would far surpass me if you would let yourself go" (930). In the pain of letting Verena go, Olive will finally be able to let herself go. Aching for the coming of the ecstasy of martyrdom, she begins her public career as a feminist, a third-sex reformer seeking to transfigure the heterosexualized social body. Living on, with the consummation of her sacrificial ecstasy deferred again and again,

64   THE SUICIDAL STATE

Olive will have to repeat her incantation over and over, "as if it were the solution of everything, as if it represented with absolute certainty some immense happiness in the future—'We must wait, we must wait!'" (877).

The consummation of death will not be brought to Olive herself, but to two other figures who follow her path, albeit in ways that are quite oblique. One is the New Woman, a fin-de-siècle feminist icon mutated from neurasthenic New England suffragists, whose insatiable desire to consume without producing would make her the new face of race suicide. In the next chapter, we will trace this figure's strange evolutionary path in the heroine of Kate Chopin's *The Awakening* (1899), following her suicidal swim into the Gulf of Mexico. The other is Olive Chancellor's distant, European cousin—so to speak—who stars in the novel that James wrote immediately after *The Bostonians* and published in the same year, *The Princess Casamassima* (1886). While James bars his neurasthenic, Anglo-Saxon heroine's sacrificial suicide, keeping her singularity intact from the mergence into the social "like the heroine that she was" (1217), he lets Hyacinth Robinson—a sensitive, delicately framed, gentle bookbinder in London—take his own life, letting his degeneracy devour him.

The two texts form a diptych. Like his American suffragist counterpart, Hyacinth Robinson is a third-sex reformer who is entranced by the ecstasy of martyrdom, "the idea of a tremendous risk and an unregarded sacrifice."[81] One day, he takes a "tremendous, terrible vow" in front of the German anarchist mastermind Diedrich Hoffendahl (327). When later asked about the nature of the vow by the eponymous Italian princess, Hyacinth answers, smiling, "I gave my life away" (327). What he awaits is Hoffendahl's cue to execute an as-yet-to-be-determined order, most likely to assassinate a dignitary in exchange for his own life. As his friend Paul Muniment says, Hyacinth has been singled out as Hoffendahl's victim for the sacred altar of revolution: "Yes, you are the boy he wants" (293). With this "consecration," his "vow to Hoffendahl, to the immeasurable body that Hoffendahl represent[s]," Hyacinth is admitted to the "innermost sanctuary" of the homosocial temple of revolutionaries (335, 384, 330).

Also like Olive Chancellor, Hyacinth Robinson is marked by a hypersensitivity that is, more than once, described as "morbid" (72, 151, 341). His morbidness is written all over his delicate body just like hers: "His bones were small. His chest was narrow, his complexion pale, his whole figure almost childishly slight" (104). But Hyacinth's morbidness has a name that is different from Olive's largely similar pathology. If neurasthenia was imagined as endemic to New England, signifying the old-stock American's refinement and decay, degeneration—or *dégénérescence*, to honor its provenance—was the name of the original wine repackaged in an American bottle. In *The Princess Casamassima,* this Old World inebriant proves more potent than its American heir, for the degenerate Hyacinth Robinson finds the expiation that his neurasthenic counterpart is denied.

Degeneration, as we have seen in the Introduction, became a popular diagnosis in France in the late 1850s, when Bénédict Augustin Morel deployed the term to nominate "*a morbid deviation from an original type.*"[82] As Daniel Pick puts it, degeneration is "the ultimate signifier of pathology"; it encompasses numbers of mental, physical, and moral anomalies, understood to be hereditarily transmissible and to cause neurosis, insanity, and finally sterility over the course of several generations.[83] Diagnoses of degeneration spread across Continental Europe against the backdrop of falling birthrates—a situation first observed in France in the 1850s, preceding that of New England by three decades.[84] Degeneration's hereditary focus was particularly strong in Italy, where Cesare Lombroso developed Morel's ideas into the science of criminal anthropology, casting criminals—including prostitutes—as hereditarily tainted degenerates, designating them "born criminals."[85] Though slower in their development, English models of degeneracy gained widespread acceptance by the 1880s and 1890s, shifting the focus from an individual diagnosis to a populational concern, especially urban vice.[86] This environmental shift in part accounts for the popularity of Max Nordau's *Degeneration* (1892, translated into English in 1895), the work that designated degeneration as emblematic of the "*fin-de-siècle* state of mind," epitomized in particular by decadent literature.[87] Similarly to the case of neurasthenia, Nordau argues that the overstimulation brought forth by modern civilization causes a disorder in the nervous system resulting in an "extraordinary emotionalism," an extremely heightened susceptibility to external stimuli that may lead the subject to "crime, madness, and suicide."[88]

Hyacinth Robinson is a walking sampler of mixed degenerative heritages, for he has "an extraordinarily mingled current in his blood" (165). On the one hand, he is an illegitimate son of "the extremely immoral Lord Frederick," an English aristocrat, from whom Hyacinth has inherited his delicate frame and his "finest sensibilities" (58, 169). On the other hand, he is a "bastard of a murderess, spawned in a gutter, out of which he had been picked up by a sewing-girl" (479). His mother Florentine Vivier—a French immigrant who became a prostitute—stabs Hyacinth's libertine father to death; after she is

66   THE SUICIDAL STATE

imprisoned for life, he is raised in a working-class London neighborhood by a spinster dressmaker, Amanda Pynsent. In a nutshell, the novel traces the way these "two currents that flowed in his nature, the blood of his passionate, plebian mother and that of his long-descended, supercivilised sire" lacerate Hyacinth from within (479).

As such, *The Princess Casamassima* showcases competing theories of degeneration through Hyacinth Robinson's family romance. The first is the Continental hereditary-transmission model, whereby Hyacinth's commitment to the revolutionary act of terror is read as criminality inherited from his French prostitute-murderess mother in a Lombrosian logic. In this model, Hyacinth's commitment to the revolutionary cause itself becomes a sign of his degeneration, for, as Daniel Pick argues, revolution was increasingly understood to be the simultaneous cause and symptom of *dégénérescence*. Especially since the rise and fall of the Paris Commune in 1871, the French Revolution had been interpreted as "a field of psychosomatic stimuli" that had left a deep scar on the collective nervous system of the French nation, "bequeath[ing] a process of degeneration which reached its apotheosis in the Franco-Prussian War and the Paris Commune."[89] Hyacinth's French degenerative heritage runs long and deep, for his namesake, Florentine's father Hyacinth Vivier, was himself "the revolutionary watch-maker who had known the ecstasy of the barricade and had paid for it with his life" (380). In short, Hyacinth Robinson is "*ab ovo* a revolutionist," as much as he is a Lombrosian born criminal (287).

The second model is that of Nordau-esque overcivilization, whereby Hyacinth's hypersensitivity is attributed to his decadent, "supercivilised sire," who belonged to "an ancient and exalted race" (479, 58). Like Captain Godfrey Sholto (an English débauché who mirrors Hyacinth's dead father), Hyacinth belongs to the line of the "finest white," "a curious and not particularly edifying English type . . . one of those strange beings produced by old societies that have run to seed, corrupt and exhausted civilizations" (273, 352). As such, even as he takes a vow to destroy that very social order, Hyacinth's sensuality is irresistibly aroused by and drawn to its opulent splendor and refinement, which, he knows, is built upon "all the despotisms, the cruelties, the exclusions, the monopolies and the rapacities of the past" (396). The last model is the environmental one, whereby he is understood as a product of the degenerate London masses, whom Hyacinth perceives as "saturated with alcohol and vice, brutal, bedraggled, obscene" (481). Hyacinth, who describes himself "a mere particle in the immensity of the people" (197), reflects upon the degenerate social body with which he is one—"what fate there could be . . . for a planet overgrown with such vermin, what redemption but to be hurled against a ball of consuming fire"—vaguely hoping for its "annihilation" (481).

Hyacinth's degeneration—reinforced threefold by his Gallic and Anglo heritages as well as his London upbringing—splits him open, pulling him in multiple directions. That is how Princess Casamassima finds Hyacinth on his bed when she rushes into his dingy room after hearing the news that he has received Hoffendahl's assassination order at last. As she opens the door, "her eyes had attached themselves to the small bed. There was something on it—something black, something ambiguous, something outstretched. . . . Hyacinth lay there as if he were asleep, but there was a horrible thing, a mess of blood, on the bed, in his side, in his heart" (590). The bullet in the revolver that Hoffendahl has sent him to shoot a Duke has found its home in Hyacinth's heart instead, causing "a mess of blood"—his degenerative heritages running against each other—to flow freely outside his little body.

With the first note of revolution forestalled, Hoffendahl's grand scenario is foiled, at least until he finds his new victim, another impressionable boy like Hyacinth. But at the same time, the novel remains skeptical that Hoffendahl's "great symphonic revolt"—symbolically revised as "great symphonic massacre" in the New York Edition—will bring forth the new social order of egalitarian "redistribution" (335, 397).[90] Hyacinth has once prophesied: "that the flood of democracy was rising over the world; that it would sweep all the traditions of the past before it; . . . that it might be trusted to look after its own" (478). But he has also apprehended: "When democracy should have its way everywhere, it would be its fault (whose else?) if want and suffering and crime should continue to be ingredients of the human lot" (478). Beheading the l'Ancien Régime-like body politic would not necessarily guarantee the end of its uneven distribution of livability. As amply proven by the headless social body crossing the Atlantic, terrorizing Sleepy Hollow on its horse with its jack-o'-lantern head in its hand, it might very well maintain its ethereal whiteness by creating the living-death within.

Rather than allowing the third-sex reformer to take part in the ritual of regenerating the rotten body politic into a white social body, rather than offering him a sacrificial victim to cover over its inequities and calling that a revolution, Henry James has Hyacinth Robinson waste the bullet and his life. Unlike his American counterpart, Hyacinth follows through with his suicidality; but his death is still devoid of the much-coveted ecstasy of martyrdom.

68 THE SUICIDAL STATE

Does this make him a traitor to the "people"? Perhaps. He dies not for the revolution, not for the *demos*, not even for himself; he dies for nothing, voiding himself and that bright white futurity by submitting to the overdetermined fate of degeneration. Dying the death of a good old degenerate, his body becomes "something black, something ambiguous, something outstretched," losing its whiteness and its singularity, whose contours are defined by the obliteration of racial subjugation, with an open wound of obscure hurt still remaining obscure (590).

2

Flirting with Death

The Awakening's Liberal Erotic Economy and the Consuming Desire of New Women

Squandering Family Property

Awakened from a long slumber on a little Louisiana island called *Chênière Caminada*, the heroine of Kate Chopin's 1899 novel, Edna Pontellier, quizzically tells the companion of her romantic escapade: "The whole island seems changed. A new race of beings must have sprung up, leaving only you and me as past relics. How many ages ago did Madame Antoine and Tonie die? and when did our people from Grand Isle disappear from the earth?"[1] Spun in the "snow-white" bed, Edna's fairy-tale-like reverie of the supersedure of her "people" by a "new race of beings" strangely resonates with race suicide's extinction narrative (35, 37). At the end of the novel, Edna drowns herself in the Gulf of Mexico to elude her two children, "who had overpowered and sought to drag her into the soul's slavery" (108). With her revolt against motherhood, Edna becomes a prototype of what Theodore Roosevelt called "a criminal against the race . . . an object of contemptuous abhorrence by all healthy people," who refuses to "recognize that the greatest thing for any woman is to be a good wife and mother."[2] Her suicidal swim into the ocean, in this context, emerges as a personal enactment of race suicide: by drowning herself, she dissipates the reproductive capacity not only of her own "white body" but also of the white American social body (109).

But what is this "new race of beings" of which Edna dreams, which has suddenly "sprung up" to supplant her "people" after race suicide's apocalyptic scenario is fulfilled? In order to pursue Edna's idiosyncratic racial fantasy, it might be helpful to start by understanding how the novel enmeshes its heroine in Progressive Era racial politics. Born the daughter of a Confederate colonel in "old Kentucky bluegrass country," Edna Pontellier is a figure molded to entice the post-Reconstruction reader's fascination with the South (6).[3] Financially and culturally invested in slavery in the antebellum period,

The Suicidal State. Madoka Kishi, Oxford University Press. © Oxford University Press 2024.
DOI: 10.1093/9780197690109.003.0003

70   THE SUICIDAL STATE

Kentucky came legally under Union control during the Civil War, becoming a putatively benign, if caricatured, emblem of the Old South after the War. Raised on a Mississippi plantation after her family moves from Kentucky, Edna later marries a white Catholic Creole, Léonce Pontellier, in opposition to her Presbyterian family's wishes. In New Orleans—the city once known as the Southern Babylon for its bacchanalian excess—she pursues her existential and sexual freedom through erotic liaisons with white Creoles until at last she drowns herself in the Gulf of Mexico.[4] Put simply, Edna Pontellier is an assemblage of motley signifiers of Progressive Era Southern whiteness— romantic, exotic, and irretrievably lost.

Edna's eponymous "awakening" into an autonomous self is also enabled by her whiteness, and is brought forth by what Michele Birnbaum incisively calls "racial midwifery."[5] The novel, as many critics have pointed out, not only heavy-handedly deploys the symbolics of black and white but also abounds in women of color whose sensual presence and intimate labor prepare the playground for the wealthy white housewife's quest for personal freedom.[6] Highly attuned to the chromatics of race, the text deploys many figures of color in its narrative tableau: the anonymous "quadroon nurse" with her "faraway, meditative air," who takes care of Edna's two children (4); the "*Griffe*" nurse, whose descriptor denotes a person with three-quarters Black heritage in Louisiana's racial taxonomy, who assists with the childbirth of Edna's white Creole friend Adèle Ratignolle (103); and the coquettish Spanish-speaking Mariequita, with her "ugly brown toes" and "pretty black eyes" (33), to name a few. In this sense, as Joyce Dyer has shown, *The Awakening* provides a textbook example of Toni Morrison's delineation of *Playing in the Dark*.[7] That is, when Edna refers to maternity as "soul's slavery," her rhetorical appropriation of racial subjugation exemplifies a longstanding tradition in which Black experience has continuously been exploited for white writers' "meditation on problems of human freedom."[8]

At the same time, when seen in the light of the novel's historical setting— New Orleans and its surroundings between the summer of 1892 and the early spring of 1893—this metaphorization of slavery seems to register a shift in modes of racialization, pointing to what Alys Eve Weinbaum calls "the race/reproduction bind": that is, the notion that the production of race is inextricably tied to biological reproduction.[9] As evidenced by the landmark Supreme Court decision *Plessy v. Ferguson* (1896), fin-de-siècle Louisiana was an especially charged site for the knotting of race and reproduction. On June 7, 1892, Homer Adolph Plessy, the son of French-speaking free

Creoles of color, boarded a whites-only coach in New Orleans. Plessy, an optically white, one-eighth Black "octoroon," declared his racial heritage upon boarding in an act of civil disobedience. Immediately dragged from the train, he was arrested for violating the Louisiana Separate Car Act. While Edna Pontellier meditates on maternity as slavery in early 1893 in the narrative world, Plessy's actual case against the constitutionality of Jim Crow was taken to the Supreme Court.[10]

The notorious 1896 ruling cemented the "separate but equal" doctrine, endorsing segregation based on so-called colored blood and white blood. Crucially, as Cheryl Harris's classic reading of the case argues, *Plessy* marked a watershed moment in the conceptualization of race—especially that of whiteness—as "status property."[11] In pointing out the arbitrariness of the color line, one of Plessy's attorneys, Albion Tourgée, strategically claimed that the Separate Car Act damaged the white-presenting Plessy's "reputation of belonging to the dominant race, in this instance the white race," which should be understood as "property in the same sense that a right of action or of inheritance is property."[12] The Court rejected Tourgée's argument: Plessy was "deprived of no property, since he is not lawfully entitled to the reputation of being a white man," while "if he be a white man and assigned to a colored coach, he may have his action for damages against the company for being deprived of his so-called property."[13] In contending that the Creole of color capable of passing as white was unlawfully claiming racial whiteness, Harris argues, the Court "lent support to the notion of race reputation as a property interest that required the protection of law through actions for damages."[14] Through *Plessy*, whiteness was thus transfigured into property with legal entitlements to enjoy the social privileges of full citizenship.

Insofar as whiteness was defined exclusively by white ancestry figured by so-called white blood, however, I would argue that whiteness was imagined not simply as property, but more specifically as family property. That is, race was not just "reproducible"; rather, it could *only* be reproduced from the supposed original—unable to be produced, acquired, or alienated unlike other forms of property—inherited and passed down exclusively by means of heterosexual intercourse.[15] The reification of whiteness as family property augmented the sociopolitical value of the white maternal body as a hereditary vessel to be protected. As Weinbaum argues, *Plessy* in this sense marks "the postbellum replacement of the black maternal body . . . by the white maternal body" as the central site of racial reproduction.[16] Under chattel slavery, the conflation of race and property had been primarily associated

72 THE SUICIDAL STATE

with Blackness, since the reproductive capacity of enslaved women was rendered a means of production and subsumed under the so-called slave owner's property accumulation, as the children of enslaved Black women assumed the status of the mother (*partus sequitur ventrem*). After abolition, however, the emphasis on the nexus binding race/reproduction/property shifted to a propertied interest in white women's bodies, which preserved and transmitted "white blood," the invisible signifier of race.

Plessy's transfiguration of whiteness into property—family property in particular—recasts how we might understand Edna's meditation on "soul's slavery." While there is no doubt that the phrase's metaphoricity casually yet violently expropriates historically specific Black suffering, Edna's conflation of maternity with slavery also seems to point to the new status transferred from the Black female body to the white female body: an apparatus reproducing racialized property contingent on procreative sex. When her husband, Léonce Pontellier, scrutinizes her complexion and remarks, "You are burnt beyond recognition," Edna is rendered "a valuable piece of personal property" (4). Her status as Léonce's "personal property" does not simply suggest her identity's subsumption under *coverture*; rather, Edna is a vessel of whiteness as family property, kept in place by the ideal of companionate marriage as "a decoy to secure mothers for the race," as one character puts it (105).[17]

In what follows, I will read Edna Pontellier's suicide as an act that squanders whiteness as family property. Her desire to dissipate herself as racialized property is, I argue, entangled with liberal logics of freedom whereby liberty is defined as the ownership of one's own person as property. Attending to Foucault's articulation of the twinned birth of the biopolitics of population and of liberalism, I will argue that *The Awakening's* narration epitomizes liberal governmentality, rendering Edna as a populational figure rather than a depth-model individual. That is, instead of uncovering and investigating the protagonist's private self, the text allows Edna to move through narrative space according to her caprice, exemplifying the *laissez-faire* ideal of freedom. This *laissez-faire* ethos—increasingly "foreign" to the Progressive Era United States—is embodied in the novel's French Creole community, which initiates Edna into their liberal erotic economy of flirtation. The autotelic play of flirtation, which seeks the prolongation of desire itself rather than any particular objects, takes new form in the burgeoning consumer economy, positing consumption as a way of avoiding the logics of property accumulation and inheritance that racial reproduction entails.

In particular, *Vogue*, in which Chopin published many of her short stories, enables her to envision a "new race of beings" that emerges from the narcissistic pleasures of consumption, figured by the mass-produced "New Woman," who propagates without biological reproduction. While Edna's suicide, in this reading, emerges as the culmination of her consumptive desire—which is ultimately directed at her own person as her property—I argue that such a liberal logic of freedom is permeated with and enabled by the consumption of Black deaths, most notably in the form of slave suicide represented in William Wells Brown's *Clotel* (1853) and Charles Chestnutt's "Dave's Neckliss" (1889).

The Alien Hands of Liberalism

As Jennifer Fleissner astutely puts it, "For someone said to be 'awakening,' Edna does quite a bit of sleeping throughout the book."[18] Despite the title's apparent emphasis on its singularity as an event—*the* awakening—Chopin depicts Edna's awakening as part of "a repetitive, rhythmic, back-and-forth movement . . . pushing against the more familiar notion of Edna's trajectory as a linear individual 'evolution' toward independence."[19] Indeed, even when the text narrates what seems to be the crucial moment of Edna's "awakening"—the night when her first swim in the Gulf suddenly makes her realize her husband's paternalistic oppression—such an awakening of "her will . . . stubborn and resistant" is immediately interrupted by the violent need to sleep: "Edna began to feel like one who awakens gradually out of a dream, a delicious, grotesque, impossible dream, to feel again the realities pressing into her soul. The physical need for sleep began to overtake her; the exuberance which had sustained and exalted her spirit left her helpless and yielding to the conditions which crowded her in" (31). The seamlessness between her "awaken[ing]" and her "physical need for sleep" here—which precludes conjunctives like "but" or "yet"—forecasts the pattern that constitutes the rest of the narrative: as Edna literally sleeps off her existential questions and moral conundrums, her physical awakening almost offsets its symbolic counterpart. In short, "each morning she awoke with hope, and each night she was a prey to despondency" (99).

To put it differently, even though *The Awakening* seems to chart the heroine's quest for personal freedom, that freedom is not necessarily imagined as an exercise of her individual will. Rather, what she pursues is

74   THE SUICIDAL STATE

"the *feeling* of freedom and independence"—as she explains her reasons for moving out of her husband's house—and the text vibrates to the rhythm of her oscillation between carefreeness and "a *feeling* of oppression" (76, 34, emphasis added). In this narrative attunement to the heroine's affective drift, *The Awakening* registers an aesthetic shift from the Victorian novel, which D. A. Miller argues is an agent of disciplinary power. Miller contends that the nineteenth-century novel represents disciplinary power's ubiquitous reach, not only via the protagonist's heroically failed attempt to resist social control, but also through "*the very practice of novelistic representation.*"[20] That is, the novel creates the protagonist as a private subject whose "integral, autonomous, 'secret' self" is minutely recorded, interrogated, and exposed by the omniscient narrator's panoptical gaze.[21] In identifying with this novelistic surveillance, readers are not only trained to understand themselves as depth-model subjects, but also led to believe that their own autonomy is beyond the purview of such control. In short, the novel constructs its reader, along with the protagonist, as a "liberal subject": "the subject whose private life, mental or domestic, is felt to provide constant inarguable evidence of his constitutive 'freedom.' "[22]

The Awakening certainly presents the tragic spectacle of a liberal subject who "dares and defies" the constraints of social convention, resolving "never again to belong to another than herself" (61, 76). The book seems to be, as Wai Chee Dimock argues, written in "the language of rights" with a grammar of liberalism.[23] As Edna declares to her lover Robert Lebrun, she defines her personal autonomy in terms of the self-ownership that undergirds the political economy of liberalism: "I am no longer one of Mr. Pontellier's possessions to dispose or not. I give myself where I choose" (102). Reclaiming her body as her private property that she is entitled to use in whatever way she chooses, she embodies the classic Lockean principle: "Every man has a *property* in his own *person.*"[24] As Dimock points out, such an account of "inviolate personality" became widely available at the turn of the century as Samuel D. Warren and Louis D. Brandeis's landmark essay, "The Right to Privacy" (1890), disseminated the conception of the "'right to one's personality' as a property right—a right whose protectability is the exclusivity of its possession."[25]

While the text thus thematizes liberal logics of freedom, however, it eludes Miller's model of the novel as a dispositif of disciplinary power in which both the character and the reader are constituted as private subjects optimized for the operation of liberal governmentality. That is, rather than uncovering or interrogating the depth of Edna's secret self, the text allows her to skid

FLIRTING WITH DEATH   75

through its narrative world, even encouraging the reader to synchronize with her whimsical movement. Tellingly, on the morning after the aforementioned scene of Edna's first "awakening," "her will [that] had blazed up" the night before seems to have already dissipated (31). Instead, "she was blindingly following whatever impulse moved her, as if she had placed herself in alien hands for direction, and freed her soul of responsibility," embarking on a romantic boat trip with Robert (32). Freedom for Edna here is paradoxically imagined as a condition in which she abandons her sovereign self and its obligations so that she can thoroughly yield herself to the "alien hands" of impulse.

The touch of these alien hands is, per Adam Smith, what also sets economic liberalism itself in motion, particularly the one characterized as *laissez-faire*. The "invisible hand," as Smith calls it in *The Wealth of Nations* (1776), stands for a coincidental harmony between a seemingly selfish pursuit of individual interests and its collective impact, which results in "the publick good."[26] Though Smith himself never used the term *laissez-faire*, the serendipitous guidance of the invisible hand became a compelling signifier of free markets throughout the nineteenth century, as it articulated faith in the market's tendency to operate most effectively when there was little—if any—governmental control. Whereas state interventions into the economy had been deemed integral to national prosperity under the previous regime of mercantilism, the liberal state limited its direct control over the economy. Instead, liberal government assumed a new responsibility: to ensure market autonomy and its expansion—both domestically and abroad—by creating social, legal, financial, or military infrastructures. In fact, as Miguel de Beistegui observes, "The paradox of laissez-faire is that it was entirely planned."[27] That is, economic liberalism was enabled by the de facto increase in state power that transpired through incorporation and various forms of social reform. The Progressive Era United States concretized this increase in state power, indicating its move away from *laissez-faire* policies into a consolidation of the administrative state.[28] To use Foucault's ventriloquizing formulation, rather than representing "the imperative of freedom," liberalism promises to manage and organize the condition of freedom: "I am going to produce what you need to be free. I am going to see to it that you are free to be free."[29]

Crucially, Foucault argues that *laissez-faire* liberalism's conceptualization of freedom as "letting things happen" at the end of the eighteenth century marks the emergence of a new form of biopower: namely, the biopolitics of

76   THE SUICIDAL STATE

population and its apparatuses of security. Just as the Physiocrats imagined the market to have an internal rhythm according to which it would regulate its own course, the new entity called the population was conceived as having its own statistical regularities, such as rates of birth, death, morbidity, or accidents. In other words, it was discovered as "a natural phenomenon that cannot be changed by decree."[30] The government's responsibility toward the population, like its responsibility toward the economy, was reimagined as securing its collective life without interfering too much in its process, managing the risk so that the damage would not exceed "a bandwidth of the acceptable."[31] As shown in Foucault's example of scarcity, the *laissez-faire* economy and the population are intertwined, rendering liberalism and biopolitics just two sides of the same governmentality. Whereas state-led mercantilism deploys a range of controls in order to avoid food shortages and their resultant revolts, liberal economy understands scarcity as "a chimera," for even when a relative shortage of food is predicted, that does not mean that the whole population will die at once.[32] Instead of trying to prevent scarcity at the cost of suppressing economic growth, then, liberal governmentality allows relative scarcity to develop, prices to increase, and part of the population to go hungry until the whole phenomenon has run its course: there will be "some scarcity, some dearness, some difficulty in buying wheat, and consequently some hunger, and it may well be that some people die of hunger after all. But by letting these people die of hunger one will be able to make scarcity a chimera."[33]

What I am driving at here through the interdigitation between *The Awakening*'s "alien hands" and liberal economy's "invisible hand" is that even though *The Awakening* exemplifies an operation of biopower, its modus operandi is not an anatomo-politics of discipline but rather a biopolitics of population. In other words, *The Awakening* simulates what Foucault calls "the game of liberalism—not interfering, allowing free movement, letting things follow their course; *laisser faire, passer et aller*."[34] That is, by letting Edna Pontellier do, move, and go as what is repeatedly called her "caprice" guides her, the novel stages liberal governmentality's ethos, which accepts the naturalness both of the market and of the population and lays the groundwork of freedom to maximize their potential (*The Awakening*, 5, 54, 76). In this context, as Foucault puts it, freedom signifies "no longer the exemptions and privileges attached to a person, but the possibility of movement, change of place, and processes of circulation of both people and things."[35] One aesthetic innovation of *The Awakening* lies in the narrative realization of this

FLIRTING WITH DEATH   77

"freedom of circulation," which is enacted by, as I argue in the next section, staging Edna's physical, affective, and romantic drift that possesses no apparent teleology, rather than portraying the depth or the development of her private self.[36]

Perhaps another way of saying this is that *The Awakening* represents Edna Pontellier not as an individual but rather as the population, both as a personification of its fluctuation and as a synecdochical part of its entity. This does not mean that the novel's rendition of Edna's mode of being—impulsive, oblivious, almost incoherent—falls short as a representation of human experience. If anything, it acutely captures what it feels to be a populational being, a newly emerging sense that one might be merely a part of some larger order of things, of what the text calls "the great unnumbered multitude of souls that come and go" (104). As we have seen in the Introduction, if discipline is a mode of individualization in which one is trained to be a self-governing subject through school, military, penal, work, and family spaces, biopolitics can be said to care not about individuals at all—even the aberrant ones—but about the population and its biological phenomenon as a whole. Even though biopolitics developed later than discipline, however, it did not supplant disciplinary power; rather, biopolitics presupposes the operation of an anatomo-politics of discipline, assuming that the population largely consists of self-governing subjects. Herein lies a paradox of the biopolitical subject, or what Foucault calls the "caesura" between the population and individuals: while individuals have become "simply . . . the instrument, relay, or condition for obtaining something at the level of the population," the security of the population largely depends on how seriously these "elements" of the population take the fiction of their own unique individuality, conducting themselves responsibly and forming desires accordingly.[37]

When Edna is said "to realize her position in the universe as a human being, and to recognize her relations as an individual to the world within and about her," this points to two different modes of existence that are intertwined in the biopolitical subject: an element of the population as a species-being on the one hand, and an autonomous, desiring personhood on the other (14). While the Pontelliers' family doctor, Mandelet, diagnoses Edna's moodiness as a "morbid condition," the hereditary explanations that applied to the two "morbid" subjects in the previous chapter—the neurasthenic Olive Chancellor and the degenerate Hyacinth Robinson—are no longer available for Edna. Mandelet's question—"Nothing hereditary?"—is met with her husband's resounding denial: "Oh, no, indeed! She comes of

78 THE SUICIDAL STATE

sound old Presbyterian Kentucky stock" (66, 63). Rather than a minoritarian pathology, Edna's mood fluctuation hypostasizes the population/individual caesura in which biopolitical beings reside: the more she realizes her liberal subjectivity and is "becoming herself," the deeper she is entangled with the population, in which "life appeared to her like a grotesque pandemonium and humanity like worms struggling blindly toward inevitable annihilation" (55, 56). If, as Miller argues, the nineteenth-century novel has successfully functioned as an apparatus of disciplinary power, *The Awakening* and other novels published toward the turn of the century—those that have been largely categorized as naturalist fiction—begin to narrate the fissure in the liberal subject disseminated through realist novels. In other words, the "naturalness" of naturalism is not only about the uncontrollable force of nature, heredity, and evolution, as it has been argued, but also about the market and the population, which are conceptualized as "natural" phenomena with their own rhythms and fluctuations. Simply put, naturalism is an aesthetic mode of the biopolitics of population, the one which *The Awakening* exemplifies with its *laissez-faire* narration.

Free Erotic Economy of Creoles

The world of *The Awakening* operates according to a cry for economic freedom attributed to seventeenth-century French merchants: *laissez nous faire*—leave us alone, let us do as we please. Edna declares to her husband, "Let me alone; you bother me," and Doctor Mandelet advises him to follow her command: "Don't bother her, and don't let her bother you. . . . It will pass happily over, especially if you let her alone" (55, 64). Léonce follows Mandelet's advice by "letting her do as she liked," even literally leaving her alone in their New Orleans residence while he pursues an investment opportunity in New York (68). The sovereign voice of his father-in-law condemns him: "You are too lenient, too lenient by far, Léonce. . . . Authority, coercion are what is needed. Put your foot down good and hard; the only way to manage a wife" (68). But the suave financier knows better; even when he learns that his wife's "whimsical turn of mind" has led her to move out of their French Quarter mansion while he is in New York, he "handled it with his well-known business tact and cleverness," circumventing reputational damage by publishing a notice in a local newspaper that their residence is undergoing "sumptuous alterations" (89). A job well-done, security restored; even Edna herself can't help but "admire[] the skills of his maneuver" (89).

Just as the term *laissez-faire* itself preserves a trace of untranslatably French flair—whose ethos Edna's Anglo-Saxon father refuses to understand—so does the environment of Edna's whimsical movement among the white Creole community, which she describes as "very French, very foreign" (52). Coming from "old Presbyterian Kentucky stock," Edna is "an American woman" through and through (63, 6). She does not belong to the "old Creole race": in the words of Edna's white Creole muse, Adèle Ratignolle, "She is not one of us; she is not like us" (62, 20). Although the white Creoles have been largely precluded in critical examinations of *The Awakening*'s race relations because of their optical whiteness, the text's demarcation of their difference attests to their liminal status in the Progressive Era's racial landscape. Put simply, Creole identity illustrates the era's complex negotiation over whiteness, as the Creoles' *laissez-faire* Frenchness has compromised their claim to whiteness as property.

As historians Virginia R. Domínguez and Joseph G. Tregle document, Creole identity underwent a dramatic change throughout the nineteenth century.[38] When the term *creole* first began to gain currency in North America after the 1803 Louisiana Purchase, it was primarily used to distinguish the descendants of French and Spanish colonists from the newly settling Anglo-Americans. The designation, "the creole," was often mythically associated with an Old World aristocratic heritage and was used to mark the group's supposed cultural superiority to Anglo-Saxon Americans, who were often depicted as "brutal and swinish 'Kaintucks,'" reminiscent of Edna's Kentucky heritage.[39] In the antebellum period, therefore, the primary emphasis of the term *creole* was on local birth and French/Spanish heritage, which often spanned racial lines. As the Emancipation dissolved preexisting social boundaries, however, white Creoles began to claim exclusive ownership over the term in order to disidentify themselves from Creoles of color.[40] To bolster their whiteness, white Creoles even started to embrace Anglo-American cultural mores. As a result, the visibility of Gallic white Creole culture was gradually starting to fade by the time of *The Awakening*'s publication, even as various preservation efforts were being made precisely at the moment of its disempowerment.[41] Chopin's choice of Grand Isle as a central setting for the novel indexes one such elegiac mode. According to Barbara C. Ewell, Chopin deliberately set her novel in the year before the 1893 Great

80 THE SUICIDAL STATE

October Storm, which devastated Grand Isle and "swe[pt] away the Creole Community that had flourished on its shore."[42]

However, the Creole was not easily assimilable to the Progressive model of whiteness for at least two reasons. For one, as we have seen in the previous chapter, Anglo-Saxonism was renewing its energy in the last decades of the nineteenth century, driving Louisiana Creole identity, with its largely Latin origin and Catholic religion, far from the center of whiteness. Anglo-Saxonism in the 1890s espoused social Darwinism in order to legitimize American imperialism, with the belief that Anglo-Saxon expansion illustrated the racial survival of the fittest whereby the principle of self-government was disseminated.[43] For thinkers like John Fiske, the Spanish-American War and the acquisition of the Philippines in 1898—a year before the publication of *The Awakening*—exemplified such Anglo-Saxon triumphs over the decaying Old World.[44] This marginalization of Latin populations—of Spanish, French, as well as Italian origins—was further driven by the rise of a new term for Anglo-Saxons and adjacent racial groups: the "English speaking race." As Thomas G. Dyer argues, while the term was widely used in the turn-of-the-century United States, Theodore Roosevelt in particular was fond of this denomination—likely because of his Dutch, and thus non-Anglo-Saxon, heritage—and was even concerned that the "French [language] might replace English" with the incursion of French Canadians in New England as early as in 1892.[45]

While the Creoles' whiteness had already been put on trial with their Gallic heritage, it was further jeopardized by their reputed intimate proximity to non-whites. In Lothrop Stoddard's *The Rising Tide of Color Against White World-Supremacy* (1920), for instance, white Creoles in the Caribbean embody the "increasing signs of degeneracy" afflicting whiteness: they are marked by "an idle and vapid existence, disdaining work as servile and debarred from higher callings by his European-born superiors."[46] This degeneration, Stoddard argues, stems from "contact with the colored races": "Despite legal enactment and social taboo, colored strains percolated insidiously into the creole stock."[47] Likewise, the Creole community in New Orleans was long associated with the quasi-institutionalized social form of plaçage, the "formal and sometimes even contractual arrangement between white men and women of color . . . which spelled out the financial terms of the[ir] relationships."[48] These white men and women of color often met at similarly institutionalized quadroon balls, where "free women of color chaperoned their daughters and bargained for extramarital alliances."[49] Even

FLIRTING WITH DEATH   81

though the custom of plaçage had primarily subsided by the 1850s, George Washington Cable's historical romances about antebellum New Orleans revived the association between Creoles and cross-racial intimacy in the 1880s.[50] As Domínguez explains, while questions about the racial purity of Creoles had been raised since the 1850s, non-Creoles in the postbellum era "began to insinuate rather openly and insistently that all Creoles had at least 'a touch of the tarbrush.'"[51] As a result, white Creoles in the 1890s vociferously insisted upon their exclusively Caucasian ancestry, fearing that optical whiteness did not necessarily guarantee the purity of their "white blood" in the American racial imaginary.

As shown in Alys Weinbaum's brilliant reading of Chopin's short story "Désirée's Baby," Chopin consciously deployed white Creoles' fraught racial status in her work.[52] Published in January 1893, immediately after *Plessy* was brought to the Supreme Court, "Désirée's Baby" features an antebellum marriage between an orphaned woman with a fair complexion, Désirée, and a Creole planter of "the oldest and proudest in Louisiana," Armand Aubigny.[53] When he beholds their newborn's dark complexion, Armand expels his wife, convinced of Désirée's hidden Black heritage. The story, however, ends with Chopin's signature ironic twist: an old letter from Armand's mother to his father reveals that it is not Désirée but Armand who "belongs to the race that is cursed with the brand of slavery."[54] Especially in the wake of *Plessy*, in which an optically white Creole with one-eighth Black ancestry had claimed racial whiteness, white Creoles were transformed into "racial 'wild card[s],'" becoming the very tokens of whiteness's vulnerability in the Progressive Era racial imaginary.[55]

Creoles in *The Awakening* also function as limit-case figures of whiteness, whose claims to whiteness as family property are under pressure because of their putative sexual laxness, an openness that erodes the privacy of the monogamous household. The text underlines the foreignness of its Creole characters, coding their intimate communications in French and representing their English as marked by "un-English emphasis and a certain carefulness and deliberation"; in contrast, Léonce Pontellier, whose English has "no accent whatever," is characterized as an Anglicized Creole eager to assimilate into mainstream American whiteness (54). It is precisely in this context that Edna's pedigreed whiteness—"com[ing] of sound old Presbyterian Kentucky stock," as Léonce proudly describes her heritage—becomes his "valuable piece of personal property," promising to strengthen both his own racial capital and that of his sons (63, 4). When Edna declares her property

82 THE SUICIDAL STATE

rights over herself—"I am no longer one of Mr. Pontellier's possessions to dispose of or not. I give myself where I choose"—her racial heritage emerges as a vital component of this private property (102). Edna's erotic liberalism thus reconfigures her body and its racial heritage as a property that only she has a right to use, invest, or dispose of.

When it comes to the erotic and the *laissez-faire*, the novel seems to say, nobody knows better than the French, for it is the white Creole women's community on Grand Isle that initiates the "American woman" into their liberal erotic economy (6). For Edna, who has "lived her own small life all within herself" in a private Anglo-Saxon household, what is most striking about the Creole women is their "freedom of expression" and "entire absence of prudery": namely, their apparent lack of a sense of privacy (14, 10, 10). For Creole women, there seems to be no such thing as sexual secrets—the constitutive core of the private self—as they talk about their bodies and bodily processes, "withholding no intimate detail" and never failing to make Edna blush (11). Even reading novels—the privateness of the act that Miller argues is crucial for constructing the reader's liberal subjectivity—becomes a public affair, as they freely circulate their books and discuss them at the table, despite Edna's desire to read in "secret and solitude" (11).

Edna becomes implicated in the circulation of their liberal erotic economy as she becomes romantically involved with Robert Lebrun. The female Creole community on Grand Isle is structured in such a way that Robert figuratively functions as its homosocial node: "Since the age of fifteen, which was eleven years before, Robert each summer at Grand Isle had constituted himself the devoted attendant of some fair dame or damsel. Sometimes it was a young girl, again a widow; but as often as not it was some interesting married woman" (11). This kind of flirtation with the Creole youth constitutes something of an initiation ritual to the homosocial circle of Creole women, and that summer the turn has fallen to Edna. It is a custom sanctioned by the whole community, about which "the Creole husband is never jealous; with him the gangrene passion is one which has become dwarfed by disuse" (12). Creole husbands, including Léonce, let their wives enjoy the erotic frisson of flirtation, and even Edna does not feel "in the least grotesque" about discussing her attachment to Robert with her husband (45).

The Awakening presents flirtation in the Creole community as the erotic counterpart of *laissez-faire* liberalism, whereby freedom is defined as the maximized circulation of desire. As the turn-of-the-century sociologist Georg Simmel theorized, in its relation to reality, flirtation is similar to the

FLIRTING WITH DEATH   83

Kantian formulation of art—" 'purposiveness without purpose' "—because it is self-contained, with no consequential interest in its object.[56] The aim of flirtation is "to captivate, to be desired, but without allowing [one]self to be taken serious[ly] in any way."[57] It is an autotelic play that has no end other than avoiding the end itself, keeping desire and intimate sociality alive and in motion. Creole women are skilled flirts, for they never mistake the play of flirtation with reality. Their erotic openness is a paradoxical sign of their impeccable self-government, "a lofty chastity which in the Creole woman seems to be inborn and unmistakable" (*The Awakening*, 10). Just as the biopolitics of population presupposes the operation of disciplinary power, the Creole women on Grand Isle enjoy the erotic liberty of flirtation precisely because their proper sexual conduct is implicitly guaranteed; despite their apparent lack of liberal private selves, they are excellent biopolitical subjects—"mother-women," as the text calls them—who conduct themselves responsibly according to codes of monogamy (9). In other words, they can take pleasure in the nonteleological *as if* of flirtation and the sociality it creates without desiring a particular object.

Though Edna learns to loosen her "mantle of reserve" to float in this liberal economy of flirtation, her "first breath of freedom" is drawn not by Robert himself but by the soft hand of the Creole "sensuous Madonna," Adèle Ratignolle (14, 19, 12). One morning during their vacation on Grand Isle, Edna and Adèle go to the beach together, carefully avoiding Robert's interference. As Edna confides to Adèle the strange feeling of disorientation that she has been experiencing lately—as if she were returning to her Kentucky childhood and "walking through the green meadow . . . idly, aimlessly, unthinking and unguided"—Adèle suddenly lays her hand on Edna's: "Seeing that the hand was not withdrawn, [Adèle] clasped it firmly and warmly. She even stroked it a little, fondly, with the other hand, murmuring in an undertone, '*Pauvre chérie.*' The action was at first a little confusing to Edna, but she soon lent herself readily to the Creole's gentle caress" (17, italics original). As Edna learns to yield herself to the sensual touch of Adèle—who is simply referred to as "the Creole" in the passage in an ungendered and unindividuated way— Adèle's hand guides Edna from existential lostness into a new erotic economy of "freedom," "muddl[ing] Edna like wine" and leaving her "flushed and . . . intoxicated" (19).

While the scene's unmistakable eroticism has been left underemphasized in *The Awakening* criticism, Adèle touch proves to be, as Mikko Tuhkanen puts it in a different context, "at once completely barren *and* intensely

84 THE SUICIDAL STATE

fecund."[58] With Adèle's initiation, the touch in *The Awakening* becomes a trope for a nonteleological eroticism that flirts with objects without consummation—the mode of sensuality that seeks no orgasmic discharge.[59] The way Edna lends herself to "the Creole's gentle caress" anticipates the scene in which Edna accepts the sexual advances of her other Creole suitor, Alcée Arobin:

> He stood up beside her and smoothed her hair with his soft, magnetic hand. His touch conveyed to her a certain physical comfort. She could have fallen quietly asleep there if he had continued to pass his hand over her hair. . . . His hand had strayed to her beautiful shoulders, and he could feel the response of her flesh. . . . He did not answer, except to continue to caress her . . . until she had become supple to his gentle, seductive entreaties. (88)

Although the scene has been understood as the awakening of Edna's sexual desire, which overpowers her romantic attachment to Robert, what matters for Edna here is not the "sexual intercourse so-called"; rather, what she desires is the continual caress of Arobin's "soft, magnetic hand."[60] As she yields herself to Arobin's caress, their flirtation's "purposiveness without purpose" seems to find closure, fulfilling Adèle's fearful prediction that Edna might one day "make the unfortunate blunder" of taking the play of flirtation too "seriously" (20). But even when the game of flirtation seemingly shifts into the reality of adultery, Edna's nonteleological drift does not end but rather augments its indifference to the object itself. Nurtured in the Creole mode of erotic liberalism, Edna's desire is no longer invested in any specific object but directed toward the constant movement from one object to another with no apparent teleology other than the circulation of desire itself. In other words, when Edna says, "To-day it is Arobin; to-morrow it will be some one else. It makes no difference to me," *The Awakening* gestures toward the ephemerality of object-desire itself (108).

Read in this way, Edna's answer to Mademoiselle Reisz's question—why she loves Robert—seems to point to the operation of a liberal economy of desire espoused by the biopolitics of population: "Because his hair is brown and grows away from his temples; because he opens and shuts his eyes, and his nose is a little out of drawing; he has two lips and a square chin, and a little finger which he can't straighten from having played baseball too energetically in his youth" (78). As Reisz interprets it, Edna's answer seemingly showcases the inevitability of her love—or romantic love in general, for that

FLIRTING WITH DEATH   85

matter—which renders the loved one a privileged object beyond any logical explanations: "Because you do, in short" (78). Yet taken at face value, her inventory of Robert's nondescript physical features bespeaks the very fungibility of the object in the calculus of population. Simply put, when Edna later realizes that "the day would come when [Robert], too, and the thought of him would melt out of her existence," she points to what might be called the biopoliticality of romantic love (108).

Parthenogenesis of the New Women

Another name for the volatility of object-desire is *vogue*; so named is the magazine that published nineteen of Chopin's short stories, "the largest number of short stories published by any single periodical in Chopin's life time."[61] As *Vogue*'s founding editor-in-chief, Josephine Redding, explains in the inaugural issue in 1892, the magazine's name was—once again—a French word that simultaneously referred to the "mode or fashion prevalent at any particular time" and the "swaying motion of a ship, the stroke of an oar."[62] Chopin's stories seem to move in tandem with *Vogue*'s everchanging, whimsical aesthetics. Since its second issue, which featured two of Chopin's stories—"A Visit to Avoyelles" and the aforementioned "Désirée's Baby"—the magazine continued to publish Chopin's stories, including what was later to become her most anthologized piece, "The Story of an Hour," and remained receptive to her fiction even after the scandalous publication of *The Awakening*.[63]

To revisit Chopin's connection to *Vogue*, I argue, helps contextualize *The Awakening*'s autotelic erotic economy by placing it against the backdrop of the burgeoning culture of consumption. As Chopin portrays with rich tactility in one of her *Vogue* stories, "A Pair of Silk Stockings" (1897), the invisible hand of the market metamorphosed into the irresistible caress of commodities at the turn of the century. A pile of silk stockings at the department store seduces a frugal, working-class young mother to "feel[] the soft, sheeny luxurious things—with both hands now, holding them up to see them glisten, and to feel them glide serpent-like through her fingers."[64] Their sensual touch leads her, like Edna, to "abandon[] herself to some mechanical impulse that directed her actions and freed her of responsibility" as she purchases one item after another until she squanders all her money.[65] To consume is to flirt with commodities, keeping the desire alive in "short-lived and necessarily incomplete pleasures."[66] Just as the young mother wishes

86   THE SUICIDAL STATE

the cable car home would "never stop anywhere, but go on and on with her forever," it is a strategy to keep the deathly weight of subjectivity at bay as long as possible.[67] When the domestic sphere—a sanctified topos of the private self—becomes the source of oppression itself, the semi-public intimate sphere of consumption furnishes one with the mass-produced pleasure and reprieve of anonymity, seducing one into the erotic life of biopolitics.

In the mode of a counter-*Künstlerroman*, *The Awakening* counterposes Edna's mode of being to that of an artist, the pianist Mademoiselle Reisz, who embodies the nineteenth-century novel's ideal of a singular, private, liberal subjectivity. Though possessing a highly attuned aesthetic sense, Edna lacks the "absolute gifts"—qualities bestowed rather than purchased—that are required to become an artist; the culmination of her aestheticism is marked not by her paintings but by the extravagant party that Arobin calls "the *coup d'état*" against her husband (61, 81). In other words, she is not an artist but an aesthete, the most refined sort of consumer, who viscerally understands and reacts to beauty. Marked by "a sensuous susceptibility to beauty," Edna's aesthetic is inextricable from her erotic sensibility (14). As Dianne Bunch argues, "If she participates in eroticism outside marriage, sends her children away, spends money extravagantly, or throws a feast for friends, Edna is living within the luxurious economy of excess: she produces nothing, and her actions are purely for pleasure."[68] Edna's consumptive desire is intertwined with her autotelic desire for the circulation of desire itself, directed against property accumulation and inheritance—the very logic that binds liberal personhood and racial reproduction. Rather than utilizing her property as a good biopolitical subject—"conduct[ing] her household *en bonne ménagère*," managing her family's financial and racial property as a good housewife—she desires to dissipate it (71). *Vogue* functioned as a textbook for such wayward consumption for bourgeois women like Edna, christening them New Women: the fin-de-siècle cultural icons of women's personal autonomy, whose singular subjectivity was paradoxically purchased through mass consumption.

Vogue's education of desire epitomizes period theorizations of consumer culture, most notably Thorstein Veblen's conspicuous consumption as a "conspicuous abstention from labour."[69] In a different key, Charlotte Perkins Gilman's *Women and Economics* (1898) critiques women's consumption as abstention not only from economic but also from reproductive labor: women are forced to engage in consumption that reinforces their sexual desirability while they evade maternity, which would depreciate their commodity value in the market of "sexuo-economic relations."[70] For Gilman, maternal capacity is a means not only to reincorporate women into the realm of production, but also to enable "racial progress": "Human motherhood must be judged as it serves its purpose to the human race. Primarily, its purpose is to reproduce the race by reproducing the individual; secondarily, to improve the race by improving the individual."[71] Among other Progressive maternalists—Margaret Sanger, Victoria Woodhull, and Lester Ward, to name a few—Gilman implicitly collapses "the human race" into the white race, deploying motherhood as collateral for the elevation of white women's social status.[72] To be better educated as mothers of the race, women should be released from the private family in which they have been consigned to compulsory consumption, and instead form collective households wherein domestic labor—including reproductive labor—will be shared. In other words, Gilman attempts to reconfigure whiteness from family property to public property.

Gilman's critique of the private family led her to conceive of an all-women utopia in her work of science fiction, *Herland* (1915), which shares, albeit obliquely, Edna Pontellier's fantasy of a "new race of beings" (*The Awakening*, 37). The eponymous gynocentric community thrives on a hidden plateau, where its all-female citizens live harmoniously with no concept of gender norms, market economy, monogamous households, or private property. The nation is "one family, all descended from one mother," who "had founded *a new race*" by parthenogenesis, a race that is symbolically named the "New Women."[73] While the heterosexual monogamous household functions to secure the patrilineage of property, sequestering women as hereditary vessels to be protected from the damage of miscegenation, the Herlandian New Women's racial property of "Aryan stock" is already secured by parthenogenesis, echoing Walter Benn Michaels' classic formulation that sterility, incest, and homosexuality all served as strategies for protecting the purity of whiteness in modernist fiction.[74] Herland's queerly singular bloodline safeguards women's reproductive capacities from racial taint and obliterates the notion of private property itself, for these citizens share everything as public property, racial or otherwise.

Vogue, to a surprising degree, shares Gilman's fantasy of the "New Woman" as a "new race," as well as her critique of the private family. Josephine Redding's editorial in the February 7, 1895 issue of *Vogue* straightforwardly embraces the ideals of New Womanhood, claiming that "personal freedom is more precious to [women] than the protection [?] [*sic*] of the best of man"; as she states

88 THE SUICIDAL STATE

in the March 15, 1900 issue, the condition in which "women were created for man's pleasure" has started to change, "when the arrogance of man met its Waterloo in the self-assertiveness of the New Woman."[75] While Gilman imagines the shared reproduction of public property as a way out of patriarchal oppression, however, *Vogue* is skeptical of the maternalist's productivism. One editorial declares that "maternal instinct theory is largely a myth": the myth is fabricated, it continues, "to beget and train children for the sake of the race, for perpetuation of the species."[76] Even when property becomes publicly shared, its reproduction still instrumentalizes women's bodies in service of the race and the species. Instead of the wholesale dismantling of private property, then, *Vogue* envisioned the New Women's liberation from the domestic sphere as a consumer capitalist project. Production, reproduction, and accumulation of property—whether private or public—were passé for *Vogue*. In its replacement of need with desire, the consumerist economy removed the productivist economy's delimited possibilities for demand, unmooring it from biological needs. This shift enabled a homologous transformation in the economic role of women's bodies. That is, whereas women were required to reproduce human bodies as sources of labor and demand under a productivist dispensation, their role enlarged with consumerism, in which they furnished insatiably circulating desire as the motor force of the market itself.[77]

Vogue self-consciously advocated for bourgeois women's autotelic aestheticism, which had no purpose other than proliferating desire by unceasingly creating eccentric trends. In *Vogue*'s second issue, Redding's tongue-in-cheek editorial defends the craze for "humps," namely, the artificial enlargement of head, shoulders, and hips in women's clothes:

> The persistent recurrence of these uncanny growths makes it doubtful whether, after all, it was quite worth while ever to have put the spelling book into woman's hands. For what value is mental development if one outcome of it is physical distortion? . . . Before so peculiar a practice as this of the humps, theory stands non-plussed. For what plausible reason can possibly be assigned for a nineteenth century woman pretending, at intervals, to the possession of big head, enlarged small of the back, abnormal growth of hip, exaggerated breadth of shoulder? . . . Impossible to account for on the ground of comfort, expediency, morality or beauty, the humps of woman's fancy must be added to the list of insoluble Whys? that forever vex the spirit of the philosopher and baffle his curiosity.[78]

FLIRTING WITH DEATH 89

Redding's cataloguing of the "uncanny growths" of humps as "physical distortion[s]" resembles Charles Darwin's list of unusual morphological features of animals in *The Descent of Man* (1871). Yet Darwin's theory of sexual selection—that creatures decorate themselves in order to be chosen as mates even at the cost of attracting their predators as well—no longer holds in the face of humps, which willfully misshape women's bodies and foil the male gaze, operating against the purpose of heterosexual attraction. Redding further states: "The hump defies classification. Each variety is unique and owes no kinship to its predecessors. A collection of them would contribute nothing to the theory of evolution."[79] Their sudden emergence short-circuits linear genealogy; each specimen is a mutant, which "owes no kinship to its predecessors."[80]

In flouting the evolutionary narrative, *Vogue*'s whimsical aesthetic presents the New Woman as impregnating and giving birth to herself with the narcissistic pleasure of consumption; narcissism, after all, is a fourth term, one that Michaels did not count among the strategies to eschew the danger of miscegenation. As shown in the cover illustration of the May 21, 1896 issue, titled "The Young Woman Has 'Arrived,'" which features a woman clad in typical New Woman attire—codified by a cigarette, a monocle, a waistcoat, and a tuxedo-jacket "humped" to the fullest on its shoulders—*Vogue* advocated New Womanhood as an aesthetic of hybrid androgyny, one that appeared suddenly out of nowhere, free of any genealogical or racial issue. Rather than a direct descendent of the New England suffragists, the New Woman is essentially an aesthetic *representation* of women's autonomy, coming out of the nowhere of evolutionary logic. Born out of narcissistic parthenogenesis from the fertile soil of consumerism, the New Woman as a new race propagates through the dissemination of mimetic desire through media like *Vogue*. Thus mass-produced, the New Woman embodies what Mark Seltzer calls the "paradoxical economy of consumption," which "deploys a rhythm of the generic and the individual": while it seems to promise the realization of one's individual desire and freedom, that realization is enabled through the standardization of the self as part of the mass, as an element of the population.[81]

While sidestepping the evolutionary reproductive imperative, as Jennifer Fleissner puts it, her sudden emergence and flourishing mean that "the New Woman *is* a fad": "fatally aligned with such consumer ephemera," such as bloomer outfits and bicycles, the New Woman was "a virtual invention of the burgeoning mass magazine," who suddenly emerged, proliferated, and

90 THE SUICIDAL STATE

disappeared within a decade.[82] In this sense, the New Woman's historical fleetingness gestures toward the original meaning of the word *consume*: to devour, to make away with something, to the extent of its extermination. As Rachel Bowlby points out, the verb's derivatives, *consumer* and *consumption*, emerged remarkably late, only with the publication of Alfred Marshall's 1890 *Principles of Economics*.[83] The residue of the word's earlier usage must have echoed loudly in its new association with economic activity in the 1890s. The parthenogenetic creation of the New Woman through narcissistic consumer pleasure was death-laden, signaling the "female resistance to futurity" even at the cost of her own consumptive death.[84]

One of Chopin's *Vogue* stories, titled "An Egyptian Cigarette" (1897) and published in the same issue as the cover featuring a New Woman with a cigarette in her mouth, captures the New Woman's consumptive drive toward pleasure, a pleasure flirting with death. As the New Woman narrator inhales the fumes of a cigarette that her male friend has brought back from Cairo, it turns out to be a hallucinogen, bringing her to an arid desert in ancient Egypt, where she crawls on the blistering sands, abandoned by her lover. Dragging herself on all fours in the desert in search of water, she drowns herself in the Nile, reminiscent of the heroine of *The Awakening*, who submerges herself in the Gulf. Her death fulfills the celestial prophecy that "after the rupture of life [she] would open [her] arms inviting death, and the waters would envelop [her]."[85] Awakened from this fifteen-minute nightmare, the narrator crumples the cigarettes left in the box, musing that their "mystic fumes" have brought her "a vision of celestial peace," "a dream of hopes fulfilled," and "a taste of rapture, such as had not entered into [her] mind to conceive."[86] In the New Woman's gender nonconforming iconography, the cigarette serves as an emblem of the very mechanism of consumptive pleasure that is captured in Oscar Wilde's famous epigram: "A cigarette is the perfect type of the perfect pleasure. It is exquisite, and it leaves one unsatisfied."[87] As Bowlby succinctly puts it, the core of this aphorism is that "pleasure entails *non*-satisfaction": "The enjoyment of the 'perfect pleasure' results not in satisfaction but in a lack of it, leaving open the demand for more, the search for the next (or the same) short-lived and necessarily incomplete pleasure."[88] The consuming desire for pleasure never settles on one object; it immortalizes itself by transferring itself from one object to another, never being consummated—except in the death of the subject of desire, the ultimate pleasure of "the sweet rapture of rest."[89]

Consummating the Consuming Desire

Marked by the instability of her object-desire, Edna Pontellier's mode of desiring is consumptive, like that of the New Woman who created, multiplied, and consumed herself in fin-de-siècle fadmongery. Edna's erotic economy operates against the utilitarian economy of production and accumulation, both in terms of the economic production and the biological reproduction of racialized property. Guided by the invisible hand of desire's sensual touch, her consumptive desire perpetuates itself by flirting with one object after another until it is finally consummated by her submergence in the Gulf of Mexico. From the beginning of the novel, "the touch of the sea" is described as "sensuous, enfolding the body in its soft, close embrace" (14). As the heroine's first swim in the Gulf coincides with her initial denial of sex with her husband—the aforementioned scene of her first "awakening"—the Gulf is the symbolic site of her nonteleological eros, "whose sonorous murmur reached her like a loving but imperative entreaty" (13). While Edna instantly recoils at her first "encounter with death" when she swims far out in the ocean toward the beginning of the narrative, she now yields her naked body to the Gulf, whose "touch" is circularly described as "sensuous, enfolding the body in its soft, close embrace" (28, 109).

Crucially, the moment that triggers Edna's suicide is the vision of Adèle Ratignolle in childbirth—the very figure who has initiated Edna into the autotelic economy of pleasure. When Edna arrives at Adèle's home, she witnesses a "scene [of] torture" in which her Creole friend groans and curses in extreme pain with "her face drawn and pinched, her sweet blue eyes haggard and unnatural" (104, 103). This scene haunts Edna as a return of the repressed reproductive body: Adèle's Rubenesque body, whose "excessive physical charm" has awakened Edna's sensuality, proves to have a straightforwardly teleological function: to reproduce the diminishing white Creole race, mechanically giving birth to a child "every two years" (14, 10). The scene of Adèle's childbirth marks a crucial moment in the novel's narrative structure as well. Even while the text seems to float freely according to Edna's caprice, its diegetic time implicitly progresses forward alongside Adèle's pregnancy, opening when she has just become pregnant with her fourth child. The way Adèle's touch awakens Edna's sensuality on the beach has also been rendered as the figuration of a fetus: "No multitude of words could have been more significant than those moments of silence, or more pregnant with the first-felt throbbing of desire" (30). As her fantasy of free-floating desire is

92 THE SUICIDAL STATE

ruptured with the physical reality of Adèle's childbirth, Edna is filled "with a flaming, outspoken revolt against the ways of Nature" (104). As Mandelet sagaciously tells Edna, the romance of personal freedom becomes purchasable only through hard labor in the service of the population: "The trouble is . . . that youth is given up to illusions. It seems to be a provision of Nature; a decoy to secure mothers for the race. And Nature takes no account of moral consequences, of arbitrary conditions which we create and we feel obliged to maintain at any cost" (105). The "arbitrary conditions" of liberal subjectivity—its desires, its hopes, its loves—bind one deeply to the matrix of the population, which now must be "maintain[ed] at any cost" in order to sustain these life-giving attachments.

In contrast to the scene of Adèle's hard labor, the way in which Edna yields her "white" procreative body to the Gulf of Mexico is filled with tenderness and sensuality: "The water was deep, but she lifted her white body and reached out with a long, sweeping stroke. The touch of the sea is sensuous, enfolding the body in its soft, close embrace" (109). Edna Pontellier's consuming desire is never satisfied by any given object; knowing no orgasmic consummation, it aims to prolong itself indefinitely, transferred from one object to another, until she consumes all her property, including her own person. It is only the ocean's touch that enables the total dissipation of her personal property, for, as Jacques Derrida says, "to touch, so one believes, is touching what one touches, to let oneself be touched by the touched, by the touch of the thing."[90] Swimming far out into the Gulf, Edna chooses to "lose herself" in "the unlimited," touched by the ocean as she touches it, letting herself be drowned rather than killing herself (Awakening, 28). Such an autoerotic touch of consumption enables the parthenogenesis of the New Woman: instead of giving birth to a child, she imaginatively returns to her own Kentucky childhood, becoming a daughter of her own. As she swims farther and farther into the ocean, she hears the distant barking of "an old dog that was chained to the sycamore tree" and the "spurs of the cavalry officer clanged as he walked across the porch," returning again to a day when she once traversed "the ocean of waving grass" (109, 18).

But even when Edna loses herself in the oceanic and escapes what she calls "soul's slavery," she purchases that very freedom by consuming the image of another woman who has drowned herself before her: a woman who heard the barking, not of her own dog chained to a tree, but of the bloodhound chasing her to enchain her in slavery again. Just as the New Woman simulated the mass-produced iconography of autonomy, Edna Pontellier's freedom is in part realized through her imitation of the eponymous heroine of William Wells Brown's *Clotel* (1853): Thomas Jefferson's illegitimate, mixed-race daughter, who leaps into the Potomac River and drowns herself to escape the slave catchers seeking to carry her back to the New Orleans slave market. But Clotel herself was a simulacrum of many other suicides before her, for prior to the vogue for white suicide in Progressive Era literature, the suicidal figure belonged most prominently to the representation of slavery. The captives' attempts at self-destruction, along with the slaveowners' brutal measures to keep their chattel alive, had been frequently reported and circulated in newspapers since the Revolutionary Era.[91] After the 1850 passage of the Fugitive Slave Act, slave suicide was increasingly seen as a "robust and existential defense" against slavery, becoming a symbol of enslaved people's last-ditch exertion to wrest themselves away from the power to keep them alive in a perpetual state of injury.[92] Black suicide, in its resistance against the bio/necropolitical instrumentalization of life, appears prototypal of the kind of counter-conduct that Edna Pontellier and other Progressive Era suicides dream of; or, more precisely, perhaps, the Progressive Era representation of suicide was already permeated with the iconography of slave suicide to begin with.

Clotel's niece, Ellen, too, kills herself after she is sold at the New Orleans slave market to "an old gentleman," knowing the true purpose of his purchase: to fornicate with "the grand-daughter[] of Thomas Jefferson," and reproduce his property as his chattel.[93] But the description of her suicide is left harrowingly unadorned: "The morning after her arrival, she was found in her chamber, a corpse. She had taken poison."[94] The suicide of the founding father's daughter, in contrast, becomes a national event, one that matches the Revolution in its symbolic significance. Clotel finds herself caught in a pincer of hostile forces on the Long Bridge just when she was on the verge of successfully escaping their pursuit: "But God by his Providence had otherwise determined. He had determined that an appalling tragedy should be enacted that night, within plain sight of the President's house and the capital of the Union, which should be an evidence wherever it should be known, of the unconquerable love of liberty the heart may inherit."[95] The self-chosen death of the President's daughter is designed to exemplify and sanctify the nation's indomitable love for freedom and will to self-government. So closes the text by singing a sardonic jubilee for the freedom-loving nation: "Hurrah for our country! hurrah! / To freedom she leaped, through drowning and death— / Hurrah for our country! hurrah!"[96]

94   THE SUICIDAL STATE

The irony becomes only more pronounced given that, as critics have noted, the title of the chapter that narrates Clotel's suicide, "Death is Freedom," reconfigures Patrick Henry's 1775 cry for independence: "Give me liberty or give me death."[97] Henry's revolutionary suicide threat (he did not have to choose death, unlike Clotel and many other enslaved people) became an archetypal declaration of the American love for liberty. Such deathly rhetoric of freedom is inscribed even deeper in the sentences that lead into Henry's *ur*-American ultimatum: "Is life so dear, or peace so sweet, as to be purchased at the price of chains and slavery? Forbid it, Almighty God! I know not what course others may take; but as for me . . . give me liberty or give me death!"[98] At stake here is not only the all-too-familiar founding hypocrisy of a lifelong slaveholder's comparison of British colonization of North America to slavery. Long before Edna Pontellier's deployment of just such a comparison to denounce biopolitical motherhood, slavery had been the primary rhetorical motor for the Revolution; it provided not only the material but also the conceptual precondition of American independence and liberalism, bolstering its claim for national sovereignty, self-ownership, and self-government.[99] Yet when Henry's rhetorical question is read in the context of *literal*, not *figurative*, slavery, and taken at face value—"Is life so dear, or peace so sweet, as to be purchased at the price of chains and slavery?"—it starts to carry a suicidal ring, one that undermines the American *raison d'état*, registering the founding paradox of the nation that loves liberty to death while that liberty is enabled by the homicidal subjugation of others. It asks itself: what makes the life, liberty, and happiness of a population secured by a racist system of subjugation so dear, so sweet?

More than one hundred years after its first utterance, the question was still ringing at the close of the nineteenth century. Crucially, *Plessy*'s logic binding whiteness, property, and (procreative) sex facilitated the intensification of the era's anti-Black violence. The 1890s witnessed not only the apex of lynching incidents, but also the spectacularization of anti-Black violence, in which the prolonged torture, burning, mutilation, and dismemberment of the victims' bodies were routinely staged in front of a large audience.[100] At the center of the lynching imaginary was the specter of the Black phallus, even as only a fraction of lynching actually involved charges—let alone cases—of sexual violation.[101] The myth of the Black rapist became a particularly cogent fiction as a result of the new status of whiteness as family property: inasmuch as whiteness was imagined as inextricably bound to reproductive sex, conceptualized through a particular kind of sex act ("sexual intercourse

FLIRTING WITH DEATH   95

so-called"), the encroachment on white entitlement took on a homologously sexual character figured as "rape" in the white imaginary.

The Black phallus was, as many critics have argued, deployed as a useful symbol to externalize white America's manifold anxieties, be it Black enfranchisement, falling white birthrates, or the shifting gender roles represented by the New Woman's increasing public presence. The imagined bind between racialized property and its sexual violation was especially taut, as we have seen in the previous chapter, where neurasthenic enervation had already threatened the very reproduction of whiteness, eventuating the discourse of race suicide. These fears were further augmented by the increasing visibility of women in public life—fighting for the ballot, owning their own property in however a limited form under the newly passed Married Women's Property Acts, as well as in the marketplace as desiring consumers. As the white woman's body, a supposed vessel of whiteness as family property, thus became increasingly exposed and putatively more vulnerable, the rise of lynching became a way for white men to monitor and curtail the movements of progressively independent white women as well as to find Black men as convenient scapegoats for their own gender anxiety. Inasmuch as whiteness as family property and its imagined security were being purchased at the price of Black deaths—social and physical, slow and quick—the parthenogenesis of the New Woman as a "new race" and her free-floating movement like a butterfly were catalyzed through the very consumption of Black deaths as well.

Take, for instance, Charles Chesnutt's "Dave's Neckliss" (1889), a story of a slave who kills himself because he thinks he is a piece of ham. Set in the Progressive Era present, Uncle Julius recounts an antebellum memory to his white employer John and his wife Annie, as he sits at their dinner table with a massive sugar-cured ham. Once smarter than anybody else on the plantation, his friend Dave slowly went out of his mind when he was made to wear a huge ham chained around his neck for six months as punishment for a theft of cured meat, of which he was innocent. Shunned even by his sweetheart and doubly consigned to social death, Dave became strangely attached to the ham, to the extent that when the meat is lifted off his neck, he misses its presence and creates an imaginary ham to comfort himself. Then he starts to believe, melancholically even, that he himself is turning into a ham, so much so that he hangs himself in the smokehouse to become a ham.

As much as "an elaborated pun [on] the 'curse of Ham,'" as one commentator aptly writes, "Dave's Neckliss" is an allegory of the flesh.[102] That is,

96   THE SUICIDAL STATE

Dave's identification with the ham is only too fitting insofar as his enslavement has already turned him into what Hortense Spillers calls the flesh: succulent, consumable, raw, and viscous animal matter, which has been marked by slavery's "lacerations, woundings, fissures, tears, scars, openings, ruptures, lesions, rendings."[103] Butchered from its original name, language, and kinship, Black flesh remains unincorporated into subjectivity's repository, "the body," be it individual or social. The meat chained around Dave's neck, then, is a punishment not so much for the theft that he did not commit as for his illicit desire for liberty and autonomy evidenced by the literacy he had illegally achieved ("'g'in de law," as Uncle Julius puts it): the ham, in short, is a metonymic reminder of his status as flesh.[104]

Adorned by a fleshy necklace, Dave's muscular physique is now queerly ungendered; or, more precisely, it looks "quare," to use an enslaved woman's derision, as he keeps muttering "quare things"—say, that he has seen a field covered with "ham-trees."[105] Dave's "quare" vision of ham-trees is an unmistakable evocation of lynching for post-Reconstruction readers. As such, the image registers the libidinal nature of gratuitous anti-Black violence, in which lynching victims were habitually dismembered, even castrated, with what Aliyyah Abdur-Rahman calls "the orgiastic fury and fervor of gang rape," becoming a centerpiece for the carnival attended by entranced audience members of all genders and ages.[106] Like the sugar-cured ham in front of Uncle Julius, the Black flesh, once carved open, "expos[es] a rich pink expanse" that never fails to arouse "the appetite of any hungry Christian."[107]

Dave hangs himself in the smokehouse, according to Uncle Julius, "ter kyo"—to cure—himself into a ham. If this story indeed is an allegory of the flesh, Dave's suicide is a "cure" for his desire for liberal subjectivity, restoring his status as consumable flesh and then preserving it as such. This curing of Black flesh has a particular resonance with the frame narrative's post-Reconstruction present, when former slaves and their descendants were entrapped into what Saidiya Hartman terms "burdened individuality."[108] Under the aegis of nominal equality and possessive individualism, Hartman argues, the emancipated were held responsible for their own struggles and injury. The volitional logic of contract concealed the severe material conditions of the newly freed Black population: through a variety of mechanisms such as debt-bondage, vagrancy laws, and the convict-release system, they were continually coerced into exploitive labor conditions sometimes not far from those under slavery. Such compulsory contracts were made possible through the inculcation of autonomy, self-possession, and self-government often initiated by the Freedmen's Bureau. By what Hartman calls "the displacement of the whip by the conscience," the emancipated internalized the disciplinary discourse that fashioned them into servile laborers.[109] That is, the liberal state communicated to the formerly enslaved people that their freedom had come at the price of the blood and treasure of the Civil War; in being free, they were indebted to the state and therefore must repay it by consenting to work. Such a logic of liberty suggests that the constrained agency and burdened volition on offer—which, in their unrestrained forms, are the hallmarks of the liberal subject—were used to exploit the newly freed.

Julius's narrative of Dave's suicide—an act "curing" the Black flesh—does not submit to this formula of the self-owning, self-governing subject. That is, where this logic reorganizes the flesh into the individual body to be disciplined and incorporated into the manageable social body, Dave's suicide aims to "cure" the Black subject of burdened individuality and preserve its fleshiness. Dave's flesh sways in the smokehouse between the zero degree of agency and something else.[110] It persists, it subsists, as Julius's tale cures Dave's flesh and preserves it as an exhibit of the gratuitous violence against Blackness. With a logic of preservation different from that of biopolitical self-preservation, Dave's Black flesh is embalmed into pink, cured meat, reminding the "Human" of what they are feasting on, nourished by, and made of. This attempt proves at least partly successful when Annie cannot eat the rest of the ham after hearing Julius's story; she cannot eat it because, as Kyla Wazana Tompkins says, eating threatens the liberal fantasy of autonomous selfhood by "blurring the line between subject and object as food turned into tissues, muscle, and nerve and then provid[ing] the energy that drives them all."[111] Eating—consuming—means letting your body be possessed against the logic of self-possession. Consuming Black death to the fullest, then, Edna Pontellier drowns herself, dreaming of escape from "soul's slavery," with the anthem celebrating the birth of a racist state, a murderous state, and a suicidal state still reverberating in the air a century after its utterance and beyond: "Hurrah for our country! Hurrah! / To freedom she leaped, through drowning and death."

3

The Spectral Lineage

Jack London, Teutonism, and Interspecies Kinship

Wolf vs. Bear

A decade after the New Woman's self-drowning in the Gulf of Mexico, another literary figure takes a suicidal leap into the ocean: Martin Eden, the eponymous hero of Jack London's 1909 semi-autographical novel. Rising from obscurity to literary fame with Franklinesque self-discipline and "the primordial vigor of life," Martin Eden, modeled largely after London himself, is the antipode not only of the bourgeois wife in *The Awakening* but also of "poodle" Henry James: he is an untamed "bulldog," "tugging hard, ... showing his teeth, and threatening to break loose."[1] And yet, untouched by the tropic sun, the underside of this ex-seafarer's bronzed arms is "very white," as fair and smooth as any "pale spirits of women" (68). As Martin says to himself while looking at the mirror, "he was a white man, after all" (68). To enter the ranks of upper-class whiteness embodied by Ruth Morse—Martin's love interest, "a pale, ethereal creature, with wide, spiritual blue eyes and a wealth of golden hair"—he remolds himself, ultimately gaining access to the bourgeois world through literary success (35). Combining blazing virility with an indomitable will to discipline himself, he is the very model of white manhood that Theodore Roosevelt would have extolled as the savior of enervated whiteness. In short, Martin Eden is "a man in a thousand—in ten thousand" (474).

But the Great White Hope is destined to be lost, and the celebrated writer chooses death.[2] Disillusioned by "the white glare of life," the glory of the bourgeois life that his fame promised him, Martin Eden dives into the Pacific from a Tahiti-bound steamer (479). His suicidal dive is the endmost assertion of his individual will, which so far has marked him as a paragon of new white manhood. As he tries to drown himself, the "will to live"—a distinct echo of the Schopenhauerian *will to life* (*Wille zum Leben*), an impersonal force that drives beings toward both species and individual preservation—keeps

Martin's arms and legs beating against his own will, bringing his body up to the surface: "The will to live, was his thought, and the thought was accompanied by a sneer. Well, he had will—ay, will strong enough that with one last exertion it could destroy itself and cease to be" (481).[3] The will to live foils Martin's will to die again and again, keeping this fine specimen of whiteness alive for the preservation of the race, until he finally "fools . . . the will to live": Martin descends deeper and deeper into the water "until his will snapped and the air drove from his lungs in a great explosive rush," so that no spasmodic movements of his limbs can drive him up to the surface (482). Thus, the would-be redeemer of the dying race asserts his private right to die, subduing the will to live that compels him and the species to live on.

It is unknowable whether the willfulness of this "bulldog" irked Roosevelt as did the effeminate "poodle" thirty years earlier. What is certain, though, is that the president's rancor was directed against London himself at the time of the novel's publication, with the still-open sore that London had inflicted on him in the previous year amidst the so-called "nature faker controversy." The contention between Roosevelt and London dated back to 1903, when a leading figure of the wilderness protection movement, John Burroughs, published an article titled "Real and Sham Natural History" in the *Atlantic Monthly*. Railing against the trend of animal stories, Burroughs argued that popular animal writers put "too much sentiment, too much literature" into their descriptions of nature; animals in their writings are "simply human beings disguised as animals; they think, feel, plan, suffer, as we do; in fact, exhibit almost the entire human psychology."[4] A long-time reader of Burroughs's work, Roosevelt wrote to him immediately after reading the *Atlantic* article, quickly striking up a friendship with this renowned nature writer. As the responses to Burroughs's criticism built into a nationwide controversy in the ensuing four years, to the surprise of many, the incumbent president himself joined this literary argument. Roosevelt published an article titled "Nature-Fakers" in *Everybody's Magazine* in 1907, with the intention to have the final word in the controversy. Endorsing Burroughs's view, Roosevelt condemned the "grave wrong" committed by animal writers, in whose works "the animals are alternately portrayed as actuated by motives of exalted humanitarianism, and as possessed of demoniac prowess and insight into motive."[5]

But Roosevelt was soon to find himself sorely bitten back by one of the writers he attacked in the article. Jack London—or "Wolf," to use his self-moniker—was evidently one of Roosevelt's "nature-fakers" without being

100 THE SUICIDAL STATE

explicitly named as such.[6] London was indebted to two canine heroes for his literary success: one named Buck, a Scotch shepherd–St. Bernard mix who becomes the leader of a wolf pack in *The Call of the Wild* (1903), the other a wolf-dog hybrid, the eponymous hero of *White Fang* (1906). Alluding to London's works, Roosevelt mockingly refers to "wolves . . . as gifted with all the philosophy, the self-restraint, and the keen intelligence of, say, Marcus Aurelius," criticizing scenes in *White Fang* as "a doubtful contest between the wolf and a lynx or a bulldog, in which the latter survives twenty slashing bites."[7]

In his 1908 essay "The Other Animals," London launched an all-out attack against Roosevelt and Burroughs, rebuffing their central belief that "Man is a voluntary agent. Animals are automatons."[8] For London, their view that nonhuman animals lack reason and agency—"wrapped up in its heredity" and operating solely on "foreordained rules"—is simply "homocentric."[9] Unfolding his interactions with two dogs in his boyhood, Rollo and Glen, London argues that nonhuman animals have the capacity for reason and will like humans. There are "no impassable gulfs" between humans and animals as Roosevelt and Burroughs presuppose; repeatedly using the phrase "kinship with the other animals," London foregrounds the continuity between nonhuman animals and "the animal man."[10] London admonishes Burroughs that to "deny your relatives, the other animals," is merely a sign of his "egotism" and "stiff-necked pride."[11] As for the president, London simply brushes him off as "an amateur": "No, President Roosevelt does not understand evolution, and he does not seem to have made much of an attempt to understand evolution."[12]

While Roosevelt made no public response to "The Other Animals," he could not let London's accusation stand unchallenged. Immediately after the publication of the essay, he wrote to the editor of *Collier's*, impugning the magazine for publishing London's essay. Roosevelt vindicated himself from London's charge, arguing that he, unlike Burroughs, believed that "the higher mammals and birds have reasoning powers, which differ in degree rather than in kind from the lower reasoning powers of, for instance, the lower savages."[13] After remonstrating against London's argument at length, Roosevelt concludes: "Now mind you, I have not the slightest intention of entering into any controversy on this subject with London. I would as soon think of discussing seriously with him any social or political reform."[14]

This odd concluding remark—about London's stance on "social or political reform"—seems to suggest the political, or rather biopolitical nature

THE SPECTRAL LINEAGE   101

of the president's argument.[15] By the time Roosevelt interposed himself into the debate, numerous commentators had expressed displeasure in the president's participation in a debate that appeared rather frivolous, considering his office. Despite these period objections, though, Roosevelt's intervention in the nature-faker controversy was precisely about his political leadership. Since his early political career, Roosevelt had long promoted his cowboy persona through such works as *Hunting Trips of a Ranchman* (1885), *Ranch Life and the Hunting-Trail* (1888), and *The Wilderness Hunter* (1892), upholding big-game hunting's regenerative effect on weakened old-stock Americans. Amidst the rapidly growing wildlife protection movement at the dawn of the new century, however, Roosevelt's "reputation as a big game hunter did not always endear him" to the public.[16] He saw the necessity of refurbishing his public image: namely, transforming himself from the "Great White Hunter" to a "mythical humanitarian."[17] Boone and Crockett, a hunting club Roosevelt founded in 1887, for instance, became one of the main vehicles for the conservationist movement during Roosevelt's presidency, aiding the passage of laws protecting natural resources and successively establishing National Parks.[18]

One episode that particularly marked the symbolic transformation of Roosevelt's political persona occurred in November 1902. During Roosevelt's hunting trip to the South, a renowned Black hunter, Holt Collier, tethered an adult female bear to a tree and arranged the terminal shot for the president. Roosevelt dismissed Collier's request, commanding him to "put it out of misery" by knife.[19] As Donna Varga argues, though, Roosevelt's refusal to shoot the bear was "not motivated by compassion for a tormented wild animal. . . . The problem facing Roosevelt on the Mississippi hunt was that the bear had been clubbed unconscious by Collier."[20] Shooting a paralyzed bear assisted by a celebrated Black hunter would violate the white man's revivification ritual; thus, Roosevelt ordered the knifing of the bear, whose meat was later consumed in three successive meals. In a series of ironic twists, however, the president's order to kill the female bear was made into a fable about his redemption of a captured male cub, culminating in the 1903 birth of that most famous of stuffed animals: the "Teddy" bear. Garbed often in "a cowboy hat, hunting rifle and axe" or "Rooseveltian riding boot[s] and [a] belt with 'U.S.' engraved on its buckle," the stuffed bear strangely fused the identities of the hunter and the hunted, creating an avatar of the president at once capably virile yet irresistibly adorable.[21] The furry form of the teddy bear softly blanketed the slaughter of the actual bear,

102   THE SUICIDAL STATE

transforming Roosevelt into a fierce and benevolent guardian of national life and the wild.

Put differently, what the "Wolf" was up against in the nature-faker controversy was "Teddy Bear Patriarchy"—Donna Haraway's apt phrase for the power administering not only human lives but also natural life.[22] Through her kaleidoscopic account of the development of the American Museum of Natural History in the Progressive Era, in which Roosevelt played a vital role, Haraway throws into relief the way in which the founders of the museum constructed a unified narrative of evolution. The evolutionary narrative not only required interspecies hierarchies, in which "the Age of Man" marked the apex of evolution; it was inextricably interwoven with the establishment of "a 20th-century primate order, with its specific and polymorphous hierarchies of race, sex, and class."[23] In an echo of Roosevelt's aforementioned belief that the reasoning capacities of "the higher mammals and birds" were comparable to those of "the lower savages," the "primitives"—Black and Native Americans in the racist imaginary of the era—were deployed as "the proper interface of the Age of Man and the Age of Mammals" in the museum's construction of a naturalized teleology of evolution.[24] In short, Roosevelt's participation in the nature-faker controversy was intimately related to Progressive racial politics: the head of the United States must also be positioned as the unchallenged master of the Great Chain of Being that controlled inter- and intraspecies hierarchies. The two ladders were tethered to each other, and to disturb one by "humanizing" nonhuman species would mean disturbing the whole order.

In this chapter, I will read Jack London's insistence on "kinship with other animals" and his fictional counterpart's suicide in *Martin Eden* as signs of the self-proclaimed Wolf's wayward revolt against the life-administering power of Teddy Bear Patriarchy. This defiance, though, is of a nature that is paradoxical and implosive, for London himself was notoriously invested in white supremacist ideologies, haunted by the white extinction narrative of race suicide. In the first section, I will examine London's early works set in the Yukon and Alaska, arguing that London's racial ideology was formed under the rubric of Teutonism rather than Anglo-Saxonism, figuring new virile whiteness through the model of a primeval tribe. By a spectral alliance with the Viking-age northern Europeans, London atavistically bypasses his hereditary ties to neurasthenic old-stock Americans. Such sidestepping of biological reproduction was, I will argue in the second section, enabled through his contact with Alaska Natives and the appropriation of their practice of totemic kinship. I argue that totemic kinship formation provided London with a model of sociality outside the constraints of the conjugal family, literalizing London's insistence on "kinship with other animals." In this context, the interspecies kinship represented in his animal stories emerged for London as an idyllic site of intimacy freed from the biopolitical mandate of racial reproduction. Crucially, however, such romantic appropriation of totemic kinship paralleled the Progressive Indian policies and their assimilationist violence, the murderousness of which haunts *The Call of the Wild* and *Martin Eden*.

London's Northland Teutonism

Born in San Francisco in 1876 and raised in a Bay Area working-class household, Jack London—né John Griffith Chaney—fully imbibed the racial tension of the West Coast at the end of the nineteenth century.[25] London's stepfather, John London, was one of many Civil War veterans who moved to the West Coast to follow the lure of fertile land, eventually finding themselves betrayed by the dream. London grew up in an environment where "white working men, particularly after the Panic of 1893, attacked and lynched Asian immigrants, who they perceived as taking their jobs."[26] Once valued as a source of cheap labor for the mining and construction of the transcontinental railroad, Chinese immigrants now became wretched refuse of the days of gold, and—as I will discuss further in the Coda—their continued entrance into the United States was barred by the Chinese Exclusion Act of 1882. Asian immigrants, though, were but one group that was subjected to racial tension. As London recalls in his autobiography, *John Barleycorn* (1913), when the family was farming in San Mateo, the area was crowded by the new wave of immigrants of southern and eastern European origin: "In all our section there was only one other old American family."[27] Proud of her "Welsh ancestry and pioneer heritage," his mother, Flora Wellman London, was particularly vocal about her antipathy toward their neighbors.[28] She and her family were "old American stock," superior to their newly immigrated neighbors; for her, "brunettes and all the tribe of dark-eyed humans were deceitful," and "the Latin races were profoundly sensitive, profoundly treacherous, and profoundly murderous."[29]

London apparently inherited his mother's race pride and was liable to endorse nativist white superiority, even though his racial ideologies were complex and often changed their shape over the course of his eventful life.[30] But

104   THE SUICIDAL STATE

especially in his early career, his nativist master trope was not his mother's pet phrase, "old American stock"; nor was it straightforwardly "Anglo-Saxon," as many London scholars have claimed.[31] London's initial sense of white superiority is better understood in the framework of Teutonism. One of the earlier manifestations of London's Teutonism is found in a letter to literary critic Cloudesley Johns written on June 12, 1899. Whereas Johns boasts that his "pure Anglo-Saxon" lineage can be "traced back to the Welsh Kings," London tells Johns that "the Welsh are farther away from the Anglo-Saxon, than are the French, Germans, Dutch, Belgians, Scandanavians [sic], Switz."[32] However, London continues that the Welsh and the Anglo-Saxon, as well as other northern Europeans, belong to "the same family": they are "the Teutonic," "the dominant race of the world."[33] In a language redolent with the social Darwinism he had espoused since his late teens, London voices his belief in the survival-of-the-fittest triumph of the Teutonic: "The negro races, the mongrel races, the slavish races, the unprogressive races, are of bad blood—that is, of blood which is not qualified to permit them to successfully survive the selection by which the fittest survive, and which the next centuries, in my opinion, will see terribly intensified."[34]

Even though the term "Teutonic" in London's oeuvre has often been conflated with "Anglo-Saxon," Teutonism had a set of values and discursive functions that were different from Anglo-Saxonism. The two terms certainly had conceptual overlaps, constituting sibling discourses with each other, for Anglo-Saxonism posited that Anglo-Saxon was the best stock in the Teutons, an ancient Germanic tribe who had originated in modern Scandinavia and northern Germany and fought against the Roman Empire. However, whereas Anglo-Saxonism idealized Saxon control before the Norman Conquest and contrasted freedom-loving Anglo-Saxons with their feudalistic Norman oppressors, Teutonism emphasized the original unity between Anglo-Saxons and Normans by looking to a moment further in the past. Anglo-Saxons and Normans, Teutonists argued, originally belonged to the same family of the Teutons, and the Norman Conquest and the Viking invasions only enabled the reunification of the once-separated branches of these Teutonic limbs. One Teutonist explained: "Anglo-Saxon, (a female race) required impregnation by the great male race,—the Norse introduction of Northman."[35] Teutonism was brought to England with the influence of German Romanticism, popularized in mid-nineteenth-century England by such writers as Thomas Carlyle, Thomas Arnold, Samuel Laing, and E. A. Freeman. However, as the historian Reginald Horsman notes, the unification

THE SPECTRAL LINEAGE   105

of "Germans, Saxons, Danes, and Normans" that the Teutonists envisioned "never achieved total acceptance in England," chiefly because of their strong belief in Anglo-Saxon superiority among the other Teutonic subgroups.[36]

Modern-day Teutonism found a more fertile ground across the Atlantic, where white populations of northern Europeans with *non*-Anglo-Saxon origins—Dutch, Irish, and Welsh, among others—were vying to find their places at the center of the white national body. London's use of "Teutonic" in this 1899 letter epitomizes a significant resurgence of this racial terminology in the United States at the turn of the twentieth century against the backdrop of the influx of so-called new immigrants from eastern and southern Europe. In 1899, leading Progressive economist William Z. Ripley popularized the term "Teutonic" in *The Races of Europe* as the name of one of the three racial groups in Europe. Deploying anthropometric data and photographs, Ripley classified the European populations into three distinct "races": tall, blond, blue-eyed "Teutons" with large skulls and fair skin, originating in northern Europe; large-skulled but short in stature, southern European "Mediterraneans" with dark hair and eyes; and the round-headed "Alpines" of central Europe with brown hair, hazel-colored eyes, and intermediate skin color. Ripley defines race as an invariable entity responsible for "peculiarities, mental or bodily, which are transmitted with constancy along the lines of direct physical descent from father to son" in a biologizing logic that mirrored the contemporaneous ruling in *Plessy*.[37] The pure whiteness of the Teutons' skin, nurtured in the northern climate, along with their height and blond hair, "constitute insignia of noble descent," marking the long history of "the splendid military and political expansion of the Teutons."[38]

Ripley's tripartite typology and its (more-or-less) implicit scientific racism found its full materialization in Madison Grant's *The Passing of the Great Race* (1916).[39] As Jonathan Spiro argues, Grant adopted Ripley's racial typology and fused it with Houston Steward Chamberlain's ideologically charged Teutonism in *The Foundation of the Nineteenth Century* (originally published in German in 1899 and translated into English in 1911).[40] Even though Chamberlain emphasized the common Aryan racial origin of all Europeans, he argued that the Teutonic branch of the Aryan race represented the finest ethos of the race. "'Teutonic' blood," which flowed in the population of every northern European nation in varying proportions, ultimately bound the apparently different groups of northern Europeans together into an "organic unity."[41] As Spiro points out, though Chamberlain deploys an anthropometric methodology similar to Ripley's, the emphasis

106 THE SUICIDAL STATE

of *The Foundation* rests more on the Teuton's "idealistic spirit, a virile sense of loyalty, and an enduring love of freedom."[42] In Chamberlain's words, the Teuton is "the poet warrior, the thinker, the freeman," forged as the ultimate antithesis of the Jew in the increasingly intensifying antisemitism in Europe—a point to which we will return in the next chapter.[43]

Grant synthesized Ripley's and Chamberlain's languages of Teutonism to proclaim the racial superiority of native-born white Americans over the newly immigrated in general, rather than over just Jewish immigrants. Following Ripley's tripartite race theory, Grant classifies the European population into "Mediterraneans," "Alpines," and, to avoid the Germanic overtone attached to "Teutonic," renamed the last one as "Nordics." Yet Grant's Nordics clearly embody Chamberlain's Teutonism, placed at the pinnacle of the European racial hierarchy and invested with overwhelmingly masculine traits: "They brought with them from the north the hardihood and vigor acquired under the rigorous selection of a long winter season, and vanquished in battle the inhabitants of older and feebler civilizations."[44] For Grant, with their "absolutely fair skin" symbolizing survival in the harsh northern climate, the Nordic stands for "the *Homo albus*, the white man par excellence."[45] Once "the nursery and broodland of the master race," Grant argues, America is now facing "serious injury" to its Nordic heritage through "reckless breeding" and the "multiplication of inferior types," the newly immigrated Alpine and the Mediterranean.[46]

After its appearance in his 1899 letter, London's use of the term "Teutonic" proliferated in his oeuvre, constantly emphasizing the Teuton's northern origin. Though scarcely commented upon, for instance, the Nordic origin of "Wolf" Larsen in *The Sea-Wolf* (1904), London's twentieth-century recast of *Moby-Dick*, should be understood in the context of US Teutonism/Nordicism at the dawn of the twentieth century rather than Anglo-Saxonism. Instead of a big white whale, the Ahabesque captain of the *Ghost* embodies absolute whiteness himself. Wolf Larsen's whiteness is otherworldly, of the nature possessed only by a "ghost." His "satiny skin," the whiteness of which captivates the narrator, Humphrey Van Weyden, is "thanks to his Scandinavian stock," reflecting the significance of the Teutons' regional origin as emphasized by Ripley, Chamberlain, and Grant.[47] With his pure Danish heritage, Wolf Larsen incarnates the "old Scandinavian myths," personifying Grant's white man par excellence.[48]

Larsen saves the overcivilized literary critic "'Sissy' Van Weyden" not only from a shipwreck but also from neurasthenic degeneration.[49] Equipped with perfectly toned muscles that are "made to grip, tear, and destroy living things," the Teuton's body manifests a supreme virility that could quash the fear of race suicide.[50] The narrative teleology of *The Sea-Wolf*, as Scott Derrick argues, "aim[s] at the construction of heterosexual masculinity," imbuing lost potency to the weakling stock through contact with the legendary Teuton.[51] Standing as "a magnificent atavism," Wolf Larsen awakens Van Weyden to the "primitive deeps of [his] nature" and his "remote and forgotten ancestry" of "hunting days and forest nights": through Larsen's discipline, the effete literary critic becomes a "protector of the weak, the fighting male," and even ultimately wins possession of a woman over Wolf Larsen himself.[52]

London's representation of Teutonic ancestry as effected by "atavism" summons a modality of racial construction different from the one defined by heredity transmission.[53] As Dana Seitler argues, atavism designates a fin-de-siècle "theory of biological reversion emerging out of modern science."[54] Derived from the Latin term "*atavus*, 'great-grandfather's grandfather,'" atavism describes a wraithlike reemergence of the prehistoric past that "skips generations."[55] In other words, while Ripley's original theorization of the Teutonic in *The Races of Europe* relies on a hereditary definition of race—physical and psychological traits linearly "transmitted with constancy along the lines of direct physical descent from father to son"—London's atavistic construction of the Teutonic heritage operates not by a process of continuity, but by a phantasmal reversal of temporality.[56] While turn-of-the-century discourse about atavism, as Seitler demonstrates, signals a fear of "infinite regress" into the primitive past with which Progressive modernity sought to break, such reversion also provided a vital refuge, especially for those who were threatened by the fear of race suicide.[57] The old-stock Americans' neurasthenic loss of sexual potency, figured most prominently by the declining birthrate of New England Anglo-Saxons as we have seen in Chapter 1, meant that they could no longer sustain their line of heredity. By claiming an atavistic, spectral affiliation with the mythic tribe, native-born white Americans sidestepped and negated their closest filiation to the weakling stock. The ghostly whiteness represented by the Teutonic tribe thus furnished a phantasmal survival narrative for the native-born white population amidst the rapid population growth of new immigrants.

Fittingly, London's Teutonism as an atavistic return seems to have been derived, at least partially, from his personal disavowal of immediate filiation. In May 1897, two years prior to his discovery of the enabling "master race" trope, twenty-one-year-old London was informed of his illegitimacy

108   THE SUICIDAL STATE

by relatives of his stepfather John London, whom London had believed to be his biological father. Excavating newspaper articles archived in the Oakland Public Library, London discovered the details of the dispute over his paternity between his mother and his putative biological father, William Chaney, a New England-born itinerant astrologer and spiritualist. The dispute reportedly culminated in Flora's two suicide attempts following Chaney's demand for an abortion, which was sensationally covered in the *San Francisco Chronicle*.[58] Tracking down Chaney's current residence in Chicago, London wrote to him and shortly heard back. Chaney opens his bitter response with a straightforward disavowal of paternity: "I was never married to Flora Wellman, of Springfield, Ohio, but she lived with me from June 11th 1874 till June 3rd 1875. I was impotent at that time, the result of hardship, privation & too much brain-work."[59] It is difficult to fathom which troubled London more: Chaney's blunt denial of paternity, or his unabashed disclosure of neurasthenic sexual impotency. The proud yet eccentric offspring of old New England families, Chaney likely personified for young London the degeneracy of the old stock and its increasing eclipse by fertile immigrants.

The young writer, as well as other native-born white Americans, needed a new trope for the master race that would replace the neurasthenic Anglo-Saxons; an atavistic return to the Teutonic, "white-skinned, fair-haired savages" who had survived the harshest environment in Europe, answered the call from the mythical, far northern lands. A decade earlier, the path to virilization would have been readily found in the American West. As Theodore Roosevelt's own revitalization by the "West cure" proved, the frontier spirit was imagined as a panacea for the weakening stock. Yet as Frederick Jackson Turner famously declared in "The Significance of the Frontier in American History" (1893), such "perennial rebirth," imagined to be enabled by the "continuous touch with the simplicity of primitive society," was put to a halt by the closure of the frontier in the last decade of the nineteenth century.[60] In the impasse of halted westward continental expansion, the year 1898 witnessed the nation thrusting itself further west by imperial expansion overseas. With the outbreak of the Spanish–American War in April 1898, the United States annexed Hawaii as a naval foothold, and in December of the same year, Spain ceded the Philippines, Guam, Puerto Rico, and Cuba—a US military victory in which Roosevelt's Rough Riders played a pivotal role. Yet immediately before the rise of US overseas expansionism, the nation experienced a last-gasp hope for regeneration within the continent, which would

THE SPECTRAL LINEAGE   109

rehash the legend of the days of gold—not in the West, but in the Northland. On July 15, 1897, San Francisco heard the news of the discovery of gold along the Yukon River valley, in the Canadian federal territory adjacent to Alaska. Ten days after the news reached San Francisco, Jack London boarded the *Umatilla*, leaving San Francisco for Alaska. His departure to the Northland occurred only a month after he had heard back from Chaney.

The hype of the frontier regained was short-lived; the Arctic climate proved too harsh for many prospectors even to reach the gold field, and for those who found their way, including London himself, the land yielded a modicum of the forty-niners' riches. As fascination with the Klondike quickly ebbed in the national consciousness, London contracted scurvy and reluctantly returned to Oakland. However, as the story goes, it was the barren soil of the Klondike that engendered the writer Jack London as the Progressive Era's iconic literary self-made man. Achieving his first breakthrough with the publication of a series of sketches and short stories set in the Yukon, London proved himself a prolific writer from then on, setting a strict agenda for his daily writing practice to keep producing, much like his fictional counterpart Martin Eden.[61]

Through his self-discipline, London mythically sired himself as a literary self-made man, one who emerged as a representative white man despite— or precisely through—the absence of a stable genealogy. One reviewer commented on the success of his collection of Klondike stories: "We cannot pay Mr. London a higher compliment than by calling him 'The Man From Nowhere,' for that was the original sobriquet of Kipling."[62] The Yukon and Alaska were the "Nowhere" of America's settler-colonialist cartography, or what London himself symbolically called "the Barrens, the bad lands of the Arctic, the deserts of the Circle, the bleak and bitter home of the musk-ox and the lean plains of wolf."[63] Much as Rudyard Kipling came from British India and rose to fame by symbolically bearing "The White Man's Burden" (1899), London became the representative white settler by claiming a spectral Teutonic lineage in the Yukon's snowbound landscape.

Many of London's early works superimpose the image of Viking-age Scandinavia onto the Yukon as the symbolic homeland of the Teutons, who would redeem the declining fate of the weakling old American stock. One such instance occurs in his first published novel, *A Daughter of the Snows* (1902). Set in the Yukon at the time of the Klondike gold rush, *A Daughter of the Snows* revolves around a young Alaskan-born woman, Frona Welse, whose name and proud Welsh heritage are reminiscent of the novelist's

110 THE SUICIDAL STATE

mother, Flora Wellman London. The novel traces a triangular relation centering Frona in the framework of Darwinian sexual selection, in which she seeks the ideal mate to pass on the legacy of "the Teuton spreading over the earth as no other race has ever spread."[64] The bleak climate of the Northland becomes an apt setting for Frona's sexual selection. As she "speak[s] for the race, . . . The north wants strong men" (38). Like the Scandinavian landscape Grant envisioned as the site of the "rigorous selection" that enabled the Nordic's "hardihood and vigor,"[65] the Arctic climate will weed out "the weak and effeminate males" for Frona, and the "history of the race, and of all races," will "seal[] her choice with approval" (87).

One of Frona's suitors, Vance Corliss—a New England-born, Yale-graduate prospector with a Freiberg mining engineering degree—criticizes Frona's blatant Teutonism as "race egotism and insular prejudice" at first (89). Yet, like Van Weyden in *The Sea-Wolf,* Corliss soon finds himself undergoing an atavistic reversion to the Teutonic heritage of "the sea-king who never slept under the smoky rafters of a roof" (146). As he acclimates to the Yukon, he finds "caverns of his being" gradually filled with the vision of archaic "bellowing of storm-winds and crash of smoking North Sea waves . . . and the sharp-beaked fighting galleys, and the sea-flung Northmen, great-muscled, deep-chested" (148). His fervid imagination amalgamates the landscape of the Yukon with Norse mythology, transforming the trails to the gold field into "the path of Hel," and Frona into "a furred Valkyrie" (147).

In the face of the Alaskan Valkyrie choosing who should be slain in the battlefield of sexual selection, Corliss's recollection of his New England mother begins to personify the decay of the white race: "his mother's women came back to him, one by one, and passed in long review—pale, glimmering ghosts, he thought, caricatures of the stock which had replenished the earth" (259). Instead of neurasthenic Anglo-Saxon women, the Alaskan-born heroine becomes "the genius of the race," reifying the Teutonic "tradition of the blood," which runs through the Scandinavian miners in the Yukon as well (111, 147). Familiar with the northern climate, Scandinavian miners thrive in the Arctic environment: for them, the toil of carrying a heavy sack on the icy trail is but "child's play," and "the joy of life was in them" (32). Scarcely understanding English, these "blond-haired giants" have little to share with Corliss and the other American miners; nonetheless, Corliss realizes that their shared endurance of the northern climate makes him feel "strangely at one with the white-skinned, yellow-haired giants of the younger world," direct descendants of the Teutons of the Viking Age (147). His spectral alliance of "race heredity" to the Teuton is, Corliss deliriously says, what "[t]he north has taught me, is teaching me" (146).

Kinship in Alaska

It is no coincidence that Madison Grant himself—of old, patrician stock from New England, who was obsessed with the potential extinction of the Nordics while producing no offspring of his own in his lifetime—was fascinated by Alaska, frequenting its wilderness for big-game hunting from the late 1890s to the early 1900s. Here lies an apparent paradox, as Jonathan Spiro observes: Grant was a blatant racist, whose work was admired as a "Bible" by one of the Third Reich's leading medical authorities, but at the same time he was the founder of the US conservation movement, who "preserved the California redwoods, saved the American bison from extinction, founded the Bronx Zoo, fought for strict gun-control laws, built the Bronx River Parkway, helped to create Glacier and Denali National Parks, and worked tirelessly to protect the whales in the ocean, the bald eagles in the sky, and the pronghorn antelopes on the prairie."[66] As Spiro explains, however, "conservation and eugenics were two sides of the same coin" for Grant, as both were an attempt to save the "endangered fauna, flora, and natural resources" that he deemed essentially American, a bio/necropolitical management of the desirability of populational life.[67] Enamored by the unsullied wilderness of Alaska and its potential promise to revivify the white race, Grant, as a prominent member of Roosevelt's Boone and Crockett Club, drafted the Alaska Game Bill in 1902 to prohibit commercial hunting. The region was, he argued, the only remaining place in the United States that "maintain[ed] primitive conditions approximating those of the whole country when first settled."[68] In lieu of New England and the Great West, the Northland thus became the regenerative topos of whiteness, splicing old-stock Americans into the mythic Teutons/Nordics. As such, the Northland emerged as a new "meeting point between savagery and civilization," which Frederick Turner believed to have defined the US national ethos until the closure of the frontier.[69] Just as the wilderness at the frontier line had divested the settler of his "European . . . dress, industries, tools, modes of travel, and thought" to make "a new product that is American," the Northland wilderness would reproduce the vigorous master race, cleansed of its overcivilized and thus degenerating Anglo-Saxon heritage.[70]

112   THE SUICIDAL STATE

The metamorphosis of old-stock Americans into Northland Teutons was, much like the frontier itself, imagined to be catalyzed by contact with Indigenous peoples. In Turner's settler-colonialist imagination, Native Americans acted as vital "consolidating agent[s]" for the European settler to become an American; stripped of the "garments of civilization," the settler would learn how to "shout[] the war cry and take[] the scalp in orthodox Indian fashion," "fit[ting] himself into the Indian clearings and follow[ing] the Indian trails."[71] The same is true for the Northland miners in London's Klondike cosmology. London's Northland Teutons are a strange hybrid of Alaska Natives and old-stock Americans. Frona Welse, "genius of the race" in *A Daughter of Snows*, is one such example. Born a daughter of a "sturdy Welsh stock" father and a "fair and flaxen-haired, typically Saxon" mother, Frona Welse also possesses a different lineage, one signified by her other name, "Tenas Hee-Hee" (56, 82, 27). After the death of her mother, she is raised under the care of the fictive Alaska Natives, the Dyea people, becoming well-versed in their native tongue. Even after being sent to the mainland for education in her teens, "the years of her culture had not weakened her" (71). Having "nursed at the breast of nature," embodied by her Dyea godmother Neepoosa, Frona boasts herself being capable of "mother[ing] the natural and strong," of becoming a Teutonic race mother in place of the "hot-house breeds" of neurasthenic New England women (24, 111).

London's atavistic construction of modern-day Teutons is enabled by what Jonathan Auerbach calls a "complex fictional system of totemic kinship," which London appropriated from Indigenous peoples in Alaska.[72] The titular story of *The Son of the Wolf* (1900), London's first published collection of short stories, depicts the conflict between white settler "Scruff" Mackenzie and Alaska Natives over a daughter of Thling-Tinneh, the chief of the Raven tribe. Rejecting Mackenzie's offer to marry his daughter Zarinska, Thling-Tinneh designates the white settlers as a totemic clan irreconcilable with his own: "O White Man, whom we have named Moose-Killer, also known as the Wolf, and the Son of the Wolf!"[73] Mackenzie embraces this designation, and the subsequent battle between the Alaska Native tribe and the white settlers is recast as one between Raven and Wolf, in which "men fought, each to his totem."[74]

As Auerbach forcibly argues, London's deep investment in the totemic designation "the Son of the Wolf" is evident in his titling of the book, which functions to "unify and establish kinship" among the otherwise only tangentially related tales of white men's survival in the Northland.[75] With the

THE SPECTRAL LINEAGE   113

trope of the "Wolf," the book becomes a short-story cycle hinging loosely on the figure of a fabled white settler "Malemute Kid," who Thling-Tinneh calls "the first of all the Wolves."[76] Sometimes appearing as an actual character and sometimes only reverently referred to in rumors, Malemute Kid furnishes an archetypal representation of Northland white men as a totemic clan. Thus, in London's fusion of Norse mythology and settler-colonialist fantasy, the Teutonic "all-conquering race" gains its totem, the "Wolf," renamed as the Son of the Wolf—a spectral genealogy that "Wolf" Larsen shares.[77]

Crucially, London's appropriation of totemic kinship allowed him to conceptualize racial mattering outside the bounds of hereditary succession. As Auerbach argues, "intimate contact with native women" plays a key role in the solidification of London's white settlers as a totemic group, though it is effected through the homosocial "traffic in women" with Indigenous men rather than actual intermarriage.[78] At the same time, London's totemic reconfiguration of whiteness points to a mode of racial mattering even more divergent from the heteronormative logic of racial reproduction. At stake here is the ideological valence assigned to the concept of "kinship" around the turn of the century, for totemic kinship was increasingly understood as a social organization that did not necessarily require procreative relatedness.

Deployed to classify certain non-Western social formations, the term "kinship" gained increasingly wide circulation in London's time with the rise of anthropology.[79] Indigenous peoples in the Americas, including Alaska Natives, furnished rich examples for period projects theorizing such alternative socialities. As David Schneider documents, the definition of the term "kinship" was murky when it originated in the mid-nineteenth century. On the one hand, it referred to "the biological system of relations," something akin to reproductive connections of consanguinity; on the other hand, it could mean "sociocultural aspects," social organizations other than strictly blood-based family relations.[80] Yet by the end of the nineteenth century, a vague consensus was reached among anthropologists to differentiate the two: as Émile Durkheim put it in his 1898 studies of Omaha and Choctaw social formation, kinship was understood to be "something completely different from the relation of consanguinity."[81] Even when certain forms of kinship functioned similarly to the Euro-American consanguine family—as a primary site of child caring, sense of belonging, or shared economy, and so on—it was understood to have an organizing logic different from procreative relatedness.

114   THE SUICIDAL STATE

Kinship's conceptual difference from consanguinity was crucial for the non-Native writers' efforts to understand totemism. Durkheim notes that in order to be recognized as a member of certain totemic kinship, "it is necessary and sufficient that one have in oneself something of the totemic being."[82] In certain cases, the relatedness to the totemic being could "result from reproduction (generation)," but biological connectedness in itself does not guarantee sharing of the totemic being; it could also "be obtained in many other ways: by tattooing, by all forms of alimentary communion, by blood contact, etc."[83] To belong to a kinship that shared such "totemic being," in other words, was understood to involve alternative theories of reproduction other than biological reproduction. In a surprising formulation of the French anthropologist Arnold Van Gennep in 1906, *procreation is not necessarily and uniquely the consequence of coitus.*[84] Such dissociation between "conception and the sexual act" was often understood, as shown in Sigmund Freud's hypothesis in *Totem and Taboo* (1913), to stem from "the long interval which is interposed between the fertilizing act and the birth of the child or the sensation of the child's first movements."[85] Freud observes, for instance, in the conception theory of an Aboriginal Australian people, the Aruntas, "the animal, plant, stone or other object" which the mother of a child senses "at the moment when she first felt herself pregnant" is believed to have "penetrated into her and was being born through her in human form."[86]

London's rendition of Alaska Natives' kinship structures in his Northland tales is itself, for the most part, anything but innovative, though such expressions as "the daughter's daughter," "mother that bore me," and "the son of my mother" register London's perception of the organizing logics of Indigenous relatedness as distinctly different from those of Western consanguine families.[87] Even so, when London deployed the totemic designation "the Son of the Wolf" as a name for the new Teutonic tribe in the Northland, and later embraced that totem as his own to call himself "Wolf," he might well have been drawn to a version of Native theories of conception, in which what he called "kinship with the other animals" in the nature-faker controversy was literalized. In totemic organizations of kinship that London adopted, a totemic animal—however metaphorical it may seem to non-Native understandings of reproduction—literally is one's progenitor. When an Alaska Native in London's work exclaims, "I am the Bear—the Silver-Tip and the Son of the Silver-Tip!" he does *not* mean that he is the son of a person called the Silver-Tip from whom he inherits his name; rather, he is the offspring and the incarnation of his totemic animal, the Silver-Tip Bear, and

THE SPECTRAL LINEAGE 115

in that he literally *is* the Silver-Tip, albeit in human form.[88] Likewise, Jack London is the Wolf and the Son of the Wolf, not the son of William Chaney, his putative biological father. If London's Teutonism, as I have argued so far, emerged partly from his desire to disown his filiation to the neurasthenic old American stock and his biological father in particular, the Alaska Native's totemic logic of kinship formation facilitated such an act of self-disinheritance.

In fact, London's appropriation of totemic kinship was diametrically opposed to turn-of-the-century conceptualizations of race, which relied heavily on a biological imaginary of hereditary succession figured by, as we have seen in the previous chapter, whiteness as family property. As Mark Rifkin argues, Progressive Era Indian politics bespeaks the ways in which "race and kinship are dialectically entwined" through "processes of heteronormalization" that seek to buttress the privatized procreative family household.[89] Heteronormalization, Rifkin argues, means more than just the institutional standardization of procreative opposite-sex relations and the regulation of erotic tendencies outside the norm. It is "an ensemble of imperatives that includes family formation, homemaking, private property holding, and the allocation of citizenship, a series of potential 'detachable parts' fused to each other through discourses of sexuality."[90] Even when Indigenous subjects participated in procreative heterosexual acts, their formation of sociality based on kinship rather than consanguinity was still perceived as a queer object in need of regulation.

The legible bequeathal of racial heritage as family property was one such component of heteronormativity. Progressive policies against Native Americans performed a regulatory heteronormalization in this sense, showcasing the intensification of intertwinement of racial identity and property holding that we have seen in Chapter 2. As epitomized in the Dawes General Allotment Act in 1887, passed under the presidency of Grover Cleveland and amended repeatedly in 1891, 1898, and 1906, Progressive regulations strove to end the Native practice of collective landholding and impose the notion of private property on Indigenous peoples. Dividing Native territory into plots and allotting them as private properties to Native Americans, the Dawes Act granted American citizenship to those who abided by the arrangement only in exchange for the dissolution of their traditional kinship network, since the allotments were "parceled out to each 'head of a family.'"[91] In the same way as their territory was divided into smaller plots, tribal kinship was atomized into "families" defined by consanguinity. Instead of the traditional name shared by their people, each family

116   THE SUICIDAL STATE

was assigned an individual patronymic surname "to keep identification and property succession clear."[92] In the wake of *Plessy*, where racial heritage became a vital component of family property, Indigenous kinship unbound by the monogamous consanguine family signified a threat to the stable racial genealogy. As exemplified in the series of anti-miscegenation laws against Native Americans reinforced in the last decades of the nineteenth century, Native Americans were increasingly quarantined for racialization in the Progressive discourse of race, which fused patrilineal property succession and racialized bloodlines.[93] Put differently, precisely at the time when Jack London expropriated the Native model of kinship to forge a chimerical model of whiteness that would sidestep the heteronormative imperative, such kinship structures in Indigenous community were severely under attack.

Composed during the period in which London wrote his Northland fiction series, *The Kempton-Wace Letters* (1903) signals London's conflict between these two models of sociality: namely, the familial imperative to propagate the race on the one hand and kinship relations that would enable him to transcend hereditary limitations on the other. *The Kempton-Wace Letters* occupies a singular space in London's oeuvre not only for its epistolary form, but also as his only collaboration with another writer. The co-author, Anna Strunsky, was a Belarusian-born Jewish immigrant and socialist activist whom London met in San Francisco in 1899. London fell in love with Strunsky and intended to propose marriage three months later; equally attracted to London, Strunsky nonetheless evaded the question of marriage, ostensibly due to her devotion to the revolutionary cause. Less than a week after his foiled marriage proposal to Strunsky, London married one of his friends, Bessie Madden, whom he reportedly forewarned that their marriage would be only for " 'breeding' potential."[94]

In the still glowing embers of tangled mutual attraction, London and Strunsky co-authored *The Kempton-Wace Letters* as a collection of letters exchanged between two men: London as Herbert Wace, a Berkeley student of economics; Strunsky as Dane Kempton, a British poet who fosters Wace after his parents die. As if to vindicate his own marriage, London, in the voice of Wace, declares to Kempton his intention to marry Hester Stebbins for "the perpetuation of the species."[95] Succeeding letters become an overwrought argument between Wace, a zealous believer in scientific breeding for the conservation of the race, and Kempton, a defender of romantic love as the kernel of every marriage.

THE SPECTRAL LINEAGE 117

Though seldom receiving serious attention from London critics, Wace's letters, composed by London, seem to exemplify the depth of his entrapment in race ideology, especially given the twisted roman-à-clef nature of the novel.[96] On the one hand, like London's Northland heroes, Wace embraces Teutonic white supremacy through and through. In a stunning moment reminiscent of Foucault's ventriloquization of the social body that we have seen in the Introduction, Wace gives voice to the genius of the Teutonic race, personifying the abstract and populational subject of race in the mold of a sovereign "I": "I conquered peoples, and organised nations and knit empires, and gave periods of peace to vast territories . . . and I multiplied myself" (46). Stebbins proves the ideal "Mother Woman" for the Teutonic race, as she represents an amalgamation of the northern European peoples (210), with "the Norman" inside her controlling her inner conflict between other heritages, "the Saxon" and "the Celt" (9).

While Wace willfully plays the role as an agent of racial propagation, his service to the biopolitical mandate is based on a fatalistic sense of resignation akin to the one articulated in *The Awakening*: "Nature tricks her creatures and the race lives on".[97] Love, which Kempton calls the "prerogative . . . high in the scale of existence," is nothing for Wace but *"a means for the perpetuation and development of the human type"* (27, 67; original emphasis). Whereas Chopin's heroine drowns herself as she refuses to become a vessel of racial property, Wace embraces the role ordained by the race with a vengeance after the same realization: he decides to "master" the "yearnings and desires, promptings of the 'abysmal fecundity'" by replacing love with eugenics. If romantic love is nothing more than "an institution necessary for the perpetuation of the species," he would outwit it to better serve the race by choosing his mate not based on romantic attraction but on the principle of scientific breeding (67). That is Wace's preferred way to "save the races from self-murder," to stop the nightmare of race suicide (157).

In having his fictional persona speak of the instrumentality of romantic love, on which the Progressive ideal of procreative conjugality rests, London delimits consanguine family as a venue for the inheritance of racial property, and nothing more. The conflict between Wace and Kempton in the novel was to be rehashed in person between their creators as they were completing the book. In two letters to Strunsky, on August 25 and 28, 1902, London responds to Strunsky's accusation that despite his continued proclamations of love to her, he has impregnated Bessie for the second time. While vindicating Bessie's pregnancy as a "work back nine months," London also

118   THE SUICIDAL STATE

acknowledges that "long, long after a child is conceived, a man may know his wife," insinuating the possibility that he might have had sex with Bessie while she was pregnant.[98] Yet, for London, fathering a child with Bessie and having an active sexual relationship with her has little to do with his love for Strunsky. He "may bribe [himself] to continue being" "by duty or desire, or both, & by these only," but his relation to Strunsky is "the last clean, pure warming I shall ever receive."[99] Though a pathetic apologia, London's words bespeak his deep entrapment in the biopolitical mandate: the propagation of the race with a native-born white American is a "work" and a "duty" he is trained to "desire," and the continuation of his "being" hinges on his service to the preservation of the race. Adherence to these decrees of race perpetuation sharply contrasts with his affective investment in a new-immigrant "Russian Jewess," as he refers to Strunsky repeatedly in his letter to his friends, with whom he can only author a book together, wherein she is disguised as his foster father.[100]

Unnatural Nuptials in *The Call of the Wild*

For Herbert Wace, the "precise value and use of this erotic phenomenon, this sexual madness, this love" is nothing but the propagation of the race (68). In a work published in the same year as *The Kempton-Wace Letters*, London again talks fervidly about the madness of love—"love that was feverish and burning, that was adoration, that was madness."[101] The "great love" in *The Call of the Wild* (1903) is similar to the one Wace is wary of, which "usurp[s] ... reason," and makes one "los[e] his head" (79). Yet this erotic phenomenon, the love that is akin to madness in *The Call of the Wild*, sabotages the precise value and use that Wace presupposes, having nothing to do with the propagation of the race, or even with the perpetuation of the species. The love in *The Call of the Wild* is destined to be infertile, because it is conceived between a man and a dog. After all, a species line was the name given to the limit of interfertility since the late eighteenth century: "The generally accepted test for distinct species, formulated by the Comte de Buffon in France and John Hunter in Britain, was that the product of sexual intercourse between them was infertile."[102] But in London's imagination, this sterile love has breeding potential for the regeneration of the white race—potential stronger than any that procreative family formations could afford. Through their interspecies kinship, a dog named Buck and a man named John Thornton become the

THE SPECTRAL LINEAGE 119

forebears of the Son of the Wolf. In tracing the dog's atavistic transmogrification into a wolf through his love for a man, *The Call of the Wild* recounts a mythical genesis of the Wolf, London's designated totem for the Northland Teutons.

Not unlike London's other overcivilized heroes, Buck, a St. Bernard–Scotch shepherd mix who had "lived the life of a sated aristocrat" in California, is brought into the Northland, undergoing the atavistic and revivifying process of "decivilization" (6, 21). Just as his human counterparts discover their phantasmal Teutonic heritage in the Northland, Buck atavistically reclaims "the old hunting days of the primordial world," which he has never experienced (79). In the "ruthless struggle for existence" in Alaska, his immediate filiation to "domesticated generations fell from him"; instead, "his ancestors, dead and dust," spectrally come alive in Buck (21, 22). As if to uncannily impregnate Buck, his "forgotten ancestors . . . quickened the old life within him," and the life that quickens inside Buck is born as a "primordial beast" (22, 24). At the end of the novel, Buck does not merely become the head of a wolf pack; he becomes more wolf than any other specimens bred between wolves. He reigns over the pack as "a gigantic wolf, larger than the largest of the breed" because of the size and weight inherited from his dog parents (77). While Buck is biologically a dog, "when he was made, the mould was broke," allowing him to become a creature other than dog (78). *The Call of the Wild* thus depicts the way in which a dog transcends his biological heritage and becomes the capitalized Wolf, who is placed at the highest notch of "the totem-pole of Alaskan fame" to lead his tribe, the Teutons (66). Just as London's Teutons are a chimerical hybrid of old-stock Americans and Alaska Natives, their totem, "Wolf," was conceived thorough an impossible crossbreeding between a man and a dog.

Kidnapped from a bourgeois household in the Santa Clara Valley and sold as a sled dog for the Klondike gold rush, Buck has undergone several different human ownerships before his fateful encounter with Thornton. He has experienced "a working partnership," "a sort of pompous guardianship," and "a stately and dignified friendship" with his previous owners; yet "love that was feverish and burning, that was adoration, that was madness, it had taken John Thornton to arouse" (60). As Michael Lundblad succinctly summarizes, interpretations of Buck's relation to Thornton in London criticism "tend to choose between either an emphasis on human sexual allegory dressed up as animal representation or an assertion of 'realistic' animal stories devoid of interspecies sexuality."[103] Critics such as Jonathan Auerbach

120   THE SUICIDAL STATE

and Scott Derrick see the passionate relationship between a male dog and a male human as a disguise of London's homoerotic desire, following Mark Seltzer's famous designation of London's canine heroes as "men in furs."[104] To read Buck as a male human wearing a canine mask is tempting, especially in the light of the term *wolf* as fin-de-siècle sexual slang referring to a working-class man who plays an insertive role in male-male sexual acts.[105] Doubtlessly, London's rendition of the relationship between Buck and Thornton, both referred to by male gender pronouns, constitutes one of the most explicit male-to-male erotic attachments in works of twentieth-century American literature. The description of their physical intimacy in which Thornton's "caressing hand" (77) puts Buck's "every part, brain and body, nerve tissue, and fibre, ... keyed to the most exquisite pitch" and makes "each hair discharge[] its pent magnetism at the contact" (78) approximates, as one critic has it, a "come-hither excerpt from the back cover of a torrid work of gay fiction."[106]

As Lundblad incisively argues, however, such readings risk missing the erotic possibilities that London's rendition of interspecies intimacy offers, which resist "the condensation of [sexual] meaning within the homo-sexual/heterosexual binary."[107] The sensual pleasure exchanged between Buck and Thornton, in contrast to the genitally organized object-choice-based sexuality, centers on "the pleasure of touch or contact," such as "petting, stroking, snuggling, kissing, scratching, touching in nongenital areas, etc."[108] Lundblad's reading of Buck and Thornton's mutual embrace richly articulates their interspecies relation as something other than what the sexual system organized by the axis of the homo/hetero binary can readily account for. Given that London unapologetically calls Buck and Thornton's definitionally infertile relationship "love" in the same year as the publication of *The Kempton-Wace Letters*, *The Call of Wild* should be understood as forging a counternarrative to that of the turn-of-the-century procreative family intertwined with race, claiming its own erotics of interspecies kinship.

Precisely because of its infertility, love between a dog and a man provides London with an idyllic model of relatedness unmediated by the biopolitical mandate. Through interspecies intimacy dissociated from procreative conjugality, London conceives an alternative sociality akin to totemic kinship: the relationality in which a nonhuman animal and a human obliterate the species lines as members belonging to the same tribe, constituting one entity in the absence of consanguinity. For Thornton, the dogs constitute his kin, even as they are not of his kind. As such, he communicates with them transcending

THE SPECTRAL LINEAGE   121

the species line: "He never forgot a kindly greeting or a cheering word, and to sit down for a long talk with them ('gas' he called it) was as much his delight as theirs" (60). Thornton and his dogs, especially Buck, develop what the text calls a "communion" through such intercourse, in which a strong affective current magnetizes and synchronizes them (61). Even when Buck sits at a distance, "the strength of Buck's gaze would draw John Thornton's head around, and he would return the gaze, without speech, his heart shining out of his eyes as Buck's heart shone out": "Such was the communion in which they lived" (61).

London's representation of interspecies communion points to a mode of intersubjective belonging that Gilles Deleuze and Félix Guattari theorize as "becoming-animal."[109] In *A Thousand Plateaus* (1980), Deleuze and Guattari conceptualize becoming-animal as "a different order than filiation," a mode of coming into being that emanates from "the domain of *symbioses*."[110] Becoming-animal happens between distinguishable subjects, pointing toward an ever-transitional mode of being that has no settled term to it. Such states of indifferentiation of becoming-animal, where "one is no longer a definite being distinguished from other beings," are understood to be effectuated by what they call an "*unnatural participation*."[111] Unnatural participations, alternately called "unnatural nuptials," have their own erotics and generative potential, constituting a different modality of "a peopling, a propagation" other than "filiation or hereditary production."[112] Instead of "the great molar powers of family, career, and conjugality" aiming to consolidate beings as autonomous subjects, becoming-animal is said to entail the decomposition of subjectivity, generating a mode of intersubjectivity through the "circulation of impersonal affects."[113]

Interspecies kinship in *The Call of the Wild* is figured in terms of such unnatural nuptials, laying the groundwork for totemic kinship between humans and nonhuman animals. Thornton and Buck affect each other to such an extent that they are altered by one another, the former becoming-dog and the latter becoming-man, forming a communion that appears to other humans "uncanny" (63). As Thornton gradates into a canine mode of being, Buck also comes "into a new existence" (59):

> Buck knew no greater joy than that rough embrace and the sound of murmured oaths, and at each jerk back and forth it seemed that his heart would be shaken out of his body so great was its ecstasy. And when, released, he sprang to his feet, his mouth laughing, his eyes eloquent, his

122   THE SUICIDAL STATE

throat vibrant with unuttered sound, and in that fashion remained without movement, John Thornton would reverently exclaim, "God! you can all but speak!" (60)

Buck's sensual joy in becoming-human is figured in terms of an "ecstasy" that shakes his "heart . . . out of his body" (60). Like Olive Chancellor's coveted "ecstasy of martyr[dom]," Buck's ecstasy is marked by a shade of death—or a modality of being beside oneself—which used to happen to him only in the bloody chase of other animals.[114] While hunting once inspired "the cry of Life plunging down from Life's apex in the grip of Death," it is now Thornton's caress that evokes "an ecstasy that marks the summit of life, and beyond which life cannot rise" (34, 33). "This ecstasy, this forgetfulness of living" constitutes "the paradox [of] living," for it marks the acme of life that becomes achievable only in the total oblivion thereof (33). Replacing hunting with Thornton's caress, Buck, in his love for Thornton, becomes ecstatic, beside himself. Thus, a man becoming-dog and a dog becoming-man forge an unnatural nuptial, inaugurating a "peopling" free of hereditary production. Such interspecies communion of becoming proffers a model for the totemic organization of white men as Teutonic "Sons of the Wolf." Put differently, London's entrapment in the biopolitical mandate finds its utopian escape in a biologically sterile, yet affectively charged, interspecies love.

But London's Northland dreamscape inevitably falls apart. As Buck returns to the camp, he finds that Thornton and his canine kin have been killed by a fictive Alaska Native tribe, the Yeehats. When Buck sees the "Yeehats . . . dancing about the wreckage of the spruce-bough lodge," he swoops upon them and destroys the tribe in revenge, wallowing in the blood of "the noblest game of all" (82, 83). As has been pointed out, the scene stages "a reenactment of the violence of national origins, that fateful encounter on frontier lands with native inhabitants."[115] Just as the frontier discursively functioned as the breeding ground for the "Americans," who had supposedly shed their European heritage through their slaughter of Indigenous peoples, the Northland spawns the Teutonic Wolf through the massacre of Alaska Natives.

But the violence reenacted in the scene is not only the one of the past, but also the one actively ongoing. Richard Henry Pratt's infamous phrase in 1892—"kill the Indian in him, and save the man"—exemplifies the murderous impetus behind the Progressive assimilationist policies taken against Indigenous peoples.[116] As Joseph M. Pierce argues, even as the primary locus of Native dispossession shifted from "war to assimilation," Indigenous lifeways were still under the exterminationist attack through "three intertwined technologies of settler colonial domination": settler-colonialist disciplining of Native children at boarding schools, their forceful adoption into white households, as well as allotment as we have seen.[117] While the discourse of the "vanishing race" had long been deployed to naturalize and legitimize the genocide of Native Americans, its rhetoric of racial extinction reached its pinnacle during the first decades of the twentieth century.[118] The sensationalist proclamation of disappearance of Native Americans was epitomized by the moniker "the last wild Indian in North America" attached to the last living member of the Yahi people, Ishi, who was studied by an anthropologist Alfred Kroebe and was made nationally famous in the 1910s.[119] By nominating Ishi as the "last wild Indian," Progressive discourse not only disavowed the continuous existence of Native Americans, but also narrated the diminishment of Indigenous populations as the natural result of evolution, camouflaging the exterminationist violence both of physical and assimilationist nature under the name of extinction.

Thornton's death and Buck's massacre of the Yeehats anticipate how the assimilationist violence against Native Americans paved the way for the birth of new whiteness in the decades following the publication of the novel. In one sense, London organizes Thornton's aptitude for becoming-animal, his affectability to the modes of being other than that of his own kind, through his close likeness to Indigenous people: "John Thornton asked little of man or nature. He was unafraid of the wild. . . . Being in no haste, Indian fashion, he hunted his dinner in the course of the day's travel; and if he failed to find it, like the Indian, he kept on travelling, secure in the knowledge that sooner or later he would come to it" (71). Such idealized proximity to the wild and "Indianness" means that he, too, must be offered as a sacrifice for the regeneration of the white race. However, it is the loss of Thornton that consummates the unnatural nuptial between him and Buck that spawns the Wolf, the totem of the Teutonic. Thornton's death "left a great void in [Buck], somewhat akin to hunger, but a void which ached and ached, and which food could not fill" (83). To fill the void in his body, Buck howls, joining the "mournful howl" of the wolves (76). For the dog to become the Wolf, he has to learn "a song of the younger world, which is the song of pack," a strain that is "pitched in minor key, with long-drawn wailings and half-sobs" (86, 31). As Deleuze and Guatarri remind us, "[a] becoming-animal always involves a pack, a band, a population, a peopling, in short, a multiplicity": it is to disintegrate oneself,

124   THE SUICIDAL STATE

to contain multiplicity in oneself, to form an assemblage by the power of affect, and to say "I am legion."[120]

If Buck's loss of Thornton—both as his cross-species lover and a proxy for Indianness—catalyzes the genesis of the Wolf, such impossible cross-species breeding stages how American Teutonism instrumentalized the coercive assimilation of Native Americans against the backdrop of the so-called new immigration. As we will discuss further in the next chapter, the year 1924 marked the passing of the Johnson-Reed Act, which severely limited the number of immigrants from eastern and southern Europe—the "Alpines" and "Mediterraneans" that American Teutonists detested. Crucially, this landmark immigration restriction coincided with the forceful enfolding of all Native Americans into US citizenry through the so-called Indian Citizenship Act. As Walter Benn Michaels famously argues, the exclusion of non-Teutonic Europeans and the inclusion of Native Americans were "complementary" movements: the native-born white Americans melancholically incorporated Native Americans, claiming true Americanness by coopting their Indigenousness.[121] Thus the "great race" whose passing Madison Grant prematurely mourned assimilated another race whose passing it had been perennially mourning, effectuating the birth of the American Teutons.

"If the Writer Is a Sorcerer"

I have argued that London's search for a regenerative trope for whiteness emanated at least partly from a desire to disown his neurasthenic father and, by extension, his hereditary relation to degenerating old-stock Americans represented by New England Anglo-Saxons. In so doing, he sought recourse to an atavistic reversion to the mythic Teutons, one that used the Northland as its medium. In the process of activating such atavism and unifying white men of varying origins under Northland Teutonism, London took up Alaska Natives' totemic kinship as a non-hereditary logic of human-animal relatedness and reproduction. London's appropriation of totemic kinship allowed him to idealize interspecies relatedness as a sanctuary of love; it created an escape both from the instrumentalization of intimacy for the racial propagation (unlike intra-racial conjugality) as well as from the threat against the purity of race (unlike miscegenation). But London's idyllic interspecies kinship was built on, enabled through, and in sync with the assimilative and

THE SPECTRAL LINEAGE   125

exterminationist violence against Indigenous peoples of the United States. Such is the genesis—or rather "becoming"—of the Son of the Wolf.

The Wolf fought back against the Bear, when the Bear accused him of nature-faking, taunting him for humanizing his canine companions. London wrote of the president: "He may know something of statecraft and of big-game shooting; he may be able to kill a deer when he sees it and to measure it and weigh it after he has shot it."[122] Roosevelt may know about the danger of race suicide, and he may attempt to re-inculcate old-stock Americans with the biopolitical mandate to reproduce and survive. But he does not know the nuptial blessing of the kinship with other animals, the unnatural participation that has its own breeding potential: "No, President Roosevelt does not understand evolution, and he does not seem to have made much of an attempt to understand evolution."[123]

London thought *he* knew something about evolution; or rather, he might have known more about what Deleuze and Guattari call "involution."[124] If "hereditary filiative evolution" means a linearity in which beings "go from something less differentiated to something more differentiated," involution signals a haunting liminality engendered between heterogeneous entities.[125] Involution is said to require beings "to involve" with each other, "form[ing] a block that runs its own line 'between' the terms in play and beneath assignable relations."[126] A dog does not evolve into a man; affected by Thornton, involved with him and in him, Buck is becoming-man and later becoming-Wolf. Such knowledge of involution, though, could cost one's life, imploding one's contained selfhood from within: "If the writer is a sorcerer, it is because writing is a becoming, writing is traversed by strange becomings that are not becoming-writer, but becoming-rat, becoming-wolf, etc. We will have to explain why. Many suicides by writers are explained by these unnatural participations, these unnatural nuptials."[127]

In 1916, Jack London died at the age of forty. Although his death was often rumored to be a suicide, critics have concluded otherwise.[128] But when London created Martin Eden largely after himself, perhaps he was modeling Martin as one such writer for whom writing was a becoming—a becoming that is a form of involution bordering on suicide. Surely, Martin Eden belongs to the spectral lineage of the Sons of the Wolf. He is an exemplar of the Teutonic ethos of what Chamberlain called "the poet warrior, the thinker, the freeman"; his fearless intellect, physical prowess, and unlimited self-discipline enable him to ascend into bourgeois whiteness, amply testifying to the Teuton's renowned capacity for self-government—the very

126   THE SUICIDAL STATE

quality that distinguished native-born white Americans from "unfit" new immigrants for period anti-immigration advocates.[129]

As an avid reader of Herbert Spencer, Martin, too, thinks he knows a lot about evolution, about the process of natural selection whereby *he* was chosen to proliferate. He is an evolutionary masterpiece: "Nature . . . had spent ten thousand centuries—ay, a hundred thousand and a million centuries . . . and he was the best she could do" (271). He is the fittest, chosen to survive, different from those miserable immigrants he sees at the socialist meeting that he was taken to by his friend Russ Brissenden. The "clever Jew" speaking at the podium immediately strikes him as "the unfit": "The man's stooped and narrow shoulders and weazened chest proclaimed him the true child of the crowded ghetto. . . . He was the figure that stood forth representative of the whole miserable mass of weaklings and inefficients who perished according to biological law on the ragged confines of life" (390). So Martin climbs the podium to represent the Teutons, giving a speech that would make Madison Grant weep in joy:

> In the struggle for existence . . . the strong and the progeny of the strong tend to survive, while the weak and the progeny of the weak are crushed and tend to perish. . . . But you slaves dream of a society where the law of development will be annulled, where no weaklings and inefficients will perish, where every inefficient will have as much as he wants to eat as many times a day as he desires, and where all will marry and have progeny—the weak as well as the strong. What will be the result? No longer will the strength and life-value of each generation increase. (391)

An avowed Nietzschean, Martin believes that "[t]he world belongs to the true noblemen, to the great blond beast, to the non-compromisers, to the 'yes-sayers'" (384). If, as Zarathustra has spoken, "Man is a rope stretched between the animal and the Superman," the Adamic Martin Eden might be that very "rope over an abyss"—the one who crosses over the evolutionary chasm to become other-than-human, to become "the magnificent blond beast avidly prowling round for spoil and victory," to become the lion, even surpassing the wolf.[130]

But as Zarathustra continues, that becoming is a "dangerous crossing."[131] Martin Eden falls off the rope, going down the abyss of involution. He dies because, as a good Teuton, he is "a good Indian" as his friend calls him (206), because "the only good Indian is a dead Indian," as the genocidal

THE SPECTRAL LINEAGE   127

aphorism goes. That phrase—commonly attributed to Phillip Sheridan's 1869 remarks—was at the height of circulation in the first two decades of the twentieth century, going side by side with the murderous assimilationist slogan: "Kill the Indian in him, and save the man."[132] Taken by Arthur Morse to his home as an exhibit of "an interesting wild man" he encountered on a ship, Martin Eden is a "a self-conscious savage, sprouting sweat at every pore in an agony of apprehension, puzzled by the bewildering minutiae of eating-implements, tortured by the ogre of a servant, striving at a leap to live at such dizzy social altitude" (47, 381). He is a savage to be educated, remolded, and assimilated by ethereally white Ruth Morse's Anglo-Saxon civilizing mission, "that common insularity of mind that makes human creatures believe that their color, creed, and politics are best and right and that other human creatures scattered over the world are less fortunately placed" (112). Thus Martin learns "correct English," reads through "a complete Shakespeare," and studies arithmetic to calculate how many cents per word he writes he can earn (113, 114). The education of possessive individualism has killed the "Indian" in Martin, and the man saved is the representative Teuton, the absolute individualist who disdains the veneer of democracy. Martin says: "The Republicans are foes to equality, though most of them fight the battle against equality with the very word itself the slogan on their lips. In the name of equality they destroy equality. . . . As for myself, I am an individualist. I believe the race is to the swift, the battle to the strong. Such is the lesson I have learned from biology" (314).

But Martin Eden dies because he is a model Teuton, a staunch individualist spawned from the dead Indian. His friend Russ Brissenden wants him to become a socialist, because he thinks it will give him "a sanction for [his] existence . . . the one thing that will save [him] in the time of disappointment that is coming to [him]"; it will have him "handcuffed to life somehow" when he is falling off the rope (389). Martin cannot, because he is "an individualist, and individualism is the hereditary and eternal foe to socialism" (314).[133] But he could, like Jack London himself, very well have been tethered to life, to others, because what distinguishes him as a writer is his "gift of sympathy," an uncontrollable affectability to channel with beings beside himself (33). Being "a fluid organism, swiftly adjustable, capable of flowing into and filling all sorts of nooks and crannies," he undergoes myriad becomings through writing (60). By that very gift of sympathetic involution, his "Nietzschean edifice seemed to shake and totter": "He grinned savagely at the paradox. A fine Nietzsche-man he was, to allow his intellectual concepts to be shaken

128   THE SUICIDAL STATE

by the first sentiment or emotion that strayed along . . . Pity and compassion had been generated in the subterranean barracoons of the slaves and were no more than the agony and sweat of the crowded miserables and weaklings" (403).

Martin Eden might have known that his precious individualist self was produced, preserved, and sustained by the network of miserables and weaklings and their ungrievable corps. With the final exertion of his will, then, he severs that rope between animals and the Superman, drowning himself in the ocean, falling deeper and deeper: "It seemed to him that he was falling down a vast and interminable stairway. And somewhere at the bottom he fell into darkness. That much he knew. He had fallen into darkness. And at the instant he knew, he ceased to know" (482). In killing himself, in asserting his own will, in resisting the biopolitical will to have him alive for the life of population, he becomes the individual that Teutonism has impelled him to be. And at that moment, Martin Eden becomes a true Teuton, because the only good Teuton is a dead Teuton.

4

Gertrude Stein's Melting Pot

Jewishness and the Excretory Pleasure of
The Making of Americans

The *Pot-au-Feu* of New Immigrants

When Henry James returned to the United States in 1904 after an absence of two decades, he immediately recognized the familiar specter of race suicide that he had once encountered in neurasthenic New England. The shadow cast over old-stock Americans seemed to have only grown darker with the massive influx of so-called new immigrants. Immigration passed the million-per-year mark in 1905 and totaled nearly nine million in the first decade alone, while each inspector at Ellis Island was said to have "examined between 400 and 500 immigrants" per day.[1] Recounting his stopover at Ellis in *The American Scene* (1907), James imagines that the sight of immigrants' incessant entrance would give any visitor a "new chill in his heart," as if he were seeing a "ghost in his supposedly safe old house."[2] His two hours at Ellis Island filled James with "a haunting wonder as to what might be becoming of us all, 'typically', ethnically, and thereby physiognomically, linguistically, *personally*."[3] What he witnessed, ultimately, was a "ceaseless process of the recruiting of our race, of the plenishing of our huge national *pot au feu*, of the introduction of fresh—of perpetually fresh so far it isn't perpetually stale—foreign matter into our heterogeneous system."[4]

James's *pot-au-feu* metaphor, in which the old American "stock" is simmered with a "hotch-potch of racial ingredients," immediately reminds us of the term that Israel Zangwill's 1908 play popularized: "the melting pot."[5] The national figuration of a crucible that would homogenize miscellaneous human materials was nothing new in itself, originally dating back at least to the early nineteenth century.[6] Yet Zangwill's invocation of a large cauldron with which the "great Alchemist" fuses "Celt and Latin, Slav and Teuton, Greek and Syrian—black and yellow" in *The Melting Pot* assumed a new potency for a nation seething with immigration debates.[7] By the end of

The Suicidal State. Madoka Kishi, Oxford University Press. © Oxford University Press 2024.
DOI: 10.1093/9780197690109.003.0005

130   THE SUICIDAL STATE

the nineteenth century, the wave of Chinese immigration that had initially sparked the race suicide controversy ebbed with the successive enactments of the Chinese Exclusion Acts. The termination of Asian immigration, however, did not bring peace for native-born white Americans. The year 1896 marked a demographic watershed, when immigrants from southern and eastern Europe—Italians comprising 17% of arrivals and Jews 14%—for the first time exceeded those belonging to the so-called Teutonic family.[8]

At stake was the new immigrants' assimilability. The presence of eastern and southern European immigrants felt uncanny to native-born white Americans, for despite their relative phenotypical familiarity, they were linguistically and culturally alien. In the words of a leading education reformer of the time, Ellwood Cubberley, newly immigrated "southern and eastern Europeans are of a very different type from the north Europeans who preceded them. Illiterate, docile, lacking in self-reliance and initiative and not possessing Anglo-Teutonic conceptions of law, order and government, their coming has served to dilute tremendously our national stock, and to corrupt our civic life."[9] The great mass of southern and eastern Europeans thus prompted the creation of what David R. Roediger calls "intrawhite racial divisions."[10] Fierce controversies occurred over whether the census should divide European immigrants into "Teutonic, Iberian, Celtic, and Slavic 'race or peoples, or more properly subdivisions of race.'"[11]

As exemplified by Jacob Riis's *How the Other Half Lives* (1890), period journalism graphicly depicted new immigrants' lifeways, exposing the "Nether Half" of the social body—a region not only sexual but excretory.[12] The social body's lower half was reimagined as becoming active with the sudden inflow of new immigrants, who were repeatedly represented in digestive terms in the national imaginary. Circulating from the turn of the century, tropes such as "racial indigestion" and "alien indigestion" signified the social body's inability to incorporate new immigrants, superimposing the digestive valence of *assimilation* onto its more familiar national meaning.[13] The racial scientist and anti-immigration zealot, G. Frank Lydston, for instance, called "paupers, prostitutes, inebriates, and [the] insane" as "the excreta of society," noting that "although foreign-born citizens constitute but one-eighth of the total population of the country, they furnish one-third of our criminals, one-third of our paupers, and one-third of our insane."[14] The foreign matter swallowed by the American social body thus turned into a not-quite-assimilable, excremental racial mass.

GERTRUDE STEIN'S MELTING POT   131

Put differently, assimilation's alimentary logic rendered new immigrants as the *abject* of the body social: neither subject nor object, as Julia Kristeva puts it, "a piece of filth, waste, or dung," muddling the border between the self and the other.[15] James's culinary take on the melting pot imagery also leads him to imagine the assimilation of immigrants as a "visible act of ingurgitation on the part of our body politic and social," a process he describes as not without a vehement foreign-body reaction.[16] Once the voracious social body ingests "gross aliens" into its system, the supposed American self is constantly threatened by the "affirmed claim of the alien, however immeasurably alien, to share in one's supreme relation," or "the idea of intimacy of relation" to his country.[17] What happens to the formerly "privileged person," the one who once firmly believed in his American identity, is a "sense of dispossession": "Who and what is an alien [?] ... Which is the American, by these scant measures?—which is *not* the alien, over a large part of the country at least, and where does one put a finger on the dividing line?"[18] New immigrants threaten to melt down the definition of the American self from within: "The abject permeates me, I become abject."[19]

Abject new immigrants invading the nation became the new face of race suicide. As a period article on race suicide puts it: "Are the people of the older stock—those of Anglo-Saxon and Teutonic descent—gradually dying out and are they being replaced by the immigrants from southern and eastern Europe? If this is the case what are the effects upon our civilization going to be? There are the questions of vital concern to Americans."[20] Henry James is no exception to this nativist imaginary when he describes what he has witnessed on the Lower East Side as "the Hebrew conquest of New York."[21] For James, more than immigrants of any other ethnicity, it was Jews who embodied the specter of race suicide. Jewish immigrants' fertility seemed to promise an eerie repopulation of the country, replacing the dwindling old-stock Americans: the "dominant note" of the "dense Yiddish quarter" was "multiplication, multiplication of everything," and, in particular, "the children swarmed above all—here was multiplication with a vengeance."[22] The "ubiquity of children" assumed an "excess of lurid meaning" for James: "they were all there for race," becoming implements of "Israel mechanically pushing through."[23]

"Multiplication, multiplication of everything" is the dominant note also of *The Making of Americans*, Gertrude Stein's thousand-page magnum opus, which was gradually composed from 1903 to 1911 (though it would

132 THE SUICIDAL STATE

remain unpublished until 1925). But the nature of multiplication in Stein's epic characterology is not the biological propagation of the Jewish race that James feared, although the text is, as I will argue, animated by questions of American identity in its relation to immigration as well as to Stein's own Jewishness.[24] The text declares its narrative purpose on its very first page in a deceivingly artless manner: "The old people in a new world, the new people made out of the old, that is the story that I mean to tell."[25] The alleged narrative goal of recounting the European immigrants' Americanization seems easily achievable, for in a young nation composed of immigrants from its outset, the history of "a real American, one whose tradition it has taken scarcely sixty years to create" will be complete if "we . . . realise our parents, remember our grandparents and know ourselves" (3). The book accordingly opens with a realist premise of "a family's progress," aiming to chronicle a three-generation history of two immigrant families, the Herslands and the Dehnings.

However, *The Making of Americans* soon begins to destroy the narrative trajectory that it sets for itself, aspiring instead to become "the history of every one" (191). Staging the narrator's quixotic struggle to create a universal typology that will supposedly encompass "every one who ever can or is or was or will be living," the text rhapsodically departs from the family saga with endless analyses of innumerable minor figures only tangentially related to the two families, stretching the limits of narrative intelligibility (171). In so doing, *The Making of Americans* radically reconfigures what Alex Woloch has memorably formulated as the "distributional matrix" of narrative attention between the one and the many, between "a strong, rounded, fully realized central protagonist and a manifold group of delimited . . . minor characters."[26] While the negotiation of narrative space in the nineteenth-century realist novel is driven by the genre's "dual impulses to bring in a multitude of characters and to bring out the interiority of a singular protagonist," Stein's text is motored by the very voiding of this distinction, or what can be called a populational imaginary. With its will to massify, to classify, and to know its inhabitants in abstract, almost statistical terms, *The Making of Americans* represents the ethos of a biopolitical state.

The Making of Americans, I argue, is a populational text, one that functions as the paragon of melting pots, which assimilates the multitudes and voids difference. Reading the text across its three versions, this chapter maps a shift in each version's narrative focus—from the individual in the first version toward the type in the second version, and ultimately, to the highest level of abstraction and impersonality in the final version. As Leon Katz's tour-de-force excavation has revealed, what he calls Stein's "first making of *The Making of Americans*" started in early 1903 in New York.[27] The story she composed in a notebook (posthumously published in 1972, hereafter referred to as "Making of the Americans" or the 1903 version) revolves around an immigrant family called the Dehnings, based largely on Stein's paternal uncle Sol Stein and his family in New York.[28] The unfinished story was left untouched for three years, until Stein started reimagining the Dehnings' family history as intertwined with that of the Herslands, whom Stein modeled after her own immediate family. In the period between 1906 to 1908, Stein envisioned a series of diegetic scenarios and drafted passages about both families in her notebooks (the second draft, or the 1908 version), but radically revised them again into their final form between 1908 and 1911 (*The Making of Americans*, or the 1911 version).[29] Written thus palimpsestically over the course of eight years, *The Making of Americans*, I argue, stages something like a recapitulation of literary history. While each version embodies a particular aesthetic—namely, realism, naturalism, and modernism—the final 1911 version fossilizes Stein's process of revision and recapitulates the gradual prominence of these literary aesthetics.

This trajectory across literary aesthetics, I argue, accompanies Stein's increasing abstraction of Jewishness. While the 1903 version imagines the process of assimilation through Jewish reproductive familialism, the 1911 version deploys an aesthetic that offers a queer alternative that would produce "Americans" as a unified mass. That is, I argue that Stein's version of the melting pot is ultimately neither an alchemical nor a culinary one: it is an excretory pot filled with abject *merde*. In Hemingway's wry words, *The Making of Americans* "began magnificently, went on very well for a long way with stretches of great brilliance and then went on endlessly in repetitions that a more conscientious and less lazy writer would have put in the waste basket": he seems to indicate that Stein—pardon my French—grandly shat out the half a million words that constitute *The Making of Americans*.[30] What Hemingway did not quite realize, though, is that Stein makes *The Making of Americans* gleefully wasteful, as the text's coprophilic poetics rescripts Americans—not just new immigrants but all Americans—as the waste matter produced by the gluttonous social body. The excretory pleasure of *The Making of Americans* culminates in the suicide of the novel's "hero," David Hersland. In killing himself by "deciding to be eating only one thing," I will argue, David aspires to become a disembodied and thus universal being

134   THE SUICIDAL STATE

(865). With this suicide, David Hersland becomes a typical and unmarked American, one who exemplifies the ethos of "race suicide."

Recovering the Absented Presence of Jewishness

While *The Making of Americans'* historical reference to Americanization has often been overshadowed by the critical conversation about its stylistic innovations, several critics have situated the text's dismantling of the "progress" narrative in the context of Progressive-Era immigration debates. For instance, Sarah Wilson argues that with its totalizing impetus to include "every one" in its characterology, *The Making of Americans* "represents a paradigmatic melting-pot text: in it, a story of immigration becomes the occasion for Stein's radical modernist deformation of conventional narratives."[31] With a similar gesture, Priscilla Wald reads *The Making of Americans* in relation to a tradition of American immigrant writings, arguing that Stein's disruption of narrative conventions performs assimilation's violent force. In contrast to the celebratory account of Americanization—epitomized by Riis's *The Making of an American* (1901), his own memoir as a Danish (read: Teutonic) immigrant—the disorienting prose of Stein's text stages immigrants' experiences as "divested of cultural narratives . . . that mark personhood," foregrounding such "a terror of displacement" as constitutive of modernity itself.[32] In these readings, Stein's stylistic experiment reflects what James recounts as a sense of dispossession amidst the large-scale populational shift—or what *The Making of Americans* calls "a horrid losing-self sense" (5).

While critics thus compellingly locate *The Making of Americans*—and, by extension, the making of American modernism—within the context of Progressive Era immigration, they are strangely reticent about Stein's own racial liminality in this discourse. Technically speaking, to characterize Stein, as Wald does, as "a white, middle-class woman" who writes about immigrant experience "self-consciously from within her limitation" is not a misnomer.[33] Born to second-generation German Jewish American parents in Allegheny, Pennsylvania, in 1874, Gertrude Stein was an American by birthright, even though her family moved to Vienna immediately after she was born and she spent the first five years of her life in Europe. At the time of Stein's birth, the US census counted those like Stein, with foreign-born grandparents and US-born parents, as white in an unmarked way, whereas those born in the

United States with foreign-born parents would still have been counted as "white" but in a separate category.[34]

Coming from a relatively well-to-do, successfully assimilated German Jewish family, Stein's relation to the question of turn-of-the-century Jewish immigration seems relatively tangential, especially when compared with that of her contemporary first-generation Jewish American authors. In contrast to the first-generation writers who richly documented their Jewish lifeways in realist detail—the Polish-born Anzia Yezierska and the Belarusian-born Abraham Cahan and Mary Antin, for instance—Stein's writing rarely features Jewishness as an explicit subject matter.[35] Even in Stein's fictional memoir of her partner, *The Autobiography of Alice B. Toklas* (1933), "despite its account of both their family histories, their Jewish roots are conspicuously absent."[36] While Emma Lazarus—whose Sephardic Jewish family's pre-Revolutionary roots in America dated from 1654—was transformed into the symbolic guardian of new immigrants as her 1883 sonnet, "The New Colossus," adorned the pedestal of the Statue of Liberty, Stein's Jewishness appears to remain, as Mary Damon suggests, "a topic that is best approached obliquely."[37]

As Amy Feinstein compellingly argues, however, although Jewishness does not appear in Stein's work in an explicit way, "Stein's Jewishness underwrites our very understanding of modernism," particularly if we understand *The Making of Americans* as recording the genesis of modernist writing.[38] As we will trace in Stein's early writings, even as the official narrative of the US census rendered her "white," her life in the turn-of-the-century United States made her acutely conscious of her Jewishness as a marker of racial difference. By the time the Steins settled in Oakland, large numbers of Jews had been exiled from czarist Russia and eastern Europe by pogroms. As a result, the US "Jewish population rose from around 270,000 in 1877 to over 4 million by 1927."[39] Though many Jewish immigrants imagined America as a safe haven, their "Promised Land"—as Antin's 1912 novel called it—was not unaffected by Europe's renewed antisemitism. Violence against Russo- and eastern European Jewish immigrants in the United States started as early as the 1880s and became increasingly widespread as the revival of the Shylock stereotype in the midst of the gold-standard controversy started to "obscure distinctions between the relatively well-to-do German Jews and the newcomers."[40] The 1915 lynching of Leo Frank, a wealthy German Jewish factory manager in Atlanta, provides one especially lurid index of such antisemitism.[41]

136   THE SUICIDAL STATE

But what was later to become *The Making of Americans* was gestated not only through Stein's self-consciousness as a Jewish American but also through its conflicted relation to her growing awareness of her queerness. When Stein wrote the original short story in 1903, she had just begun what she would later describe as the "fateful twenty-ninth year" of her life (437). The beginning of her twenty-ninth year was indeed a "tumultuous" one, in which "all the forces that have been engaged through the years of childhood, adolescence and youth in confused and sometimes angry combat range themselves in ordered ranks" (436–437). Leaving Johns Hopkins Medical School in 1901, she was about to move into 27 rue de Fleurus, Paris, to join her brother Leo Stein. As Katz and others have speculated, her ambition to become a psychologist—as her former mentor William James had hoped—was aborted at least partly because of her triangular relationship with May Bookstaver and Mabel Haynes at Johns Hopkins.[42] The frustrated love affair was dramatized in Stein's first completed novel, *Q.E.D*, which was written a few months after the original draft of "The Making of Americans."[43] Stein's fictional counterpart, Adele, says to Helen, the Bookstaver figure in *Q.E.D.*: "You have a foolish notion that . . . to cherish the ideals of respectability and decency is to be commonplace and that to be the mother of children is to be low."[44] What initially prevents Adele from acknowledging her attraction to Helen—characterized as a pleasure-loving, individualistic, "blooming Anglo-Saxon"—is "the failing of [Adele's] tribe," that is, a belief in "strong family affection and great respect for ties of blood."[45]

Though Stein ascribes her fictional counterpart's disavowal of same-sex desire to "the Calvinistic influence that dominates American training," a more likely explanation seems to be that it is related to her conception of Jewishness.[46] Stein's 1896 essay written at Radcliffe College, which Feinstein has recovered—titled "The Modern Jew Who Has Given up the Faith of His Fathers Can Reasonably and Consistently Believe in Isolation"—evinces Stein's early investment in Jewish separatism and reproductive familialism. Advocating for the preservation of Jewish "race-feeling," Stein condemns Jewish "intermarriage with an alien" as "the death-blow of the race."[47] In order for the Jewish race to fulfill its original "great destiny in the sense of being a great power," that is, to aspire to effect "a nation standing by itself, ethical, civilizing, blessing other nations but apart from them," Jews in America should not embrace assimilation in their intimate lives, even if they commingle with Gentiles in their social lives: "In the sacred precincts of the home, in the close union of family and of kinfolk he must be a Jew

GERTRUDE STEIN'S MELTING POT   137

with Jews; the Gentile has no place there."[48] Her "race-feeling," which she equated with "an enlargement of the family tie," grew steadily as she entered Johns Hopkins and encountered the increasing antisemitism of the 1890s.[49] In London in 1902, immediately before writing "The Making of Americans" and *Q.E.D.*, she was befriended by one of the most prominent spokesmen of the World Zionist Organization, Israel Zangwill, whom she praised as an inseminator of "a strong revival of Jewish feeling."[50]

In this context, *The Making of Americans*' manifested goal to chronicle "a decent family progress respectably lived"—a phrase taken almost verbatim from the 1903 version, "a family progress respectably lived"—ceases to appear as a mere effigy for the modernist conflagration (*Making*, 33; "Making," 144). Rather, it records Stein's conflicted relation to Jewish familialism at the outset of her project, her negotiation of the desire to endorse what she describes in *Q.E.D.* as "the ideals of respectability and decency" in which "to be the mother of children" was valued as a means of the preservation of the race, even as it inhibited the realization of her same-sex desire. Set in the 1880s, "twenty years before the fever to be an Anglo Saxon and a gentleman" had become widespread, the original 1903 version reflects Stein's anti-assimilationist views, reminiscent of her Radcliffe essay ("Making," 137). The story opens with an almost identical passage to the one in the completed 1911 version: "It has always seemed to me a rare privilege this of being an American, a real American *and yet* one whose tradition it has taken scarcely sixty years to create" ("Making," 137; italics added). The phrase "and yet," which was to be replaced with a comma in the 1911 version ("a real American, one whose tradition"), implies that she originally envisioned a sharper distinction between "Anglo Saxon" Americans and naturalized immigrants, and the story to be told was a history of an immigrant family whose Americanization was believed to have been achieved in three generations in the state's official narrative, the one that made Stein "white" (*Making*, 3).

Inspired by the then-ongoing divorce suit of Gertrude's erstwhile favorite cousin, Bird Stein (whose fictional counterpart was named Julia Dehning), "The Making of Americans" charts a typical generational conflict between first-generation parents and their Americanized children. Growing up under "the breaking Anglo Saxon wave," the Dehning children seek to pursue individualism against their immigrant parents' Old World counsel, but not with much success. Their frustrated attempt is epitomized by Julia's foolhardy marriage to Henry Hersland, who turns out to be after Julia's father's money

138 THE SUICIDAL STATE

(141).[51] The paterfamilias of the Dehnings in the 1903 version bears a responsibility to guide not only his children but also the young nation, something akin to the civilizing mission that Stein had ascribed to Jewishness in her Radcliffe essay. "Even here in the heart of individualistic America," the narrator declares, the "straightened bond of family is the one thing always healthy, human, vital and from which has always the best the world can know" ("Making," 144–145). The Dehnings are summoned to provide a model for such familialism:

> We need not turn Chinese but till some more effective method proves itself some process more successful than any we Americans have yet discovered for remaining simple honest and affectionate I recommend you all to laud the bourgeois family life at [the] expense if need be of the individual and to keep the old world way of being born in a middle class tradition from affectionate honest parents whom you honor for those virtues and so come brother Americans come quickly and for your own soul's sake and listen while I tell you further of the Dehning family. ("Making," 145)

With an abrupt reference to "Chinese[ness]," the Dehnings' Jewish version of reproductive familialism is presented as a viable alternative to Chinese immigrants' threatening fertility—the original fear of race suicide, as we will discuss in the Coda—and is imagined instead as a remedy for the alienating effects of American individualism. "The Making of the Americans" thus starts recounting the story of a Jewish family's recovery of "simple honest and affectionate" ways of living in America, while simultaneously depicting its clash with the Dehning children's growing sense of liberal selfhood within a classic grammar of realism (145).

The 1903 version, however, was left unfinished in her notebook until Stein revisited it in April 1906.[52] In this revision, the original focus on Julia Dehning's marriage and divorce was to be massively expanded with the three-generation history not only of the Dehnings but also of the family of Julia's (ex-)husband, who was renamed Alfred Hersland. As Leon Katz's reconstruction of Stein's notebooks shows, her writings from the period between 1906 to 1908 evince that she modeled the Herslands closely after her own family in California. For instance, though Henry/Alfred Hersland had originally been inspired by Bird Stein's former husband, Louis Sternberger, he now also took on the personal traits and anecdotes of Gertrude's oldest brother, Mike Stein, while the eldest of the Hersland children, Martha, was

GERTRUDE STEIN'S MELTING POT   139

shaped by Gertrude's observations of her older sister Bertha.[53] The youngest of the three, David Hersland—whom Stein described as the most "singular," with a "certain genius" inside him—was reminiscent of Leo and herself.[54] As Stein recounts in one of her notebooks, David became the 1908 version's new focal point, since he became the confidant of his sister-in-law Julia, just as Stein and Leo had tried (and failed) to be Bird's: "I need not be in a hurry to give birth to my hero because it will be an enormous task to struggle his development."[55]

However, repeatedly called "LeonDave," "David-Leon," "Leon David" or simply "Leon" in the notebooks, young David Hersland is also a portrait of Leon Solomons: Stein's closest friend and her collaborator in lab experiments on automatic writing at the Harvard Psychological Laboratory, with whom, she indicates, she had shared a brief Platonic intimacy before she fully realized her lesbianism.[56] Particularly germane to David Hersland's characterization was Solomons's death in 1900. The death of young David Hersland became a new center of her project in the 1908 version, as she repeatedly wrote about his death wish in her notebooks: "David constantly surrounded with the thought of death, puts it away from him then endeavors to embrace it to dead in a [death?] to conquer it almost never quite."[57] Referring to David as "Leon" and Julia as "Bird" based on their respective models, Stein wrote about her plan to shape David's self-willed death after Solomons's: "Use for Leon . . . the part about 29 years old when he decides on cancer ultimately separates him from Bird . . . ultimately kills himself, through operation like Leon's."[58] Alice B. Toklas commented on this entry as follows:

> Leon Solomons chose his death; he practically committed suicide. He had an organic disorder and thought that a diet would cure him, and so he went on a little bit like Leo. Finally, he saw that he was weakening, but he persisted until he died. Gertrude said he willed his death.
>
> Late in the writing of the David chapter, when she saw what was coming, Gertrude said, Don't type for a few days. Then—It's finished. And that was the day, the day her hero died, that Gertrude went to see Mildred Aldrich. The book is done, Gertrude told her. What happened? My hero was killed last night. And Mildred said, shocked, How could you have killed him?[59]

Pointing to the similarity between Leon Solomons's dietary practice and Leo Stein's Fletcherism (a Progressive Era eating regimen that advocated for the total mastication of food for the purification of feces), Toklas explains here

140   THE SUICIDAL STATE

how Stein conceived of David's slow demise by "going on eating almost only one thing" (*Making*, 899).[60] The death of her "hero" David—the most singular one, or "the one" in Woloch's terminology—would provide her with an apt ending for the family history, which was now imagined to be fully novelized.

Denaturalizing Procreative Familialism

What was completed in 1911 as *The Making of Americans*, however, was a total departure from the realist narrative that had first revolved around those characters. The ethnic marker "german" in the 1908 version attributed to the characters based on her Jewish German family was changed to "certain" in the 1911 version, and the narrative trajectory and diegetic details planned in the notebooks were rendered almost thoroughly unintelligible.[61] After the first approximately seventy-five pages of the 1911 version, which expanded the 1903 version's account of the Herslands' history, the family stories of the Herslands and the Dehnings are increasingly decentered by the narrator's typological endeavor to construct the character system of "bottom nature." Starting with the description of the neighboring families of the Herslands, the narrator starts to classify "every one" around the two families into the ever-elusive categories of "independent dependent" and "dependent independent," trying to explicate the organizing logics of the personalities that lie beneath people's repeated patterns of behaviors.

Still bearing the subtitle *Being a History of a Family's Progress*, the final 1911 version's relentlessly democratic endeavor to include every being in sight reconfigures the notion of family as a socially sanctioned, closed unit of intimacy defined by heritage.[62] This undoing of the master plot of biological reproduction is arguably driven by what Laura Doyle calls "lesbian 'deviance,'" for the beginning of Stein's final revision in 1908 largely coincided with that of Stein and Toklas's union.[63] Given that it was Toklas who first recognized the value of *The Making of Americans* and started to type its manuscript, to say that *The Making of Americans* is a product of the literary symbiosis of "Gertrice/Altrude," as Stein called their alliance, is more than a tired cliché that romanticizes their relationship.[64] As the narrator in the 1911 version says: "Then somebody says yes to it, to something you are liking, or doing or making and then never again can you have completely such a feeling of being afraid and ashamed that you had then when

GERTRUDE STEIN'S MELTING POT   141

you were writing or liking the thing and not any one had said yes about the thing" (485).

Stein's queer reconfiguration of the family narrative is inextricable also from her reconceptualization of race, particularly in the Progressive Era racial landscape, in which heterosexual reproduction and racial production were inseparable from each other. Doyle puts it succinctly: "Race is a narrative concept. Whether or not it becomes the basis for social hierarchy or gets configured in binary oppositions, 'race' is at its base the idea that characteristics are passed from one generation to the next through time."[65] For Stein, however, "racialized heterosexual reproduction" is a logic associated not so much with what Doyle calls "Anglo-American virtue and sensibility" as with the Jewish familialism that Stein had upheld in the original 1903 version.[66] Even though Stein's own anti-Oedipal commentary about *The Making of Americans*, "fathers are depressing," has often been cited by critics, surprisingly little attention has been paid to how her complaint, "There is too much fathering going on," is made in relation to Jewishness: "The Jews . . . come into this because they are very much given to having a father and to being one and they are very much given not to want a father and not to have one, and they are an epitome of all this that is happening the concentration of fathering to the perhaps there not being one."[67]

What Stein articulates here as the simultaneous over-presence and absence of the Jewish father figure can be understood in relation to the discursive reformulation of Jewish masculinity at the turn of the century. Since the mid-nineteenth century, European scientific racism had constructed the "Jew" as the antithesis of the Aryan, a biologically defined, hereditarily tainted, "degenerate" group.[68] In degeneration theory, Jewish men in particular were often associated with the inversion model of homosexuality, both through the Jewish ritual of circumcision—which non-Jews often associated with castration—and through traditional Talmudic culture's male ideal, which was distinctly different from the Aryan model of manliness.[69] In response to the pathologizing discourse of Jewish effeminacy, a call for the masculinization of Jewishness arose from within Jewish communities. Such an endeavor is best exemplified by Max Nordau, the primary advocate of the ideals of "Muscular Judaism" and a cofounder of the World Zionist Organization, also known for his sexological attack on fin-de-siècle decadence, *Degeneration*. As Daniel Boyarin maintains, Nordau's call for the remaking of the male Jewish body was "literally a body politics" in which Zionism was imagined as a "heterosexualizing project" that would make

142 THE SUICIDAL STATE

Jewish men "physically strong and active, the head of the family, dominant in the public world of politics at home and abroad."[70]

Assimilation into the United States was no less a "heterosexualizing project" for Jewish immigrants, for monogamous marriage and heterosexuality were primary organizing structures for the new immigrants' formation of American identity. As Margot Canaday documents, the Bureau of Immigration used the public charge clause to target aliens who "exhibited gender inversion, had anatomical defects, or engaged in sodomy."[71] Jewish immigrants often came under strict scrutiny, leading immigration officers to note "the frequency with which . . . hidden sexual complexes among Hebrews" were detected.[72] Though marriage and a strong father figure were prominent features of the works of first-generation Jewish authors, such preeminence was, as Warren Hoffman argues, "not the product of heterosexuality but [an] enabling device and centrally defining act that would make sure that Jews could pass as straight" and by extension, pass as desirable "American" citizens.[73] In this context, what Stein describes in *The Making of Americans* as "the right kind of marrying," in which "decent well to do fathers and good mothers are always existing who have a decent loyal feeling of the right kind of loving and they have their children and so they keep on going," emerges as a mechanism integral to the production of Americans out of immigrants, particularly for those with Jewish heritage (*Making*, 69).

Yet the 1911 version rejects "the right kind of marrying" as the central machinery of national and racial reproduction (21). If same-sex desire is "the ungenerating-ungenerated terror of the family, because it produces itself without reproducing," as Guy Hocquenghem says, Stein needs to find another machinery to generate Americans.[74] Deploring the middle-class sensibility "that has within it a little of the fervor for diversity," the narrator abruptly addresses "Brother Singulars":

> Brother Singulars, we are misplaced in a generation that knows not Joseph. We flee before the disapproval of our cousins, the courageous condescension of our friends who gallantly sometimes agree to walk the streets with us, from all them who never any way can understand why such ways and not the others are so dear to us, we fly to the kindly comfort of an older world accustomed to take all manner of strange forms into its bosoms. (21)

Singularity—or "vital singularity," as the narrator also calls it—designates the quality of "being free inside it," a sign of one's uniqueness, individuality

GERTRUDE STEIN'S MELTING POT   143

unfettered by conventions, or even of genius, as we have seen in relation to Stein's conceptualization of David (21, 47). At the same time, as Susan Lanser argues, the word *singular* had also been a signifier of same-sex eros since the late eighteenth century, particularly "used frequently ... to describe women suspected of homoerotic desires."[75] With reference to Joseph, the third Hebrew patriarch's favored son, who is sold into slavery by his brothers, the narrator bemoans the failed incorporation of fellow "Brother Singulars" into the American family narrative: "No brother singulars ... there is no place in an adolescent world for anything eccentric like us" (*Making*, 47). Ill-adapted to the logic of *re*production—replication of the sameness, of the homeostasis of the nation—the eccentricity of Brother Singulars renders them unfit for assimilation into the New World, spurring them to flee to the Old World, which offers them "kindly comfort" and embraces "all manner of strange forms" of intimacy.

Brother Singulars' exodus resonates with that of Stein herself, who left the United States in 1903 for the liberal atmosphere of the Left Bank. At the same time, however, Stein repeatedly asserted her Americanness and remained an American citizen even while spending her whole life in Paris: "After all I am American alright. Being there does not make me more there."[76] Perhaps, though, it is more accurate to say that being not there made her more there, inasmuch as self-expatriation enabled her to lay claim to Americanness. The distance from her home country allowed Stein to "play the part of an eccentric, patriotic American abroad," not a Jewish American alienated from the generational narrative of Americanization.[77] Even against the backdrop of the Dreyfus affair, which fueled French antisemitism, Stein and Toklas were "most often described as Americans, never as Jews."[78] In this regard, the gradual re-composition of *The Making of Americans* after Stein's departure from the United States seems to chronicle the making of an American as well, insofar as the eccentric Americanness that Stein donned in Europe allowed her to become an American in a racially unmarked way.

The erasure of ethnic markers as well as the dismantling of the family narrative in the 1911 version signals Stein's own parting with a heredity-based logic of Jewishness. This departure was catalyzed by the introduction of the abstract characterology of "bottom nature," Stein's term for the essential human character that purportedly emerges through a subject's repeated pattern of unconscious action. Beginning in 1908, Stein started to write numerous character observations not only of her own family, but also of her friends on both sides of the Atlantic (one of the first and most extensive

144   THE SUICIDAL STATE

notes, in fact, was about Alice Toklas), as well as historical and celebrity figures (Lucrezia Borgia, Shakespeare, and Van Gogh, to name a few).[79] Her
aim was to classify them into various character types and create networks
of these categories. Even though the characterology of the final version was
to be boiled down into "independent dependent" and "dependent independent," Stein's notebooks showcase the eclectic menagerie of character
types that she originally devised. Some categories are gender-based: "Pure
Lady," "Pure Prostitute," "Lady Masculine," "Servant Girl," and "Spinster
Kind," for instance, are female types, whereas "The Man of the World," "The
'Kantian' Man," "Boy," and "Earthy Boy" are male types.[80] Others are putatively organized by race—namely "The Anglo-Saxon" and "The Jew," who are
respectively associated with "Attacking" and "Resisting/Earthy"—though
the race of the individuals classified in these categories does not always align
with Stein's taxonomy. For instance, her sister Bertha and her sister-in-law
Sarah "Sally" Stein (both Jewish) are described as "type Anglo Saxon and
American," whereas Goethe and Frederick the Great were categorized as
"jewish types."[81]

Stein's notebooks from this period capture, so to speak, her shift from the
realist phase to the naturalist one, exemplifying what Jennifer Fleissner memorably calls the "naturalist problematic of the 'compulsion to describe.'"[82] If
naturalism is, as Fleissner argues, a genre motored by the will to describe that
short-circuits realism's narrative trajectory and denaturalizes its "reality"
along with its models of selfhood, Stein's near-obsession with dissecting
everybody's "bottom nature" closely aligns with Fleissner's account. As
Barbara Will argues, Stein's idea of bottom nature is rooted in her earlier
neuropsychological interest in and investigations of automatism, which she
conducted with Leon Solomons at the Harvard Psychological Laboratory.[83]
Stein's notebooks from 1908, especially the one titled "The Diagram Book,"
show the continuation of this bent with a number of web graphs, line graphs,
and tables that strive to scientifically render individuals into types.

Such an impulse to classify humans into predictable types is shared by period racial science, as well as sexological, sociological, and anthropological
writings, which aimed to produce what Mark Seltzer calls "models for the generic, typical, or average man."[84] As Seltzer argues, social science's statistical
imaginary that naturalism shares is "closely bound up with the emergence
of a biopolitics of population."[85] As it aims to depersonalize and massify
its subjects, this biopolitical mode devises "'the naturalist machine' as a
counter-model of the generation of persons," ultimately creating the "'typical

GERTRUDE STEIN'S MELTING POT   145

American'—that is . . . the American *as* typical, standard, and reproducible."[86] Through her typological endeavor, Stein ultimately found her naturalist machine, the one that would produce Americans as types in place of biological reproduction. In other words, *The Making of Americans* illustrates how naturalism's populational imaginary inaugurates new aesthetic and ontological possibilities through its departure from the realist model of private selfhood, whose construction is inseparable from heteropatriarchal domesticity and its procreative narrative.

The completed 1911 version, particularly up to the David Hersland chapter, is undoubtedly still charged with the naturalist compulsion to describe—in one sense, even more so, in its willful and repetitive insistence on explaining its "completed system of kinds of men and women" (*Making*, 334). However, composed simply of two types, "independent dependent" (roughly corresponding to the one formerly called "attacking" or "Anglo Saxon") and "dependent independent" (corresponding to "resisting" or "Jew"), the characterology of the 1911 version is thoroughly "abstracted from the contingencies of race, gender, and sexuality."[87] In this bipartite matrix, gender-based and race-based category names disappear along with the phenotypical attributes associated with certain types—such as "independent dependent" as "blue-eyed" and "dependent independent" as "dark-eyed."[88]

What becomes the center of the text instead is the narrator's act of classifying and describing itself. Or more precisely, as E. L. McCallum compellingly argues, while the text stalls the legible narrative trajectory with the narrator's compulsively repetitive description, "the narrator's emotional reflections serve to manifest and sustain her phenomenological dimension," lending the text an emotional motor force and an orientation for the reader's sense-making process.[89] Upon introducing the two categories, the narrator offers a basic definition, albeit in a characteristically abstruse way. The "dependent independent" are described as "always somehow own[ing] the ones they need to love them" and "loving them give to such of them strength in domination"; the "independent dependent," in contrast, "have it in them to love only those who need them, such of them have it in them to have power in them over others only when these others have begun already a little to love them" (*Making*, 165). Still, what these types exactly signify remains elusive, and much of *The Making of Americans* dramatizes the narrator's struggle to explicate these categories as distinct and complementary types, a struggle that ultimately leads her to an epistemological and emotional crisis. In one striking moment, for instance, the narrator collapses under the weight of her

146   THE SUICIDAL STATE

own project: "Sometimes I am almost despairing. Yes it is very hard, almost impossible I am feeling now in my despairing feeling to have completely a realising of the being in any one, when they are telling it when they are not telling it, it is so very very hard to know it completely in one the being in one" (458).

In their inevitable inadequacy as categories, "independent dependent" and "dependent independent" in the 1911 version constitute what Eve Kosofsky Sedgwick terms a "nonce taxonomy": "the making and unmaking and remaking and redissolution of hundreds of old and new categorical imaginings concerning all the kinds it may take to make up a world."[90] The oddly Steinian cadence of Sedgwick's prose here captures Stein's project of world-making, in which familiar categories of identity—race, sexuality, or gender—no longer become the central markers of beings and instead become replaced with ad hoc categories. Through this typology, as Maria Farland argues, Stein conceives of "the matrix of a potentially infinite taxonomic system of all conceivable types of individuals."[91] Regardless of their biological sex, virtually every being who appears in *The Making of Americans* is assigned one of the fundamental constituents of these two categories.[92] The law of opposite attraction is at work in Steinian typologies and brings the two types together, but in a logic that differs from heterosexual coupling, since "dependent independent/resisting" and "independent dependent/attacking" are themselves free of gender construction: "Mostly for successful living two living together, man and woman or two women or two men, there should be in them two kinds of them, one independent dependent the other dependent independent, one with attacking as the natural way of fighting, the other resisting as the way of being" (228). The combination of "independent dependent" and "dependent independent" that is said to be essential for any successful coupling simply results in the further proliferation of "independent dependent" and "dependent independent" types.

Ultimately, as Melanie Taylor puts it, Stein's matrix of the bottom nature renders "symbolic notions of difference . . . meaningless through a proliferation of increasingly nonsensical categories and types."[93] From the outset, as suggested by their very names, "dependent independent" and "independent dependent" themselves are interdependent categories, representing how "dependent" and "independent" portions exist to varying degrees in every being. Accordingly, despite the narrator's invocational utterance— "sometime oh sometime, really truly sometime there will be a description a complete description of every one"—the narrator's attempt at a complete description of these types becomes inevitably self-defeating, since the combination of degrees of "dependent" and "independent" in one being is literally infinite (*Making*, 549). Even in the category of "independent dependent," which is alternatively called "attacking" beings, there are numerous variants—"sensitive attacking," "trembling attacking," "piercing attacking," "cowardly attacking," "withdrawing attacking," "steady attacking," "enthusiastic attacking," "narrow attacking," "dutiful attacking," "wobbling attacking" among others—while the "dependent independent," or "resisting" being, also has variations like "vacant resisting," "solemn resisting," "intermittent resisting," "confused resisting," and even "attacking resisting" (605–606). To conclude the necessarily incomplete list of variations of the two bottom natures, the narrator guilelessly presents a truism that undercuts the explanatory device with which she intends to differentiate the two categories: "In short there are very many kinds of ways of having loving feeling in men and women" (606). With the multiplication of subtypes, the difference between the two categories becomes exponentially murky, so much so that the concept of difference itself becomes voided. Such murkiness takes, as we will see, a particularly queer ontological shape, one associated with both same-sex desire and the history of immigration: excrement.

Mr. Pottie and the Fantasy of Anal Pregnancy

"It takes time to make queer people," the narrator of *The Making of Americans* wistfully observes; for "machine making does not turn out queer things like us" (*Making*, 21, 47). The prolixity of the text attests to the way Stein does take time—tremendous time—to make queer people out of her idiosyncratic characterology, rejecting procreative marriage as the central machinery to produce Americans out of immigrants. Neither Zangwill's conjugal model nor James's culinary model of the melting pot is encompassing enough; the melting pot that Stein conjured for the American social body is instead the "pot" that she would daily find her Baby Precious—as Stein called the ever-constipated Toklas in her private notes—"sit[t]ing on."[94] As indicated by one of Toklas's pet names for Stein, "Mr. Pottie," Stein metamorphoses into a huge excretory pot for her home country, rescripting an assimilation plot to make it capacious enough to embrace everybody, even those who have been excluded by the procreative narrative.[95]

148   THE SUICIDAL STATE

To read *The Making of Americans* as a text rejoicing in excretory pleasure is not as labored a joke as one would imagine, not least because of the text's preoccupation with eating, to which we will return especially in light of David's Fletcherite self-starvation. In his rumination on Stein's coprophilic aesthetic in her poetry, Christopher Schmidt observes that "Stein was equally interested in both portals of the digestive body—its intake and its output."[96] Similarly, I would argue that Stein's taxonomy of *bottom* nature— with its excretory connotations—reimagines the narrator as the social body with a huge digestive organ, anally giving birth to Americans in its singular characterology, immigrants and native-born alike. If, as Will Stockton argues, "queer bodies are often degenerate and wasteful by definition, differentiated from the reproductive telos of . . . body politics, and produced by the purgative movements of a heteronormative social order," Stein draws on the resources of naturalism to fashion a coprophilic aesthetic to produce Americans.[97]

As Lisa Ruddick's radical and yet attentive reading shows, the dominant mode of pleasure in *The Making of American* is arguably an excretory one. Decentering the time-honored metaphor of literary maternity associated with the narrative act, Ruddick likens the controlling narrational pattern of *The Making of Americans* to defecation, marked by the rhythmic repetition of retention and expulsion: for the narrator, "to tell is to enjoy the feeling of filling up with material and then excreting it."[98] Countless examples can be found in the text to support Ruddick's reading, in which a plethora of sensory data about various beings—both with and without names—enters through the narrator's "ears and eyes and feelings and the talking," filling up the narrator until they are verbally discharged as a "whole one," or an explanation of either of the two abstract character types (*Making*, 300).

In trying to explain the nature of Alfred Hersland as a specimen of "dependent independent," for instance, the narrator begins to be filled up by numerous beings that belong to his group: "I am full up very full up now with a whole large group who are all more or less connected in kind with him, . . . I have then so many men and women in me now who are of his kind in men and women and they are in me now, I am completely full up with them now, completely filled up with them filled up with them as men and women" (507–508). Like Henry James's social body, which tries to ingest immigrants and suffers racial indigestion, the large group of beings whom the narrator greedily swallows creates "a depressing solemn load inside" (321). For the narrator, "the only way to loosen" the grip of the inhabitants inside the body is "to tell it" (313). In a most successful case, it will "come out completely from me leaving me inside me just then gently empty, so pleasantly and weakly gently empty" without the narrator's "straining" and "pressing" it (586). In other cases, the narrator says, it comes out "very slowly," "sharply," "to amuse me," "as a way of doing a duty for me," "brilliantly," "as a way of playing by me," "repeatingly," "willingly," or "not very willingly," but "always then it comes out of me" (327). Sometimes the narrator finds that her ingestion is not quite large enough for the pleasure of expulsion: "I will wait again and soon then I will be full up with him, I am not then not completely full up with him" (513). The "waiting" itself constitutes a pleasure of retention: "All this is in me in waiting and I like very well doing waiting and now perhaps a little more I will be waiting and I like well doing waiting and now perhaps a little more I will be waiting but always I am a little near to beginning and now once more again I am waiting and now I am contenting myself again with waiting and that is a very pleasant feeling a pleasant thing for any one content inside them with it in them" (514).

One Steinian portmanteau in *Tender Buttons* (1914) in particular encapsulates the ethos of this fusion between excretion and creation: to "excreate."[99] Kathryn R. Kent describes "excreation" in these terms: "a condensation of signifiers that makes writing into both excretion and procreation . . . an alternative form of both production and reproduction."[100] It is only natural that *The Making of Americans*, the work that Toklas's daily act of typing enabled Stein to create, exemplifies the logic of "excreation," considering Stein's loving attention to Toklas's daily bowel movement. The collection of love notes exchanged between them, a portion of which were edited by Kay Turner as *Baby Precious Always Shines*, is filled with the enigmatic repetition of the word "cow."[101] Against the dominant understanding of "cow" as Stein's code word for female orgasm (a reading popularized in relation to the poem "As a Wife Has a Cow: A Love Story"), Turner forcibly presents a new interpretation of "cow": "More than a third of notes demonstrate unequivocally that 'cows' are Toklas's feces or stools, as Stein defines them in one example: 'And / what is a stool. That was / the elegant name for a cow.'"[102] Infamously chain-smoking, Toklas seems to have tried every stimulant on top of cigarettes for her bowel movement—coffee, warm baths, enemas, and so on. Stein attempts to invoke Toklas's defecation with her incantatory language: "A cow ahoy, a cow now sweet smelly and complete."[103]

Written after Stein's nightly writing and then hidden in various places for Toklas to find before she would start typing Stein's manuscript in the

150 THE SUICIDAL STATE

morning, Stein's notes present "cow" as a triplex signifier for Toklas's excretory production, her own literary production, as well as their lovemaking:

> Baby precious, the pen seems to
> be writing beautifully and not
> blotting at all, I thought it was
> because it was not full enough,
> I think it blots when it needs filling,
> and my baby needs filling with love
> every second and she is she is
> she is filled up full every
> second, and a cow comes out.[104]

In order for the smooth coming out of literary/fecal production, a pen/body needs to be "full enough." The act of filling up becomes equivalent to the act of making love for Stein, as her love for Toklas becomes the best laxative: "I / am so full of tenderness and delight in / my blessed wifie that it must overflow / in a cow out of she."[105] In Stein's imagination, her love, which fills up Toklas's body, "overflow[s]" in Toklas's fecal production, just as Toklas's love overflows in Stein's literary production. Clearly, Stein regards Toklas's excretion as a product of her act of insemination, that is, breeding prompted by her writing, when she calls her own literary product a "cow": "His cow / will make her cow."[106] For Stein, who apologizes for the burden of typing that her literary prolificacy will cause, "I made so many babies and I am / so sorry I was naughty," literary production is both associated with Toklas's fecal production and imagined as the act of breeding.

With this logic of excreation, which fuses the narrative/digestive/procreative process, the narrator of *The Making of Americans* contains the miscellaneous multitudes and discharges them into a single mass of characterology—giving birth to them as "typical" Americans. In so doing, the text recasts the heteronormative plot associated with the dominant melting pot trope, rejecting what the 1903 version calls "the science of heredity" ("Making," 147). If the procreative logic of heredity prescribes a linear succession of genetic traits that differentiate one family or one race from others, Stein's excretory production radically levels such differences, aiming toward abstracted universality. In its universalizing impulse, I argue, Stein's fecal imagination finds a strange parallelism with Sigmund Freud's theorization of anal pregnancy. There is little doubt that Stein was conversant with Freudian concepts through her brother Leo, who became an avid Freud reader when his sister was working on the final version of *The Making of Americans*.[107] However, my aim here is not to establish Freudian influence on the text, but to attend to the ways in which both Stein and Freud sought to erase racial markers of Jewishness from their work in order to establish a universalizing logic of their respective theories.[108] Harold Bloom's question about Freud's Jewishness—"What is most Jewish about Freud's work?"—might be instructive here. To this question, Bloom answers: "The center of Freud's work, his concept of repression, as I've remarked, does seem to me profoundly Jewish, and in its patterns even normatively Jewish. Freudian memory and Freudian forgetting are a very Jewish memory and a very Jewish forgetting."[109] What I suggest here is that we could almost replace "Freud" with "Stein" in this passage. That is, for both of them, "repression"—or preservation through displacement—of Jewishness becomes the key to a universal theory of human nature, constituting itself as a paradoxically Jewish gesture; and the central site of their "forgetting" is the intimate vacuum of the rectum.

Just as Stein erased the racial markers of Jewishness in her Icarian endeavor to establish a democratic characterology of "every body," Freud sought to "distance psychoanalysis from the label 'Jewish science.'"[110] Freudian psychoanalysis claimed "a universalization of human experience and an active exclusion of the importance of race from its theoretical framework" in the heyday of racial science and its determinist logic.[111] One of the most salient examples of psychoanalysis's universalizing impetus is its paradigm shift of same-sex desire from the theory of "inversion" to that of "homosexuality." While the inversion model—in which male homosexuals were imagined to have a female soul and vice versa—was predicated on a "heterosexual paradigm" of attraction, the homo/hetero binary of Freudian psychoanalysis established a distinction between the desire for sameness and the desire for difference.[112] Same-sex desire and perversion from procreative sex are, Freud repeatedly asserts, "something innate in *everyone*, though as a disposition it may vary in its intensity and may be increased by the influences of actual life."[113] By postulating an autoerotic desire for sameness that *universally* exists, Freud resisted the minoritizing and racializing logic undergirding inversion theory, which often rendered Jewish men hereditarily determined inverts. Thus Freud directly confronted the speciation of racial science by declaring the universalizing logic of psychoanalysis: "Psycho-analytic research is most decidedly opposed to any attempt at

152 THE SUICIDAL STATE

separating off homosexuals from the rest of mankind as a group of a special character."[114]

If Freud's rejection of inversion theory was at least partially rooted in his desire to dissociate Jewishness from degeneracy, so was his theorization of the castration complex and Oedipal model. As Daniel Boyarin and Sander Gilman have argued, Freud's initial conceptualization of the castration complex in *Analysis of a Phobia in a Five-Year-Old Boy* (1909) is haunted by the specter of Jewish effeminacy.[115] The case revolves around a boy with a horse phobia, "Little Hans," who has discovered that there is no penis on his mother's body.[116] At a critical moment, when Freud narrates Hans's horror that his penis might be taken away to make him a "woman"—that is, a penis-less being like his mother—Freud makes a strange interjection:

> I cannot interrupt the discussion so far as to demonstrate the typical character of the unconscious train of thought which I think there is here reason for attributing to little Hans. The castration complex is the deepest unconscious root of antisemitism; for even in the nursery little boys hear that a Jew has something cut off his penis—a piece of his penis, they think—and this gives them a right to despise Jews.[117]

Though Freud does not mention it explicitly, "Little Hans," or Herbert Graf, was also Jewish and had a circumcised penis. As Boyarin speculates, the elision of this racial marker from Little Hans's case was likely motivated by Freud's desire to establish the Oedipal complex as a universal model, rather than the one informed by specifically Jewish experience.[118] Insofar as Freud's castration complex is a fantasy universally held by *all* infants, and insofar as their relinquishment of mother-desire *universally* amounts to their symbolic castration by the father, the circumcised penis of Jewish men no longer stands as an overdetermined racial marker defining their putatively anomalous psychopathology.

Though left unremarked-on by critics, Freud's universalization of Jewish experience in "Little Hans" takes yet another route. If the circumcised penis functions simultaneously as a racial marker (a specifically Jewish phenomenon) and a sexual marker (quasi-femininity, as a sign of castrated phallus), the sexual difference inscribed therein must also be excised. Freud remarks that Little Hans finds a "happier solution" to his castration complex.[119] Instead of submitting himself to symbolic castration and giving up his desire for the mother, he envisions himself giving birth to a child, identifying with his mother by delivering an imaginary baby, a "lumf"—that is, feces. The orifice for Hans's imaginary child is, as he calls it, a "behind-hole."[120]

Hans's fantasy constitutes an early example of Freud's theorization of the infantile fantasy of anal pregnancy, which he calls a "cloacal theory."[121] Especially important for the development of cloacal theory is the chapter "Anal Erotism and the Castration Complex" in *The History of an Infantile Neurosis* (1914). Freud ascribes the chronic intestinal troubles that his patient has suffered from his youth—diarrhea, constipation, intestinal pain, and fear of having blood in his feces—to a notion the patient unconsciously has held onto: "the notion, namely, that sexual intercourse takes place at the anus."[122] As in Hans's case, the patient's castration fear was activated by the discovery of his mother's vagina (i.e., a castratory wound used in coitus), but it was also fueled by "the ritual circumcision of Christ and of the Jews in general."[123] The patient's solution to this fear also resembles Hans's: "He rejected castration, and held to his theory of intercourse by the anus."[124] By clinging to the fantasy that the anus is the only orifice in human bodies, the patient disavows the existence of the vagina as a source of castration fear; the anus, in his imaginary, is thus transformed into a universal hole that functions triply for excretion, coitus, and parturition regardless of sex, even though, as a result, he assumes the pain of childbirth in his intestinal pain as well.[125] If the castration complex emerges, at least partially, from seeing a Jew's circumcised penis, the anus, in the cloacal fantasy, functions as a site for rejecting the complex itself, since it expels racial and sexual difference. Thus, as Guy Hocquenghem puts it, the anus creates "a loss of identity": "Seen from behind we are all women; the anus does not practice sexual discrimination," nor does it practice antisemitism.[126]

I have been arguing that Freud's attempt to excise Jewishness from psychoanalysis's universalizing project ultimately leads him to theorize the anus as a phantasmal black hole that absorbs racial and sexual difference. Stein's anal propagation through the characterological matrix in *The Making of Americans* functions in a similar way. To put it in a Freudian register, being Jewish and a woman, Stein is discursively formulated as a doubly castrated subject, whose status is deployed to establish a phallic identity that is synonymous with the status of being a legitimate "American." Such a stable identity is given only to those who participate in the stabilization of racial and sexual identity through biological reproduction, be they native-born or immigrant. Dislodged from the procreative narrative even more forcibly than Little Hans, Stein rejects castration and

154 THE SUICIDAL STATE

the phallic logic of castration itself, instead holding onto the cloacal theory with a vengeance.

For Stein, the anus becomes a fecund organ with the triple function of coitus, excretion, and parturition, through which she produces Americans with Toklas as she types the manuscript of *The Making of Americans*. In the narrator's imaginary body, human material and its concomitant diverse identitarian markers are devoured, digested, and merged into universal oneness, and excretorily spawned into the abstract characterology. Ostensibly deploring this approaching implosion of her typological endeavor, the narrator finds solace in the undifferentiated oneness that she has inadvertently created: "It is a very wonderful thing," after all, "to be all loving and certain that they are really all loving," despite the surface difference in the way they love (605). The narrator suddenly realizes that to be filled with beings in the construction of a universal typology itself constitutes an act of love: "Loving being, I am filled just now quite full of loving being in myself and in a number of men and women. Loving is to me just now an interesting, a delightful a quite completely realised thing. I have loving being in me more than I knew I could have in me. It was a surprising thing to find it so completely in me" (604). In the intimate void that is the anus, the phallic logic of difference between the circumcised and the intact penis (as a racial marker) and the existent and the absent penis (as a sexual marker) is nullified: every one lovingly becomes one, discharged as a single mass of magnificent cow.

Populational Imagination of "Each One Is One"

Stein's paean to universal oneness reaches its climax in the final chapter, titled "David Hersland." This chapter revolves around the life of the youngest child of the Herslands, who inherits the name David both from his father and grandfather. The three-generation history of the Herslands closes with the young David Hersland, who "was a dead one before he was a middle aged one" (*Making*, 725). From his youth, he is "interested in dying, in loving, in talking, in listening, in ways of eating, in ways of being going on being in living," and ultimately ends his life by "going on eating almost only one thing" (899). By this self-chosen slow death, he terminates the successive line of the name "David Hersland," for "David Hersland was never really wanting to be needing to have much feeling about having babies in being one being living. He did not have any of them" (792). By concluding the history of the

GERTRUDE STEIN'S MELTING POT   155

family with the death of the name-bearer of the Herslands, *The Making of Americans* seems to insist on "putting an end not only to history but to the ideology of family as the basis for all that is good, human, and American."[127]

At the same time, however, the "David Hersland" chapter marks the much-longed-for completion of the excretory making of Americans. Though titled "David Hersland," the final chapter is not about David Hersland, either as an individual character or as a specimen of a certain type. Unlike the preceding chapters, which, albeit nominally, describe the focal characters' life events in order to place them into the characterological system, even the now-familiar terms "independent dependent/attacking" and "dependent independent/resisting" cease to appear in the "David Hersland" chapter, along with the personal pronoun "I," which has so far represented the narrator. As Tanya Clement argues in her pathbreaking distant reading of *The Making of Americans*, the use of the narrator's first-person pronoun "declines precipitously in the middle of the text" and virtually disappears in the "David Hersland" chapter.[128] The staged presence of the narrator grappling with her typological endeavor, which has so far lent the novel an affective scaffolding, is now exponentially replaced by "one" as "a new primary character": "*One* encompasses all the characters in the text, proving Stein's supposition that everyone is *one*."[129]

Even more than what her sophisticated use of algorithmic methods affords us, Clement's distant reading *feels* right. That is, with its ample usage of charts and graphs, Clement's reading seems to break open the hermeneutic stalemate of *The Making of American* scholarship's "unreadability" debate, partly because its treatment of the text as a set of linguistic data simulates the text's affect, especially the one toward the end: namely, its impersonal, statistical conceptualization of the human aggregate. In this demographic imaginary, "one" becomes 1) a generic pronoun (as in "One can only hope"), 2) a state of collective unification ("The two became one that night"), as well as 3) a numerical designation ("He is just one of them"). While the first two valences of oneness embody the abstract universalism that I have been discussing in relation to Freud and Stein, an additional third valence in the "David Hersland" chapter points to the text's operational shift. That is, with this numerical connotation, "one" becomes a signifier of a new awareness of human fungibility, and, in so doing, it initiates the text's final turn to modernist aesthetics.

If the middle part of *The Making of the Americans* represents the biopolitical management of the population with its naturalist compulsion to

156   THE SUICIDAL STATE

describe, classify, and totalize, the "David Hersland" chapter and the ensuing epilogue titled "History of a Family's Progress" are doing something else, both in terms of their aesthetic mode and their emulation of statecraft. Even though the final part also performs a modality of the biopolitics of population, it is no longer about its taxonomizing impulse. Rather, it represents what we can call biopolitics's computational imaginary, in which subjects become arbitrary samples for its management. Along with "one," what populates the chapter is the generic, indefinite, and impersonal plural pronoun, "some." A typical passage reads:

> Some are certain that each one could be one being certain of something. Some are certain that some could be ones being certain of something, some are not at all certain about any one being certain of anything, some are quite certain about every one being certain about one thing, some are quite certain that every one is certain about the same thing, some are not at all certain about every one being certain about the same thing. (742)

What the text presents here is various permutations of beliefs about knowability. The first part of the quotation, for instance, can be paraphrased like this: some people believe that "*everyone* knows about something for certain," some others believe that "*some people* know about something for certain," and yet other people believe that "*nobody* knows about anything for certain." Subjects denoted by "some" in this passage become fully fungible with any set of subjects, being a mere permutation of every other set.

This evaporation of personhood into replaceable elements becomes a hallmark of political discourse in the panic over race suicide—the much-discussed "extinction of the older native stock and its replacement with the newer immigrant stocks."[130] At the same time, it also becomes a central feature of modernist literary aesthetics and of Stein's prose in particular: its circularity and self-referentiality, in which, as Natalia Cecire puts it, "phrases like 'rose is a rose is a rose is a rose' represent a recognizable Steinian *style* that was both utterly distinctive and endlessly imitable and imitated."[131] This Steinian style, as Cecire further argues, has been treated by a tradition of reading—or rather, dismissive "not reading"—of Stein's oeuvre as "a consistent quality that can be sampled arbitrarily (any given chunk of it will do to make the point)."[132] Yet the very samplability of Stein's prose—epitomized in the passage above—points to its synecdochical alertness to human fungibility, a feeling of modernity that was to grow ever more acute with the coming two great Wars.

This fungibility of generic, numeric oneness is realized in the figure of David Hersland. David Hersland "was completely certain that being existing is not anything," since existing as an individuated being in the world signifies nothing of particular importance in Stein's rhapsody of universal oneness (810). David Hersland fully realizes the Steinian maxim: "Each one is one. David Hersland was completely remembering that each one is one, he was completely remembering this thing that each one is one. He was then loving one of them and he was then completely remembering that each one is one" (872). For David Hersland, the felt exceptionality that usually differentiates the object of love from others dissolves into the universalization of "each one is one." "Loving one of them" becomes no different from loving others, and the loved one loses its privileged uniqueness.

This axiom applies to himself: "He was one. He was very often not telling anything about that thing about being one. He was not ever telling any one he was almost needing telling about his being one. He was one" (868). The supposed "singularity" of his selfhood—the heroic quality that makes one "*the* one*," a quality Stein had associated most closely with David—is voided as he is abstracted into a generalized "one." Paradoxically, even as his singularity makes him an Emersonian representative man, its synecdochical typicality evacuates his particular being: "Some love themselves so much immortality can have no meaning for them, the younger David Hersland was such a one" (505). The sentence sounds counterintuitive at first, for, as the narrator notes a little earlier, when people love themselves they typically do "not want to lose themselves," and "immortality can to them mean nothing but this thing"; that is, self-love usually leads to the desire for self-preservation (480). Yet because David Hersland believes in the universal oneness in himself that represents everyone else in the world, the preservation of his own life has no particular significance; even if he dies, the "one" that is himself will continue to exist in "each one."

This paradoxical self-love ultimately leads him to disintegrate himself into the abstract mass of the population. He loves himself because he is "connected with every other one," and "it was a pleasant thing to him to know then that everything means something, that he was a part of every one who was a part of him" (862). David de-individuates himself in such a way that he becomes not an individual but an indistinguishable part of the

158   THE SUICIDAL STATE

population: he is a part of every one and everyone is part of him. Becoming one with the population, he is merely a numeric "one" in the many, with no specificity in his own eyes or those of the state. David's self-disintegration thus signifies his total integration into the population, in which his individual body becomes one with the social body. Such oneness with every one through self-disintegration constitutes "a pleasant thing" for him. If the pleasant, as Samuel Delany theorizes, is a "pleasure in its most generalized form (though pleasure no less important or social for that)," David's effacement of the self into the population emanates with the ambient erotics of biopolitical sociality.[133]

Ultimately, it is through his abdication of life that David Hersland comes to personify the populational "oneness" produced by Stein's melting-pot imagination. As death finally effaces the last vestiges of his individuality, David becomes one with the American race that is said to kill itself. In bringing his own line to an end, he enacts a vision of the race that is defined not through biological reproduction and heredity but through a suicidal desire that aims to abrogate selfhood. His way of dying—"not eating anything but one thing"—epitomizes the population's disembodied oneness produced by Stein's excretory melting pot. If the anus nullifies racial and sexual difference by negating the logic of castration, its product still retains a trace of bodiliness with its stench. David Hersland's olfactory sensitivity detects his own effluvium, which reminds him that he still has an individual body: "David Hersland was sometimes smelling something, he was sometimes interested in smelling something, he was sometimes smelling himself when he was smelling something, he was not completely interested in smelling himself when he was smelling something" (850). In order for him to attain a completely universal existence, the odor that reminds him of his fleshly being must be extinguished. Thus, recalling the Fletcherite purification of the feces reminiscent of his models Leon Solomons and Leo Stein, he eats minimally in order to excrete minimally, approximating the rarified being that ubiquitously exists in every one. So "he came to be a dead one," dying a slow death of starvation that eludes the dramatic demise that marks the singularities of Hyacinth Robinson, Edna Pontellier, and Martin Eden (903). David's death is no longer a special narrative event, but just another episode: as the epilogue recapitulates it, "any one has come to be a dead one," while "family living can go on existing" without them (907).

Such disembodiedness is, Stein says through the mouth of the Alice Toklas in her fictional autobiography, quintessentially American:

GERTRUDE STEIN'S MELTING POT 159

> She always says that americans can understand spaniards. That they are the only two western nations that can realise abstraction. That in americans it expresses itself by disembodiedness, in literature and machinery, in Spain by ritual so abstract that it does not connect itself with anything but ritual.... Americans, so Gertrude Stein says, are like spaniards, they are abstract and cruel. They are not brutal they are cruel.[134]

The cruelty of American disembodied abstractionism that Stein speaks of here might be that of American optimism—particularly the optimism that is, as Lauren Berlant argues, debilitating in its impossible achievement and yet simultaneously indispensable in sustaining otherwise unlivable lives.[135] While sidestepping the heteropatriarchal logic of racial and national reproduction, *The Making of Americans'* excretory production of disembodied Americans also captures the double bind of hope that entrapped those who yearned to belong to this nation. Many immigrants believed that once the abject stench—of their poverty, of their food, of their eccentric mannerisms, of their laughter, of their accent—wore off, they could become one with that disembodied social body. If they worked hard enough, if they waited long enough, someday it would happen, perhaps finally in three generations.

The warm glow of cruel optimism emanating from the Mother of Exiles' torch guided new immigrants with the promise of "world-wide welcome," only to burn them like moths.[136] In the same year that part of *The Making of Americans* first appeared in the *Transatlantic Review*, the Immigration Act of 1924 marked the end of open immigration from Europe.[137] Following the 1917 Act, which limited the entry of immigrants by making literacy a prerequisite for immigration, the 1924 Act introduced the national quota system, setting an annual ceiling on immigrants from each country and admitting up to two percent of each group already present in 1890. The use of the 1890 census—conducted before the start of large-scale immigration from southern and eastern Europe—was initially proposed by Madison Grant's Sub-Committee on Selective Immigration of the Eugenic Committee. Lady Liberty's hollowness, then, could very well be the American social body's ego ideal, gorging itself on aliens and purging clean their abject mass altogether. And yet, somehow, the wretched refuse cannot help but expect her embrace, particularly when we see her smiling sweetly in her homeostasis with those blank eyes that would never return our gaze.

The race suicide panic was thus contained by closing the insatiable mouth of the social body, which was now disciplined to eat only one thing in order

160 THE SUICIDAL STATE

to maintain its ethereal whiteness. But a century later, the cry of "you will not replace us, Jews will not replace us" echoed once again at the Unite the Right Rally held in Charlottesville in 2017. The ghost of the race that kills itself has now metamorphosed into the so-called Great Replacement, once again bemoaning the coming of white extinction. Renaud Camus, the father of modern-day replacement theory, philosophizes: "*Replacing* is the central gesture of contemporary societies. For better or worse, everything is being replaced by something else."[138] The omnipresent work of replacement marks modernity itself, as "stone masonry is being replaced by ferroconcrete, concrete by plaster, marble by chip aggregate, timber by PVC" and "natives by non-natives, Europeans by Africans, White Anglo-Saxons by Afro-Americans and Latinos."[139]

Replacement theory has continued to summon the existential terror of biopolitical fungibility, actuating it and propagating it in the form of white supremacist terrorism.[140] It mobilized the shooter who stormed into the Tree of Life synagogue with an AR-15, killing eleven congregants in Pittsburgh in 2018. What Henry James once called "the Hebrew conquest of New York" was transfigured into a "Hispanic invasion of Texas" in 2019, when twenty-three shoppers, most of them Latinx, were shot to death at a Walmart in El Paso. The shooter left behind a four-page manifesto rehashing replacement theory, emulating the one written earlier the same year in advance of the mosque shooting in Christchurch, New Zealand, which left fifty-one people dead. Three years later, another believer in the Great Replacement, this time with a hundred-and-eighty-page manifesto, murdered ten Black shoppers at a Tops Friendly Markets in Buffalo, New York. When the much-touted singularity of whiteness is threatened by its awareness of fungible oneness, mass murder melds racial differences of any color—be it Jews, Arabs, Latinx, or Blacks—in the abstracting cauldron of the population, leaving numbers as the only metric to talk about the incommensurable loss. And then, as *The Making of Americans* prophesized, "any one has come to be a dead one," while the white social body keeps living on, threatening again and again to kill itself (907).

Coda

Hindsight 20/20, or Asiatic Im-Personality

Thrown into the temporal middle of nowhere, Frank Kermode says, we hanker after the sense of an ending. Jittery anticipations of the capitalized End allow us to make sense of our lives in the nebula of the present. The imaginary end, then, forges our relation to the unknown beginning that has fatally preceded us, restoring the illusory order of things in which "the end is in harmony with the beginning, the middle with beginning and end."[1] But every apocalypse is a broken apocalypse: "The great crises and ends of human life do not stop time."[2] Having awkwardly survived the much-trumpeted Age of Crisis, most of us are suspended once again in the unmeaning banality of here and now. In the disjointed aftermath of circumvented calamities, apocalyptic feeling perpetuates itself, carried on by weary survivors.

The fear of race suicide was a manifestation of such apocalyptic feeling suffusing the fin de siècle, whose cultural identity, as its name suggests, hinged on the sense of an ending. The collective hysteria of the passing of the master race in effect forged its unknown beginning, creating the mythic origins of "the race." The dying race was vivified precisely through the manufactured crisis and reinstated the system of dominance, be it New England Anglo-Saxonism, Jim Crow, or Teutonism. While the suicidality of the race was touted as a sign of its indomitable will and agency, some dreamed of an escape from the very logic of such liberal subjectivity, trying to fulfill their desire for the end. Progressive literature imagined suicidal characters attempting to evade the biopolitical control that sutures individual bodies into the social body's self-preservation, in whose name too many lives were, and still are, trampled. Yet the apocalyptic scenario of race suicide, as with most narratives of calamity, did not materialize. The furor over the suicidal race calmed to a whisper with the success of immigration restrictions toward the end of the 1920s. The American social body, then, survived its crisis by absorbing the remainder of what it had once refused as foreign bodies, appropriating the new immigrant's fertility in order to regenerate itself in a

The Suicidal State. Madoka Kishi, Oxford University Press. © Oxford University Press 2024.
DOI: 10.1093/9780197690109.003.0006

162   THE SUICIDAL STATE

new shroud of whiteness. The deaths of suicidal Progressives neither stopped time nor undid the all-devouring racial purity agenda of the American social body. No race has ever yet committed suicide.

Since the anticlimactic closure of the race suicide panic, we have survived another fin de siècle, which coincided with the end of a millennium no less. There have been periodic proclamations of global crises ever since, in which the flickering signs of the End beckons biopolitical hands to securitize the population according to its calculus of life. The COVID-19 pandemic was one of the most recent of such biopolitical crises. Seeing the masked faces in a small city in the US South brought me a strangely melancholic feeling, as the sight reminded me of the Japanese winter, when everyone wears a mask to avoid the flu, allergies, brisk air, or yet another task of affective labor. Then one day I saw a picture on the internet of a person holding a sign that read "I am not a virus." There was something mesmerizing about the declaration; it slowly enabled me to reconnect with a project I had abandoned, along with my former life as an aspiring full-time academic and everything else I had left in Japan, evoking the *ur*-scene of the discourse of race suicide, which so far, strangely, I had sidestepped. So here is a little coda, a retrospective, a hindsight brought to me in 2020: one more time with feeling, even if that affective demand is just another biopolitical imperative.[3]

* * *

In the wake of the intensifying anti-Asian racism in France that followed the COVID-19 lockdown in Wuhan, China, a hashtag, #JeNeSuisPasUnVirus, started on Twitter on January 28, 2020.[4] This hashtag was rapidly shared worldwide, translated into a multitude of languages—#NoSoyUnVirus, #Nonsonounvirus, #ichbinkeinVirus, #IAmNotAVirus, #我不是病毒, #私はウイルスじゃない, among many others.[5] The rapidity and multilinguality of the hashtag's spread unexpectedly brought into relief the otherwise-inconspicuous omnipresence of Asian immigrants in the West, showcasing the affinities between Asians and the virus in the Western imaginary: an invisible, swarming horde that furtively proliferates in the host (social) body.

Symptomatically enacting the Asian virality that it constatively disavows, "I am not a virus" exposes an ontological instability that has haunted Asianness by inviting a question: "What *are* you, then?" Since the mid-nineteenth century, Colleen Lye argues, Asians have signified for the West a "kind of difference that is marked by the lack of difference between individuals."[6]

CODA   163

Lye calls this amorphous irrepresentability of Asians—imagined always as an unindividuated, faceless, teeming mass—"Asiatic racial form."[7] Perhaps, then, one aspect of the phrase "I am not a virus" that makes it particularly striking is the contrast between the singular subjectivity asserted by "I am" and the unindividuated collectivity often associated with Asians. In this respect, the phrase's very object of disidentification—an uncountable mass noun, "virus"—lends a much more convincing figuration of Asianness than the individuated subjecthood of an "I."

The notion of a virus, in fact, historically served as one figuration of Asiatic racial form, deployed for the purpose of immigration restriction in the United States. As the historian Nayan Shah documents, starting in the late nineteenth century, Chinese exclusion was promoted in part under the rubric of public health. Amidst heightened anti-Chinese sentiment in 1870s California, for instance, the spread of syphilis was attributed almost exclusively to Chinese prostitutes, resulting in the enactment of the first federal immigration ban, the Page Act of 1875. As one of its first symptoms, the appearance of "copper-colored blotches," was associated with Asiatic complexion, syphilis was believed to be a "generic condition of the Chinese race."[8] One leading medical professional testifies that "nine-tenths" of syphilis cases he saw in white boys came from Chinese prostitutes, who they describe "do not care how old the boys are, whether five years old or more, as long as they have money."[9] As Shah further details, leprosy (Hansen's disease) similarly became heavily associated with Asianness when a case was discovered in a Chinese migrant laborer in 1871. It was often conceived as a hereditary disease, endemic to the Chinese people (dubbed "Asiatic leprosy") and transmittable to whites through intimate physical contract.[10] Because of the intense process of bodily disintegration that was believed to transfigure those infected until they became unrecognizable, the spread of leprosy emblematized, for nativists, "the fate of American society after years of intimate contact and miscegenation with the Chinese."[11]

Crucially, Edward Alsworth Ross's conceptualization of race suicide was also catalyzed by the ominous spread of Asiatic racial form, or what he calls a "heavy influx of a prolific race from the Orient."[12] Prior to its printed debut in Ross's "The Causes of Race Superiority" (1901), the term "race suicide" made its first passing appearance in a speech that he gave at a mass meeting in the San Francisco Metropolitan Hall on May 7, 1900. With the impending expiration of the 1892 Geary Act—which had extended the Chinese Exclusion Act of 1882 for ten years—the San Francisco audience demanded the Act's

164   THE SUICIDAL STATE

indefinite extension as well as the addition of a provision totally excluding Japanese immigration.[13] In his impassioned speech, Ross decried immigration from China, India, and Japan as the "invasion of cheap labor from the teeming Orient" into California, the "latest and loveliest seat of the Aryan race."[14] The text of Ross's speech almost exactly prefigures the argument of his 1901 article, which I have discussed in the Introduction. While Asiatics copiously reproduce even under precarious conditions, he claims, white Americans refrain from procreation as they become wary of the severe financial outlook. Ross ventures: "To let this go on, to let the American be driven by coolie competition, to check the American birth-rate in order that the Japanese birth-rate shall not be checked, to let an opportunity for one American boy be occupied by three Orientals so that the American will not add that boy to his family, is to reverse the current of progress, to commit race suicide."[15]

Ross's rhetoric—which finds a distinct echo in replacement theory's cry in the twenty-first century, "You will not replace us"—encapsulated the views of many at the meeting. As one participant put it, Asian immigrants' subservient laboriousness lent the silent replacement of whites a particularly sinister cast: "The Japanese . . . are only automatons, mere machines, in which their physical endurance and mode of living cheaply weighed heavily against the American workingman and his better social condition."[16] Asian immigrants at the turn of the century—the Japanese in particular here— extend the historically earlier figuration of the Chinese "coolie" that Eric Hayot has theorized.[17] Submissive, efficient, seemingly impervious to minor pain, and thus optimized for menial labor, the figure of the "coolie" was the nightmare of modernity: while it stood for everything that the liberal subject should *not* be, the "coolie" body was tailor-made for the coming age of standardization, automation, and mass production. Asian immigrants' supposed fecundity underwrote this foreboding coming of modernity in biopolitical terms. Like the virus replicating itself, Asians were thought to re-produce undifferentiated sameness in the mode of mass production, laying bare the fungible logic of biological *re*production. In other words, the figure of the over-fertile Asiatic, which underscored the very replaceability of humans in the populational calculus, was a model for the biopolitics of population.

If Asians at the turn of the century figured the menacing fungibility of the biopolitical subject, how is such fungibility different from the one that has, as scholars of Afro-pessimism argue, marked Blackness? Drawing on Saidiya Hartman, Hortense Spillers, and Orlando Patterson, among others,

CODA   165

Frank Wilderson III argues that the contours of Blackness are defined by slavery: the ontological foundation of Blackness is "accumulation and fungibility," which are derived from the slave's "condition of being owned and traded."[18] Conceived as an interchangeable and replaceable commodity, Blackness is a figuration of the "anti-Human, a position against which Humanity establishes, maintains, and renews its coherence."[19] The Human, conversely, is a mode of being constituted by anti-Black violence, the brutal force that constantly demarcates what is not the Human. Inasmuch as the Human is defined as non-Blackness (rather than whiteness), Asians in the West, too, are part of this "race of Humanism," along with Whites, Arabs, and Latinx.[20] Non-Black racialized subjects, Wilderson says, are the "junior partners of civil society": "Latinos and Asians stand in *conflictual relation* to the Settler/Master, that is, to the hemisphere and the United States writ large.... They do not register as antagonists."[21]

Indeed, the fungibility of Blackness, in its consignment to fleshy commodity, is fundamentally different from that of the Asiatic. Even as the "importation" of Chinese indentured laborers was devised to compensate for the labor shortage expected after the end of the slave trade in Britain, even as most "coolies" were taken by deception and carried in the vessels often known as "floating hells" with exceptionally high mortality rates, and even as the conditions of their labor were so atrocious as to be deployed to justify slavery's benevolence, the coolies were no chattel to be owned or disposed of.[22] They were not the "anti-Human," the brutal subjugation of which functioned as a ritual to establish the free, self-possessed, property-owning, and self-governing human being.

Still, in a process of racialization different and yet inseparable from that of Blackness, the Asiatic was also relegated to the ontological background against which modern subjecthood was established. While Blackness is reduced to the flesh—whereby life itself is denuded of symbolics and marked by an excess of "animatedness"—the Asiatic is defined by its low positioning within what Mel Y. Chen calls the "animacy hierarchy."[23] As its prototypical figuration as an automaton exemplifies, the Asiatic is imagined as devoid of agency, volition, emotion, character, or sentience—all those things that constitute what is called "personality."[24] Or perhaps it is more accurate to say that the Asiatic stands at the periphery of what is called a "person": an elusive category that seems to point toward, to use Clifford Geertz's expansive description of personhood, "a bounded, unique, more or less integrated motivational and cognitive universe, a dynamic center of awareness, emotion,

166   THE SUICIDAL STATE

judgment and action, organized into a distinctive whole and set contrastively against other such wholes and against a social and natural background."[25]

Hovering in proximity to the human being (as a species being) and the citizen (as a rights-bearing human subject belonging to a state), the "person" became an especially contested category of being in the Progressive Era.[26] With a new concept of artificial personhood established in *Santa Clara County v. Southern Pacific Railroad* (1886)—the case that famously extended the Fourteenth Amendment's Equal Protection Clause to corporations—the ever-shifting category of personhood became even murkier.[27] In effectively declaring that the categories of the person and of the human were not coextensive, this case demarcated a new category of non-human being—corporate personhood—worthy of personhood's imprimatur. Simultaneously, there existed a category of beings—namely, Asiatics—who seemingly were human and yet lacking in certain qualities that would have made them fit for liberal society, most notably the capacity for self-determination and self-government. In other words, whereas the negation of Blackness has defined the Human, what was established through the negation of the Asiatic was the Person. Where Blackness stands for the "anti-Human," the Asiatic represents the anti-Person.

Or rather, it could more precisely be termed the "im-person," inasmuch as Asians have perpetually been marked as impersonal: inscrutable, self-effacing, and polite to the extent of impassivity.[28] Such Asiatic im-personality simultaneously threatened and fascinated turn-of-the-century America and Europe. While the Yellow Peril represented the Asiatic as a swarming horde of automatons, Japonism and the revival of chinoiserie conflated the Asiatic with the region's commodities, fetishizing particularly Asian women in the mode of what Anne Anlin Cheng calls "ornamental personhood": "a peculiar state of being produced out of the fusion between 'thingliness' and 'personness.' "[29] Asiatic im-personality simultaneously lures and repels the West, in part because—to use Sharon Cameron's evocative phrase—"we don't know what the *im* of impersonality means."[30] Rather than a simple negation of the person or personality, im-personality might permeate, penetrate, or dislocate the boundary of autonomous personhood.

At least, that is one reason why impersonality per se (if not its Asiatic permutation) became a privileged site of modernist aesthetics. Since Maud Ellman's classic study, *The Poetics of Impersonality*, many scholars have underscored the centrality of the doctrine of impersonality to modernism, most prominently theorized in T. S. Eliot's 1919 essay "Tradition and the

CODA 167

Individual Talent." In Heather Arvidson's gloss, impersonality has become "shorthand for the fragmented forms, intellectual detachment, and imperious command of abstraction and allusion conventionally associated with modernism."[31] Yet to a surprising degree—perhaps because it feels too obvious—the Asiatic's relation to the poetics of impersonality has been left largely unexamined. Even as scholars have written in depth about modernist Orientalism—Pound's fascination with China, his translational practice, haiku-inspired imagism, and his collaboration with Yeats on Noh plays—the Asiatic im-persons themselves remain, to use Josephine Nock-Hee Park's memorable phrase, apparitional.[32] What could Eliot's implicit point of reference have been, for instance, when he wrote, "Poetry is not a turning loose of emotion, but an escape from emotion; it is not the expression of personality, but an escape from personality. *But of course, only those who have personality and emotions know what it means to want to escape from these things*"— who are these beings without personality or emotions to begin with, against whom the modernist poet's universal impersonality was constructed?[33]

Unlike Eliot, though, there were some modernists who were fascinated with Asiatic im-persons. Percival Lowell—a brother of the imagist poet Amy Lowell—wrote a whole book to explain the enigma of "the peculiar atmosphere of impersonality that pervades" Japan, as well as Korea and China.[34] Like many other members of the elite New England Anglo-Saxons dubbed "Boston Brahmins" (whose self-designation, devised by Oliver Wendell Holmes, was already saturated with Orientalism), Lowell was obsessed with Asia. He lived in Japan for almost a decade after serving in 1883 as a foreign secretary in Korea and went on to write four books on "the Far Orientals."[35] Lowell's *The Soul of the Far East* was published in 1888, when Japan was yet to be paired with China as the other wing of the Yellow Peril's double menace, a threat that emerged with its rise as an imperial power.[36] Enchantedly lost in a country that he perceives as "one huge, comical antithesis" of his homeland, Lowell realizes that what lies at the bottom of this difference is the degree of individuality:

> The sense of self grows more intense as we follow in the wake of the setting sun, and fades steadily as we advance into the dawn. America, Europe, the Levant, India, Japan, each is less personal than the one before. We stand at the nearer end of the scale, the Far Orientals at the other. If with us the I seems to be of the very essence of the soul, then the soul of the Far East may be said to be impersonality.[37]

168 THE SUICIDAL STATE

Self-consciousness's painful awakening, it seems, has not yet touched the Japanese, leaving them quite innocent and unindividuated from each other. This, Lowell claims, explains everything about Japan and its people—their enthusiastic spirit of imitation, which compensates for their lack of originality; their language, which is strangely devoid of personal pronouns, gender distinctions, or plural nouns; their blind obedience to the imperative of the patriarchal family system; their marriage, which knows no love and stands in stark contrast with their almost erotic passion for nature; and, of course, their religion, which seeks the blissful nothingness of Nirvana. All these things connote the Japanese's indifference to difference, his readiness to be immersed into entities larger than himself. In short, the Japanese sees himself merely as "a fraction of the universe—one might almost say as a vulgar fraction of it, considering the low regard in which he is held."[38]

For Lowell, such absence of ego could at times be quite agreeable, to be sure. The Far Orientals (Lowell's favorite designation for East Asians) are artistic because their impersonality makes them susceptible to nature's calling, alive to the sentience of the natural world. Their politeness, "one of the most marked results of impersonality," comes from their tenuous sense of self and its concomitant attentiveness to others.[39] But at bottom, there is something uncanny about Asiatic impersonality. Their lack of self-consciousness reminds Lowell of both the state of infancy and that of senility—because, after all, the Orient is ancient, though it appears beguilingly innocent—leading him to wonder if "personality is but its passing phase from a vast impersonal on the one hand to an equally vast impersonal on the other."[40] Lowell mutters to himself: "Can it be that the personal, progressive West is wrong, and the impersonal, impassive East right? Surely not."[41] Even as he immediately denies it, this self-doubt continues to resurface: "If the ego be but the passing shadow of the material brain, at the disintegration of the gray matter what will become of us? Shall we simply lapse into an indistinguishable part of the vast universe that compasses us round?"[42] In short, Asiatic impersonality, with its disintegration of individuality and personhood, smells like death. Ultimately, as Lowell realizes, the Asiatic lack of personality connotes their nearly defunct "instinct of self-preservation," in which death ceases to register as a threat to "the continuance of the ego."[43]

Marked by their indifference to self-preservation (or even selfhood itself), Lowell's impersonal Asiatics begin to appear as a mirror image of the race that kills itself. What he witnesses is the impending, inevitable disappearance of the Asiatic: "No weak spot in their social organization destroyed them

CODA 169

from within; no epidemic, in the shape of foreign hordes, fell upon them from without."[44] Rather, solely because of their indifference to selfhood and survival, "vanish they will off the face of the earth and leave our planet. . . . Their Nirvana is already being realized." [45] If Lowell's premature mourning of the passing of the Asiatic strangely echoes Ross's elegy for the old-stock American—"There is no bloodshed, no violence, no assaults of the race that waxes upon the race that wanes. The higher race quietly and unmurmuringly eliminates itself"—such resonance is probably not a coincidence.[46] For one thing, Ross himself was once quite intrigued by the idea of Nirvana's promise of equilibrium. Published ten years prior to his coinage of race suicide, Ross's "Turning towards Nirvana" (1891) is an observation (rather an unexpected one from a then-political economist) on the prevalence of pessimism in fin-de-siècle European literature and philosophy. As its title suggests, Ross attributes Europe's culture of despair to its fascination with "a black pessimism [in] Hindoo thought . . . allied to that strange exotic cult of Eastern religions that has enabled Neo-Buddhism."[47]

But European intellectuals' infatuation with such nihilistic Eastern thought, Ross argues, has its roots in their disenchantment with "personality" itself. The idea of personality—defined here as continuous consciousness with a faculty of rational decision making—is besieged on many fronts; the burgeoning fields of hereditary science and neuroscience in particular have "dissolve[d] the personality into temperaments and susceptibilities, predispositions, and transmitted taints, atavisms, and reversions," revealing that "choice is the greatest of illusions."[48] If "science finds no ego, self, or will that can maintain itself against the past," no wonder those intellectuals find solace in the sublime nonexistence of the self in Oriental thoughts. So Ross argues, showing off his rather surprising familiarity with the Hindu and Buddhist lexicon: "Sansara, the unabiding pain-world; Nirvana world of rest and reabsorption; the deceptive veil of Maya, the wheel of life, the melting bubbles poured from the bowl of Saki, the Brahma fallen from unity and serenity into multiplicity and pain, the illusion of birth and death, the evil of all individual existence, the retreat from life, the euthanasia of the will and the return to non-existence."[49]

Asiatic impersonality—their indifference to individuation, selfhood, and ultimately, the continuation of life itself—thus seems to lie at the core of race suicide's imaginary in at least in two senses. On the one hand, the nightmare of Asian immigrants' automated reproduction was seen as an immediate threat to old-stock Americans, whose preoccupation with individuality and

170   THE SUICIDAL STATE

its quality of life, according to Ross, had caused the decrease in their fertility rate. On the other hand, the Oriental detachment from life was imagined as an alternative way of being outside the confines of "personality," as the concept came increasingly under the attack of science. Suicide itself emerges as an act realizing such Asiatic impersonality: "the retreat from life, the euthanasia of the will and the return to non-existence." In other words, Asiatic impersonality is simultaneously the cause and the model of the old-stock American's racial suicide: while the Asiatic's indifference to individuality allegedly results in the biological mass-(re)production that outbreeds the old-stock American, it also provides an alluring way out of life and a quiet retreat from the sordid struggle for existence.

In fact, suicide was registered in the turn-of-the-century US imaginary as an act marked as peculiarly Asiatic—or more specifically, Japanese. The Japanese self-killing known as *seppuku* or *hara-kiri* has been an object of exotic fascination since the concept's first introduction to the United States in the 1870s.[50] Instituted in medieval Japan, *seppuku* was a ritualized form of suicide by disembowelment (which was, in most cases, followed immediately by decapitation by a swordsman). It was considered an honorable death, granted only to members of the warrior class when they sought to expiate their crimes, atone for their guilt, or honor their dead masters. Even as the practice itself had largely become outmoded in Japan with the abrogation of the warrior class, Japanese intellectuals visiting the U.S. at the dawn of the twentieth century fueled such Orientalist fascination in an effort to glorify Japanese imperialism.

The practice, for instance, figures prominently in Nitobe Inazo's *Bushido: The Soul of Japan* (1900), a book that reportedly fascinated Theodore Roosevelt with its explication of the Japanese "race feelings" that supposedly outlined the samurai moral code.[51] For Nitobe, *seppuku* is an act that ultimately crystalizes the samurai ideal: "a sense of calm trust in Fate, a quiet submission to the inevitable, that stoic composure in sight of danger or calamity, that disdain of life and friendliness with death."[52] Fearing that such a fatalistic sense of detachment (or what Lowell has called "impersonality") would confound the Western reader, Nitobe seeks to give an account of the "inner working of [Japanese] minds which often present an appearance of callousness."[53] Far from connoting impassivity, he explains, *seppuku* carries the "most touching pathos" for the Japanese sensibility, since the abdomen was believed to be "the seat of the soul and of the affections"; to lay open one's guts was to say, "I will open the seat of my soul and show you how it fares with it. See for yourself whether it is polluted or clean."[54] For Nitobe, in short, *seppuku* becomes an act of outpouring affect that is otherwise tightly contained in the body.

As such, *seppuku* was aestheticized, and even eroticized, in its climactic affective discharge. "Some flowers glory in death—certainly the Japanese cherry blossoms do as they freely surrender themselves to the winds," writes Okakura Kakuzo, a Japanese art critic cherished by the Boston circle of Japanophiles.[55] His *Book of Tea* (1906) is a philosophical exposition of the highly stylized art of the Japanese tea ceremony, in which, as he explains, total surrender to generic form—in contrast to Western celebrations of individual genius—becomes the artistic ideal. It is only fitting, then, that this slim volume should close with the *seppuku* of the sixteenth-century tea master, Sen no Rikyu. When he incurs the wrath of the ruler and his patron Toyotomi Hideyoshi, Rikyu is granted "the honour of dying by his own hand."[56] Okakura narrates Rikyu's death as the apotheosis of his aestheticism, noting that "he only who has lived with the beautiful can die beautifully."[57] After he finishes his last tea ceremony, during which he has calmly and silently made a final farewell to his friends, Rikyu sits in his white death robe and "tenderly . . . gazes on the shining blade of the fatal dagger. . . . With a smile upon his face Rikyu passed forth into the unknown."[58]

The tenderness and intoxication that visits Rikyu as he slits open his abdomen is, of course, Okakura's fantasy (*seppuku* was, after all, usually accompanied by decapitation performed by a trusted swordsman, because of its unbearable pain). This fantasy of death effecting a blissful union with the unknown, the acme of aesthetic refinement, is undoubtedly akin to, or even exemplary of, what Susan Sontag calls "fascists aesthetics": "Fascist art glorifies surrender, it exalts mindlessness, it glamorizes death."[59] Japanese impersonality at the turn of the century, with its dream of the self's eccstatic surrender, seems exceptionally susceptible to totalitarianism and its aesthetic seductions. Around the time Nitobe and Okakura exalted the spiritualized and aestheticized militarism of the *seppuku* tradition, Japan was fighting in the First Sino-Japanese War (1894–1895) and Russo-Japanese War (1904–1905), expanding its colonial rule over Taiwan and Korea. It is easy to see how, decades later, such glorification of "honorable death" morphed into the WWII *kamikaze* suicide attackers' ecstatic cry of *Tennōheika Banzai*: Long live the Emperor, because as I sacrifice my life, my soul will amalgamate with yours.

172   THE SUICIDAL STATE

Hindsight is 20/20—a bad joke, for sure, but only with a nervous laugh could I admit that it had taken me a decade and a global pandemic to realize that my interest in the trope of race suicide, and its weird fantasy of a self-surrender that exceeds the biopolitical imperative to survive, was likely informed by my Japanese sensibility. Japan's cultural legacy idealizing impersonality has probably formed me as an im-person, a not-quite-person, who is lured by the phantasmatic tenderness of self-surrendering. Even as my whole being is disgusted by what that ideology has wrought, wasn't I projecting my own escapist fantasy onto those white characters precisely because I had been formed as a part of "the race" to be preserved, while the biopolitical state has continuously neglected and consigned to death those living outside the putative homogeneity of ethnic Japaneseness? But dare I say—dare I also say—that the fantasy of self-surrender was constructed as a crucial ideal for post-War Japan to reckon with its imperial past, even as it has been failing miserably in that attempt? Article Nine of the Japanese Constitution, written under the supervision of the Allied Powers and enacted in 1947, pledges that "the Japanese people forever renounce war as a sovereign right of the nation and the threat or use of force as means of settling international disputes," adding that "the right of belligerency of the state will not be recognized."[60] That impossible promise of renouncing the sovereign right to belligerency, of assuming suicidal vulnerability as a state, has also formed me and this project, particularly during the years when I witnessed, from across the Pacific, the radical attacks on Article Nine by right-wing administrations, while at the same time I have realized the painful hypocrisy and emptiness of that very promise—for, after all, Japan's post-war security has been procured through its dependence on and collusion with American neocolonial power, as well as through Japan's own furtive militarization in the name of self-defense and world peace.

Asiatic im-personality is a fantasy both abject and alluring for the moderns. While its obscuring of the self's singularity threatens the ideal of liberal personhood and flirts with totalitarianism, its seductions of cosmic immersion and self-surrender promise to appease the narcissistic wound inflicted by modernity: there you will be freed from painful alienation, from the hierarchy of difference, from the grueling bearing of your "historical self."[61] In its ready evacuation of the self, its jubilant abandonment of self-mastery and self-defense, Asiatic im-personality invites—to borrow the title of Tim Dean's study about the intense sexual excitement of the transmission

CODA   173

of death through HIV—the coming of "unlimited intimacy," in which erotic relationality is disentangled from personhood.[62]

That's partly why Asiatic im-personality lies at the heart of what David Henry Hwang calls "the archetypal East-West romance that started it all"—namely, the story of Madame Butterfly. The eponymous Japanese *geisha* in the story (Cho-Cho-San, in her own language) kills herself out of love for an American naval officer stationed in Nagasaki, who has married her on a whim and deserts her when he leaves Japan. Through her suicide, she is immortalized as an archetype—or even a geopolitical symbol—of Oriental submission to the West. As such, the Butterfly story had been retold innumerable times across genres, long before it was adapted by Hwang's postcolonial queer retelling, *M. Butterfly* (1988), or metamorphosed into the Broadway spectacle of the Vietnam War, *Miss Saigon* (1989). Marked by its proliferation and mercurial mutation, the story itself seems to constitute another figural variant of Asiatic racial form. Even the supposed original, John Luther Long's 1898 short story "Madame Butterfly," was a rewriting (if not a daring plagiarism) of French novelist Pierre Loti's fictionalized memoir, *Madame Chrysanthème* (1888, translated into English in 1889). Shortly thereafter, Long's short story was adapted by David Belasco into a one-act play, *Madame Butterfly: A Tragedy of Japan*, which premiered as a sideshow in New York in 1900. It reached global fame when Giacomo Pucccini developed Belasco's play into an opera, *Madama Butterfly* (which premiered in Milan in 1904 and in Washington, D.C., and New York in 1906), inspiring numerous adaptations—at least four silent films and eleven sound films, as well as three film-operas, among many others.[63] In its constant retelling and reinterpretation, the Butterfly story feels almost mythical, or, as one critic puts it, "a tale that has no beginning."[64]

Still, tracing its transfiguration from its earliest identifiable form helps us narrate and understand an elusive history of im-personhood. The premise of Loti's *Madame Chrysanthème* is almost identical to the successive Butterfly stories. A French naval officer, the narrator of the novel, decides to marry a Japanese woman as a pastime while he is stationed in Nagasaki, procuring a wife (or, more precisely, a concubine, as their relationship is based on a financial agreement) through a local broker, and then leaving her when he moves to China at the end of the novel. But Loti's Madame Chrysanthème does not kill herself, for she still is not so much a butterfly as a chrysalis. Callous, dormant, and uncannily inscrutable, she is Asiatic impersonality

174   THE SUICIDAL STATE

incarnate, or, as the narrator refers to her, a "doll," indistinguishable from the numerous other "Niponese dolls" he encounters in Japan, whose "little narrow eyes open and seem to reveal an unexpected something, almost a soul, under these trappings of marionettes."[65]

To the extent that Loti's exquisitely rendered, if glaringly racist, ethnographic sketch has a plot, it revolves around the narrator's initial question when he encounters Madame Chrysanthème: "Is it a woman or a doll? Well, time will show."[66] In other words, the question is: What if a person falls in love with an im-person devoid of interiority, or as Anne Cheng puts in her theorization of yellow femininity, an "object-person who is radically undone yet luminously constructed—that is, meticulously and aesthetically composed yet degraded and disposable"?[67] Even though the narrator despises the possibility of love (and Chrysanthème herself), and even though his desire is clearly directed at his best friend Yves (whom, in a Girardian triangle of desire, the narrator tries to have his wife seduce), he cannot deny that "habit turns into a makeshift of attachment."[68] At some point, he even starts to see a modicum of personhood in Chrysanthème, calling her name in her native tongue—"*Kikou, Kikou-San*"—to which, he thinks, she responds with "almost a bitter curve of triumph and disdain about her lips."[69] But such impassiveness feels soothing to him, as when, on the day he leaves Nagasaki, he finds her—instead of killing herself from sadness—counting the silver dollars that he has paid her in fulfillment of their initial agreement. The chill in his spine at this sight feels almost delightful to him, because hasn't he, like Eliot's poet, wanted to escape from emotions, escape from personality, from the very beginning? He finds what he has been seeking amidst "the swarming crowd of this Liliputian curtseying people—laborious, industrious, greedy of gain, tainted with a constitutional affectation, hereditary insignificance, and incurable monkeyishness": a release from the depth-model of personhood, from the imperative to feel, to know, and to love.[70]

The American hero of Long's "Madame Butterfly," grandly named Benjamin Franklin Pinkerton, is not as blasé as his French counterpart. Though described as "impervious," or "hard to comfort—humanly speaking," Pinkerton still tries to put a soul in his Pygmalion—and succeeds in his attempt.[71] Severed from her relatives (for she has "an appalling horde" of them), given a secure boudoir and its promise of privacy ("through the courtesy of her American husband"), and even newly endowed with the ability to reason (again, "as he had taught her"), Madame Butterfly is no longer an impersonal, un-individuated, Asiatic racial form; as the American consul Sharpless bitterly observes, Pinkerton "[took] this dainty, vivid, eager, formless material, and mold[ed] it to his most wantonly whimsical wish."[72] Chirping incessantly in pidgin English, delightfully coquettish yet faithfully, fatally, in love, she is "an American refinement of a Japanese product, an American improvement on a Japanese invention."[73] As such, she even gives birth to a son (unbeknownst to Pinkerton, who leaves Japan when she is still early in her pregnancy), who is free of the markers of the Asiatic *re*production of sameness: a blond baby with purple eyes, a "miracle" indeed, defying the principles of Mendelian genetics.[74]

Transformed from an im-person to an almost-person, Madame Butterfly is now ready for Long's creative leap from Loti's original novel: her self-killing. When Sharpless asks her what she would do if Pinkerton does not return, she answers: "Me? I could—dance, mebby, or—or die?"[75] But the almost-person immediately realizes that it was not an appropriate answer to her American interlocutor, and she corrects herself (a rare moment, fittingly, when she speaks in more or less standardized English): "Well, it is not so easy to die as it was—before he came . . . He make my life more sweet."[76] Because of her love for Pinkerton, she has lost the Asiatic im-personality that would make death a blissful release from life's suffering, just as it was for her father, who killed himself when he lost in the war—fighting for the Emperor, fighting against modernity's arrival—with a sword bearing the inscription: "To die with Honor / When one can no longer live with Honor."[77]

Her personality's awakening lends her subsequent relinquishment of life a tragic cast; suicide becomes a painful renouncement only when there is a self to begin with. Butterfly decides to end her life after she encounters Pinkerton's American wife, Adelaide, who has come to Japan with her husband. Adelaide has learned of Pinkerton's dalliance with Butterfly and decided to adopt his biracial son, all the while not knowing his concubine is standing right next to her as she breathlessly informs Sharpless of her plans. When she notices the Japanese woman's presence, Adelaide is charmed by her immediately though remaining unaware of Butterfly's identity, so much so that she impulsively asks for a kiss (and is denied), calling her "you pretty—*plaything*."[78] Butterfly trembles with shame—"She—she thing me—jus'a—plaything"—as she is pushed back into the status of an im-person, a soulless doll that straddles the line between a person and a thing.[79] Shame flashes when one's narcissistic self-recognition is not reciprocated by the other's gaze; that is why she decides to "die with Honor," with her father's sword.[80] As she cuts her throat, she thinks: "They had taught her how to die, but he had taught her how to

176 THE SUICIDAL STATE

live—nay, to make life sweet. Yet that was the reason she must die. Strange reason!"[81] She must die because she has almost been made into a person; through the strange reasoning of liberal personhood, only her choice to end her life can prove the existence of her inchoate personhood.

Even her attempt at killing herself, of course, does not make her into a full-fledged person. The scene of Butterfly's throat-cutting is narrated in the grammar of aestheticized and eroticized Japanese suicide, tracing the blood that flows "down her neck," "divided on her shoulder," and then becomes "the larger stream going down her bosom . . . making its way daintily between her breasts."[82] What was once a flimsy little insect with disproportionately big wings is now, at least, endowed with some flesh; but the explicitness of the description, which would not have been allowed in the case of a white woman's body, indicates that this flesh is still marked as disposable in its very aestheticization. Besides, *she fails in her attempt to kill herself.* A little surprise, for we tend to believe that it is her suicide that embalms the little butterfly into the haunting symbol of Oriental femininity; but the original Butterfly drops her sword when her loving maid, Suzuki, pushes the crying baby into the room to stop her attempt. Suzuki binds up her wound and disappears with Butterfly and her son; the story ends when Adelaide, who has come to adopt Butterfly's son, finds their house empty.[83]

Crucially, Butterfly was immortalized through death only when she was embodied by *white* women. The performance that established Butterfly's suicide as a staple ending was David Belasco's 1900 one-act play *Madame Butterfly, A Tragedy of Japan*, produced in collaboration with Long. Except for this Butterfly's climactic death, the play largely follows Long's story, even closely adapting the original's use of pidgin English in its dialogues. Butterfly, performed first by Blanche Bates and then by Valerie Bergere alongside other members of an all-white cast, became a breakthrough role for these hitherto little-known actresses; the character demanded the virtuosic delivery of intense pathos behind comically eccentric speech and quaint mannerisms (the stage directions copiously feature *salaaming*, indicating the Orientalist merging of the Middle and Far East). This career-making trend continued with another Belasco protégée, the Irish-Canadian Mary Pickford, who starred in Sydney Olcott's 1915 silent movie *Madame Butterfly* before she was launched into stardom as "America's Sweetheart."[84]

Period audiences seem to have found something irresistible about white actresses embodying—or, to use a contemporary term for enacting, "impersonating"—the Asiatic im-person. Raving over the play's artistic

CODA 177

achievements and Bergere's flawless "impersonation of Cho-Cho San," one contemporary reviewer reported on the way Belasco directed the actress:

> Mr. Belasco demands of the impersonator of Cho-Cho San that that she shall wear a costume closely associated in the theater-goer's mind with comic opera and musical comedy, that she shall toddle instead of walking, that her poses and gestures shall all be queer, stiff, "unnatural," that she shall talk in a distinctly comic dialect and embellish her speech with much American slang and a little American profanity . . . and that, so handicapped, she shall be always real, vivid, "sympathetic," most convincingly human, pathetic and tragic and mose [sic] seriously accepted as all these by an average audience, with no conventions, or precedents or traditions to help her.[85]

Belasco's direction here captures the mechanism of what Sianne Ngai theorizes as an aesthetic category of modernity: "cuteness." Having emerged in the second half of the nineteenth-century United States, cuteness has aligned itself with commodity fetishism, casting the "illusion of . . . animated personhood" over inanimate objects and thereby providing consumers with a fantasy of control as the guardians of those objects.[86] Cuteness, then, is "an aestheticization of powerlessness": its aesthetic quality is heightened by the object's comically exaggerated pitifulness, smallness, and even sometimes, deformity, all of which indicate its "pliancy . . . to the will of others."[87]

Asiatic im-personality's eerie proximity to inert objecthood is transformed into the source of such cuteness when it is impersonated by the fully realized personalities of white actresses; just as when nonhuman objects are anthropomorphized, it achieves the illusion of an animated yet flimsy personhood, one that seduces the audience with its powerful vulnerability. Conversely, when a white actress assumes the "queer, stiff, 'unnatural,'" objecthood of Asiatic impersonality, her autonomous personhood is compromised in such a way as to achieve irresistible "cuteness," demanding a powerful affective response from the audience. For, as Ngai says, "The cute object seems to insist on *getting something* from us (care, affection, intimacy) that we in turn feel compelled to give."[88] Thus, the white actress's performance of the Asiatic im-person's deformed personhood, in its departing from realist verisimilitude, paradoxically renders the character "real, vivid, 'sympathetic,' most convincingly human." In other words, the affective demands of the cuteness that floats between objecthood and personality pave the way

178 THE SUICIDAL STATE

for the white actress to attain the so-called "It-Effect"; for, as Anne Cheng reminds us, the "It" is simultaneously "the vernacular term used to indicate ultrapersonality" and "the pronoun that designates nonpersonhood."[89]

If Butterfly, when performed by white actresses, becomes a literal "It girl," that it-ness is crystalized as she is turned into a particularly lifelike inanimate object—a corpse. Belasco's play departs from Long's text at its very end. When Suzuki, her servant, sends the baby into the room where Butterfly is preparing for her death, this time the child's cry does not stop Butterfly's endeavor: "*Madame Butterfly drops the sword and takes the baby in her arms. . . . She sets the child on a mat, puts the American flag in its hand, and, picking up the sword, goes behind the screen that the child may not see what she is about to do.*"[90] Escaping Long's pornographic rendering of the scene, Belasco's white Butterfly cuts her throat as she goes literally "off the stage," enacting the etymology of the *obscene*. In this private moment of death, Butterfly is transformed into a "race mother"—albeit a surrogate one.[91] Unlike contemporary white women who evade the imperative to procreate, this white Butterfly is charged with the Asiatic im-person's reproductive capacity. She has given birth to a simulacrum not of her Asiatic self but of Benjamin Franklin Pinkerton, a baby endowed with "jus' his face, same hair, same blue eye" (a subtle revision from Long's purple-eyed baby, which further Americanizes the child).[92] Her status as a surrogate race mother becomes even more pronounced at the end of the play. When Pinkerton finally returns to their house to find his ersatz concubine with a blood-soaked scarf wrapped around her neck, she "*waves the child's hand which holds the flag*" as she expires in Pinkerton's arms; the curtain falls.[93]

Through her surrogacy and her suicide, Butterfly bequeaths a white child to the infertile nation and is commemorated as America's It-girl just like the actresses who have performed her. Titled "French by Birth, She is American by Choice," Valerie Bergere's interview reports on this cosmopolitan actress's backstage transformation into Butterfly.[94] Described as "of French birth, a true American and a lover of the people of the Orient," Bergere is said to have intensely studied Japanese women's "stoic way of living," so much so that while preparing for the stage, she "unconsciously sat on her foot on a low stool as near the floor as possible."[95] Her transformation, of course, involves yellowface:

"I must be transported to another land of different features and deeper coloring," she said as she browned her complexion and rouged her face and lips with deep carmine. "No, these paints are not injurious to our complexion . . . but on the contrary, the grease and the constant massage we actresses give our complexions in applying and removing the paints keep us free from wrinkles and make us younger looking."[96]

Her yellowface does not compromise her whiteness; on the contrary, it only enhances its pearly glow. Ultimately, through her impersonation of the Asiatic im-person, Bergere is transformed into "a true American"; for the Japanophile French-born actress's naturalization "by Choice" underwrote the melting-pot fantasy embodied in the "world-wide welcome" of immigrants by the Statue of Liberty, itself a gift from France.[97] The dream that Emma Lazarus's "The New Colossus" summoned felt tangible for some, especially on the eve of the poem's inscription into the pedestal of the Statue in 1903. But to others, the promise extended by the poem's "Mother of Exile"—written for the fundraising of the Statue's pedestal in 1883, the year after the passage of the Chinese Exclusion Act of 1882—sounded as hollow as Lady Liberty herself. As Saum Song Bo, a Chinese immigrant in New York, wrote to the *New York Sun* in 1885: "The statue represents Liberty holding a torch which lights the passage of all nations who come into this country. But are the Chinese allowed to come? . . . Are they allowed to go about everywhere free from the insults, abuse, assaults, wrongs and injuries from which men of other nationalities are free?"[98]

While white actresses were learning to bow, toddle, or kneel, the Asiatics they impersonated were severely denied entry to the United States. Even though the era's anti-Asian sentiments emerged primarily as a result of the labor competition posed by male Chinese migrant laborers, immigration laws prior to the 1882 Exclusion Act had explicitly targeted Chinese women.[99] Although the first federal immigration law, the Page Law of 1875, on the surface prohibited the entry of all contract laborers and felons as well as Asian prostitutes, it was Chinese women who became the exclusive object of the law's enforcement.[100] Because the law prohibited "the immigration of any subject of China, Japan, or any Oriental country" coming with "lewd and immoral purposes," it further underscored the Asiatic's failure to meet liberalism's logic of volition. In repeating the specific bar against the entry of "any subject of China, Japan, or any Oriental country, without their free and voluntary consent," the law reinforced the discursive construction of Asians as im-persons lacking agency, not fit for immigration to the US and its governmentality.[101] In the American imaginary, the Chinese practice

180 THE SUICIDAL STATE

of polygamy and concubinage particularly left Chinese female immigrants prone to the charge of involuntary prostitution; like their fictional Japanese counterparts, Chrysanthème and Butterfly, they must have been sold by their destitute families into concubinage and prostitution because they were, after all, "female coolies" without volition.[102] Simply put, while Chinese men were imagined to be depriving white men of labor opportunities, Chinese women were constructed as prostitutes infiltrating the white family, spreading leprosy and syphilis, or worse, spawning miscegenated children. Ultimately, as one medical professional in San Francisco testified in 1877, the Asiatic imperson was the carrier of death: "The virus of the cooly [sic], in my opinion, is almost sure death to the white man. That is my opinion because I have seen it. There are cases of syphilis among the whites that originated from these Chinese prostitutes that are incurable."[103]

So they were killed, instead.

On March 16th, 2021, a shooting spree took place in Atlanta, targeting three different Asian massage spas. Eight people were murdered; six of them were Asian women. At the virtual vigil organized by the Korean American Coalition Metro Atlanta Chapter, the names of the victims were not mentioned because some of their families wished for their names not to be shared in association with the killing.[104] Because, according to the investigators, the shooter said that he had killed them as a result of his sex addiction; he claimed that he wanted to eliminate his temptations, denying that these murders were racially motivated. But that reticence at the vigil, that non-mentioning of their names, that tender impersonality, felt strangely Asian to me, perhaps all the more so because of its contrast with the powerful invocation of #SayHerName. Because we—at least some of us—don't care much about names. Having our names constantly mispronounced is part of the formative experience, even the basic condition, of being Asian immigrants. Knowing our real name, American people profusely apologize, because aren't the names important for our identities, our cultural legacies? Shouldn't we be proud of our names?

But I can be just a Monica, like I am at the local Asian massage clinic in Baton Rouge. I am strangely attached to this name under which I seem to be registered after I told them my name for the first time on the phone. I haven't corrected it since, partly because I am also probably mispronouncing theirs when I yelp and ask them to go a bit softer, to which they typically respond with a laugh that might sound mildly mocking to non-Asians. But I know that it is an expression of anonymous endearment because that's how those

CODA   181

who nurtured me used to laugh as they helped me up when I fell on the ground. Their precise fingers detect the knots of pain and disentangle those hardened spots in my neck left by a car accident—not only physically but emotionally as well, because that Asian massage clinic is one of those rare places in this Southern town where I get to see faces that resemble my own, feeling that I won't be judged, won't have to try hard, just entrusting my body as a Japanese Monica.

I know their hands and their warmth—that's what shook me so hard after the shooting in Atlanta. I could feel their touch, their voices, and their laughter; and then, their degraded care labor, their invisibility, and their endurance with a smile that covers over their indignation and perhaps shame, as the customers' sticky voices tell them to reach down a bit further. Their hands—that's what rocked me so hard. So I practiced saying their names, one by one, obsessively watching a video tutorial made by women who— or perhaps whose mothers, grandmothers, or great grandmothers—came from the countries that my country had fought against, slaughtered in, or colonized—those whose ancestors my ancestors called by the name of comfort women. Now I can say your name—even though far from perfectly— because your impersonal intimacy has taught me what it means to be an Asian in this country, how to live on in a suicidal state, swaying together between a broken apocalypse and a broken hallelujah.

Acknowledgments

Inasmuch as every book records the writer's own shifting sense of self, what is chronicled here is the making of an immigrant. Strange, because when I decided to write my dissertation on the turn-of-the-century racial panic over immigrants ten years ago, I did not expect that I would become one myself. I was a foreigner, a visitor, somebody who had a home elsewhere to return to, and this language was still alien on my tongue, sometimes curdling there and other times choking my throat. I still hesitate to call this country or this language mine. I have learned that this feeling of estrangement is part and parcel of a migrant being, binding me to others who live with their own apparitions of home. Nevertheless, I still live, here and now, because of those to whom I feel indebted for the new life given to me, of those to whom I will never be able to express my gratitude adequately, in this language or any other.

Somewhat embarrassingly, when I first moved to Louisiana to start my PhD in 2010, it was the very first time I had lived outside my family home in Tokyo, and my life was literally sustained by the sheer kindness of other people. Yoshiko Fukuda—whose friendship I've been blessed with for more than two decades now—flew to Baton Rouge to help me set up life here, providing me with all the life's necessities and emotional sustenance that I needed. I am still astonished by the depth of the Morikawas' generosity—Atsuko-san, Eiji-san, Shoko, and Ayuko—who held me together as I toddled into the US way of life, anchoring me with a sense of Japanese American home when I felt out of place everywhere else. In the Department of English and the wider campus community at LSU, I learned that friendship is a true gift, one that you can never return in its bounty, especially when you feel constantly abridged in your capacity to repay the debt of daily acts of care. I am deeply grateful for Stephanie Alexander, Stacey Amo, Matt Dischinger, Al Dixon, Rian Hill, Juliette Highland, Josef Horáček, Ryan McGuckin, Peter Pappas, Cristina Rosell, Jordan VonCannon, Michael VonCannon, and Deighton Zerby. Conversations with these brilliant and kind-hearted people not only afforded me many discoveries that helped launch this project, but also introduced me to the unknown affective depths and vivacities of a language that I had previously known only how to read and write.

184 ACKNOWLEDGMENTS

From my first semester at LSU, Elsie Michie's dazzling presence, insight, and jaw-dropping necklaces have cast light upon my scholarly path. Bill Boelhower has been a master mariner on my intellectual voyage, showing me how to embrace the disorientation of an *étranger* as an intellectual project. Hours of conversation in Lauren Coats's office initiated me into the pleasure of getting lost in the archives. The late John Lowe, whose work on Zora Neale Hurston first led me to LSU, taught me what it means to live fully, extravagantly, and generously—in a word, to be a *bon vivant.*

In addition to the support of these mentors and so many others in the department, I've now had the pleasure of knowing them as friends—a pleasure that feels all the more serendipitous because my return to Baton Rouge was not without trepidation. I feel eternally indebted to Chris Barret, Michael Bibler, and Chris Rovee, who welcomed me back, carved out a space for me to thrive, and have continuously ensured me a sense of belonging as I complete this book, each in their own special, magical ways. My intellectual and affective life has been sustained also by members of the English Department and the Women's, Gender, and Sexuality Studies Program, as well as their loved ones, particularly Mae Asaba, Megumi Asaba, Kathryn Barton, Sarah Becker, Elena Castro, Peter Cava, Giovanna Ceserani, Ferdoss Al Chaarani, Areendam Chanda, Keya Chanda, Anaya Chanda, Alexandra Chiasson, Mary Clinkenbeard, Allan Edmunds, Lara Glenum, Cat Jacquet, Kal Heck, Joseph Kronick, Seohye Kwon, Liam Lair, Michelle Massé, Todd McCarty, Saumya Lal, Jiwon Min, Subbah Mir, Eta Nurulhady, Arendt Owl, Shima Patrovian, Casey Patterson, Ankita Rathour, Irina Shport, Austin Svedjan, Ashley Thibodeaux, Denis Waswa, and Sue Weinstein. Rei Asaba and I have been unexpected travel companions from Tokyo to Louisiana for almost twenty years, and I'm grateful for his unwavering willingness to bear witness to my pain and joy while letting me do the same for him. I am also deeply thankful for my fellow founding members of the Asian, Asian American, Pacific Islander Caucus at LSU: Asiya Alam, Sumit Jain, Samithamby Jeyaseelan, Yong-Hong Lee, William Ma, Jim Nguyen Spencer, George Xue, Le Yan, Yao Zeng, and our fierce leader, Margot Hsu Carroll. Their friendship and support were vital for me as I was becoming an Asian immigrant and reshaping this project as one. Without the blazing brilliance and vivifying passion of Pallavi Rastogi, neither the A/AAPI Caucus nor my ceaseless revising would have been sustained. Literally hundreds of hours of conversation with her taught me about racialization, migrant lives' entwinement with geopolitics, and the boundlessness of care, richer than that

ACKNOWLEDGMENTS 185

recorded in any book of theory. Every page of this book is touched by her wisdom and love, and it is her magnetic presence and the lilt in her laugher that helped me call Baton Rouge my home.

I am also immensely fortunate to have a wider community of intellectual exchange and support to draw on, including such wonderful US-based friends as Henry Abelove, J. B. Capino, Lee Edelman, Scott Herring, Olivia Loksing Moy, James Mulholland, and Shane Vogel. One of the greatest pleasures of knowing these people is to realize that scholars that I've long admired are even more exceptional as people—which feels impossible, considering the stunning brilliance of their works. I've been buoyed and inspired countless times by my queer reading group extraordinaire: Teagan Bradway, Jonathan Flatley, Kathryn Kent. Our leader Brian Glavey's supernatural capacity to relate the shy whisper of so many queer texts, as well as that of this book, has immeasurably improved my work and my life. Adam Thompson was one of the very first readers of the whole manuscript, miraculously animating it into the frontispiece of the book, which now welcomes readers as the Statue herself purports to do. My readers understood this project in ways that I myself could never have, and their anonymous gift bestowed the project with a new foundation and the guidance to make it feel truly mine. This manuscript has also been expertly held by the whole Oxford team, especially Gigi Clement, Rajeswari Srinivasan, and Samantha Pious. No words can describe my gratitude for my editor Hannah Doyle, who saw the potential of this project and believed in it despite my unconventional background. Her warmth, passion, and vision dissolved the petrifying fear and doubt that enshrouded me and enabled me to keep on writing.

One thing I realized through the process of revision was the depth of my intellectual debt to the Department of English at the University of Tokyo, which was my alma mater and also my first job after finishing my PhD. To call it home feels painfully cliché, but still my scholarly self, as well as my youth, was shaped by the people I met there in ways that only the word home can describe, even if it means that I had to part ways with them. Almost all the literary works I have discussed in this project—including *The Making of Americans*—I first read in the graduate seminar of Takaki Hiraishi. Revising the manuscript felt like resubmitting to him the assignments which I had received incompletes, and his deep voice always was, and will be, in the back of my head whenever I write. Motoyuki Shibata and his works of translation literally saved my life as a teenager, and the training I received in his classes to attune my ears to the textual voice is still the backbone of my

186   ACKNOWLEDGMENTS

reading practice. I am also deeply grateful for those who patiently tended to my slow footsteps as I grew into the profession, especially Noriko Imanishi, Miyako Miyagawa, Hideki Nakajima, and Yoichi Ohashi. My work and existence have also been moored by the larger network of scholars and their families in Japan, including Michiko Amemiya, Yuki Katsuta, Kyoko Shoji Hearn, Kaita Takeda, Kanna Takeda, Masaaki Takeda, as well as Tomoyuki Zettsu, who has introduced me into queer studies and its protean intimacies. Yoshiaki Furui has been my rock and my compass for almost two decades, and his work, unwaveringly pointing to true north, continues to inspire me to be a person deserving of his friendship. Ikuko Endo, for me, is life's warmest, balmiest, most restorative light. Even when we are thousands of miles or kilometers apart, her presence has illumed my path home, with the still-lingering aroma of the many meals that we cooked together in our dingy grad apartment in Baton Rouge.

When I was originally writing the chapter on *The Making of Americans* for my dissertation, I did not in the least expect that I would become part of a Jewish family. Many Passovers, Rosh Hashanahs, Bat Mitzvahs and Hanukkahs with the ever-radiant Kahans and Barons—Michael, Jennifer, Sophia, Lila, Alma, Jeremy, Sarah, Joanna, Elliott—have taught me not only the enduring vivacity of the things we carried to this country but also the labor of love to keep them alive. The term "in-laws" always feels grossly inadequate to describe them, especially when I find myself cocooned in the love of Susie and Joel Kahan. Their constant care and exuberant encouragement, as well as their *naches* in me, have made me feel as if I were reliving my childhood in this country. My family in Japan—I miss them daily, more than I would usually allow myself to express or even to feel. My sister Mizuki's razor wit never fails to make me laugh till tears roll down, and it was her incisive understanding of my crisis, an illumination that I have witnessed her cast on innumerable works of art, that enabled me to keep on living a life that might have been unaccountable to anybody else. I'm grateful for Hiroaki Hashiguchi, who brought so much serenity and balance to our often-turbulent family life, and for my father Yoichi, whose resolve to stay in the family, albeit in an unconventional way, has enabled each of us to flourish. My mother Yasuko, who bears and embraces solitude in the most dignified way I know, has also been the keeper of my mother tongue. Since Covid-19's emergence, it has become our custom to Facetime every night at 1:00 AM after my writing is done, talking of the haiku she has read and written, of the small lives she has found and tended in her garden. Our conversation every

ACKNOWLEDGMENTS 187

so often circles back to the memories of her mother and my grandmother Shizu Maruyama, with whom we lived together until the end of her life, who gave us our resplendent lives in the small family home she had built, and whose sonorous voice saying the Buddhist mantra I now emulate nightly.

Benjy Kahan is the reason I'm here, still writing, still pulsating. He was there when this project was still in its embryonic stage, and he has been here with me and my project ever since, tending it as every word was written, deleted, and written again. So many nights of writing I felt myself rotting away, caught in self-doubt and despair; every time, he gathered my shattered self together and carried me forward in his arms, running toward the light with his characteristic beaming smile and jet-like propulsion, without ever looking back. He has given me my life back, breathing new life into what I had many times abandoned. For all the splendiferous things that you have given me, I have not much to give you back other than my love. But this book, certainly, I dedicate to you, because it is as much yours as mine, because we wrote it together.

Notes

Introduction

1. Willa Silbert Cather, "Paul's Case," in *The Troll Garden* (New York: McClure, Philips & Co., 1905), 252.
2. José Esteban Muñoz, *Cruising Utopia: The Then and There of Queer Futurity* (New York: New York University Press, 2009), 148.
3. Cather, *Troll Garden*, 214, 216.
4. Ibid., 217, 214, 214.
5. On Cather's reaction to Max Nordau's *Degeneration* and its relationship to "Paul's Case," see Scott Herring, "Willa Cather's Lost Boy: 'Paul's Case' and Bohemian Tramping," *Arizona Quarterly* 60, no. 2 (2004): 95–96.
6. Cather, *Troll Garden*, 235.
7. Lauren Berlant, "On the Case," *Critical Inquiry* 33, no. 4 (2007): 663. Michel Foucault, *Security, Territory, Population: Lectures at the Collège de France, 1977–78* (New York: Picador, 2007), 60.
8. Cather, *Troll Garden*, 253.
9. Michel Foucault, *"Society Must Be Defended": Lectures at the Collège de France, 1975–1976* (New York: Picador, 2003), 241.
10. Ibid., 138.
11. Ibid., 139.
12. Ibid.
13. For the technological advancements in the Progressive Era and their impact on views of humans as statistical, technologically reproducible beings, see Mark Seltzer, *Bodies and Machines* (New York: Routledge, 1992), and Martha Banta, *Taylored Lives: Narrative Productions in the Age of Taylor, Veblen, and Ford* (Chicago: University of Chicago Press, 1993). Jennifer L. Fleissner's *Women, Compulsion, Modernity: The Moment of American Naturalism* (Chicago: University of Chicago Press, 2004) and Dana Seitler's *Atavistic Tendencies: The Culture of Science in American Modernity* (Minneapolis: University of Minnesota Press, 2008) also provide important accounts of counter-narratives to the forward-looking ethos of Progressivism.
14. "Topics of the Times," editorial, *Woman's Exponent* (Salt Lake City, UT), September 15, 1886, 61.
15. "The Increase in Suicide," *Saint Paul Daily Globe* (Saint Paul, MN), August 4, 1895, 4.
16. "The Increase of Suicide," *The Word and Way: A Weekly Baptist Journal* (Kansas City, MO), May 19, 1904, 1.
17. "The Increase in Suicide," *Seymour Daily Republican* (Seymour, IN), April 11, 1910, 2.
18. Theodore Roosevelt, Prefatory Letter to Mrs. John Van Vorst and Marie Van Vorst, *The Woman Who Toils: Being the Experiences of Two Ladies as Factory Girls* (New York: Doubleday, Page, and Company, 1903), viii, vii.
19. Ibid., viii.
20. From Roosevelt's first reference to the term "race suicide" in *Woman Who Toils* in 1903 to 1925, there were approximately 4,000 newspaper articles on race suicide, which are found in *America's Historical Newspapers* (of those 4,000, a total of 1,290 articles use "race suicide" in their headline). The subject also ignited debates in the nascent field of sociology. For major works on race suicide published in the Progressive Era, see, for instance, Robert Reid Rentoul, *Race Culture; Or, Race Suicide? (A Plea for the Unborn)* (London: Walter Scott, 1906), Myre St. Walde Iseman, *Race Suicide* (New York: Cosmopolitan Press, 1912), and Warren Thompson's serial essays "Race Suicide in the United States" I–III, published in *Scientific Monthly* (1917).
21. Francis Amasa Walker, "Immigration and Degradation," *Forum* 11 (1891): 634–644. Walker was the superintendent of the 1870 and 1880 censuses. On Walker as the initiator of the race suicide discourse, see Thomas C. Leonard, *Illiberal Reformers: Race, Eugenics, and American Economics* (Princeton, NJ: Princeton University Press, 2016), 144–145.

190 NOTES

22. Edward A. Ross, "The Causes of Race Superiority," *Annals of the American Academy of Political and Social Science* 18 (1901): 86.

23. Ibid., 88.

24. Madison Grant was a prominent member of the Boone and Crockett, a hunting club Roosevelt founded in 1887. Upon the publication of *The Passing of the Great Race*, Roosevelt's passionate endorsement of Grant's ideas in his personal letter was used for promotion by Scribner's: "The book is a capital book. . . . It shows a fine fearlessness in assailing the popular and mischievous sentimentalities and attractive and corroding falsehoods which few men dare assail. It is the work of an American scholar and gentleman; and all Americans should be sincerely grateful to you for writing it." Quoted in Jonathan Spiro, *Defending the Master Race: Conservation, Eugenics, and the Legacy of Madison Grant* (Burlington: University of Vermont, 2008), 154. I discuss *The Passing of the Great Race* in detail in Chapter 3.

25. Émile Durkheim, *On Suicide*, trans. Robin Buss (New York: Penguin, 2006), 19, italics original.

26. Cather, *Troll Garden*, 224.

27. Michel Foucault, *The History of Sexuality, Vol. 1: An Introduction*, trans. Robert Hurley (New York: Pantheon Books, 1978), 139.

28. Judith Butler, *Frames of War: When is Life Grievable?* (New York: Verso, 2009), 15, 14.

29. Ibid., 24.

30. Lee Edelman, *No Future: Queer Theory and the Death Drive* (Durham, NC: Duke University Press, 2004), 3.

31. Heather Love, *Feeling Backward: Loss and the Politics of Queer History* (Cambridge, MA: Harvard University Press, 2007), 146.

32. Michel Foucault, *"Society Must Be Defended": Lectures at the Collège de France, 1975–1976*, trans. David Macey (New York: Picador, 2003), 256, 260.

33. Foucault, *"Society"*, 242, 245.

34. Ibid., 246.

35. Ibid., 246. While the emergence of biopolitics in the second half of the eighteenth century followed the historical development of anatomo-politics, this was by no means a supersession; Foucault instead describes their relation as biopolitics "dovetail[ing] into," "integrat[ing]," and "us[ing]" anatomo-politics, even though they exist on different planes and operate at different scales (242).

36. Michel Foucault, *Security, Territory, Population: Lectures at the Collège de France, 1977–1978*, trans. Graham Burchell (New York: Picador, 2007), 71. Often glossed as the "conduct of conducts," governmentality for Foucault exceeds the sphere of the state's political apparatus; it points to the comprehensive mode of guiding, directing, or organizing of acts and behaviors, even including government of the self, on which the liberal notion of subjectivity lies. On the "conduct of conducts," see Colin Gordon, "Governmental Rationality: An Introduction," in *The Foucault Effect: Studies in Governmentality*, ed. Graham Burchell, Colin Gordon, and Peter Miller (Chicago: University of Chicago Press, 1991), 2, and Michel Foucault, "The Subject and Power," in *Power*, trans. Robert Hurley et al. (New York: New Press, 1997), 341.

37. Foucault, *Security*, 70.

38. Ibid., 352.

39. Ibid., 6.

40. Michel Foucault, *The Birth of Biopolitics: Lectures at the Collège de France 1978–1979*, trans. Graham Burchell (New York: Picador, 2008), 66.

41. Thomas Lemke, "The Risks of Security: Liberalism, Biopolitics, and Fear," in *The Government of Life: Foucault, Biopolitics, and Neoliberalism*, ed. Vanessa Lemm and Miguel Vatter (New York: Fordham University Press, 2014), 65, 68.

42. Foucault, *Security*, 72, 75. For Foucault in *Security*, one site of such penetrability, where disciplinary anatomo-politics and biopolitics interdigitate to govern the population, is desire. Among the countless variants that characterize and surround human life, desire is "one invariant," since every individual invariably acts to pursue their desire. That is, the "production of the collective interest through the play of desire" provides an access point for population management (73).

43. Ibid., 107.

44. Foucault, *History of Sexuality*, 147.

45. Foucault, *"Society"*, 251.

46. Foucault, *History of Sexuality*, 105, and Penelope Deutscher, *Foucault's Futures: A Critique of Reproductive Reason* (New York: Columbia University Press, 2017), 1.

NOTES 191

47. For a foundational essay on the populational implications of sexuality, see Henry Abelove, "Some Speculations on the History of Sexual Intercourse during the Long Eighteenth Century in England," in *Deep Gossip* (Minneapolis: University of Minnesota Press, 2005), 21–28.

48. See, for example: Ann Laura Stoler, *Race and the Education of Desire: Foucault's "History of Sexuality" and the Colonial Order of Things* (Durham, NC: Duke University Press, 1995); Alys Eve Weinbaum, *Wayward Reproductions: Genealogies of Race and Nation in Transatlantic Modern Thought* (Durham, NC: Duke University Press, 2004); Ladelle McWhorter, *Racism and Sexual Oppression in Anglo-America: A Genealogy* (Bloomington: Indiana University Press, 2009); Jasbir K. Puar, *Terrorist Assemblages: Homonationalism in Queer Times* (Durham, NC: Duke University Press, 2007); and Kyla Schuller, *The Biopolitics of Feeling: Race, Sex, and Science in the Nineteenth Century* (Durham, NC: Duke University Press, 2017).

49. Stoler, 46.

50. Schuller, 8.

51. Timothy Campbell, Translator's Introduction to Robert Esposito, *Bios: Biopolitics and Immunity* (Minneapolis: University of Minnesota Press, 2008), vii.

52. Ernst H. Kantorowicz, *The King's Two Bodies: A Study in Medieval Political Theology* (Princeton, NJ: Princeton University Press, 1957), 4.

53. On the nineteenth-century popularization of the term "social body," see Mary Poovey, *Making a Social Body: British Cultural Formation 1830–1864* (Chicago: University of Chicago Press, 1995), 7–8.

54. "Copy of the Declaration of Rights As Finally Decreed By the National Assembly of France, on Thursday, August 27," *Times* (London), September 3, 1789, 3.

55. Mitchell Dean, *Critical and Effective Histories: Foucault's Methods and Historical Sociology* (London: Routledge, 1994), 156.

56. Eric Santner, *The Royal Remains: The People's Two Bodies and the Endgames of Sovereignty* (Chicago: University of Chicago Press, 2011), xv.

57. Ibid., xv.

58. Foucault, *"Society"*, 256, 257.

59. Achille Mbembe, "Necropolitics," trans. Libby Meintjes, *Public Culture* 15, no. 1 (2003): 11. It is perhaps no coincidence that Mbembe contemplates suicide bombing at the end of his rearticulation of Foucauldian biopower. Taking Gaza and the West Bank as necropower's manifestation par excellence, Mbembe argues that late-modern colonial occupation combines bio- and necropolitical controls; it not only disposes a large number of victims with a highly mechanized means of killing, but also keeps the colonized in a constant state of injury by orchestrating a systematic control of lifelines. In this context, we can read Mbembe's sudden—and rather disorienting—turn to suicide bombing in Palestine toward the end of "Necropolitics" as portraying suicide bombing as an appropriation of the power—necro and bio—that instrumentalizes human existence for the eugenic calculus of population. First, like the process of late-modern colonial occupation itself, suicide bombing intends to rupture the spaces of everyday life, indiscriminately targeting unarmed civilian populations. The terror that suicide bombing inspires continuously permeates and controls the quotidian life, refusing to be quarantined in the extremities of the globalized social body. Second, suicide bombing transforms the "body" itself—the very site of biopolitical control—into a weapon. Literally instrumentalizing their own body, the suicide bomber explodes the façade of biopower that seductively consigns autonomy, agency, and privacy to the body. The body, both of their own and that of the victims, is reduced to "the status of pieces of inert flesh, scattered everywhere, and assembled with difficulty before the burial" (Mbembe, 36–37). Mirroring biopower's suturing of the individual and the population through procreative sex, suicide bombing ultimately makes death "not simply that which is *my own*, but always goes hand in hand with the death of the other," binding the death of the individual and that of the population (Mbembe, 37).

60. Foucault, *"Society"*, 255.

61. I here refer to Lauren Berlant's term "slow death." Lauren Berlant, "Slow Death (Sovereignty, Obesity, Lateral Agency)," *Critical Inquiry* 33, no. 4 (2007): 754–780.

62. Madison Grant, *The Passing of the Great Race, Or the Racial Basis of European History* (New York: Charles Scribner's Sons, 1916), 81.

63. Roosevelt, Prefatory Letter to *The Woman Who Toils*, vii.

64. Theodore Roosevelt, "Message," in *The Abridgement 1906: Containing the Annual Message of the United States to the Two Houses of Congress* (Washington, D.C.: Government Printing Office, 1907), 1:36.

192 NOTES

65. Audrey Smedley and Brian Smedley, *Race in North America: Origin and Evolution of a World View* (Boulder, CO: Westview, 2011), 37. Classic discussions of the shifting and competing definitions of race include Thomas F. Gossett, *Race: The History of an Idea in America* (New York: Oxford University Press, 1963, rpt. 1997), Michael Banton, *Racial Theories* (Cambridge: Cambridge University Press, 1987), and Smedley and Smedley. Before the conceptualization of race as a signifier of sets of biological differences, human classifications that *resemble* the biologized notion of race existed. For instance, German physician John Friedrich Blumenbach developed some of the racial lexicon used in nineteenth and twentieth centuries in *On the Natural Variety of Mankind* in 1775. Blumenbach presented the fivefold classification using the newly developed method of craniology: Caucasian, Mongolian, Ethiopian, American, and Malayan. The hierachization of these "variations" of mankind, placing Europeans on the top and Africans on the bottom, was already prevalent in the early nineteenth century. However, in the eighteenth and the early nineteenth centuries, these "types" based on physiological differences were not regimented under the term *race* per se.
66. Even by then, competing taxonomies of race uneasily coexisted. As late as 1888, "the total number of races was a point of great contention" among experts, ranging from two to sixty-three. Reynolds J. Scott-Childress, "Race, Nation, and the Rhetoric of Color: Locating Japan and China, 1870–1907," in *Race and the Production of Modern American Nationalism*, ed. Reynolds J. Scott-Childress (New York: Routledge, 1999), 4.
67. Grant, 47.
68. Schuller, 178, 179.
69. Ed Cohen, *A Body Worth Defending: Immunity, Biopolitics, and the Apotheosis of the Modern Body* (Durham, NC: Duke University Press, 2009), 6. Whereas such killing for Foucault remains ambiguously vital yet ancillary to biopower, for others this deathly function is hard-wired at the core of the power invested in life, which paradoxically has produced deaths of unprecedented scale, brutality, and systematicity. Among those frameworks that designate this inextricability—such as thanatopolitics (Giorgio Agamben) or necropolitics (Achille Mbembe)—Robert Esposito's immunization paradigm illuminates the centrality of the somatization of the social in this welding. Esposito argues that as a term used both in biomedical and politico-judicial fields, *immunity* illuminates the jointure between biology and politics in biopolitics. Derived from the Latin *immunitas* (the negation or lack of *munus*, an obligation, duty, or gift), immunity designates a privileged exemption from a common condition applied to its conceptual counterpart, *communitas* (community, those who share *munus*). As such, immunity designates both the exemption from legal obligation and the nonsusceptibility to a particular disease. Securitization, in the context of race suicide, operates according to what Esposito calls the immunization paradigm. The term *immunity*'s jointure of the biological and political-juridical fields enables biopolitics' fusion of biology and politics, somatizing the social body as an organism to be protected. Giorgio Agamben, *Homo Sacer: Sovereign Power and Bare Life*, trans. Daniel Heller-Roazen (Stanford, CA: Stanford University Press, 1998); Achille Mbembe, "Necropolitics," trans. Libby Meintjes, *Public Culture* 15, no. 1 (2003): 11–40; and Roberto Esposito, *Bios: Biopolitics and Philosophy*, trans. Timothy Campbell (Minneapolis: University of Minnesota Press, 2008). For a robust and incisive mapping of the relation between these various thinkers and differences in their theorizations, see Deutscher, especially 102–104.
70. Benjamin Kahan, *The Book of Minor Perverts: Sexology, Etiology, and the Emergences of Sexuality* (Chicago: University of Chicago Press, 2019), 172 note 43.
71. Ross, "Causes of Race Superiority," 88.
72. Eithne Luibhéid, *Entry Denied: Controlling Sexuality at the Border* (Minneapolis: University of Minnesota Press, 2002), 31–54.
73. Lisa Lowe, *Immigrant Acts: On Asian American Cultural Politics* (Durham, NC: Duke University Press, 1996), 187; Jennifer Ting, "Bachelor Society: Deviant Heterosexuality and Asian American Historiography," in *Privileging Positions: The Sites of Asian American Studies*, ed. Gary Y. Okihiro et al. (Pullman: Washington State University Press, 1995), 271–279.
74. Ross, 88.
75. Mae M. Ngai, *Impossible Subjects: Illegal Aliens and the Making of Modern America* (Princeton, NJ: Princeton University Press, 2004), 11.
76. Nancy Tomes, *Gospel of Germs: Men, Women, and the Microbe in American Life* (Cambridge, MA: Harvard University Press, 1998).
77. Nayan Shah, *Contagious Divides: Epidemics and Race in San Francisco's Chinatown* (Berkeley: University of California Press, 2001), 185.

NOTES 193

78. William Z. Ripley, *The Races of Europe: A Sociological Study* (New York: D. Appleton and Company, 1899).
79. Ellwood P. Cubberley, *Changing Conceptions of Education* (Boston: Houghton Mifflin, 1909), 15.
80. Quoted in Thomas C. Leonard, "'More Merciful and Not Less Effective': Eugenics and American Economics in the Progressive Era," *History of Political Economy* 35, no. 4 (2003): 696.
81. For a more extensive discussive of the impact of eugenics on US immigration policy, see Daylanne K. English, *Unnatural Selections: Eugenics in American Modernism and the Harlem Renaissance* (Chapel Hill: University of North Carolina Press, 2004); Nancy Ordover, *American Eugenics: Race, Queer Anatomy, and the Science of Nationalism* (Minneapolis: University of Minnesota Press, 2003); and Daniel Kelves, *In the Name of Eugenics: Genetics and the Uses of Human Heredity* (New York: Knopf, 1985).
82. Ordover, 11.
83. Ibid., 25.
84. Quoted in ibid., 8.
85. Elaine Tyler May, *Barren in the Promised Land: Childless Americans and the Pursuit of Happiness* (Cambridge, MA: Harvard University Press, 1997), 92. While still deploying the familiar rhetoric of race suicide as "the unpardonable crime against the race," Roosevelt, in his "Twisted Eugenics" (1914), advocated for sterilization: "I wish very much that the wrong people could be prevented entirely from breeding.... Criminals should be sterilized, and feeble-minded persons forbidden to leave offspring behind them." Theodore Roosevelt, "Twisted Eugenics," *Outlook* 106 (1914): 32.
86. Grant, 47, 46, 47, 46.
87. May, 106.
88. Holmes's description here of "three generations of imbeciles" refers to Carrie Buck, an eighteen-year-old white woman sterilized without consent under the Virginia Eugenic Sterilizing Act, her daughter, and her mother. Buck's mother had been institutionalized as "feebleminded," the same condition that was ascribed to Carrie Buck when she conceived a daughter out of wedlock (by rape). Likewise, Buck's daughter was described in the testimony as "abnormal." As scholars have pointed out, "feeblemindedness" was both understood to be a hereditary condition and one deployed to control and police female sexuality. *Buck v. Bell*, 274 U.S. 200 (1927).
89. Weinbaum, 1.
90. Ibid., 5.
91. Ibid., 4.
92. Brian Connolly, *Domestic Intimacies: Incest and the Liberal Subject in Nineteenth-Century America* (Philadelphia: University of Pennsylvania Press, 2014), 172.
93. On the discourse of hereditary danger of miscegenation and hybridity (cross-species reproduction), see Robert Young, *Colonial Desire: Hybridity in Theory, Culture, and Race* (New York: Routledge, 1995).
94. On anti-miscegenation laws enacted in the Progressive Era, see Michael Grossberg, *Governing the Hearth: Law and the Family in Nineteenth-Century America* (Chapel Hill: University of North Carolina Press, 1988), 135–141, and Peggy Pascoe, *What Comes Naturally: Miscegenation Law and the Making of Race in America* (Oxford: Oxford University Press, 2010). The bans against intermarriage between Blacks and whites were strengthened and added in twenty states and territories between 1880 and 1920. The growing anti-Asian sentiment propagated under the rubric of "yellow peril" first set its sights on Chinese women, who were believed to circulate sexually transmitted disease through prostitution. The Page Act of 1875, the first federal restrictive immigration law, was aimed at Asian women entering "under contract for 'lewd and immoral purposes.'" Nancy Cott, *Public Vows: A History of Marriage and the Nation* (Cambridge, MA: Harvard University Press, 2000), 136. In a similar vein, the longstanding tolerance for white–Native American matrimony gradually ebbed. Even though Native American–white marriage had even been upheld in the first half of the century as a means of assimilation, toward the end of the nineteenth century, it began to encounter legal prohibitions. By the end of the century, Arizona, North Carolina, Nevada, and Oregon had banned Native American–white intermarriage.
95. "The Virginia 'Act to Preserve Racial Integrity' of 1924," in *Interracialism: Black-White Intermarriage in American History, Literature, and Law*, ed. Werner Sollors (Oxford: Oxford University Press, 2000), 24.
96. Ibid., 23.

194   NOTES

97. It might be more accurate to say the law conceives of race as primarily a biological problem for it contains a stubbornly political problem: namely, that many elite whites proudly traced their lineage to the marriage between the famous "Indian Princess" Pocahontas and John Rolfe. See Richard B. Sherman, "'The Last Stand': The Fight for Racial Integrity in Virginia in the 1920s," *Journal of Southern History* 54, no. 1 (1988): 69. This so-called "Pocahontas exception" ensured the legal whiteness of Virginia's planter class. See Kevin Noble Maillard, "The Pocahontas Exception: The Exemption of American Indian Ancestry from Racial Purity Law," *Michigan Journal of Race and Law* 12, no. 3 (2007): 351–386.

98. Pascoe, 140.

99. Ladelle McWhorter, "Enemy of the Species," in *Queer Ecology: Sex, Nature, Politics, Desire*, ed. Catriona Mortimer-Sandilands and Bruce Erickson (Bloomington: Indiana University Press, 2010), 91.

100. Melissa N. Stein, *Measuring Manhood: Race and the Science of Masculinity, 1830–1934* (Minneapolis: University of Minnesota Press, 2015), 243.

101. Ibid., 228. On *furor sexualis*, see Hunter McGuire and G. Frank Lydston, *Sexual Crimes among the Southern Negroes* (Louisville, KY: Renz and Henry, 1893), and James G. Kiernan, "Race and Insanity: The Negro Race," *Journal of Nervous and Mental Disease* 12, no. 3 (1885): 290–293.

102. Thomas Dixon, *The Clansman: An Historical Romance of the Ku Klux Klan* (New York: A. Wessels, 1907), 306. Here, I see Marion Lenoir's suicide—unlike other suicides I examine in the book—as an embodiment of the alarmist, white-supremacist discourse of race suicide, rather than its figural counterpart *race suicide*, which symptomatically undermines its imperative.

103. Richard Dyer, "Into the Light: The Whiteness of the South in *The Birth of a Nation*" in *Dixie Debates: Perspectives on Southern Cultures*, ed. Richard King and Helen Taylor (New York: New York University Press, 1996), 173. In D. W. Griffith's *The Birth of a Nation*, Marion Lenoir is rewritten as Flora Cameron, who jumps off a cliff in order to escape from the assault, thereby keeping her whiteness intact. As Melvyn Stokes states, *The Birth of a Nation* was the first "blockbuster" in the American movie industry and its screening was literally a national event: "it was the first movie to be shown at the White House, the first to be projected for judges of the Supreme Court and members of Congress, the first to be viewed by countless millions of ordinary Americans." Melvyn Stokes, *D. W. Griffith's "The Birth of a Nation": A History of "the Most Controversial Motion Picture of All Time"* (Oxford: Oxford University Press, 2007), 1. As Stokes argues, the climactic scene of the Klan ride was enthusiastically cheered by Northern and Southern audiences alike. See Stokes, especially 125–127.

104. Jonathan Ned Katz, *The Invention of Heterosexuality* (New York: Dutton, 1995), 86.

105. Ibid., 87.

106. Abelove, 26, 23.

107. On race suicide as antifeminism, see Laura L. Lovett, *Conceiving the Future: Pronatalism, Reproduction, and the Family in the United States, 1890–1938* (Chapel Hill: University of North Carolina Press, 2007), 77–108, and Linda Gordon, *The Moral Property of Women: A History of Birth Control Politics in America* (Champaign: University of Illinois Press, 2002), 86–108.

108. Stein, 179.

109. Ibid., 183.

110. Ralph Werther–Jennie June ("Earl Lind"), *The Female-Impersonators*, ed. Alfred W. Herzog (New York: Medical Legal Journal, 1922), 49.

111. Ibid., 196.

112. As Melissa Stein argues, the archive of American sexology is populated almost entirely by case studies of white men, whose homosexuality or inversion is conceptualized as being congenital. When non-whites do appear in the archive, their same-sex sexual practices are usually attributed to vice, immorality, and/or sexual excess. As Stein puts it: "While members of either race could engage in homosexual sex, the *homosexual* was implicitly white" (201). Stein's claim enables us to pressurize Foucault's skepticism about the centrality of procreation—or what Deutscher calls the "repudiation of a procreative hypothesis"—in the construction of sexuality (1). Ventriloquizing a possible objection to his thesis about the proliferation of sexual discourse, Foucault writes: "[I]s it not motivated by one basic concern: to ensure population, to reproduce labor capacity, to perpetuate the form of social relations: in short, to constitute a sexuality that is economically useful and politically conservative?" (*History of Sexuality*,

NOTES 195

36–37). While Foucault remains agnostic about this question—"I still do not know whether this is the ultimate objective"—we can say that, at least in the US context, the speciation of the homosexual was catalyzed in relation to the failed reproduction of the white race (*The History of Sexuality*, 37). We might, then, rephrase Foucault's famous dictum. The sodomite had been a temporary aberration; the homosexual was now a race, rather than a species.

113. David M. Halperin, *How to Do the History of Homosexuality* (Chicago: University of Chicago Press, 2002), 131.

114. Reginald Horsman, *Race and Manifest Destiny: The Origins of American Racial Anglo-Saxonism* (Cambridge, MA: Harvard University Press, 1981), 5.

115. Matthew Frye Jacobson, *Whiteness of a Different Color: European Immigrants and the Alchemy of Race* (Cambridge, MA: Harvard University Press, 1998), 40. In its emphasis on the interconnectedness between whiteness and heterosexuality, my project owes a particular debt to works such as Julian Carter, *The Heart of Whiteness: Normal Sexuality and Race in America, 1880–1940* (Durham, NC: Duke University Press, 2007); Mason Stokes, *The Color of Sex: Whiteness, Heterosexuality, and the Fictions of White Supremacy* (Durham, NC: Duke University Press, 2001); and Richard Dyer, *White: Essays on Race and Culture* (London: Routledge, 1997). While their works offer brilliantly nuanced accounts of whiteness, when it comes to analyzing sexuality, they seem to depend too much on the homo/hetero binary, as do Roderick Ferguson's *Aberrations in Black: Toward a Queer of Color Critique* (Minneapolis: University of Minnesota Press, 2004) and Siobhan Somerville's *Queering the Color Line: Race and the Invention of Homosexuality in American Culture* (Durham, NC: Duke University Press, 2000). For the production of whiteness with a particular emphasis on Progressive Era racial politics, see, for instance, Jacobson, Horsman, and Thomas G. Dyer, *Theodore Roosevelt and the Idea of Race* (Baton Rouge: Louisiana State University Press, 1992).

116. Stein, 217–250. G. Frank Lydston argues that venereal disease causes male infertility and is one of the chief causes of race suicide in *Sex Hygiene for the Male and What to Say to the Boy* (Chicago: Riverton Press, 1912), 17, 206.

117. G. Frank Lydston, *Diseases of Society* (Philadelphia: J. B. Lippincott, 1906).

118. Ibid., 36.

119. Ibid., 197.

120. "Increase of Suicide: Laurence Irwell Spoke of 'Racial Deterioration,'" *Detroit Free Press* (Detroit, Michigan), August 11, 1897, 2.

121. Andrew Bennett, *Suicide Century: Literature and Suicide from James Joyce to David Foster Wallace* (Cambridge: Cambridge University Press, 2017), 40. Quoted in Howard Kushner, *Self-Destruction in the Promised Land: A Psychocultural Biology of American Suicide* (New Brunswick, NJ: Rutgers University Press, 1989), 15.

122. Richard Bell, *We Shall Be No More: Suicide and Self-Government* (Cambridge, MA: Harvard University Press, 2012), 20.

123. Foucault, *History of Sexuality*, 138.

124. Kushner, 35–61.

125. S. A. K. Strahan, *Suicide and Insanity: A Physiological and Sociological Study* (London: S. Sonnenschein & Co., 1893), 66, 30.

126. Ian Marsh, *Suicide: Foucault, History and Truth* (Cambridge, MA: Cambridge University Press, 2010), 127.

127. Strahan, 78.

128. Ibid., 70.

129. Marsh, 126–127.

130. Holly A. Laird, "Between the (Disciplinary) Acts: Modernist Suicidology," *Modernism/modernity* 18, no. 3 (2011): 538.

131. Marsh, 173.

132. Sigmund Freud, *Three Essays on the Theory of Sexuality*, trans. James Strachey (New York: Basic Books, 2000), 50.

133. Sigmund Freud, *Beyond the Pleasure Principle*, trans. James Strachey (New York: W. W. Norton, 1989, rpt. 1961), 67, 76, 77.

134. Richard von Krafft-Ebing, *Psychopathia Sexualis: With Especial Reference to the Antipathic Sexual Instinct*, trans. Franklin S. Klaf (New York: Arcade, 2011), 46.

135. Lee Edelman, *No Future: Queer Theory and the Death Drive* (Durham, NC: Duke University Press, 2004), 3.

196 NOTES

136. José Esteban Muñoz, *Cruising Utopia: The Then and There of Queer Futurity* (New York: New York University Press, 2009), 95.
137. Edelman, 4, 15.
138. Foucault, "*Society*," 256, 260.
139. Ibid., 259.
140. Ibid., 260.
141. Esposito, 138.
142. Ibid., 116.
143. Jacques Derrida, *Rogues: Two Essays on Reason* (Palo Alto, CA: Stanford University Press, 2005), 18; Giovanna Borradori, *Philosophy in the Time of Terror: Dialogues with Jürgen Habermas and Jacques Derrida* (Chicago: University of Chicago Press, 2003).
144. Derrida, *Rogues*, 35.
145. Ibid., 36.
146. Ibid., 52.
147. Ibid., 45.
148. Ibid., 157.
149. Foucault, *History of Sexuality*, 83.
150. Ibid., 35, 138.
151. Foucault, *Security*, 194, 195.
152. Arnold Davidson, Introduction to Michel Foucault, *Security, Territory, Population: Lectures at the Collège de France, 1977–78* (New York: Picador, 2007), xxx.
153. Ibid., xxxi.
154. Michel Foucault, "Passion According to Werner Schroeter," in *Foucault Live: Collected Interviews, 1961–1984*, trans. Lysa Hochroth and John Johnston (South Pasadena, CA: Semiotext[e], 1996), 318.
155. Michel Foucault, "The Simplest of Pleasures," in *Foucault Live: Collected Interviews, 1961–1984*, trans. Lysa Hochroth and John Johnston (South Pasadena, CA: Semiotext[e], 1996), 296.
156. Love, 12.
157. For the genre's influential self-definition, see Émile Zola, *The Experimental Novel, and Other Essays*, trans. Belle Sherman (New York: Cassell Publishing, 1893), 1–56. For classic arguments on American naturalism in particular, see Malcom Cowley, "'Not Men': A Natural History of American Naturalism," *Kenyon Review* 9, no. 3 (1947): 414–435, and Donald Pizer, *Realism and Naturalism in Nineteenth-Century American Literature* (Carbondale: Southern Illinois University Press, 1966).
158. D. A. Miller, *The Novel and the Police* (Berkeley: University of California Press, 1989).
159. Georg Lukács, *Writer and Critic and Other Essays*, trans. Arthur Kahn (London: Merlin, 1970), 134, 133.
160. Emily Steinlight, *Populating the Novel: Literary Form and the Politics of Surplus Life* (Ithaca, NY: Cornell University Press, 2018), 3, 18.
161. On corporate personhood, see Walter Benn Michaels, *The Gold Standard and the Logic of Naturalism: American Literature at the Turn of the Century* (Berkeley: University of California Press, 1987), 181–214. On "statistical persons," see Mark Seltzer, *Bodies and Machines* (New York: Routledge, 1992), esp. 91–110.
162. Jennifer L. Fleissner, *Women, Compulsion, Modernity: The Moment of American Naturalism* (Chicago: University of Chicago Press, 2004), 27.
163. On literary suicide, see Jeffrey Berman, *Surviving Literary Suicide* (Amherst: University of Massachusetts Press, 1999); Nathaniel Miller, "'Felt, Not Seen Not Heard': Quentin Compson, Modernist Suicide, and Southern History," *Studies in the Novel* 37, no. 1 (2005): 37–49; Laird; Jared Stark, *A Death of One's Own: Literature, Law, and the Right to Die* (Evanston, IL: Northwestern University Press: 2018), esp. Chapter 1, "Preferring Not to: Living Wills, Assisted Suicide, Bartleby"; Benjamin Bateman, *The Modernist Art of Queer Survival* (Oxford: Oxford University Press, 2018), esp. Chapter 5, "Cather's Survival by Suicide"; Dana Seitler, "Willing to Die: Addiction and Other Ambivalence of Living," *Cultural Critique* 98 (Winter 2018): 1–21; Dana Seitler, "Suicidal Tendencies: Notes toward a Queer Narratology," *GLQ* 25, no. 4 (2019): 599–616; and Deanna P. Koretsky, *Death Rights: Romantic Suicide, Race, and the Bounds of Liberalism* (Albany, NY: SUNY Press, 2021). For historical and theoretical texts, see Kushner; Susan Morrissey, *Suicide and the Body Politic in Imperial Russia* (Cambridge: Cambridge University Press, 2006); Marsh; Bell; Jasbir Puar, "Coda: The Cost of Getting Better: Suicide, Sensation, Switchpoints," *GLQ* 18, no. 1 (2012): 149–158.

NOTES   197

164. Bennett, 2.
165. Seitler, "Suicidal Tendencies," 602.
166. Benjamin Bateman, *The Modernist Art of Queer Survival* (Oxford: Oxford University Press, 2018), 4.
167. For more discussion about human fungibility under biopolitics, see Chapter 4, and for the concept's relation to Black fungibility as discussed by scholars of Afro-pessimism, see the Coda. Replacement theory, also called "the Great Replacement," after Renaud Camus's 2011 book *Le Grand Remplacement*, is a right-wing conspiracy theory spread both in Europe and the United States, which is "predicated on the notion that white women are not having enough children and that falling birthrates will lead to white people around the world being replaced by nonwhite people" (Nellie Bowles, " 'Replacement Theory,' a Racist, Sexist Doctrine, Spreads in Far-Right Circles," *New York Times*, March 18, 2019, https://www.nytimes.com/2019/03/18/technology/replacement-theory.html). In the United States, replacement theory or "white genocide" discourse has been used to coordinate and reinforce a number of the Republican Party's policy positions—including anti-abortion, anti-immigration, and American jingoism—and is espoused by such figures as Steve King, Ann Coulter, Newt Gingrich, and Tucker Carlson. While this theory circulated in the rightwing media ecosystem for much of Barack Obama's presidency, it came to increasing prominence with the deadly "Unite the Right" rally in Charlottesville, Virginia, on August 11 and 12, 2017.
168. Eve Kosofsky Sedgwick, *Touching Feeling: Affect, Pedagogy, Performativity* (Durham, NC: Duke University Press, 2003), 179.
169. Jack London, *Martin Eden* (New York: Penguin, 1993), 482.
170. My thinking here has been inspired by Lee Edelman's claim that "*queerness teaches us nothing*," both in the sense that this pedagogy points toward "nothing"—what has been foreclosed from the ontological field as a condition of life's mattering—and in the sense that its pedagogical reach necessarily fails to grasp that "nothing," thereby suspending the learner within meaninglessness. Lee Edelman, *Bad Education: Why Queer Theory Teaches Us Nothing* (Durham, NC: Duke University Press, 2023), xvii.

Chapter 1

1. "Mr. Roosevelt's Creed," *New York Times*, October 19, 1884: 2. My references to Roosevelt in this section are drawn from Philip Horne, "Henry James and 'the Forces of Violence': On the Track of 'Big Game' in 'The Jolly Corner,' " *Henry James Review* 27, no. 3 (2006): 234–247. Horne's article traces the decade-long relationship between James and Roosevelt. Underscoring James's ambivalence to the hyper-masculine President, Horne sees Roosevelt as an inspiration for the protagonist of James's 1908 story "The Jolly Corner."
2. "Mr. Roosevelt's Creed," 2. See also Philip Horne, " 'Poodle and Bull Moose': What Henry James, Theodore Roosevelt Felt about War, America, and Each Other," *Times Literary Supplement* 5802 (June 13, 2014): 13–15.
3. Quoted in Horne, "Henry James," 237.
4. Ibid., 239.
5. Kevin Murphy, *Political Manhood: Red Bloods, Mollycoddles, and the Politics of Progressive Era Reform* (New York: Columbia University Press, 2009), 14.
6. Murphy, 15, 28, 27.
7. Quoted in ibid., 28.
8. Edmund Morris, *The Rise of Theodore Roosevelt* (New York: Modern Library, 1979), 425. According to Horne, this remark was scribbled in blue pencil and deciphered only by Morris. The existent collection of Roosevelt's letters by Cambridge does not record it. See Horne, "Henry James," 240.
9. Gail Bederman, *Manliness and Civilization: A Cultural History of Gender and Race in the United States, 1880–1917* (Chicago: University of Chicago Press, 1995), 170.
10. Quoted in Morris, 144.
11. Quoted in Bederman, 175.
12. On Henry James's celibacy, see Benjamin Kahan, *Celibacies: American Modernism and Sexual Life* (Durham, NC: Duke University Press, 2013), 52–55.
13. Henry James, *The Complete Letters of Henry James, 1884–1886, Vol 1*, ed. Michael Anesko and Greg W. Zacharias (Lincoln: University of Nebraska Press, 2020), 11. According to Horne, evidence that James heard of the details of Roosevelt's speech has not yet been found. Horne, "Henry James," 240.

198 NOTES

14. Theodore Roosevelt, *The Letters of Theodore Roosevelt*, vol. 1, *The Years of Preparation, 1868–1898*, ed. Elting E. Morison (Cambridge, MA: Harvard University Press, 1951), 123. James would not become a British citizen until 1915.

15. Ibid., 390.

16. Theodore Roosevelt, "True Americanism," in *American Ideals and Other Essays, Social and Political* (New York: G. P. Putnam's Sons, 1904), 60–61. This essay, as Horne notes, was first published as "What Americanism Means" in *The Forum* in April 1894. Horne, "Henry James," 240.

17. Roosevelt, "True Americanism," 55.

18. Henry James, *The Notebooks of Henry James*, ed. F. O. Matthiessen and Kenneth B. Murdock (New York: Oxford University Press, 1947), 47, italics original.

19. Ibid., 47, italics original.

20. Henry James, "Anthony Trollope," *The Century Illustrated Monthly Magazine* (July 1883): 391.

21. James, *Notebooks*, 47.

22. Henry James, *The Bostonians*, in *Novels 1881–1886*, ed. William T. Stafford (New York: Library of America, 1985), 832. All other references to the text will be cited parenthetically.

23. Theodore Roosevelt, *The Letters of Theodore Roosevelt*, vol. 2, *The Years of Preparation, 1898–1900*, ed. Elting E. Morison (Cambridge, MA: Harvard University Press, 1951), 1053.

24. Theodore Roosevelt, *The Winning of the West: An Account of the Exploration and Settlement of Our Country from Alleghanies to the Pacific* (New York: The Current Literature Publishing Company, 1889, rpt. 1905), 1:39.

25. On US Anglo-Saxonism, see Richard Hofstadter, *Social Darwinism in American Thought* (Boston: Beacon Press, 1944), 170–184; Barbara Miller Solomon, *Ancestors and Immigrants: A Changing New England Tradition* (Chicago: University of Chicago Press, 1956), 59–81; Thomas Gossett, *Race: The History of an Idea in America* (Dallas, TX: Southern Methodist University Press, 1963), 84–122; Reginald Horsman, *Race and Manifest Destiny: The Origin of American Racial Anglo-Saxonism* (Cambridge, MA: Harvard University Press, 1981); and Eric P. Kaufman, *The Rise and Fall of Anglo-America* (Cambridge, MA: Harvard University Press, 2004). Anglo-Saxonism originated in the English Reformation as an attempt to break away from Roman Catholicism by returning to an imagined pre-Norman Conquest past centered in modern-day Germany. Similar views have been held in the United States since before the Founding regarding the Americas as the lands where the Anglo-Saxon would find true freedom. However, due to the remaining anti-British sentiment, Anglo-Saxonism was not fully embraced until the mid-nineteenth century, when an influx of Irish Catholic immigrants into Boston and New England generally spurred its uptake. While Henry Adams's 1873–1874 seminar on Anglo-Saxon history was crucial to the formation of US Anglo-Saxonism, Adams himself generally kept his distance from Anglo-Saxonism's claims to racial superiority. Anglo-Saxon racial superiority was proclaimed by such thinkers as John Fiske and Herbert Baxter Adams, who were influenced by the thought of the British Anglo-Saxonist Edward Freeman.

26. Roosevelt observes in his review of Brooks Adams's 1896 *The Law of Civilization and Decay* that New Englanders, "the most highly civilized races, and . . . the most highly civilized portions of all races," were starting "to lose the power of multiplying, and even to decrease." See "The Law of Civilization and Decay (Review)," in *The Works of Theodore Roosevelt in Fourteen Volumes*, vol. 1, *American Ideals and Administration—Civil Service* (New York: G. P. Putnam's Sons, 1897), 354. Francis Amasa Walker, another New England intellectual and the director of the United States Census Bureau since 1870, was the first to realize this racial change after the 1870s census, sounding the alarm against open immigration and laying the groundwork for Edward Ross's 1901 christening of the issue as "race suicide" more than two decades later. See Solomon, 71–81.

27. Nathan Allen, "Changes in New England Population," *Popular Science Monthly* 23 (1883): 435.

28. Solomon, 43.

29. Barrett Wendell, *Barrett Wendell and His Letters*, ed. Mark Antony DeWolfe Howe (Boston: Atlantic Monthly Press, 1924), 47.

30. Wendy Graham, *Henry James's Thwarted Love* (Stanford, CA: Stanford University Press, 1999), 146.

31. David G. Schuster, *Neurasthenic Nation: America's Search for Health, Happiness, and Comfort, 1869–1920* (New Brunswick, NJ: Rutgers University Press, 2011), 2. For other exemplary work on neurasthenia, see Julian Carter, *The Heart of Whiteness: Normal Sexuality and Race in America, 1880–1940* (Durham, NC: Duke University Press, 2007), 42–74, and Tom

NOTES 199

Lutz, *American Nervousness, 1903: An Anecdotal History* (Ithaca, NY: Cornell University Press, 1991).

32. John Ellis, *Deterioration of the Puritan Stock and Its Causes* (New York: Published by the Author, 1884), 3, 16.

33. Ibid., 6.

34. George M. Beard, *American Nervousness: Its Cause and Consequences* (New York: Putnam's, 1881), vi (repeated verbatim on 96), viii. As I discuss later in the chapter, Max Nordau, in his *Degeneration* (1892, translated into English in 1895), similarly argues that "the little shocks of railway travelling... the perpetual noises, and the various sights in the streets of a large town... the constant expectation of the newspaper, of the postman, of visitors" and other elements of "the present conditions of civilized life" are the causes of degeneration, the European precursor of neurasthenia. Max Nordau, *Degeneration* (Lincoln: University of Nebraska Press, 1993), 39, 41.

35. Schuster, 21.

36. Beard, 26.

37. Schuster, 22.

38. Carter, 47.

39. Ibid., 44.

40. George M. Beard, *Sexual Neurasthenia: Its Hygiene, Causes, Symptoms, and Treatment* (New York: E. B. Treat, 1884). In this posthumous volume, Beard primarily tackles the kind of neurasthenia that manifests in "conditions of genital debility in the male—impotence and spermatorrhoea, prostatorrhoea, irritable prostate," seeing masturbation as a major cause of such sexual neurasthenia (23). At the same time, he argues that "woman is man, pathologically; all the symptoms of sexual neurasthenia, as described by me here or elsewhere, are found in females as well as males" (200–201).

41. On Silas Weir Mitchell's "rest cure," which was made famous by Charlotte Perkins Gilman's nightmarish representation of her treatment in "The Yellow Wallpaper" (1892), see Schuster, 29–31, and Jennifer Fleissner, *Women, Compulsion, Modernity: The Moment of American Naturalism* (Chicago: University of Chicago Press, 2004), 52–55. On Mitchell's "West cure" (also known as "camp cure"), see Barbara Will, "The Nervous Origin of the American West," *American Literature* 70, no. 2 (1998): 293–316, and Schuster, 134–139. Tom Lutz sees Theodore Roosevelt's trips to the Dakotas in the 1880s as part of a West cure for his "asthmatic neurasthenia" (63). Gail Bederman, however, remains skeptical of Lutz's account, for despite Roosevelt's numerous ailments there is no written evidence that Roosevelt was ever diagnosed as a neurasthenic (275).

42. In contrast, the Mississippian Basil's complexion is marked as "brown" (*The Bostonians*, 1031), and he himself is conscious that his "Southern complexion" causes "a prejudice" among his clients (973). As mentioned earlier, Beard underlines that neurasthenia is endemic to the North: "Contrasting the North and the South, we not only find that nervous diseases of all kinds steadily diminish as we go towards the Gulf" (186).

43. Ruth Bernard Yeazell, Introduction to *The Death and Letters of Alice James* (Berkeley: University of California Press, 1981), 3.

44. For the James family's neurasthenic history, see also Graham, 159. For neurasthenia as "Americanitis," see, for instance, Paul Stephens, "'Reading at It': Gertrude Stein, Information Overload, and the Makings of Americanitis," *Twentieth Century Literature* 59, no. 1 (2013): 126–156. According to Stephens, although William James is credited for this epithet, there is no printed record that he ever used this term (131).

45. For Henry and Alice's cohabitation in Boston, see Leon Edel, "Portrait of Alice James," in *The Diary of Alice James* (New York: Dodd, Mead & Co., 1934), 8–10.

46. Yeazell, 4, 3.

47. Quoted in ibid., 15.

48. Quoted in Edel, 15–16.

49. Quoted in ibid., 16.

50. Quoted in ibid., 13. According to Edel, Henry became acquainted with Loring during his two visits to the United States between 1881 and 1883, and Alice and Loring visited Henry in London in 1884. He was deeply grateful for Loring's abiding care of Alice and described her in his letter to his mother "'the most perfect companion' Alice could have found" (10).

51. Graham, 149.

52. Quoted in Yeazell, 12.

53. Graham, 150.

200 NOTES

54. Ibid., 154; Theodore Roosevelt, Preface to Mrs. John Van Vorst and Marie Van Vorst, *The Woman Who Toils: Being the Experiences of Two Ladies as Factory Girls* (New York: Doubleday, Page, and Company, 1903), viii.

55. Quoted in Scott Herring, *Queering the Underworld: Slumming, Literature, and the Undoing of Lesbian and Gay History* (Chicago: University of Chicago Press, 2007), 35. Herring argues that clubwoman were associated with the "perversion of spinsterhood" (35).

56. Graham, 152. How to interpret Olive Chancellor's sexuality has been a subject of debate. For instance, see Phillip Rahv, Introduction to Henry James, *The Bostonians* (New York: Dial, 1945), v–ix; Terry Castle, *The Apparitional Lesbian: Female Homosexuality and Modern Culture* (New York: Columbia University Press, 1993), 150–184; Hugh Stevens, *Henry James and Sexuality* (Cambridge, MA: Cambridge University Press, 1998), 90–116; David Van Leer, "A World of Female Friendship: *The Bostonians*," in *Henry James and Homo-erotic Desire,* ed. John R. Bradley (New York: St. Martin's, 1999), 93–109; Kahan, *Celibacies*, 33–55; Peter Coviello, *Tomorrow's Parties: Sex and the Untimely in Nineteenth-Century America* (New York: New York University Press, 2013), 168–189; Natasha Hurley, *Circulating Queerness: Before the Gay and Lesbian Novel* (Minneapolis: University of Minnesota Press, 2018). At the time of the novel's publication, the intensity of Olive's relation to Verena was strangely disregarded. In the words of Phillip Rahv, who first designated Olive as a "Lesbian" in his introduction to the 1945 reprint of the novel (ix), the absent reference to Olive's sexuality at the time of the novel's publication bespeaks its contemporary reviewers' incapability of "seeing a relationship of this kind in a clear clinical light" and "approach[ing] it in their minds with any degree of candor" (vi). Critics after Rahv have almost unanimously adopted the repressive hypothesis, regarding contemporary imperceptions of Olive's sexuality as a sign of an unconscious refusal to know. Accordingly, the lack of explicit articulation of their sexual relationship in the novel, which could potentially pre-empt lesbian readings, has often been reframed in terms of the double fold of unrepresentability. On the one hand, this invisibility is ascribed to the author's strategic conformation to the literary decorum of his time. Terry Castle's insightful reading, for instance, places *The Bostonians* in the French literary tradition of "Sapphic love," shedding light on the palimpsestic rhetoric whereby James subtly inscribes the corporeal dimension of lesbianism as a "kind of intertextual ghost effect" (Castle, 169–170). On the other hand, this nonrepresentationality also seems to arise from the lack of a name for same-sex desire itself, at the time of the novel's publication, that preceded sexological discourse. Peter Coviello reads the "earliness and expectancy" of Olive's non-heteronormative love, which misrecognizes reformist feminism as "the closest approxima-tion of a language" for her passion for Verena (Coviello, 171). Although my argument highlights same-sex intimacy between Olive and Verena without physical consummation, I contend, in the sections that follow, that Olive's erotic attachment to Verena is neither repressed or unrep-resented; rather, like Kahan, who finds celibate eroticism in *The Bostonians*, I argue that Olive's eroticism is metaphysical. Kahan, *Celibacies*, 44.

57. Stevens, 97, italics original.

58. Kahan, *Celibacies*, 44.

59. As Michiel Arnoud Cor de Vaan argues, the etymology of morbid can be traced to *moriri*, meaning "to die," and etymologically linked to *mori*. Michiel Arnoud Cor de Vaan, *Etymological Dictionary of Latin and the Other Italic Languages* (Leiden: Brill, 2008), 389. For a related reading of Olive Chancellor's morbidness as a representation of Henry James Senior's idea of "sick soul," see Madoka Kishi, "'The Ecstasy of the Martyr': Lesbianism, Sacrifice, and Morbidness in *The Bostonians*," *Henry James Review* 37, no. 1 (2016): 100–116.

60. Melvin Stokes, *D. W. Griffith's "The Birth of a Nation": A History of "the Most Controversial Motion Picture of All Time"* (Oxford: Oxford University Press, 2007), 180. On the Lost Cause and the reunion narrative, see *The Myth of the Lost Cause and Civil War History*, ed. Gary W. Gallagher and Alan T. Nolan (Bloomington: Indiana University Press, 2000), and David W. Blight, *Race and Reunion: The Civil War in American Memory* (Cambridge, MA: Harvard University Press, 2001).

61. Arthur J. Bond, "'Applying the Standards of Intrinsic Excellence': Nationalism and Arnoldian Cultural Valuation in the *Century Magazine*," *American Periodicals* 9 (1999): 55.

62. Nina Silber, *The Romance of Reunion: Northerners and the South, 1865–1900* (Chapel Hill: University of North Carolina Press, 1993). For exemplary accounts of Civil War readings of *The Bostonians*, see Leland Person, "In the Closet with Frederic Douglass: Reconstructing Masculinity in *The Bostonians*," *Henry James Review* 16, no. 3 (1995): 292–298; Aaron Shaheen, "Henry James's Southern Mode of Imagination: Men, Women, and the Image of the South in *The*

Bostonians," *Henry James Review* 24, no. 2 (2003): 180–192; Susan M. Ryan, "*The Bostonians* and the Civil War," *Henry James Review* 26, no. 3 (2005): 265–272; and Barbara Hotchman, "Reading Historically/Reading Selectively: *The Bostonians* in the *Century*, 1885–1886," *Henry James Review* 34, no. 3 (2013): 270–278. Hotchman's argument in particular situates the novel's Civil War theme in the context of the *Century*'s post-Reconstruction nationalism.

63. Ann Brigham, "Touring Memorial Hall: The State of the Union in *The Bostonians,*" *Arizona Quarterly* 62, no. 3 (2006): 14.

64. Henry James, *Notes of a Son and Brother*, in *Notes of a Son and Brother and The Middle Years: A Critical Edition*, ed. Peter Collister (Charlottesville: University of Virginia Press, 2011), 194. Further citations will appear parenthetically.

65. Tess Hoffmann and Charles Hoffmann, "Henry James and the Civil War," *The New England Quarterly* 62, no. 4 (1989): 533. See also Leon Edel, *Henry James: The Untried Years, 1843–1870* (New York: Avon, 1953); Paul John Eakin, "Henry James's 'Obscure Hurt': Can Autobiography Serve Biography?" *New Literary History* 19, no. 3 (1988): 675–692; John Halperin, "Henry James's Civil War," *Henry James Review* 17, no. 1 (1996): 22–29.

66. This date was two months after his name was found on the list of Newport youth drafted by lottery, though James never mentions the drafting anywhere in his writing. See Hoffman and Hoffman, 529.

67. Edel, *Untried*, 176.

68. Halperin, "Henry James's Civil War," 24.

69. Graham, 12.

70. Wendy Brown, "Wounded Attachments," *Political Theory* 21, no. 3 (1993): 390–410.

71. Ibid., 403, 398.

72. Ibid., 407.

73. Eve Sedgwick, *Touching Feeling: Affect, Pedagogy, Performativity* (Durham, NC: Duke University Press, 2003), 64.

74. Person, 295.

75. Judith Butler, *Undoing Gender* (New York: Routledge, 2004), 20.

76. Georges Bataille, *Erotism: Death and Sensuality* (San Francisco: City Lights Books, 1986), 22.

77. Herring, 27.

78. Ibid., 59.

79. For a reading of this image, see Thomas Bertonneau, "Like Hypatia before the Mob: Desire, Resentment, and Sacrifice in *The Bostonians* (An Anthropoetics)," *Nineteenth-Century Literature* 53, no. 1 (1998): 56–90.

80. Kahan, 52. Leslie Petty discusses a 1887 fan fictionalization of *The Bostonians* by Cecilia B. Whitehead, who used the pseudonym "Henrietta James." This pamphlet, titled "Another Chapter of 'The Bostonians,' " imagines the narrative's aftermath, in which Olive becomes a feminist lecturer and later is reunited with Verena (who, at the end, marries Henry Burrage). Leslie Petty, "The Political is Personal: The Feminist Lesson of Henry James's *The Bostonians*," *Women's Studies* 34 (2005): 398–402.

81. Henry James, *The Princess Casamassima* (New York: Penguin, 1987), 574. The Penguin edition is based on the first Macmillan edition of 1886. All other references to the text will be cited parenthetically.

82. Quoted in Nordau, 16.

83. Daniel Pick, *Faces of Degeneration: A European Disorder, c. 1848–1918* (Cambridge, MA: Cambridge University Press, 1989), 8. For some important accounts of degeneration, see Robert A. Nye, *Crime, Madness and Politics in Modern France: The Medical Concept of National Decline* (Princeton, NJ: Princeton University Press, 1984), and *Degeneration: The Dark Side of Progress*, ed. J. Edward Chamberlin and Sander L. Gilman (New York: Columbia University Press, 1985).

84. Robert A. Nye, "Sociology and Degeneration: The Irony of Progress," in *Degeneration: The Dark Side of Progress*, ed. J. Edward Chamberlin and Sander L. Gilman (New York: Columbia University Press, 1985), 60.

85. On Cesare Lombroso and his idea of "born criminals," see Pick, 109–154; Mary Gibson, *Born to Crime: Cesare Lombroso and the Origins of Biological Criminology* (Westport, CT: Praeger, 2002); and David G. Horn, *The Criminal Body: Lombroso and the Anatomy of Deviance* (New York: Routledge, 2003).

86. Pick, 222.

87. Nordau, 1.

202 NOTES

88. Ibid., 25, 40.
89. Pick, 68, 72. Nordau expresses a similar view, explaining the French people's particular predisposition to degeneration from the perspective of the historical trauma of the Revolution, which resulted in "the awful catastrophe of 1870" (42). He also draws on Lombroso, arguing that "it can scarcely be doubted that the writings and acts of revolutionists and anarchists are also attributed to degeneracy" (22).
90. Henry James, *The Princess Casamassima*, vol. 2 (London: Macmillan, 1921), 50.

Chapter 2

1. Kate Chopin, *The Awakening* (New York: Norton, 1899, rpt. 1994), 37. All other citations will be given parenthetically.
2. Theodore Roosevelt, Preface to Mrs. John Van Vorst and Marie Van Vorst, *The Woman Who Toils: Being the Experiences of Two Ladies as Factory Girls* (New York: Doubleday, Page & Co., 1903), viii.
3. Even though *The Awakening* was published in 1899 and does not explicitly specify the year in which the narrative is set, Barbara Ewell and Pamela Glenn Menke convincingly argue that the novel is set in the period from the summer of 1892 to the early spring of 1893. Grand Isle and Chênière Caminada were thoroughly destroyed by the Great October Storm of 1893, and the novel's passing mention of "the meeting of a branch Folk Lore Society" (72) attests that it is set in the year before the storm, since the New Orleans Association of the American Folklore Society was founded in February 1892. See Barbara C. Ewell and Pamela Glenn Menke, "*The Awakening* and the Great October Storm of 1893," *Southern Literary Journal* 42, no. 2 (2010): 1–11.
4. For New Orleans and its reputation as the "Southern Babylon," see Alecia P. Long, *The Great Southern Babylon: Sex, Race, and Respectability in New Orleans, 1865–1920* (Baton Rouge: Louisiana State University Press, 2004).
5. Michele A. Birnbaum, "'Alien Hands': Kate Chopin and the Colonization of Race," *American Literature* 66, no. 2 (1994): 307.
6. For some exemplary works on *The Awakening* and race, see Elizabeth Ammons, *Conflicting Stories: American Women Writers at the Turn into the Twentieth Century* (New York: Oxford University Press, 1991), 59–85; Sandra Gunning, *Race, Rape, and Lynching: The Red Record of American Literature, 1890–1912* (Oxford: Oxford University Press, 1996), 108–135; Phillip Barrish, "*The Awakening*'s Signifying Mexicanist Presence," *Studies in American Fiction* 28, no. 1 (2000): 55–76; Allison Berg, *Mothering the Race: Women's Narratives of Reproduction, 1890–1930* (Urbana: University of Illinois Press, 2002), 52–78.
7. Joyce Dyer, "Reading *The Awakening* with Toni Morrison," *Southern Literary Journal* 35, no. 1 (2002): 138–154; Toni Morrison, *Playing in The Dark: Whiteness and the Literary Imagination* (Cambridge, MA: Harvard University Press, 1992).
8. Morrison, 37.
9. Alys Eve Weinbaum, *Wayward Reproductions: Genealogies of Race and Nation in Transatlantic Modern Thought* (Durham, NC: Duke University Press, 2004), 5.
10. On November 18, 1892, Judge John H. Ferguson handed down the ruling against Plessy's claim in *Homer Adolph Plessy v. The State of Louisiana*; immediately, the Citizen's Committee took the case to the Louisiana Supreme Court, which upheld the original decision on November 22. In January 1893, the case now known as *Plessy v. Ferguson* was brought to the United States Supreme Court, but the case was suspended for a long time before the infamous 1896 decision was handed down. For another important reading of *Plessy*'s relation to *The Awakening*, see Wai Chee Dimock, *Residues of Justice: Literature, Law, Philosophy* (Berkeley: University of California Press, 1996), 227–231.
11. Cheryl I. Harris, "Whiteness as Property," *Harvard Law Review* 106, no. 8 (1993): 1714.
12. Quoted in Abraham Davis and Barbara Graham, *The Supreme Court, Race, and Civil Rights: From Marshall to Rehnquist* (Thousand Oaks, CA: Sage Publications, 1995), 51.
13. Ibid., 51.
14. Harris, 1749.
15. Weinbaum, 16.
16. Ibid., 21.
17. As Margit Stange points out, in Louisiana in the 1890s, when the Napoleonic Code was still in force, wives "had no separate legal or proprietary identity and could not own property in their own right." Margit Stange, *Personal Property: Wives, White Slaves, and the Market in Women* (Baltimore: Johns Hopkins University Press, 1998), 26. See also Dimock, 193–194.

NOTES 203

18. Jennifer L. Fleissner, *Women, Compulsion, Modernity: The Moment of American Naturalism* (Chicago: University of Chicago Press, 2004), 240.
19. Ibid., 241.
20. D. A. Miller, *The Novel and the Police* (Berkeley: University of California Press, 1989), 20, original emphasis.
21. Ibid., 162.
22. Ibid., x.
23. Dimock, 192.
24. John Locke, *Second Treatise of Government* (Indianapolis, IN: Hackett, 1690, rpt. 1980), 19.
25. Dimock, 194–195.
26. Adam Smith, *An Inquiry into the Nature and Causes of the Wealth of Nations* (Oxford: Clarendon Press, 1776, rpt. 1979), 456.
27. Miguel de Beistegui, *The Government of Desire* (Chicago: University of Chicago Press, 2018), 59.
28. On the Progressive Era's consolidation of state power and departure from *laissez-faire* economics, see Thomas C. Leonard, *Illiberal Reformers: Race, Eugenics, and American Economics in the Progressive Era* (Princeton, NJ: Princeton University Press, 2016).
29. Michel Foucault, *The Birth of Biopolitics: Lectures at the Collège de France, 1978–79*, trans. Graham Burchell (New York: Picador, 2008), 63.
30. Michel Foucault, *Security, Territory, Population: Lectures at the Collège de France 1977–1978*, trans. Graham Burchell (New York: Picador, 2007), 71.
31. Ibid., 6.
32. Ibid., 38.
33. Ibid., 42.
34. Ibid., 48.
35. Ibid., 48–49.
36. Ibid., 49.
37. Ibid., 42.
38. Joseph G. Tregle Jr., "Creoles and Americans," in *Creole New Orleans: Race and Americanization*, ed. Arnold R. Hirsch and Joseph Logsdon (Baton Rouge: Louisiana State University Press, 1992), 131–188, and Virginia R. Domínguez, *White by Definition: Social Classification in Creole Louisiana* (New Brunswick, NJ: Rutgers University Press, 1986).
39. Tregle, 135.
40. The term *Creole of color*, as Tregle explains, came into usage only after Black emancipation, as the term *creole* had been used without reference to color, sometimes even attached to animals and plants native to Louisiana. See Tregle, 137–141. Prior to the end of the Civil War, free Creoles of color were primarily called *gens de couleur libre*, or simply *gens de couleur*. In Louisiana, *gens de couleur libre* formed a prominent population because the custom of *plaçage*, a system of mixed-race concubinage whereby white male participants often gave manumission to their children as well as to their concubines, facilitated its growth. For a detailed account of *gens de couleur libre* and the custom of interracial concubinage, see Domínguez, 23–36; Joan Martin, "*Plaçage* and the Louisiana *Gens de Couleur Libre*: How Race and Sex Defined the Lifestyles of Free Women of Color," in *Creole: The History and Legacy of Louisiana's Free People of Color*, ed. Sybil Kein (Baton Rouge: Louisiana State University Press, 2000), 57–70.
41. On the white Creole organizations founded after Reconstruction to preserve their Gallic heritage and claim their whiteness, see Domínguez, 146–147.
42. Ewell and Menke, 7.
43. For Anglo-Saxonism's co-option of social Darwinism, see Richard Hofstadter, *Social Darwinism in American Thought* (Boston: Beacon, 1944, rpt. 1992), 170–200, and Eric T. L. Love, *Race over Empire: Racism and U.S. Imperialism, 1865–1900* (Chapel Hill: University of North Carolina Press, 2004), 1–26.
44. Hofstadter, 176–178.
45. Dyer, *Theodore Roosevelt*, 144. Nearly one million French-speakers migrated to the United States between 1840 and 1930 from what is now Canada, particularly from Québec and the region once known as Acadia (*Acadie*). The largest part of this immigrant population settled in New England and were often discriminated against for their French-speaking Roman Catholic heritage. After the Great Expulsion of Acadians between 1755 and 1764, some Acadians fled to Louisiana, where they later came to be known as "Cajuns." For a detailed history of French-Canadian migration to the United States, see David Vermette, *A Distinct Alien Race: The Untold Story of Franco-Americans* (Montréal, QC: Baraka Books, 2018).

204 NOTES

46. Lothrop Stoddard, *The Rising Tide of Color Against White World-Supremacy* (New York: Charles Scribner's and Sons, 1920, rpt. 1921), 107, 108.
47. Stoddard, 108.
48. Long, 7.
49. Anna Shannon Elfenbein, *Women on the Color Line: Evolving Stereotypes and the Writings of George Washington Cable, Grace King, and Kate Chopin* (Charlottesville: University of Virginia Press, 1989), 17. On *plaçage* and quadroon balls, see also Martin.
50. Among the most famous works of Cable's representation of interracial liaisons in the antebellum Creole community are a short story, "'Tite Poulette" (collected in *Old Creole Days*, published in 1879), *The Grandissimes: A Story of Creole Life*, and *Madame Delphine* (1881). In these works, Cable, representing Creole communities still clinging to their aristocratic heritage after the Louisiana Purchase, implicitly portrayed the postbellum white Creoles' anxiety over the Northerners' incursion into New Orleans. Through this dual representation, Cable critiqued the Creoles' hypocrisy and obsession with their racial lineage. As a result, Cable, a non-Creole born in New Orleans, came to be known as the "most cordially hated little man in New Orleans," opening himself to vociferous attacks from white Creoles and their non-Creole supporters, most notably Grace King (quoted in Tregle, 131). For an excellent account of Cable's critique of racial inequality in his Creole stories and Grace King's response, see Elfenbein.
51. Domínguez, 141.
52. Weinbaum, 15–20.
53. Kate Chopin, "Désirée's Baby," in *Kate Chopin: Complete Novels and Stories* (New York: Library of America, 2002), 242. For an important reading of this story, see Brigitte Fiedler, *Relative Races: Genealogies of Interracial Kinship in Nineteenth-Century America* (Durham, NC: Duke University Press, 2020), 1–3.
54. Chopin, "Désirée's Baby," 247.
55. Weinbaum, 16.
56. Georg Simmel, *On Women, Sexuality, and Love*, trans. Guy Oaks (New Haven, CT: Yale University Press, 1984), 144.
57. Ibid., 146.
58. Mikko Tuhkanen, "Breeding (and) Reading: Lesbian Knowledge, Eugenic Discipline, and *The Children's Hour*," *MFS* 48, no. 4 (2002): 1002. For lesbian readings of *The Awakening*, see, for example, Kathryn Lee Seidel, "Art is an Unnatural Act: Mademoiselle Reisz in *The Awakening*," *Mississippi Quarterly* 46, no. 2 (1993): 199–214; Elizabeth LeBlanc, "The Metaphorical Lesbian: Edna Pontellier in *The Awakening*," *Tulsa Studies in Women's Literature* 15, no. 2 (1996): 289–307; and Mary Biggs, "'Si tu savais': The Gay/Transgendered Sensibility of Kate Chopin's *The Awakening*," *Women's Studies* 33, no. 2 (2010): 145–181.
59. Rachel Bowlby, *Shopping with Freud* (London: Routledge, 1993), 8.
60. Henry Abelove, "Some Speculations on the History of Sexual Intercourse during the Long Eighteenth Century in England," in *Deep Gossip* (Minneapolis: University of Minnesota Press, 2005), 23. Abelove argues that "cross-sex genital intercourse (penis in vagina, vagina around penis, with seminal emission uninterrupted)" might have become the dominant form of what we conceive as "sex" only in the late eighteenth century (23). He sees the correlation between the Industrial Revolution and population growth in eighteenth-century England as a manifestation of productivism. Accordingly, he hypothesizes that diverse sexual acts such as "mutual masturbation, oral sex, anal sex, display and watching" were "reconstructed and reorganized in the late eighteenth century as foreplay . . ., relegated and largely confined to the position of the preliminary" (27). Read in this context, Edna's attachment to "foreplay" rather than sexual intercourse so-called could be seen as a sign of the decline of productivism at the dawn of the consumerist economy.
61. Bonnie James Shaker, *Coloring Locals: Racial Formation in Kate Chopin's "Youth's Companion" Stories* (Iowa City: University of Iowa Press, 2002), 10. The list of Chopin's short stories published in *Vogue* is as follows: "Désirée's Baby" (January 14, 1893), "A Visit to Avoyelles" (January 14, 1893), "Caline" (May 20, 1893), "A Lady of Bayou St. John" (September 21, 1893), "Ripe Figs" (August 1893), "Doctor Chevalier's Lie" (October 5, 1893), "La Belle Zoraïde" (January 1894), "A Respectable Woman" (February 15, 1894), "The Story of an Hour" (originally titled "The Dream of an Hour") (December 6, 1894), "The Kiss" (January 17, 1895), "Her Letters" (April 18 and 25, 1895), "Two Summers and Two Souls" (August 7, 1895), "The Unexpected" (September 19, 1895), "The Recovery" (May 21, 1896), "A Pair of Silk Stockings" (September 16, 1897), "The Blindman" (May 13, 1897), "Suzette" (October 21, 1897), "An Egyptian Cigarette" (October 21,

NOTES 205

1897), and "The White Eagle" (July 12, 1900). After Josephine Redding was let go from her post as the chief editor of *Vogue* in 1900, *Vogue* ceased to publish Chopin's works. Other than *Vogue*, only *Youth's Companion* printed her works after *The Awakening*. "The Wood-Choppers" and "Polly" were published, respectively, on May 29, 1902 and July 3, 1902.

62. Josephine Redding, editorial, *Vogue*, December 17, 1892, 2. Daniel Deils Hill points to three factors—fashion journalism, ready-to-wear manufacturing, and fashion advertising—that enabled the inauguration of those magazines: "During the last quarters of the nineteenth century, numerous women's magazines made their debut: *Delineator* (1873), *McCall's* (1876), *Ladies' World* (1880), *Ladies' Home Journal* (1883), *Good Housekeeping* (1885), and *Cosmopolitan* (1886), to name a few." Daniel Deils Hill, *As Seen in Vogue: A Century of American Fashion in Advertising* (Lubbock: Texas Tech University Press, 2004), 4.

63. Of Chopin's nineteen *Vogue* short stories, ten were to be collected in her third book, *A Vocation and a Voice*, in 1900. The book, however, would not see the light of day until 1991, as Herbert S. Stone & Co. cancelled her publication contract. The cancellation was presumably because of the stir caused by *The Awakening*, as the book was described by many contemporary reviewers as "sick," "morbid," and "sex fiction," which "can hardly be described in language fit for publication." See Chopin, *The Awakening*, 162, 163, 166.

64. Kate Chopin, "A Pair of Silk Stockings," in *Kate Chopin: Complete Novels and Stories* (New York: Library of America, 2002), 817.

65. Ibid., 818.

66. Bowlby, 8. For exemplary works on turn-of-the-century consumerism, see Rita Felski, *Gender of Modernity* (Cambridge, MA: Harvard University Press, 1995), 61–90; Mark Selzer, *Bodies and Machines* (New York: Routledge, 1992), especially 119–146; and Fleissner, 161–200.

67. Chopin, "A Pair of Silk Stockings," 820.

68. Dianne Bunch, "Dangerous Spending Habits: The Epistemology of Edna Pontellier's Extravagant Expenditures in *The Awakening*," *Mississippi Quarterly* 55, no. 1 (2002): 49.

69. Thorstein Veblen, *The Theory of the Leisure Class* (Oxford: Oxford University Press, 2009), 30.

70. Charlotte P. Gilman, *Women and Economics: A Study of the Economic Relation Between Men and Women as a Factor in Social Evolution* (Boston: Small, Maynard & Company, 1898), 120.

71. Ibid., 59, 178.

72. For some exemplary accounts of the interrelation between eugenics and Progressive Era maternalism, see, for instance, Gail Bederman, *Manliness and Civilization: A Cultural History of Gender and Race in the United States, 1880–1917* (Chicago: University of Chicago Press, 1995), 121–169; Berg, *Mothering the Race*, 55–67; Fleissner, 233–274; Daylanne K. English, *Unnatural Selections: Eugenics in American Modernism and the Harlem Renaissance* (Chapel Hill: University of North Carolina Press, 2004), 141–170; Weinbaum, 61–105; and Dana Seitler, *Atavistic Tendencies: The Culture of Science in American Modernity* (Minneapolis: University of Minnesota Press, 2008), 175–198.

73. Charlotte Perkins Gilman, *Herland, The Yellow Wall-Paper, and Selected Writings* (New York: Penguin, 1999), 58, 59, 58; italics added.

74. Ibid., 55. Walter Benn Michaels, *Our America: Nativism, Modernism, and Pluralism* (Durham, NC: Duke University Press, 1995), 12.

75. Josephine Redding, editorial, *Vogue* 113, February 7, 1895; Josephine Redding, Editorial, *Vogue*, March 15, 1900.

76. Josephine Redding, editorial, *Vogue*, May 24, 1895.

77. For an analysis of the relation between productivism, consumerism, and sexuality to which these points are indebted, see Lawrence Birken, *Consuming Desire: Sexual Science and the Emergence of a Culture of Abundance, 1871–1914* (Ithaca, NY: Cornell University Press, 1988).

78. Josephine Redding, editorial, December 24, 1892.

79. Ibid.

80. Ibid.

81. Seltzer, 58, 56.

82. Fleissner, 143, 44, 136.

83. Bowlby, 14.

84. Fleissner, 159.

85. Kate Chopin, "An Egyptian Cigarette," in *Kate Chopin: Complete Novels and Stories* (New York: Library of America), 895.

86. Ibid., 896, 897.

87. Oscar Wilde, *The Picture of Dorian Gray* (New York: Penguin, 2000), 123.

206 NOTES

88. Bowlby, 8, 7–8.
89. Chopin, "An Egyptian Cigarette," 896.
90. Jacques Derrida, "Le Toucher: Touch/To Touch Him," *Paragraph* 16, no. 2 (1993): 136.
91. Richard Bell, *We Shall Be No More: Suicide and Self-Government in the Newly United States* (Cambridge, MA: Harvard University Press, 2012), 39, 201–246. As Bell argues, since the seventeenth century, US discourse on slave suicide had oscillated between two interpretive frameworks: whether to see it as "an act of principled yet costly resistance to tyranny" or as "abject victimhood that begged for humanitarian intervention" (203). Put differently, slave suicide presented itself as a problematic straddling the opposite ends of agency's spectrum: either the ultimate form of self-mastery or absolute passivity. By the mid-nineteenth century, the first understanding gradually became dominant.
92. Bell, 239. This discursive trend continued after Emancipation. Frederick Douglass's *Life and Times of Frederick Douglass* (1881) records one example, in which Demby, an enslaved man, chooses death by an overseer's bullet.
93. William Bells Brown, *Clotel; or, the President's Daughter: A Narrative of Slave Life in the United States*, ed. Robert S. Levine (Boston: Bedford, 2000), 197.
94. Ibid.
95. Ibid., 205.
96. Ibid., 209.
97. See for instance, Bell, 240–241; Russ Castronovo, *Necro Citizenship: Death, Eroticism, and the Public Sphere in the Nineteenth-Century United States* (Durham, NC: Duke University Press, 2001), 35–50; and Paul Gilroy, *The Black Atlantic: Modernity and Double-Consciousness* (New York: Verso, 1993), 63, 233 n. 65.
98. William Wirt, *Sketches of the Life and Character of Patrick Henry* (Philadelphia: James Webster, 1818), 123.
99. For slavery's rhetorical role in the Founding, see Peter A. Dorsey, "To 'Corroborate Our Own Claims': Public Positioning and the Slavery Metaphor in Revolutionary America," *American Quarterly* 55, no. 3 (2003): 353–386. For slavery's foundational role in the American Revolution, see, for instance, Orlando Patterson, *Slavery and Social Death: A Comparative Study* (Cambridge, MA: Harvard University Press, 1982), especially 340–342, and Frank B. Wilderson III, *Red, White and Black: Cinema and Structure of U.S. Antagonisms* (Durham, NC: Duke University Press, 2010), especially 17–23. For the relationship between biopolitics, liberalism, and slavery, see Achille Mbembe, *Critique of Black Reason*, trans. Lauren Dubois (Durham, NC: Duke University Press, 2017), particularly 79–84.
100. On lynching in the Progressive Era, see, for instance, Trudier Harris, *Exorcizing Blackness: Historical and Literary Lynching and Burning Rituals* (Bloomington: Indiana University Press, 1984); Bederman, 45–76; Robyn Wiegman, *American Anatomies* (Durham, NC: Duke University Press, 1995); Gunning; Phillip Dray, *At the Hands of Persons Unknown: The Lynching of Black America* (New York: Random House, 2002), 1–251; Jacqueline Goldsby, *A Spectacular Secret: Lynching in American Literature* (Chicago: University of Chicago Press, 2006); and Manfred Berg, *Popular Justice: A History of Lynching in America* (Chicago: Ivan R. Dee, 2011), 90–116.
101. Harris, 54–81. See also Ida B. Wells, *On Lynchings* (Amherst, NY: Humanity Books, 2002).
102. John N. Swift and Gigen Mamoser, "'Out of the Realm of Superstition': Chesnutt's 'Dave's Neckliss' and the Curse of Ham," *American Literary Realism* 42, no. 1 (2009): 2.
103. Hortense J. Spillers, "Mama's Baby, Papa's Maybe: An American Grammar Book," *Diacritics* 17, no. 2 (1987): 67, 72.
104. Charles W. Chesnutt, "Dave's Neckliss," *Atlantic Monthly* 64 (1889): 502.
105. Chesnutt, 504, 505. On "quare," see E. Patrick Johnson, *Sweet Tea: Black Gay Men of the South* (Chapel Hill: University of North Carolina Press, 2008), and Michael Bibler, "Queer/Quare," in *Keywords for Southern Studies*, ed. Scott Romine and Jennifer Rae Greeson (Athens: University of Georgia Press, 2016), 200–212.
106. Aliyyah Abdur-Rahman, *Against the Closet: Identity, Political Longing, and Black Figuration* (Durham, NC: Duke University Press, 2012), 51. On the libidinal nature of lynching, see also Trudier Harris, *Exorcizing Blackness: Historical and Literary Linching and Burning Rituals* (Bloomington: Indiana University Press, 1984); Orlando Patterson, *Rituals of Blood: Consequences of Slavery in Two American Centuries* (New York: Basic Books, 1998); Melissa Stein, *Measuring Manhood: Race and the Science of Masculinity, 1839–1934* (Minneapolis: University of Minnesota Press, 2015); and Robyn Wiegman, *American Anatomies* (Durham, NC: Duke University Press, 1995).

NOTES 207

107. Chesnutt, 500.
108. Saidiya Hartman, *Scenes of Subjection: Terror, Slavery, and Self-Making in Nineteenth-Century America* (Oxford: Oxford University Press, 1997), 127.
109. Hartman, 140.
110. In attempting to elucidate this something else, I think in concert with Kevin Quashie, who finds that "an overemphasis on death simplifies the nuanced insights of black pessimism and its related discourses." Kevin Quashie, *Black Aliveness, or A Poetics of Being* (Durham, NC: Duke University Press, 2021), 9.
111. Kyla Wazana Tompkins, *Racial Indigestion: Eating Bodies in the 19th Century* (New York: New York University Press, 2012), 3.

Chapter 3

1. Jack London, *Martin Eden* (New York: Penguin, 1909, rpt. 1993), 106, 211. All other citations will be given parenthetically in the text. For an argument about "poodle" Henry James, see Chapter 1.
2. London wrote an extensive reportage for the *New York Herald* in July 1910 on the boxing match between the "Great White Hope," a former heavy-weight world champion James Jefferies, and a Black heavy-weight world champion, Jack Johnson. Johnson's defeat of Jefferies in what was called the "Fight of the Century" led to incidents of white supremacist violence across the country. London's ten-day report on the two boxers is collected in *Jack London: Stories of Boxing*, ed. James Bankes (Dubuque, IA: William C. Brown, 1992), 151–187. London likens Jefferies to "the legendary Teutonic warrior," the race ideal that, I will argue throughout this chapter, was central to London's early career development as well as to the anti-immigration arguments of the turn of the twentieth century (159).
3. I would like to thank Benjy Kahan for pointing me to the importance of the Schopenhauerian valence of "the will to live" here, especially its double relation to the species and the individual continuance. For Kahan's argument on Schopenhauer's relation to the history of sexuality, see his forthcoming *Sexual Aim and Its Misses*. For the procreative imperative of the will to live, see Arthur Schopenhauer, *The World as Will and Representation*, vol. 2 (Cambridge: Cambridge University Press, 2018), 526–532. Additionally, while for Martin suicide is the way to negate the will to live, Schopenhauer specifically discounts suicide's capacity to do so. For Schopenhauer's argument on suicide, see Arthur Schopenhauer, *The World as Will and Representation*, vol. 1 (Cambridge: Cambridge University Press, 2010), 425–429.
4. John Burroughs, "Real and Sham Natural History," *The Atlantic Monthly* 91 (1903): 299. Burroughs's primary target in this article is American naturalist and minister Reverend William J. Long, as well as Canadian writers such as Ernest Thompson Seton and Charles G. D. Roberts. For a detailed account of the nature faker controversy, see Ralph H. Lutts, *The Nature Fakers: Wildlife, Science and Sentiment* (Charlottesville: University Press of Virginia, 1990).
5. Theodore Roosevelt, "Nature-Fakers," in *Roosevelt's Writings: Selections from the Writings of Theodore Roosevelt*, ed. Maurice Garland Fulton (New York: Macmillan, 1920), 266, 263.
6. London's nickname "Wolf" was originally given by one of his most intimate friends, George Sterling. London signed his letters as "Wolf" to Sterling and his second wife Charmian, called his dream house in Beauty Ranch "Wolf House," and created a custom-made wolf-head insignia to mark his literary property. On London's Wolf-identification, see Jonathan Auerbach, *Male Call: Becoming Jack London* (Durham, NC: Duke University Press, 1996), 9; Jeanne Campbell Reesman, *Jack London's Racial Lives: A Critical Biography* (Athens: University of Georgia Press, 2009), 61–62; and Michael Lundblad, *The Birth of a Jungle: Animality in Progressive-Era U.S. Literature and Culture* (Oxford: Oxford University Press, 2013), 49–74.
7. Roosevelt, "Nature-Fakers," 262.
8. Jack London, "Other Animals," in *Revolution and Other Essays* (New York: Macmillan, 1910), 245.
9. Ibid., 245, 245, 240.
10. Ibid., 259, 250.
11. Ibid., 265–266, 266, 265.
12. Ibid., 240, 241.
13. Theodore Roosevelt, *The Letters of Theodore Roosevelt*, vol. 6, *The Big Stick, 1907–1909*, ed. Elting E. Morison (Cambridge, MA: Harvard University Press, 1952), 1221.

208   NOTES

14. Ibid., 1223.
15. Jonathan Berliner interprets this line as Roosevelt's indirect attack on London's socialism. See "Jack London's Social Darwinism," *American Literary Realism* 41, no. 4 (2008): 52–78.
16. Lutts, *Nature Fakers*, 1.
17. Donna Varga, "Teddy's Bear and the Transfiguration of Savage Beasts into Innocent Children, 1890–1920," *Journal of American Culture* 32, no. 2 (2009): 98.
18. On Boone's and Crockett's conservation movement, see Jonathan Spiro, *Defending the Master Race: Conservation, Eugenics, and the Legacy of Madison Grant* (Burlington: University of Vermont Press, 2008), 15–29.
19. Quoted in Varga, 99.
20. Ibid., 100.
21. Ibid., 108. Ironically enough, some period critics accused the teddy bear as "destructive of the instincts of real motherhood and perhaps leading to race suicide" as the stuffed bear's popularity surpassed that of the dolls that had been cherished not only by girls but also by adult women. See Laura Lovett, *Conceiving the Future: Pronatalism, Reproduction, and the Family in the United States, 1890–1938* (Chapel Hill: University of North Carolina Press, 2007), 95.
22. Donna Haraway, "Teddy Bear Patriarchy: Taxidermy in the Garden of Eden, New York City, 1908–1936," *Social Text* 11 (1984–1985): 20–64.
23. Ibid., 42–43.
24. Ibid., 53.
25. Though he was called "Johnny" at home, London adopted "Jack" as his pen name from his nursemaid Virginia Prentiss's pet name for him. The Prentisses were Black neighbors of the Londons, and Virginia (whom London called "Aunt Jennie") became particularly close to young London. For detailed accounts of London's relation to Virginia Prentiss, see Reesman, 23–30.
26. Reesman, 4.
27. Jack London, *John Barleycorn: Alcoholic Memoirs* (New York: Century, 1913), 22.
28. Reesman, 22.
29. London, *John Barleycorn*, 26, 22.
30. Reesman's *Jack London's Racial Lives* provides the most comprehensive and nuanced account of London's shifting racial ideologies throughout his life.
31. London's alignment with scientific racism has been understood almost exclusively within the framework of Anglo-Saxonism. On London's Anglo-Saxonism, see, for instance, Andrew J. Furer, "'Zone-Conquerors' and 'White Devils': The Contradictions of Race in the Works of Jack London," in *Rereading Jack London*, ed. Leonard Cassuto and Jeanne Campbell Reesman (Stanford, CA: Stanford University Press, 1996), 158–171; Agnes Malinowska, "From Atavistic Gutter-Wolves to Anglo-Saxon Wolf: Evolution and Technology in Jack London's Urban Industrial Modernity," in *The Oxford Handbook of Jack London*, ed. Jay Williams (Oxford: Oxford University Press, 2017), 438–455. It is certainly true that Teutonism cannot be completely disarticulated from Anglo-Saxonism and that London sometime put more emphasis on (Anglo-)Saxonism, especially in his later career (in such works as *The Valley of the Moon* [1913], whose protagonist is named Saxon). However, as I will discuss further in this chapter, London's race ideals in the 1890s and the early 1900s are often figured as an ethnic amalgamation of the Saxon and the Celt (such as Frona Welse in *A Daughter of the Snows* or Stebbins in *The Kempton-Wace Letters*), and this inclusion of the Celts (who had been excluded from the center of whiteness because of their association with Catholicism) at the center of whiteness, as well as the emphasis on the Scandinavian origin of whiteness, are two of the discursive features of American Teutonism and Nordicism of his time.
32. Jack London, *The Letters of Jack London*, ed. Earle Labor et al. (Stanford, CA: Stanford University Press, 1988), 86.
33. Ibid., 86, 87.
34. Ibid., 87. For London's relation to social Darwinism, see Berliner, as well as Lawrence I. Berkove, "Jack London and Evolution: From Spencer to Huxley," *American Literary Realism* 36, no. 3 (2004): 243–255.
35. Quoted in Reginald Horsman, *Race and Manifest Destiny: The Origins of American Racial Anglo-Saxonism* (Cambridge, MA: Harvard University Press, 1981), 76.
36. Ibid., 38.
37. William Zebina Ripley, *The Races of Europe: A Sociological Study* (New York: D. Appleton and Co., 1899), 32, 1.

NOTES   209

38. Ibid., 457, 470.
39. For the detailed discussion of Ripley's impact on Grant, see Spiro, 92–100.
40. Ibid., 123.
41. Houston Steward Chamberlain, *The Foundation of the Nineteenth Century*, trans. John Lees (New York: John Lane, 1912), 257.
42. Spiro, 109; Chamberlain, xlviii.
43. Chamberlain, xlviii.
44. Madison Grant, *The Passing of the Great Race, or the Racial Basis of European History* (New York: Charles Scribner's Sons, 1916), 155.
45. Grant, 23.
46. Grant, 187, 44.
47. Jack London, *The Sea-Wolf*, in *Jack London: Novels and Stories* (New York: Library of America, 1982), 593.
48. Ibid., 557.
49. Ibid., 552.
50. Ibid., 593–594.
51. Scott Derrick, "Making a Heterosexual Man: Gender, Sexuality, and Narrative in the Fiction of Jack London," in *Rereading Jack London*, ed. Leonard Cassuto and Jeanne Campbell Reesman (Stanford: Stanford University Press, 1996), 111.
52. London, *Sea-Wolf*, 557, 712.
53. John Bruni also focuses on the concept of atavism in his analysis of *The Call of the Wild*, arguing that atavism in the novel functions as "the nostalgic desire for recovery of the lost frontier and a hope that the 'frontier spirit' might be resurrected." John Bruni, "Furry Logic: Biological Kinship and Empire in Jack London's *The Call of the Wild*," *Interdisciplinary Studies in Literature and Environment* 14, no. 1 (2007): 27.
54. Dana Seitler, *Atavistic Tendencies: The Culture of Science in American Modernity* (Minneapolis: University of Minnesota Press, 2008), 1.
55. Ibid., 2.
56. Ripley, 1.
57. Seitler, 3.
58. For London's discovery of his illegitimacy, see Joan London, *Jack London and His Times: An Unconventional Biography* (New York: Book League of America, 1939), 134–135. The incident was covered in an article published in the *San Francisco Chronicle*, June 4, 1875, titled "A Discarded Wife: Why Mrs. Chaney Twice Attempted Suicide," which is reprinted in Russ Kingman, *A Pictorial Life of Jack London* (New York: Crown, 1979), 15–17.
59. Quoted in Kingman, 18. Chaney wrote twice to London, suggesting London's potential fathers in the first letter (June 4, 1897) and detailing Flora's "loose character" and promiscuity in the second (June 14, 1897). Both of letters are reprinted in Kingman, 18–21.
60. Frederick Jackson Turner, "The Significance of the Frontier in American History," in *The Frontier in American History* (New York: Henry Holt and Co., 1920), 2–3.
61. London's strict discipline about his writing quota has often been discussed in association with the mass-producing ethos of the Progressive Era. Jonathan Auerbach, for instance, reads it as "a kind of literary Taylorism" (22), while Mark Seltzer, analyzing "an erotics of discipline" in London's works, sees it as a form of "nonbiological and autonomous reproduction" that attempts to replace heterosexual biological reproduction. See Mark Seltzer, *Bodies and Machines* (New York: Routledge, 1992), 33, 169.
62. Quoted in Reesman, 62.
63. Jack London, *Children of the Frost* (New York: Century, 1902), 3.
64. Jack London, *A Daughter of the Snows* (Philadelphia: J. B. Lippincott Company, 1902), 86, 146. All other citations will be given parenthetically in the text.
65. Grant, 155.
66. Spiro, xii.
67. Ibid., xiii.
68. Quoted in ibid., 72. The bill was passed shortly with the strong support of Grant's old friend and president, Theodore Roosevelt, and it became one of the earliest wilderness protection acts.
69. Turner, 3.
70. Ibid., 4.
71. Ibid., 15, 4.
72. Auerbach, 48.

210 NOTES

73. Jack London, *Son of the Wolf: Tales of the Far North* (Boston: Houghton, Mifflin and Company, 1900), 30.
74. Ibid., 37.
75. Auerbach, 57.
76. London, *Son of the Wolf*, 31.
77. Ibid., 26.
78. Auerbach, 58, 60.
79. The first recorded usage of the word "kinship" in the *OED* is in 1833, in the sense of "relationship by descent; consanguinity." The second definition, whose first recorded usage appeared in 1866, is more closely related to anthropological discourse: "The recognized ties of relationship, by descent, marriage, or ritual, that form the basis of social organization."
80. David Schneider, *A Critique of the Study of Kinship* (Ann Arbor: University of Michigan Press, 1984), 97.
81. Quoted in Marshall Sahlins, *What Kinship Is and Is Not* (Chicago: University of Chicago Press, 2013), 17. For a vital intervention into kinship studies, see Teagan Bradway and Elizabeth Freeman, ed., *Queer Kinship: Race, Sex, Belonging, Form* (Durham, NC: Duke University Press, 2022).
82. Quoted in Sahlins, 18.
83. Quoted in ibid., 18.
84. Quoted in Schneider, 104, original emphasis.
85. Sigmund Freud, *Totem and Taboo: Resemblances between the Psychic Lives of Savages and Neurotics*, trans. A. A. Brill (London: George Routledge and Sons, 1919), 193, 194.
86. Ibid., 193.
87. London, *Children of the Frost*, 37, 79, 126.
88. London, *Son of the Wolf*, 41.
89. Mark Rifkin, *When Did Indians Become Straight? Kinship, the History of Sexuality, and Native Sovereignty* (New York: Oxford University Press, 2011), 36.
90. Ibid., 37.
91. Ibid., 153.
92. Nancy Cott, *Public Vows: A History of Marriage and the Nation* (Cambridge, MA: Harvard University Press, 2000), 121.
93. On anti-miscegenation laws regarding the marriage between Native Americans and whites, see Peggy Pascoe, *What Comes Naturally: Miscegenation Law and the Making of Race in America* (Oxford: Oxford University Press, 2010), 94–104. Pascoe argues that while matrimony between white men and Indigenous women had been largely sanctioned in the first half of the nineteenth century because of its bolstering effect on white land settlement, it began to be regulated in the 1860s, when the states of Washington, Nevada, Idaho, and Arizona added "Indians" to the targets of their miscegenation laws. These laws were increasingly enforced in the 1890s, especially after the Dawes Act of 1887.
94. Reesman, 50.
95. Jack London and Anna Strunsky, *The Kempton-Wace Letters* (New York: Macmillan, 1903), 7. All further citations will be given parenthetically in the text.
96. As Auerbach writes, *The Kempton-Wace Letters* is "probably the least-read work" of London, "perhaps for the very reason that the shared billing complicates our image of London as an independent self-made author" (149). Auerbach's *Male Call* is an important exception, providing a rich account of London's complex relation to Jewishness and of his fetishization of Strunsky as a "Jewess." See Auerbach, 148–177.
97. Kate Chopin, *The Awakening* (New York: Norton, 1899, rpt. 1994), 123.
98. London, *Letters*, 307.
99. Ibid., 309.
100. On the relationship between authorship, fatherhood, and race, see Yoshiaki Furui, " 'No One Is His Own Sire': Dead Letters and Kinship in Melville's *Pierre*," *Journal of the American Literature Society of Japan* 8 (2010): 1–17.
101. Jack London, *The Call of the Wild*, in *Jack London: Novels and Stories* (New York: Library of America, 1982), 60. All other citations will be given parenthetically in the text.
102. Robert J. C. Young, *Colonial Desire: Hybridity in Theory, Culture, and Race* (New York: Routledge, 1995), 7.
103. Lundblad, 49.

NOTES   211

104. Seltzer, 166.
105. For a detailed account of the "wolf," see George Chauncey, *Gay New York: Gender, Urban Culture, and the Making of the Gay Male World, 1890–1940* (New York: Basic Books, 1994), 65–98. Both Jonathan Auerbach and Michael Lundblad refer to this sexual figuration in their discussions of London's wolf-identification. For Auerbach's reading of the "wolf" in relation to Wolf Larsen in *The Sea-Wolf*, see Auerbach, 198. Lundblad's reading of the "wolf" also draws on Chauncey, arguing that the wolf's non-identitarian figuration before the calcification of "homosexual" identity signals a form of sexuality that does "not depend upon the object choice" (68).
106. Marjorie Garber, *Dog Love* (New York: Touchstone, 1996), 120. Though Garber's reading of London's canine stories is brief (120–121), her book takes the position that interspecies love between a human and a dog "is not an evasion or a substitution" for an intra-human relationship (14).
107. Lundblad, 66.
108. Ibid., 70, 68.
109. Gilles Deleuze and Félix Guattari, *A Thousand Plateaus: Capitalism and Schizophrenia*, trans. Brian Massumi (Minneapolis: University of Minnesota Press, 1987), 14.
110. Ibid., 238.
111. Ibid., 240, original emphasis.
112. Ibid., 240, 241.
113. Ibid., 233.
114. Henry James, *The Bostonians: Henry James, Novels 1881–1886*, ed. William T. Stafford (New York: Library of America, 1985), 935. For a longer reading of this quotation see Chapter 1.
115. Bruni, 42. For a similar argument about this scene's restaging of settler-colonialist violence, see Amy Kaplan, "Nation, Region, and Empire," in *Columbia History of the American Novel*, ed. Emory Elliot (New York: Columbia University Press, 1991), 240–266.
116. The popularized phrase "Kill the Indian, save the man" is drawn from the 1892 speech by Richard Henry Pratt, the longtime superintendent of the Carlisle Indian Industrial School: "A great general has said that the only good Indian is a dead one, and that high sanction of his destruction has been an enormous factor in promoting Indian massacres. In a sense, I agree with the sentiment, but only in this: that all the Indian there is in the race should be dead. Kill the Indian in him, and save the man." Richard H. Pratt, "The Advantages of Mingling Indians with Whites," in *Americanizing the American Indians: Writings by the "Friends of the Indian" 1880–1900*, ed. Francis Paul Prucha (Cambridge, MA: Harvard University Press, 1973), 261–262.
117. Joseph M. Pierce (Cherokee Nation), "In Good Relations: Native Adoption, Kinstillations, and the Grounding of Memory," in *Queer Kinship: Race, Sex, Belonging, Form*, ed. Teagan Bradway and Elizabeth Freeman (Durham, NC: Duke University Press, 2022), 103. For an excellent overview of the history of boarding schools, see David Wallace Adams, *Education for Extinction: American Indians and the Boarding School Experience, 1875–1928* (Lawrence: University Press of Kansas, 1995).
118. On the discourse of the "vanishing race," see Patrick Brantlinger, *Dark Vanishings: Discourse of the Extinction of the Primitive Races, 1800–1930* (Ithaca, NY: Cornell University Press, 2003), especially 45–67, and James M. O'Brien, *Firsting and Lasting: Writing Indians Out of Existence in New England* (Minneapolis: University of Minnesota Press, 2010), especially 105–144.
119. Joshua Schuster, *What Is Extinction? A Natural and Cultural History of Last Animals* (New York: Fordham University Press, 2023), 68. See also Charles L. Crow, "Ishi and Jack London's Primitives," in *Rereading Jack London*, ed. Leonard Cassuto and Jeanne Campbell Reesman (Stanford, CA: Stanford University Press, 1996), 46–54.
120. Deleuze and Guattari, *A Thousand Plateaus*, 239.
121. Walter Benn Michaels, *Our America: Nativism, Modernism, and Pluralism* (Durham, NC: Duke University Press, 1995), 31.
122. Jack London, "Other Animals," 240–241.
123. Ibid., 241.
124. Deleuze and Guattari, 238.
125. Ibid., 238.
126. Ibid., 239.
127. Ibid., 240.

212 NOTES

128. On London's death and the extensive rumors about his suicide, see Earle Labor, *Jack London: An American Life* (New York: Farrar, Straus and Giroux, 2013), 381, 425. Labor forcefully argues that the suicide is a myth.

129. Chamberlain, xlviii. Woodrow Wilson exemplifies this anti-immigration argument about self-government as a constitutive feature of white native-born Americans: "Our own temperate blood, schooled to self-possession and to the measured conduct of self-government, is receiving a constant infusion and yearly experiencing a partial corruption of foreign blood. Our own equable habits have been crossed with the feverish humors of the restless Old World. We are unquestionably facing an ever-increasing difficulty of self-command with ever-deteriorating materials, possibly with degenerating fibre." Woodrow Wilson, "Character of Democracy in the United States," in *An Old Master and Other Political Essays* (New York: Charles Scribner's and Sons, 1893), 126.

130. Friedrich Nietzsche, *Thus Spoke Zarathustra*, trans. Thomas Common (New York: The Modern Library, 1917), 8.

131. Ibid.

132. For the origin and the circulation of the phrase "The only good Indian is a dead Indian," see Wolfgang Mieder, "'The Only Good Indian Is a Dead Indian': History and Meaning of a Proverbial Stereotype," *Journal of American Folklore* 106, no. 419 (1993): 38–60. Mieder attributes the origin of the phrase not to Phillip Sheridan but to a congressman from Montana, James Michael Cavanaugh. During a debate on an Indian Appropriation Bill in May 1868, Cavanaugh remarked: "I have never in my life seen a good Indian except when I have seen a dead Indian" (42).

133. Martin Eden, in this sense, represents what Yoshiaki Furui terms *lonely individualism*, the heavy emotional tax of desolation that comes with American individualism's lionization of lofty solitude. To use Frui's words describing Ahab in *Moby-Dick*, the task assigned to Martin Eden is "to test the limits of individualism, not in theory, but in his own person." Yoshiaki Furui, "Lonely Individualism in *Moby-Dick*," *Criticism* 62, no. 4 (2020): 613.

Chapter 4

1. Elliott Robert Barkan and Michael C. LeMay, *U.S. Immigration and Naturalization Laws and Issues: A Documentary History* (Westport, CT: Greenwood, 1999), 47.

2. Henry James, *The American Scene* (London: Chapman and Hall, 1907), 85. For an interpretation of this passage in a different key, as well as queer readings of southern and eastern European immigrant literature, see Madoka Kishi, "Queering Immigration and the Social Body, 1875–1924," in *The Cambridge History of Queer American Literature*, ed. Benjamin Kahan, (Cambridge: Cambridge University Press, 2024), 89–109.

3. Ibid., 64, italics original.

4. Ibid., 64, italics original.

5. Ibid., 121.

6. For a brief history of the origin of the "melting pot," see Philip Gleason, "The Melting Pot: Symbol of Fusion or Confusion?" *American Quarterly* 16, no. 1 (1964): 22–23.

7. Israel Zangwill, *The Melting-Pot: Drama in Four Acts* (New York: Macmillan, 1909), 199. Among the audience of the first performance of *The Melting Pot* in Washington, D.C., in October 1908 was the then-president Theodore Roosevelt, who reportedly "leaned over his box and shouted to Zangwill: 'That's a great play, Mr. Zangwill, that's a great play.'" Quoted in Guy Szuberla, "Zangwill's *The Melting Pot* Plays Chicago," *MELUS* 20, no. 3 (1995): 3.

8. Thomas J. Archdeacon, *Becoming American: An Ethnic History* (New York: Free Press, 1983), 113; Aristide Zolberg, *A Nation by Design: Immigration Policy in the Fashioning of America* (Cambridge, MA: Harvard University Press, 2006), 187.

9. Ellwood P. Cubberley, *Changing Conceptions of Education* (Boston: Houghton Mifflin, 1909), 15.

10. David R. Roediger, *Wages of Whiteness: Race and the Making of the American Working Class* (New York: Verso, 2007), 50.

11. Ibid., 17.

12. Jacob A Riis, *How the Other Half Lives: Studies Among the Tenements of New York* (New York: Dover, 1970), 201.

13. See, for example, "Racial Indigestion," *Atlanta Constitution* (Atlanta, GA), October 6, 1913, 13; "Great Scott! Doesn't the Judge Know That I'm Suffering from Alien Indigestion?" *Greenville Democrat* (Greenville, TN), May 2, 1923, 4; "'Cyclone Mack' Says—," *Portsmouth Daily Times* (Portsmouth, OH), January 16, 1925.

NOTES 213

14. G. Frank Lydston, *The Diseases of Society (The Vice and Crime Problem)* (Philadelphia: J. Lippincott Company, 1904), 28, 130.
15. Julia Kristeva, *Powers of Horror: An Essay on Abjection*, trans. Leon S. Roudiez (New York: Columbia University Press, 1982), 2.
16. James, *American Scene*, 84.
17. Ibid., 231, 85, 85.
18. Ibid., 85, 86, 124.
19. Kristeva, 11.
20. Warren S. Thompson, "Race Suicide in the United States," *Scientific Monthly* 5, no. 1 (1917): 22.
21. James, *American Scene*, 132.
22. Ibid., 130, 131, 131.
23. Ibid., 132.
24. For a reading of Stein's text in relation to epic, see Václav Paris, *The Evolutions of Modernist Epic* (New York: Oxford University Press, 2021).
25. Gertrude Stein, *The Making of Americans: Being a History of a Family's Progress* (Normal, IL: Dalkey Archive Press, 1995), 3. All further citations will be made parenthetically in the text.
26. Alex Woloch, *The One vs. the Many: Minor Characters and the Space of the Protagonist in the Novel* (Princeton, NJ: Princeton University Press, 2003), 20, 34.
27. Leon Katz, "The First Making of *The Making of Americans*: A Study Based on Gertrude Stein's Notebooks and Early Versions of Her Novel," Columbia University, 1963 (unpublished diss.).
28. Gertrude Stein, "The Making of Americans," in *Fernhurst, Q.E.D., and Other Early Writings* (London: Peter Owen, 1972), 137–174. All further citations will be made parenthetically in the text.
29. Unlike the 1903 version ("The Making of Americans") and the 1911 version (*The Making of Americans*), the 1908 version does not exist in a complete manuscript form. My argument about this version relies on Katz's laborious and careful reconstruction from Stein's notebooks. Gertrude Stein, *The Notebooks of Gertrude Stein for "The Making of Americans," 1903–1912*, ed. Leon Katz (Orlando, FL: Lightning Source, 2021). This volume encompasses the commentaries of both Katz himself and Alice B. Toklas (made as Katz interviewed Toklas from November 1952 to February 1953), as well as Stein's notes and drafts. Section 4, "The Buried Narrative" (567–586), is drawn from Katz's dissertation, assembling the full diegetic trajectory of the 1908 version.
30. Ernest Hemingway, *A Moveable Feast: The Restored Edition*, ed. Seán Hemingway (New York: Scribner, 2010), 27.
31. Sarah Wilson, *Melting-Pot Modernism* (Ithaca, NY: Cornell University Press, 2010), 165.
32. Priscilla Wald, *Constituting Americans: Cultural Anxiety and Narrative Form* (Durham, NC: Duke University Press, 1995), 239, 243.
33. Wald, 242.
34. Roediger, 20.
35. For an important contextualization of these writers, see Mark Whalan, *American Culture in the 1910s* (Edinburgh: Edinburgh University Press, 2010), 29–31. There are only a few pieces in which Stein directly writes about Jewishness. The most notable are her college essay, written in 1896, "The Modern Jew Who Has Given Up the Faith of His Fathers Can Reasonably and Consistently Believe in Isolation," which I will discuss in the first section, and her 1920 poem "The Reverie of the Zionist." On Stein's essay, see Gertrude Stein, "The Modern Jew Who Has Given up the Faith of His Fathers Can Reasonably and Consistently Believe in Isolation (1896)," ed. Amy Feinstein, *PMLA* 116, no. 2 (2001): 416–428. For an excellent reading of "Reverie," see Barbara Will, "Gertrude Stein and Zionism," *MFS* 51, no. 2 (2005): 437–455.
36. Amy Feinstein, "Gertrude Stein, Alice Toklas, and Albert Barnes: Looking Like a Jew in *The Autobiography of Alice B. Toklas*," *Shofar* 25, no. 3 (2007): 48. In contrast, Stein's and Toklas's friends often commented on their "Jewishness" as marked in their appearance. For instance, Hemingway describes Stein as having "a strong German-Jewish face" with "lovely, thick, alive immigrant hair" (Hemingway, 24). Stein's friend Mabel Dodge portrays Toklas as "slight and dark, with beautiful gray eyes hung with black lashes—and she had a drooping, Jewish nose, and her eyelids drooped, and the corners of her red mouth and the lobes of her ears drooped and the black folded Hebraic hair, weighted down, as they were, with long heavy Oriental earrings." quoted in Janet Hobhouse, *Everybody Who Was Anybody: A Biography of Gertrude Stein* (New York: Putnam, 1975), 64.

214 NOTES

37. Maria Damon, "Gertrude Stein's Jewishness, Jewish Social Scientists, and the 'Jewish Question,'" *MFS* 42, no. 3 (1996): 492. As Damon argues, there has been a long tradition of critically foreclosing "the Jewish question" in Stein studies. Other notable exceptions are Maria Damon, "Gertrude Stein's Doggerel 'Yiddish': Women, Dogs, and Jews," in *The Dark End of the Street: Margins in American Vanguard Poetry* (Minneapolis: University of Minnesota Press, 1993), 202–245; Barbara Will, *Gertrude Stein, Modernism, and the Problem of Genius* (Edinburgh: Edinburgh University Press, 2000); Barbara Will, *Unlikely Collaboration: Gertrude Stein, Bernard Faÿ, and the Vichy Dilemma* (New York: Columbia University Press, 2011); and Amy Feinstein, *Gertrude Stein and the Making of Jewish Modernism* (Gainesville: University Press of Florida, 2020).

38. Feinstein, *Gertrude Stein and the Making of Jewish Modernism*, 1.

39. Barkan and LeMay, 47.

40. John Higham, *Strangers in the Land: Patterns of American Nativism, 1860–1925* (New Brunswick, NJ: Rutgers University Press, 1955), 93.

41. On the Leo Frank case, see Matthew Frye Jacobson, *Whiteness of a Different Color: European Immigrants and the Alchemy of Race* (Cambridge, MA: Harvard University Press, 1998), 62–68.

42. On Stein's relationship to Bookstaver and Haynes, see Leon Katz, Introduction to *Fernhurst, Q.E.D., and Other Early Writings* (London: Peter Owen, 1972), i–xxxiv.

43. Like "The Making of Americans," *Q.E.D.* was also restored from Stein's notebooks and published in 1972 (it was originally titled "Quod Erat Demonstrandum" in her notebooks). Donald Gallup, "A Note on the Texts," in *Fernhurst, Q.E.D., and Other Early Writings* (London: Peter Owen, 1972), vii. Before the 1972 publication, it had been published in 1950, four years after Stein's death, under the title *Things as They Are*, with slight modifications of names and phrases. For a detailed record of the novel's production, see Katz, Introduction.

44. Stein, *Fernhurst, Q.E.D., and Other Early Writings*, 56.

45. Ibid., 80, 57, 74.

46. Ibid., 103.

47. Stein, "The Modern Jew," 423.

48. Ibid., 425, 423.

49. Ibid., 426. On Stein's experience at Johns Hopkins, see Linda Wagner-Martin, *"Favored Strangers": Gertrude Stein and Her Family* (New Brunswick, NJ: Rutgers University Press, 1995), 49.

50. Stein, "The Modern Jew," 424. On Stein's friendship with Zangwill, see Will, "Gertrude Stein and Zionism," 446.

51. On Bird Stein's divorce from Louis Sternberger, see Stein, *Notebooks*, 170. Even though Bird had once been Gertrude's closest cousin, the two had a falling out during Bird's divorce, partly because Gertrude felt moral repugnancy over Bird's growing intimacy with her lawyer, Howard Gans. See Stein, *Notebook*, 116, 157–158.

52. "The Making of Americans" abruptly ends in the middle of the fifth chapter. Katz explains, "The rest of the leaves written on in the notebook—about the same number as still remain—are sliced out" (Introduction, xxiv). In Stein's notebook, however, there remains what seems to be the original conclusion of the 1903 version. This paragraph begins: "And now having carried all my generation into marriage and into middle life and having seen them all start a posterity on the road to make for itself again a fortune a character and a career we must content ourselves to leave them." Stein, *Notebooks*, 74.

53. This is repeatedly attested in the notebooks. See, for example, Stein, *Notebooks*, 84, 88, 106, 115, 128. Stein also composed a table of characters and their real-life counterparts. Stein, *Notebooks*, 159.

54. Stein, *Notebooks*, 95, 127.

55. Stein, *Notebooks*, 387. Stein's notebooks often record the impact of her falling out with Bird when discussing the plot during this period of revision: for instance, "The real drama is Dave Hersland and Julia Dehning. Dave's final split like mine with Bird because of her not realizing him and her dishonesty when in in a hole." Stein, *Notebooks*, 87.

56. Stein, *Notebooks*, 86, 87, 89, 106. When Solomons was at the Harvard Psychological Laboratory, he and Stein published a paper together on automatic writing. Leon M. Solomons and Gertrude Stein, "Normal Motor Automatism," *Psychological Review* 3 (1896): 492–512. Stein had a different interpretation of the experiments they collaborated on, and she later published another paper under her name alone. Gertrude Stein, "Cultivated Motor Automatism: A Study of Character in Its Relation to Attention," *Psychological Review* 5 (1898): 295–306. On

NOTES   215

their scientific collaboration, see Will, *Gertrude Stein*, 23–27, and Steven Meyer, *Irresistible Dictation: Gertrude Stein and the Correlation of Writing and Science* (Stanford, CA: Stanford University Press, 2001), 221–227. As Stein wrote down her ideas for David Hersland's character development, she repeatedly referred to Solomons and her romantic entanglement as one of the sources for David's "college life and love experiences." Stein, *Notebooks*, 100. See also Leon Katz's commentary in Stein, *Notebooks*, 115–116, 141–142.

57. Ibid., 176.
58. Ibid., 82.
59. Ibid.
60. A dietary practice initiated by the health reformer known as "the Great Masticator," Horace Fletcher, Fletcherism advocated for the most through digestion possible, chewing food until it became completely liquified. As I discuss later, the aim of this regimen was to minimize the waste and purify the feces. On Fletcherism in general and its influence on Henry James's writing, see Tim Armstrong, "Disciplining the Corpus: Henry James and Fletcherism," in *American Bodies: Cultural Histories of the Physique*, ed. Tim Armstrong (New York: New York University Press, 1966), 101–119. For a detailed analysis of the relation between Fletcherism, Gertrude Stein, and Leo Stein, see Christopher Schmidt, *The Poetics of Waste: Queer Excess in Stein, Ashbery, Schuyler, and Goldsmith* (New York: Palgrave, 2014), 27–56. See also Leon Katz's commentary on Leon Stein's Fletcherism in Stein, *Notebooks*, 182–183.
61. For instance, compare the following two almost-verbatim passages from the 1908 version and the 1911 version, in which the 1908 version represents the exceptionality of Jewish familialism:

> These german men and women our grandfathers and grandmothers with their children born and unborn with them, some whose children had gone ahead to prepare a home to give them, other countries too were full of men and women who brought their many children, but only german men and women and the children they had in them to make many generations for them this history for us of a family and its progress. (Stein, *Notebooks*, 75)

> These certain men and women, our grandfathers and grandmothers, with their children born and unborn with them, some whose children were gone ahead to prepare a home to give them; all countries were full of women who brought with them many children; but only certain men and women and the children they had in them, to make many generations for them, will fill up this history for us of a family and its progress. (Stein, *Making of Americans*, 3)

62. Stein's radical project of inclusion is often compared with Whitman's. See, for example, Matt Miller, "Making of Americans: Whitman and Stein's Poetics of Inclusion," *Arizona Quarterly* 65, no. 3 (2009): 39–59.
63. Laura Doyle, "The Flat, the Round, and Gertrude Stein: Race and the Shape of Modern(ist) History," *Modernism/Modernity* 7, no. 2 (2000): 263.
64. As Catherine R. Stimpson points out, "Gertrice/Altrude" appears in Stein's manuscript. See Catherine R. Stimpson, "Gertrice/Altrude: Stein, Toklas, and The Paradox of the Happy Marriage," in *Mothering the Mind: Twelve Studies of Writers and Their Silent Partners*, ed. Ruth Perry and Martine Watson Brownley (New York: Holmes & Meier, 1984), 122–139. Stimpson examines the critical ambivalence about the Stein–Toklas alliance in queer studies, as ostensibly their relation is heavily prescribed in the traditional gender binary.
65. Doyle, 250.
66. Ibid., 263.
67. Gertrude Stein, *Everybody's Autobiography* (London: Virago, 1937, rpt. 1985), 121.
68. Sander Gilman argues that in the 1840s, the basis of the definition of the Jew was still a religious one. Sometime in the 1870s, the "Jews" become a biologically defined racial category, the antithesis of the "Aryans." Sander Gilman, *Freud, Race, and Gender* (Princeton, NJ: Princeton University Press, 1993), 9–36. Gilman also argues that the construction of the "Jew" as a scientifically determined racial group coincided and overlapped with the invention of the "homosexual" as a sexual type, as observed in the simultaneous origination of the terms "homosexuality" and "anti-Semitism" in 1869. Sander Gilman, *The Jew's Body* (New York: Routledge, 1991), 126.
69. This model of male ideal is called *Edelkayt*, which can be loosely translated as "delicacy and gentleness." See Daniel Boyarin, *Unheroic Conduct: The Rise of Heterosexuality and the Invention of the Jewish Man* (Berkeley: University of California Press, 1997), 23. For another account of the imbrication between Jewishness and homosexuality, see Jonathan Freedman, "Coming Out

216 NOTES

of the Jewish Closet with Marcel Proust," in *Queer Theory and the Jewish Question*, ed. Daniel Boyarin, Daniel Itzkovitz, and Ann Pellegrini (New York: Columbia University Press, 2003), 521–555.

70. Boyarin, *Unheroic Conduct*, 246, 231.

71. Margot Canaday, *The Straight State: Sexuality and Citizenship in Twentieth-Century America* (Princeton, NJ: Princeton University Press, 2009), 21.

72. Quoted in ibid., 31. The other factor that made Jewish immigrants particularly prone to intense investigation was the custom of arranged marriage. As Nancy Cott argues, along with Asians, Jews were "more easily accused of masking prostitution as marriage" because of the popular notion of matchmaking as "overt economic bargaining." Nancy Cott, *Public Vows: A History of Marriage and the Nation* (Cambridge, MA: Harvard University Press, 2000), 149. The charge of prostitution was not directed exclusively toward Jewish women. The Lower East Side, the nation's largest Jewish quarter, and the Bowery in particular, where Yiddish theater flourished, was reported to be the "principal resort in New York for degenerates," populated by male prostitutes. Quoted in George Chauncey, *Gay New York: Gender, Urban Culture, and the Making of the Gay Male World, 1890–1940* (New York: Basic Books, 1994), 33.

73. Warren Hoffman, *The Passing Game: Queering Jewish American Culture* (Syracuse, NY: Syracuse University Press, 2009), 8.

74. Guy Hocquenghem, *Homosexual Desire*, trans. Daniella Dangoor (Durham, NC: Duke University Press, 1993), 107.

75. Susan S. Lanser, "'Queer to Queer': The Sapphic Body as Transgressive Text," in *Lewd and Notorious: Female Transgression in the Eighteenth Century*, ed. Katharine Kittredge (Ann Arbor: University of Michigan Press, 2003), 36.

76. Stein, *Everybody's Autobiography*, 94.

77. Timothy K. Nixon, "Gertrude Stein's Performance of Patriotism," *Studies in American Humor* 3, no. 24 (2011): 45.

78. Feinstein, "Gertrude Stein, Alice Toklas, and Albert Barnes," 48.

79. Stein's notebooks contain many of her observations about Toklas, but for one of the earliest and most sustained, see Stein, *Notebooks*, 337. On Lucrezia Borgia, Shakespeare, and Van Gogh, see Stein, *Notebooks*, 240–241.

80. Stein classifies herself as a male type, an "earthy boy." See Stein, *Notebooks*, 313. For an important reading of Stein in relation to transness, see Chris Coffman, *Gertrude Stein's Transmasculinity* (Edinburgh: Edinburgh University Press, 2018).

81. See Stein, *Notebooks*, 233, 431. For a detailed analysis of "Jewish" and "Anglo-Saxon" types, see Feinstein, *Gertrude Stein and the Making of Jewish Modernism*, 62–86.

82. Jennifer L. Fleissner, *Women, Compulsion, Modernity: The Moment of American Naturalism* (Chicago: University of Chicago Press, 2004), 254.

83. On the relation between Stein's experiments on automatism and her conceptualization of bottom nature, see Will, *Gertrude Stein*, 22–43 and 51–58.

84. Mark Seltzer, *Bodies and Machines* (New York: Routledge, 1992), 105.

85. Ibid.

86. Ibid., 95, 5.

87. Will, *Gertrude Stein*, 64.

88. Stein, *Notebooks*, 294. As critics have pointed out, Stein's bipartite characterology was partly inspired by Jewish-Austrian author Otto Weininger's *Sex and Character* (1903), which Stein is said to have read for the first time in 1907 with great enthusiasm. Weininger's book posits "a permanent bisexual condition," in which all human beings, regardless of sex assigned at birth, are "sexually intermediate forms" that combine M (maleness) and F (femaleness) in varying degrees; any erotic magnetism between two beings is effectuated by the law of opposite attraction, wherein one being's M and F components are complemented by those of the other. See Otto Weininger, *Sex and Character* (New York: A. L. Burt, 1906), 7, 79. For the foundational argument regarding Weininger's influence on *The Making of Americans*, see Leon Katz, "Weininger and the Making of Americans," *Twentieth Century Literature* 24, no. 1 (1978): 8–26. See also Will, *Gertrude Stein*, 62–66, and Maria Farland, "Gertrude Stein's Brain Work," *American Literature* 76, no. 1 (2004): 117–148.

89. E. L. McCallum, *Unmaking* The Making of Americans: *Toward an Aesthetic Ontology* (Albany: State University of New York Press, 2018), 118.

90. Eve Kosofsky Sedgwick, *Epistemology of the Closet* (Berkeley: University of California Press, 1990), 23.

NOTES 217

91. Farland, 128.
92. For instance, a portion of those in the "independent dependent" categories are David Hersland II, Martha Hersland, Julia Dehning, Phillip Redfern, Mabel Linker, and Mary Maxworthing. In the "dependent independent" categories, we find Fanny Hersland, David Hersland III, Alfred Hersland, Cora Dounor, Minnie Mason, and the narrator.
93. Melanie Taylor, "A Poetics of Difference: *The Making of Americans and Unreadable Subjects*," *NWSA Journal* 15, no. 3 (2004): 30.
94. Gertrude Stein, *Baby Precious Always Shines: Selected Love Notes Between Gertrude Stein and Alice B. Toklas*, ed. Kay Turner (New York: St. Marin's Press, 1999), 58.
95. Kay Turner, "This 'Very Beautiful Form of Literature': An Introduction to the Love Notes Between Gertrude Stein and Alice B. Toklas," in *Baby Precious Always Shines: Selected Love Notes Between Gertrude Stein and Alice B. Toklas*, ed. Kay Turner (New York: St. Marin's Press, 1999), 4.
96. Schmidt, 37.
97. Will Stockton, *Playing Dirty: Sexuality and Waste in Early Modern Comedy* (Minneapolis: University of Minnesota Press, 2011), xix. For another brilliant reading of the erotics of defecation, see Scott Herring, "Eve Sedgwick's 'Other Materials,'" *Angelaki* 23, no. 1–2 (2018): 5–18.
98. Lisa Ruddick, *Reading Gertrude Stein: Body, Text, Gnosis* (Ithaca, NY: Cornell University Press, 1990), 77.
99. Gertrude Stein, *Tender Buttons* (New York: Clair Marie, 1914), 58.
100. Kathryn R. Kent, *Making Girls into Women: American Women's Writing and the Rise of Lesbian Identity* (Durham, NC: Duke University Press, 2003), 163.
101. As Turner notes, the complete collection of love notes—totaling over three hundred—is kept at the Beinecke Rare Book and Manuscript Library at Yale University. These notes most likely were donated by mistake by Toklas to the Beinecke, and they were made unavailable to the public by Toklas's request until 1981. None of them are dated, but Turner speculates that they were written in the last decade of the Stein–Toklas alliance (6–7). On the constitution of the Beinecke's archive, see Melanie Micir, *The Passion Projects: Modernist Women, Intimate Archives, Unfinished Lives* (Princeton, NJ: Princeton University Press, 2019), 88–94.
102. Turner, 25. "As a Wife Has a Cow" was originally published in Paris in 1926 and reprinted in *Selected Writings of Gertrude Stein*, edited by Stein and Toklas's friend Carl Van Vechten in 1946, immediately before Stein's death. For readings of "cows" as female orgasm, see, for example, Stimpson.
103. Stein, *Baby Precious*, 67.
104. Ibid., 98.
105. Ibid., 64.
106. Ibid., 74.
107. Ruddick, 93. Ruddick comments on the Freudian undertones in *The Making of Americans* in arguing for the connection between Stein's repetitive style and repetition compulsion as theorized in *Beyond the Pleasure Principle*, rather than in the context of anal eroticism.
108. For the "assimilation" of Freud, see, for instance, Jay Geller, "Freud, Blüher, and *Secessio Inversa*: Männerbünde, Homosexuality, and Freud's Theory of Cultural Formation," in *Queer Theory and the Jewish Question*, ed. Daniel Boyarin, Daniel Itzkovitz, and Ann Pellegrini (New York: Columbia University Press, 2003), 90–120.
109. Harold Bloom, *The Strong Light of the Canonical: Kafka, Freud, and Scholem as Revisionists of Jewish Culture and Thoughts* (New York: City College Press, 1987), 43.
110. Geller, 93. For the most comprehensive work on Freudian psychoanalysis's relation to Jewishness, see Gilman, *Freud*. For other accounts, see Geller; Boyarin, *Unheroic*, 189–220; and Daniel Boyarin, "Homophobia and the Postcoloniality of the 'Jewish Science,'" in *Queer Theory and the Jewish Question*, ed. Daniel Boyarin, Daniel Itzkovitz, and Ann Pellegrini (New York: Columbia University Press, 2003), 166–198.
111. Gilman, *Freud*, 6.
112. George Chauncey Jr., "From Sexual Inversion to Homosexuality: The Changing Medical Conceptualization of Female 'Deviance,'" in *Passion and Power: Sexuality in History*, ed. Kathy Peiss and Christina Simmons (Philadelphia: Temple University Press, 1989), 93, 94.
113. Sigmund Freud, *Three Essays on The Theory of Sexuality (1905)*, in *The Standard Edition of the Complete Psychological Works of Sigmund Freud*, trans. James Strachey (London: Hogarth, 1995), 12:171, italics original.
114. Ibid., 145.
115. Boyarin, "Homophobia," 167–173; Gilman, *Freud*, 77.

218   NOTES

116. Though the actual term "Oedipus complex" appears for the first time in "A Special Type of Choice of Object Made by Men" (1910), Freud calls Little Hans "little Oedipus" twice in this case study. Sigmund Freud, "Analysis of a Phobia in a Five-Year-Old Boy (1909)," in *The Standard Edition of the Complete Psychological Works of Sigmund Freud*, trans. James Strachey (London: Hogarth, 1995), 10:97, 111.
117. Ibid., 36.
118. Boyarin, *Unheroic*, 234, 232.
119. Freud, "Analysis," 97.
120. Ibid., 96.
121. Ibid., 68.
122. Sigmund Freud, *The History of An Infantile Neurosis* (1914), in *The Standard Edition of the Complete Psychological Works of Sigmund Freud*, trans. James Strachey (London: Hogarth, 1995), 17:78.
123. Ibid., 86.
124. Ibid., 84.
125. Freud develops the concept of the anus displacing the vagina via the passivity of the mucous membrane of the rectum in *The History of Infantile Neurosis* and "Transformation of Instinct as Exemplified in Anal Erotism" (1917). Freud argues that if the passivity of the mucous membrane is envisioned as something similar to the vagina in cloacal theory, it is "the column of faeces" that "behaves just as the penis does." Freud, *History*, 84. At the same time, since the cloacal theory bequeaths the functions of excretion, coition, and childbirth to the anus, the fecal mass becomes simultaneously equivalent to both penis and baby. Further, as Freud elaborates in "Transformation" and "Character and Anal Erotism" (1908), since excreta function as the infant's first gift to those he loves, it is translated also into something valuable, gold and money (and thus his famous theorization of the "anal" character as "parsimonious" in "Character"). Ultimately, therefore, excrement comes to represent three things: penis, baby, and money. As David Hillman suggests, the link between feces and money points toward the unconscious association of Jewishness with Freud's conceptualization of anality. Not only did "medieval and early modern anti-Semitic fantasies associate[] Jews with both faeces and anal intrusiveness," the age-old association between the Jew and usury regarded usury as an "unnatural breeding" of money not unlike fecal production. David Hillman, "Freud's Shylock," *American Imago* 70, no. 1 (2013): 15–16.
126. Hocquenghem, 101.
127. McCallum, 6.
128. Tanya Clement, "The Story of One: Narrative and Composition in Gertrude Stein's *The Making of Americans*," *Texas Studies in Literature and Language* 54, no. 3 (2012): 438.
129. Ibid., 443.
130. Thompson, 22.
131. Natalia Cecire, "Ways of Not Reading Gertrude Stein," *ELH* 82, no. 1 (2015): 282.
132. Ibid., 292.
133. Samuel Delany, *Times Square Red, Times Square Blue* (New York: New York University Press, 1999), 121.
134. Gertrude Stein, *The Autobiography of Alice B. Toklas* (New York: Modern Library, 1993), 123.
135. Lauren Berlant, *Cruel Optimism* (Durham, NC: Duke University Press, 2011).
136. Emma Lazarus, "The New Colossus," *The Poems of Emma Lazarus in Two Volumes*, vol. 1, *Narrative, Lyric, and Dramatic* (Boston: Houghton Mifflin, 1889), 202. "The New Colossus" was written immediately after the passage of the Chinese Exclusion Act of 1882 and inscribed at the foot of the Statue of Liberty in 1903. As Max Cavitch points out, "How could these words ever have been heard as anything other than a ruse?" Max Cavitch, "Emma Lazarus and the Golem of Liberty," *American Literary History* 18, no. 1 (2006): 19.
137. Despite his wry commentary on *The Making of Americans*, Hemingway enabled its appearance in the *Transatlantic Review*. For a detailed publication history of *The Making of Americans*, see Donald Gallup, "Appendix: The Making of *The Making of Americans*," in Gertrude Stein, *Fernhurst, Q.E.D., and Other Early Writings* (London: Peter Owen, 1972), 173–214.
138. Renaud Camus, *You Will Not Replace Us!* (Plieux, France: Chez l'auteur, 2018), 11.
139. Ibid., 14.
140. This existential terror parallels what Calvin Warren calls the "ontological terror" of Blackness. Warren argues that "black being" is excluded from the ontological realm of the human and positioned under the erasure of "being": "black being incarnates metaphysical nothing . . .

NOTES 219

The function of black(ness) is to give form to a terrifying formless (nothing)." Anti-Black violence is, in this sense, "violence against nothing," by which the human desperately tries to dominate and eradicate the nothing projected onto Blackness. Calvin Warren, *Ontological Terror: Blackness, Nihilism, and Emancipation* (Durham, NC: Duke University Press, 2018), 5, 21. For an elaboration of Black fungibility, see the Coda.

Coda

1. Frank Kermode, *The Sense of An Ending: Studies in the Theory of Fiction* (Oxford: Oxford University Press, 1967, rpt. 2000), 6.
2. Ibid., 90. My thinking about the temporality of ending and catastrophe here has also been inspired by Pallavi Rastogi's brilliant theorization of postcolonial disaster's ongoingness. Postcolonial disaster fiction, Rastogi argues, "teaches us how to live within the all-pervasiveness of catastrophe while simultaneously resisting it." Pallavi Rastogi, *Postcolonial Disaster: Narrating Catastrophe in the Twenty-First Century* (Evanston, IL: Northwestern University Press, 2020), 11.
3. For an excellent account of disaffection as a way to navigate this affective imperative, especially in its relation to Asianness, see Xine Yao, *Disaffected: The Cultural Politics of Unfeeling in Nineteenth-Century America* (Durham, NC: Duke University Press, 2021), particularly 171–210.
4. With a picture of himself holding a paper captioned "Je Ne Suis Pas Un Virus," French-Chinese Lou Chengwang wrote on Twitter: "Je suis Chinois / Mais je ne suis pas un virus!! / Je sais que tout le monde a peur au virus, mais pas de préjugé, svp.! # JeNeSuisPasUnVirus" (I'm Chinese, but I'm not a virus! I know everyone's scared of the virus but no prejudice, please! #IamNotAVirus). Lou Chengwang, Twitter post, January 28, 2020, https://twitter.com/chengwangl?lang = en. This tweet spread rapidly when the BBC cited it the next day. "Coronavirus: French Asians hit back at racism with 'I'm not a virus,'" *BBC News*, BBC, January 29, 2020, https://www.bbc.com/news/world-europe-51294305.
5. See, for instance, Gille Roland, Twitter post, January 29, 2020, https://twitter.com/gilles_rol and?lang = en; Jason Oliver Chang, Twitter post, January 30, 2020, https://twitter.com/chin otronic?lang = en; Luke Bowe, Twitter post, February 10, 2020, https://twitter.com/lmbowe; Judith Sunderland, Twitter post, February 3, 2020, https://twitter.com/sunderland_jude; Lani7, Twitter post, February 28, 2020, https://twitter.com/Lani_NG16; and Ricky Oishi, Twitter post, January 30, 2020, https://twitter.com/iromiud0211.
6. Colleen Lye, *America's Asia: Racial Form and American Literature, 1893–1945* (Princeton, NJ: Princeton University Press, 2005), 8.
7. Ibid., 7.
8. Nayan Shah, *Contagious Divides: Epidemics and Race in San Francisco's Chinatown* (Berkeley: University of California Press, 2001), 88.
9. Ibid., 86.
10. Ibid., 99. "Asiatic leprosy" is an extremely common term used frequently in newspaper articles. It also appears in literary works; for instance, Charles Warren Stoddard uses the term "Asiatic leprosy" in his reportage on Hawaiian leper colonies, ending his account with a warning to US readers: "The seeds of the plague are sown in the track of the Chinese cooly [*sic*]." Charles Warren Stoddard, *The Lepers of Molokai* (Notre Dame, IN: Ave Maria Press, 1885), 10, 79.
11. Shah, 79.
12. Edward A. Ross, "The Causes of Race Superiority," *Annals of the American Academy of Political and Social Science* 18 (1901): 88.
13. "Many Voices for Japanese Exclusion: Prominent Citizens Say that Coolies from the Mikado's Kingdom Are as Bad as Chinese Labor, and That Their Coming Should Be Checked by Law Before It Is Too Late," *The San Francisco Examiner* (San Francisco, CA), May 8, 1900, 7.
14. "Japanese Competition: The Protection American Labor Wants Is Restriction and Exclusion Laws Against the Cheaper Man," *Organized Labor* 1, no. 16 (1900): 1. Ross's entire speech is reprinted in this article. As Laura Lovett details, Ross's anti-Asian commentary in this speech exasperated Jane Stanford, a co-founder of Stanford University, who called for Ross's resignation shortly afterward. More than eight hundred newspapers applauded Ross's statement against this impingement on academic freedom, which he published shortly after his resignation. For more details on the so-called "Ross affair," see Laura L. Lovett, *Conceiving the Future: Pronatalism, Reproduction, and the Family in the United States, 1890–1938* (Chapel Hill: University of North Carolina Press), 82–85.

220 NOTES

15. "Japanese Competition," 1.
16. "Many Voices for Japanese Exclusion," 7.
17. Eric Hayot, *The Hypothetical Mandarin: Sympathy, Modernity, and Chinese Pain* (Oxford: Oxford University Press, 2009), 135–171. I place the term "coolie" in quotation marks because it is a derogatory term and one that does not have any legal status. It primarily refers to Asian migrant laborers working as contract laborers in such regions as Hawai'i, Cuba, and Peru. Some scholars have argued that Asian migrants in the United States were not technically "coolies" because they worked under a "credit-ticket system." However, as scholars like Moon-Ho Jung and Elliott Young have argued, there was little difference in terms of their labor conditions, and drawing too great a distinction reifies American exceptionalism. See Moon-Ho Jung, *Coolies and Cane: Race, Labor, and Sugar in the Age of Emancipation* (Baltimore: Johns Hopkins University Press, 2006), and Elliott Young, *Alien Nation: Chinese Migration in the Americas from the Coolie Through World War II* (Chapel Hill: University of North Carolina Press, 2014). Regardless of this debate, virtually all Asian laborers, including Indian, Chinese, and Japanese people, were referred to in common parlance as "coolies" well into the early twentieth century.
18. Frank B. Wilderson III, *Red, White Black: Cinema and the Structure of U.S. Antagonisms* (Durham, NC: Duke University Press, 2010), 14.
19. Ibid., 11.
20. Ibid., 20.
21. Ibid., 28, 45.
22. Quoted in Hayot, 23 n. 3. The "coolie" in the British Caribbean, as Lisa Lowe argues, figured the "alleged transition from slavery to freedom." Claims about their "labor as 'freely' contracted" were deployed to cover over their "racialized and coerced" labor conditions, which were akin to slavery. Lisa Lowe, *The Intimacies of Four Continents* (Durham, NC: Duke University Press, 2015), 24. Their exceptionally high mortality rate rivaled "that of the infamous Middle Passage," occasionally reaching as high as seventy percent (Young, 30). Pro-slavery forces in the United States during the antebellum period held up the Caribbean "coolie" system as a nightmarish alternative to slavery, one they believed to be so deplorable as to justify the benevolence of slavery in comparison (Hayot, 137).
23. Sianne Ngai, *Ugly Feelings* (Cambridge, MA: Harvard University Press, 2005), 89–125; Mel Y. Chen, *Animacies: Biopolitics, Racial Mattering, and Queer Affect* (Durham, NC: Duke University Press, 2012), 5. Here, I borrow Ngai's term "animatedness," although I disagree with her aggregation of both Blacks and Asians under the sign of "animatedness." Instead, I see the perceived scarcity of animacy—"agency, awareness, mobility, and liveness"—as marking the Asian body (Chen, 2).
24. As Warren Susman argues the concept of personality came into vogue in the first decade of the twentieth-century United States. This widespread terminological flourishing was reflected in the U.S. self-help literature which transitioned from a focus on character (based on morality) in the nineteenth century to a focus on personality (based on uniqueness) in the twentieth century. Warren Susman, "'Personality' and the Making of Twentieth-Century Culture," in *Culture as History: The Transformation of American Society in the Twentieth Century* (Washington, D.C.: Smithsonian Institute Press, 2003), 271–286.
25. Clifford Geertz, "'From the Native's Point of View': On the Nature of Anthropological Understanding," *Bulletin of the American Academy of Arts and Sciences* 28, no. 1 (1974): 31.
26. Robert Esposito, *Third Person: Politics of Life and Philosophy of the Impersonal*, trans. Zakiya Hanafi (Malden, MA: Polity, 2012), 70.
27. *Santa Clara v. Southern Pacific Railroad*, 118 U.S. 394 (1886). Stephen Best succinctly summarizes this case: "In *Santa Clara*, the U.S. Supreme Court took as its task the determination of whether the equal protection clause of the Fourteenth Amendment barred California from taxing corporate property—in this case, railroad property—differently from individual property." Stephen Best, *The Fugitive's Properties: Law and the Poetics of Possession* (Chicago: University of Chicago Press, 2004), 281 n. 6. As Peter Jaros elaborates, the case "put corporations on par with natural persons for the purposes of Fourteenth Amendment protections." Peter Jaros, "A Double Life: Personifying the Corporation from *Dartmouth College* to Poe," *Poe Studies* 47 (2014): 28 n. 8.
28. For an excellent account of Asian inscrutability and its negotiation with neoliberal visibility, see Vivian L. Huang, *Surface Relations: Queer Forms of Asian American Inscrutability* (Durham, NC: Duke University Press, 2022).

29. Anne Anlin Cheng, *Ornamentalism* (New York: Oxford University Press, 2019), 18.
30. Sharon Cameron, *Impersonality: Seven Essays* (Chicago: University of Chicago Press, 2007), ix.
31. Heather Arvidson, "Personality, Impersonality, and the Personified Detachment of Wyndham Lewis," *Modernism/modernity* 25, no. 4 (2018): 791.
32. For a brilliant discussion of Pound in relation to Asian American studies, see Josephine Nock-Hee Park, *Apparitions of Asia: Modernist Form and Asian American Poetics* (Oxford: Oxford University Press, 2008). Carrie Preston, in her experimental work fusing memoir and modernist scholarship, explores the tension between the Western liberal subject and Noh's pedagogical cultivation of an "impersonal self." Carrie Preston, *Learning to Kneel: Noh, Modernism, and Journeys in Teaching* (New York: Columbia University Press, 2016), 16.
33. T. S. Eliot, *The Sacred Wood: Essays on Poetry and Criticism* (London: Methuen and Co., 1920), 58.
34. Percival Lowell, *The Soul of the Far East* (New York: MacMillan, 1911), 27.
35. On the Boston Brahmins' Japanism, see Christopher Reed, *Bachelor Japanists: Japanese Aesthetics and Western Masculinities* (New York: Columbia University Press, 2017), 117–200.
36. Lye, 17.
37. Lowell, 15.
38. Ibid., 125.
39. Ibid., 88.
40. Ibid., 23.
41. Ibid., 24.
42. Ibid., 16–17.
43. Ibid., 197, 198.
44. Ibid., 9.
45. Ibid., 226.
46. Ross, "The Causes of Race Superiority," 88.
47. Edward A. Ross, "Turning Towards Nirvana," *The Arena*, 4, no. 24 (1891): 741.
48. Ibid., 739–740.
49. Ibid., 743.
50. For an overview of the history of *seppuku*, see Toyomasa Fusé, "Suicide and Culture in Japan: A Study of *Seppuku* as an Institutionalized Form of Suicide," *Social Psychiatry* 15 (1980): 57–63. *Seppuku* became popular in the United States even as the Japanese government was debating its abolition in the 1870s in an effort to Westernize Japan. As a result of this effort, the Japanese government banned *seppuku* as a method of execution.
51. Inazo Nitobé, *Bushido: The Soul of Japan, An Exposition of Japanese Thought* (New York: G. P. Putnum's Sons, 1907), 15.
52. Ibid., 11.
53. Ibid., 109.
54. Ibid., 112, 114.
55. Kakuzo Okakura, *The Book of Tea* (New York: G. P. Putnum's Sons, 1906), 146.
56. Ibid., 157.
57. Ibid., 156.
58. Ibid., 160.
59. Susan Sontag, "Fascinating Fascism," in *Under the Sign of Saturn* (New York: Vintage, 1981), 91.
60. Article 9 in its entirety reads: 第九条　日本国民は、正義と秩序を基調とする国際平和を誠実に希求し、国権の発動たる戦争と、武力による威嚇又は武力の行使は、国際紛争を解決する手段としては、永久にこれを放棄する。○2　前項の目的を達するため、陸海空軍その他の戦力は、これを保持しない。国の交戦権は、これを認めない。[Aspiring sincerely to an international peace based on justice and order, the Japanese people forever renounce war as a sovereign right of the nation and the threat or use of force as means of settling international disputes. 2) In order to accomplish the aim of the preceding paragraph, land, sea, and air forces, as well as other war potential, will never be maintained. The right of belligerency of the state will not be recognized.] For an English translation of the article, see https://japan.kantei.go.jp/constitution_and_government_of_japan/constitution_e.html
61. I repurpose this term from Claudia Rankine, *Citizen: An American Lyric* (Minneapolis, MN: Graywolf Press, 2014), 14.
62. Tim Dean, *Unlimited Intimacy: Reflections on the Subculture of Barebacking* (Chicago: University of Chicago Press, 2009), 45–46. It is suggestive that Dean, in arguing that T. S. Eliot's doctrine of impersonality elsewhere, aligns his reading against the Western conception of selfhood,

222 NOTES

states: "The critical genealogy I have been tracing suggests just how hard it is, in the individualist societies of the West, to contemplate seriously the implications of divesting the self of its authority. These implications run counter to Enlightenment notions of individual sovereignty and self-possession, upon which rests a fundamental idea of political liberty. . . . The basic incompatibility between Enlightenment and impersonalist models of the self helps explain critics' inability to view impersonality as anything but a politically dubious enterprise." Tim Dean, "T. S. Eliot, Famous Clairvoyante," in *Gender, Desire, and Sexuality in T. S. Eliot*, ed. Cassandra Laity and Nancy K. Gish (Cambridge: Cambridge University Press 2004), 50. Even though Dean does not mention the so-called East, impersonalist models of the self are rooted in non-Western constructions of selfhood.

63. For an extensive list of "Madame Butterfly" adaptations, see W. Anthony Sheppard, "Cinematic Realism, Reflexivity and the American 'Madame Butterfly' Narrative," *Cambridge Opera Journal* 17, no. 1 (2005): 60.

64. Sheppard, 59.

65. Pierre Loti, *Madame Chrysanthéme*, trans. Laura Ensor (London: George Routledge and Sons, 1897), 74, 290. After Loti's 1888 novel was made into an opera in France in 1893, a French illustrator, Félix Régamey, published a rewriting of the novel in the magazine *La Plume*, in the form of Chrysanthème's fictional diary, titled *Le Cahier Rose de Madame Chrysanthéme* (*The Pink Notebook of Madame Chrysanthéme*). Written from the perspective of Chrysanthème, Régamey's short piece narrates her secret love for the impervious "Monsieur Loti," ending with Chrysanthème's suicide attempt: "*Here the notes in the pink notebook end. The epilogue is very Japanese. Forsaken, she wanted to end her existence and hurled herself into the sea. Around her neck hung one hundred silver coins tied with a bit of rare silk. She was saved.*" The Chrysanthème Papers: *The Pink Notebook of Madame Chrysanthéme and Other Documents of French Japonism*, trans. and ed. Christopher Reed (Honolulu: University of Hawai'i Press, 2010), 90–91, emphasis his.

66. Ibid., 64.

67. Cheng, 1.

68. Loti, 112.

69. Ibid., 280, 281.

70. Ibid., 328.

71. John Luther Long, "Madame Butterfly," in *Madame Butterfly and A Japanese Nightingale: Two Orientalist Texts*, ed. Maureen Honey and Jean Lee Cole (New Brunswick, NJ: Rutgers University Press 2002), 30.

72. Ibid., 31, 36, 44, 64.

73. Ibid., 36.

74. Ibid., 37–38.

75. Ibid., 61.

76. Ibid., 62.

77. Ibid., 78.

78. Ibid., 75.

79. Ibid., 76.

80. On shame and its wounded narcissism, see Eve Kosofsky Sedgwick, *Touching Feeling: Affect, Pedagogy, Performativity* (Durham, NC: Duke University Press 2003), 35–65.

81. Ibid.

82. Long, 78.

83. Even though the ending of Long's story is slightly ambiguous as to whether Butterfly dies or not, in a 1935 interview he asserts that Butterfly does not die at the end of his story. See, for example, Arthur Groos, "Madame Butterfly: The Story" *Cambridge Opera Journal* 3, no. 2 (1991): 131 n. 18.

84. Elizabeth Binggeli argues that even though Mary Pickford with her honey-blonde ringlets is now remembered as an icon of whiteness, she played a number of racialized characters at the beginning of her career, including a Native American, a Filipino, and a "Hindu girl." The last of these roles and the one that cemented her whiteness was Butterfly. Elizabeth Binggeli, "Blood and Sympathy: Race and the Films of Mary Pickford," in *Mary Pickford: Queen of the Movies*, ed. Christel Schmidt (Louisville: University Press of Kentucky, 2012), 187–204.

85. "Amusements," *Democrat and Chronicle* (Rochester, NY), December 29, 1900, 13.

86. Sianne Ngai, *Our Aesthetic Categories: Zany, Cute, Interesting* (Cambridge, MA: Harvard University Press, 2012), 61.

NOTES 223

87. Ibid., 64.
88. Ibid., 98.
89. Cheng, 76.
90. David Belasco, *Six Plays: Madame Butterfly, Du Barry, the Darling of the Gods, Adrea, the Girl of the Golden West, the Return of Peter Grimm* (Boston: Little, Brown, 1929), 32.
91. "Race mother" is a period term to describe (white) woman's reproductive responsibility for eugenic "race betterment" and was widely understood to be essential to the health of the race. According to this concept, the maternal body became the central locus of positive eugenics. The term appears most prominently in Margaret Sanger's writing. See, for instance, Margaret Sanger, *Woman and the New Race* (New York: Eugenics Publishing Company, 1920), 232.
92. Belasco, 24.
93. Ibid., 32.
94. Sara Hirschfield Kessel, "Dainty Valerie Bergere: Talented Actress Talks Interestingly of Her Likes and Dislikes," *Buffalo Courier*, January 13, 1901: 2 (Buffalo, NY).
95. Ibid., 2.
96. Ibid., 2.
97. Emma Lazarus, "The New Colossus" in *The Poems of Emma Lazarus in Two Volumes*, vol. 1, *Narrative, Lyric, and Dramatic* (Boston: Houghton Mifflin, 1889), 202–203.
98. Saum Song Bo, "A Chinese View of the Statue of Liberty," in *Chinese American Voices: From the Gold Rush to the Present*, ed. Judy Yung, Gordon H. Chang, and Him Mark Lai (Los Angeles: University of California Press, 2006), 56.
99. As Kerry Abrams points out, Chinese prostitutes constituted "uniquely identifiable legal targets"; even though there were many prostitutes of other races and ethnicities, state laws often singled out Chinese prostitutes not only for the purpose of immigration restriction, but also for the regulation of brothels. See Kerry Abrams, "Polygamy, Prostitution, and the Federalization of Immigration Law," *Columbia Law Review* 105, no. 3 (2005): 641–716.
100. As Abrams points out, even though the Page Law of 1875 was the first federal immigration law, it has been overshadowed by the 1882 Chinese Exclusion Act and remains "surprisingly understudied" (645). For a detailed analysis of the law, see also Eithne Luibhéid, *Entry Denied: Controlling Sexuality and the Border* (Minneapolis: University of Minnesota Press, 2002), especially 31–54.
101. Asian women's lack of volition was an extremely common discourse. For instance, in 1874, then-President Ulysses Grant claimed: "The great proportion of the Chinese immigrants who come to our shores do not come voluntarily . . . but come under contracts with headmen who own them almost absolutely. In worse form does this apply to Chinese women" (quoted in Luibhéid, 36).
102. Abrams, 651. Abrams argues that while a large portion of female Chinese immigrants actually engaged in prostitution, the census overestimated the number of Chinese prostitutes, as the census-takers did not understand the pre-revolutionary family system in China, which allowed a husband to have a second wife and concubines. Many of the female Chinese immigrants who were mistaken as prostitutes were actually "secondary wives," as the first wife often stayed with the husband's family in China (Abrams, 656).
103. Quoted in Luibhéid, 35. Luibhéid argues that the development of germ theory accelerated anti-Chinese sentiments, as Chinese immigrants were understood as carriers of distinct germs. In particular, Chinese prostitutes were believed to spread leprosy and syphilis to white men, prompting the American Medical Association to study "whether Chinese prostitutes were poisoning the nation's blood stream" (Luibhéid, 37).
104. "Worldwide Vigil for the Victims of the Atlanta Shooting," hosted by KAC-Metro Atlanta, March 26, 2021, https://326vigil.org.

Bibliography

Abdur-Rahman, Aliyyah. *Against the Closet: Identity, Political Longing, and Black Figuration.* Durham, NC: Duke University Press, 2012.

Abelove, Henry. "Some Speculations on the History of Sexual Intercourse during the Long Eighteenth Century in England." In *Deep Gossip*, 21–28. Minneapolis: University of Minnesota Press, 2005.

Abrams, Kerry. "Polygamy, Prostitution, and the Federalization of Immigration Law." *Columbia Law Review* 105, no. 3 (2005): 641–716.

Adams, David Wallace. *Education for Extinction: American Indians and the Boarding School Experience, 1875–1928.* Lawrence: University Press of Kansas, 1995.

Agamben, Giorgio. *Homo Sacer: Sovereign Power and Bare Life.* Translated by Daniel Heller-Roazen. Stanford, CA: Stanford University Press, 1998.

Allen, Nathan. "Changes in New England Population." *Popular Science Monthly* 23 (1883): 433–444.

Ammons, Elizabeth. *Conflicting Stories: American Women Writers at the Turn into the Twentieth Century.* New York: Oxford University Press, 1991.

Archdeacon, Thomas J. *Becoming American: An Ethnic History.* New York: The Free Press, 1983.

Armstrong, Tim. "Disciplining the Corpus: Henry James and Fletcherism." In *American Bodies: Cultural Histories of the Physique*, edited by Tim Armstrong, 101–119. New York: New York University Press, 1966.

Arvidson, Heather. "Personality, Impersonality, and the Personified Detachment of Wyndham Lewis." *Modernism/modernity* 25, no. 4 (2018): 791–814.

Auerbach, Jonathan. *Male Call: Becoming Jack London.* Durham, NC: Duke University Press, 1996.

Banta, Martha. *Taylored Lives: Narrative Productions in the Age of Taylor, Veblen, and Ford.* Chicago: University of Chicago Press, 1993.

Banton, Michael. *Racial Theories.* Cambridge: Cambridge University Press, 1987.

Barkan, Elliott Robert, and Michael C. LeMay. *U.S. Immigration and Naturalization Laws and Issues: A Documentary History.* Westport, CT: Greenwood, 1999.

Barrish, Phillip. "*The Awakening*'s Signifying Mexicanist Presence." *Studies in American Fiction* 28, no. 1 (2000): 55–76.

Bataille, Georges. *Erotism: Death and Sensuality.* San Francisco: City Lights Books, 1986.

Bateman, Benjamin. *The Modernist Art of Queer Survival.* Oxford: Oxford University Press, 2018.

Beard, George M. *American Nervousness: Its Cause and Consequences.* New York: Putnam's, 1881.

Beard, George M. *Sexual Neurasthenia: Its Hygiene, Causes, Symptoms, and Treatment.* New York: E. B. Treat, 1884.

Bederman, Gail. *Manliness and Civilization: A Cultural History of Gender and Race in the United States, 1880–1917.* Chicago: University of Chicago Press, 1995.

Beistegui, Miguel de. *The Government of Desire.* Chicago: University of Chicago Press, 2018.

Belasco, David. *Six Plays: Madame Butterfly, Du Barry, the Darling of the Gods, Adrea, the Girl of the Golden West, the Return of Peter Grimm.* Boston: Little, Brown, 1929.

226 BIBLIOGRAPHY

Bell, Richard. *We Shall Be No More: Suicide and Self-Government in the Newly United States.* Oxford: Oxford University Press, 2012.

Bennett, Andrew. *Suicide Century: Literature and Suicide from James Joyce to David Foster Wallace.* Cambridge: Cambridge University Press, 2017.

Berg, Allison. *Mothering the Race: Women's Narratives of Reproduction, 1890–1930.* Urbana: University of Illinois Press, 2002.

Berg, Manfred. *Popular Justice: A History of Lynching in America.* Chicago: Ivan R. Dee, 2011.

Berkove, Lawrence I. "Jack London and Evolution: From Spencer to Huxley." *American Literary Realism* 36, no. 3 (2004): 243–255.

Berlant, Lauren. "On the Case." *Critical Inquiry* 33, no. 4 (2007): 663–672.

Berlant, Lauren. *Cruel Optimism.* Durham, NC: Duke University Press, 2011.

Berlant, Lauren. "Slow Death (Sovereignty, Obesity, Lateral Agency)." *Critical Inquiry* 33, no. 4 (2007): 754–780.

Berliner, Jonathan. "Jack London's Social Darwinism." *American Literary Realism* 41, no. 4 (2008): 52–78.

Berman, Jeffrey. *Surviving Literary Suicide.* Amherst: University of Massachusetts Press, 1999.

Bertonneau, Thomas. "Like Hypatia before the Mob: Desire, Resentment, and Sacrifice in *The Bostonians* (An Anthropoetics)." *Nineteenth-Century Literature* 53, no. 1 (1998): 56–90.

Best, Stephen. *The Fugitive's Properties: Law and the Poetics of Possession.* Chicago: University of Chicago Press, 2004.

Bibler, Michael. "Queer/Quare." In *Keywords for Southern Studies*, edited by Scott Romine and Jennifer Rae Greeson, 200–212. Athens: University of Georgia Press, 2016.

Biggs, Mary. "'Si tu savais': The Gay/Transgendered Sensibility of Kate Chopin's *The Awakening.*" *Women's Studies* 33, no. 2 (2010): 145–181.

Binggeli, Elizabeth. "Blood and Sympathy: Race and the Films of Mary Pickford." In *Mary Pickford: Queen of the Movies*, edited by Christel Schmidt, 187–204. Louisville: University Press of Kentucky, 2012.

Birken, Lawrence. *Consuming Desire: Sexual Science and the Emergence of a Culture of Abundance, 1871–1914.* Ithaca, NY: Cornell University Press, 1988.

Birnbaum, Michele A. "'Alien Hands': Kate Chopin and the Colonization of Race." *American Literature* 66, no. 2 (1994): 301–323.

Blight, David W. *Race and Reunion: The Civil War in American Memory.* Cambridge, MA: Harvard University Press, 2001.

Bloom, Harold. *The Strong Light of the Canonical: Kafka, Freud, and Scholem as Revisionists of Jewish Culture and Thoughts.* New York: City College Press, 1987.

Bo, Saum Song. "A Chinese View of the Statue of Liberty." In *Chinese American Voices: From the Gold Rush to the Present*, edited by Judy Yung, Gordon H. Chang, and Him Mark Lai, 56. Los Angeles: University of California Press, 2006.

Bond, Arthur J. "'Applying the Standards of Intrinsic Excellence': Nationalism and Arnoldian Cultural Valuation in the *Century Magazine.*" *American Periodicals* 9 (1999): 55–73.

Borradori, Giovanna. *Philosophy in the Time of Terror: Dialogues with Jürgen Habermas and Jacques Derrida.* Chicago: University of Chicago Press, 2003.

Bowe, Luke. Twitter post, February 10th 2020. https://twitter.com/lmbowe.

Bowlby, Rachel. *Shopping with Freud.* London: Routledge, 1993.

Bowles, Nellie. "'Replacement Theory,' a Racist, Sexist Doctrine, Spreads in Far-Right Circles." *New York Times*, March 18, 2019. https://www.nytimes.com/2019/03/18/technology/replacement-theory.html.

Boyarin, Daniel. "Homophobia and the Postcoloniality of the 'Jewish Science.'" In *Queer Theory and the Jewish Question*, edited by Daniel Boyarin, Daniel Itzkovitz, and Ann Pellegrini, 166–198. New York: Columbia University Press, 2003.

Boyarin, Daniel. *Unheroic Conduct: The Rise of Heterosexuality and the Invention of the Jewish Man.* Berkeley: University of California Press, 1997.

BIBLIOGRAPHY 227

Bradway, Teagan and Elizabeth Freeman, eds. *Queer Kinship: Race, Sex, Belonging, Form.* Durham, NC: Duke University Press, 2022.

Brantlinger, Patrick. *Dark Vanishings: Discourse of the Extinction of the Primitive Races, 1800–1930.* Ithaca, NY: Cornell University Press, 2003.

Brigham, Ann. "Touring Memorial Hall: The State of the Union in *The Bostonians.*" *Arizona Quarterly* 62, no. 3 (2006): 5–29.

Brown, Wendy. "Wounded Attachments." *Political Theory* 21, no. 3 (1993): 390–410.

Brown, William Wells. *Clotel; or, the President's Daughter: A Narrative of Slave Life in the United States.* Edited by Robert S. Levine. Boston: Bedford, 2000.

Bruni, John. "Furry Logic: Biological Kinship and Empire in Jack London's *The Call of the Wild.*" *Interdisciplinary Studies in Literature and Environment* 14, no. 1 (2007): 25–49.

Bunch, Dianne. "Dangerous Spending Habits: The Epistemology of Edna Pontellier's Extravagant Expenditures in *The Awakening.*" *Mississippi Quarterly* 55, no. 1 (2002): 43–61.

Burroughs, John. "Real and Sham Natural History." *Atlantic Monthly* 91 (1903): 298–309.

Butler, Judith. *Frames of War: When is Life Grievable?* New York: Verso, 2009.

Butler, Judith. *Undoing Gender.* New York: Routledge, 2004.

Cameron, Sharon. *Impersonality: Seven Essays.* Chicago: University of Chicago Press, 2007.

Campbell, Timothy. Translator's Introduction to *Bios: Biopolitics and Immunity*, by Robert Esposito, vii–xlii. Minneapolis: University of Minnesota Press, 2008.

Camus, Renaud. *You Will Not Replace Us!* Plieux, France: Chez l'auteur, 2018.

Canaday, Margot. *The Straight State: Sexuality and Citizenship in Twentieth-Century America.* Princeton, NJ: Princeton University Press, 2009.

Carter, Julian. *The Heart of Whiteness: Normal Sexuality and Race in America, 1880–1940.* Durham, NC: Duke University Press, 2007.

Castle, Terry. *The Apparitional Lesbian: Female Homosexuality and Modern Culture.* New York: Columbia University Press, 1993.

Castronovo, Russ. *Necro Citizenship: Death, Eroticism, and the Public Sphere in the Nineteenth-Century United States.* Durham, NC: Duke University Press, 2001.

Cather, Willa Silbert. "Paul's Case." In *The Troll Garden*, 211–253. New York: McClure, Philips & Co., 1905.

Cavitch, Max. "Emma Lazarus and the Golem of Liberty." *American Literary History* 18, no. 1 (2006): 1–28.

Cecire, Natalia. "Ways of Not Reading Gertrude Stein." *ELH* 82, no. 1 (2015): 281–312.

Chamberlain, Houston Steward. *The Foundation of the Nineteenth Century.* Translated by John Lees. New York: John Lane, 1912.

Chamberlin, J. Edward and Sander L. Gilman, eds. *Degeneration: The Dark Side of Progress.* New York: Columbia University Press, 1985.

Chang, Jason Oliver. Twitter post, January 30, 2020. https://twitter.com/chinotronic?lang=en.

Chauncey, George. *Gay New York: Gender, Urban Culture, and the Making of the Gay Male World, 1890–1940.* New York: Basic Books, 1994.

Chauncey, George. "From Sexual Inversion to Homosexuality: The Changing Medical Conceptualization of Female 'Deviance.'" In *Passion and Power: Sexuality in History*, edited by Kathy Peiss and Christina Simmons, 87–117. Philadelphia: Temple University Press, 1989.

Chen, Mel Y. *Animacies: Biopolitics, Racial Mattering, and Queer Affect.* Durham, NC: Duke University Press, 2012.

Cheng, Anne Anlin. *Ornamentalism.* New York: Oxford University Press, 2019.

Chengwang, Lou. Twitter post, January 28, 2020. https://twitter.com/chengwangl?lang=en.

Chesnutt, Charles W. "Dave's Neckliss." *Atlantic Monthly* 64 (1889): 500–508.

Chopin, Kate. *The Awakening.* New York: Norton, 1899. Reprinted 1994.

Chopin, Kate. "Désirée's Baby." In *Kate Chopin: Complete Novels and Stories*, 242–247. New York: Library of America, 2002.

228 BIBLIOGRAPHY

Chopin, Kate. "An Egyptian Cigarette." In *Kate Chopin: Complete Novels and Stories*, 894–897. New York: Library of America, 2002.

Chopin, Kate. "A Pair of Silk Stockings." In *Kate Chopin: Complete Novels and Stories*, 816–820. New York: Library of America, 2002.

Clement, Tanya. "The Story of One: Narrative and Composition in Gertrude Stein's *The Making of Americans*." *Texas Studies in Literature and Language* 54, no. 3 (2012): 426–448.

Coffman, Chris. *Gertrude Stein's Transmasculinity*. Edinburgh: Edinburgh University Press, 2018.

Cohen, Ed. *A Body Worth Defending: Immunity, Biopolitics, and the Apotheosis of the Modern Body*. Durham, NC: Duke University Press, 2009.

Connolly, Brian. *Domestic Intimacies: Incest and the Liberal Subject in Nineteenth-Century America*. Philadelphia: University of Pennsylvania Press, 2014.

"Copy of the Declaration of Rights as Finally Decreed by the National Assembly of France, The Times (London), on Thursday, August 27." September 3, 1789. 3.

Cor de Vaan, Michiel Arnoud. *Etymological Dictionary of Latin and the Other Italic Languages*. Leiden: Brill, 2008.

"Coronavirus: French Asians hit back at racism with 'I'm not a virus.'" *BBC News*, BBC, January 29, 2020. https://www.bbc.com/news/world-europe-51294305.

Cott, Nancy. *Public Vows: A History of Marriage and the Nation*. Cambridge, MA: Harvard University Press, 2000.

Coviello, Peter. *Tomorrow's Parties: Sex and the Untimely in Nineteenth-Century America*. New York: New York University Press, 2013.

Crow, Charles L. "Ishi and Jack London's Primitives." In *Rereading Jack London*, edited by Leonard Cassuto and Jeanne Campbell Reesman, 46–54. Stanford, CA: Stanford University Press, 1996.

Cubberley, Ellwood P. *Changing Conceptions of Education*. Boston: Houghton Mifflin, 1909.

"'Cyclone Mack' Says—." *Portsmouth Daily Times*. January 16, 1925. Scioto County, OH.

Damon, Maria. "Gertrude Stein's Doggerel 'Yiddish': Women, Dogs, and Jews." In *The Dark End of the Street: Margins in American Vanguard Poetry*, 202–235. Minneapolis: University of Minnesota Press, 1993.

Damon, Maria. "Gertrude Stein's Jewishness, Jewish Social Scientists, and the 'Jewish Question.'" *MFS* 42 no. 3 (1996): 489–506.

Davidson, Arnold. Introduction to *Security, Territory, Population: Lectures at the Collège de France 1977–78*, by Michel Foucault, xviii–xxxiv. New York: Picador, 2007.

Davis, Abraham and Barbara Graham. *The Supreme Court, Race, and Civil Rights: From Marshall to Rehnquist*. Thousand Oaks, CA: Sage Publications, 1995.

Dean, Mitchell. *Critical and Effective Histories: Foucault's Methods and Historical Sociology*. London: Routledge, 1994.

Dean, Tim. "T.S. Eliot, Famous Clairvoyante." In *Gender, Desire, and Sexuality in T. S. Eliot*, edited by Cassandra Laity and Nancy K. Gish, 43–65. Cambridge: Cambridge University Press, 2004.

Dean, Tim. *Unlimited Intimacy: Reflections on the Subculture of Barebacking*. Chicago: University of Chicago Press, 2009.

Delany, Samuel. *Times Square Red, Times Square Blue*. New York: New York University Press, 1999.

Deleuze, Gilles, and Félix Guattari. *A Thousand Plateaus: Capitalism and Schizophrenia*. Translated by Brian Massumi. Minneapolis: University of Minnesota Press, 1987.

Derrick, Scott. "Making a Heterosexual Man: Gender, Sexuality, and Narrative in the Fiction of Jack London." In *Rereading Jack London*, edited by Leonard Cassuto and Jeanne Campbell Reesman, 110–129. Stanford, CA: Stanford University Press, 1996.

Derrida, Jacques. *Rogues: Two Essays on Reason*. Palo Alto, CA: Stanford University Press, 2005.

Derrida, Jacques. "Le Toucher: Touch/To Touch Him." *Paragraph* 16, no. 2 (1993): 122–157.

BIBLIOGRAPHY 229

Deutscher, Penelope. *Foucault's Futures: A Critique of Reproductive Reason.* New York: Columbia University Press, 2017.

Dimock, Wai Chee. *Residues of Justice: Literature, Law, Philosophy.* Berkeley: University of California Press, 1996.

Dixon, Thomas. *The Clansman: An Historical Romance of the Ku Klux Klan.* New York: A. Wessels, 1907.

Domínguez, Virginia R. *White by Definition: Social Classification in Creole Louisiana.* New Brunswick, NJ: Rutgers University Press, 1986.

Dorsey, Peter A. "To 'Corroborate Our Own Claims': Public Positioning and the Slavery Metaphor in Revolutionary America." *American Quarterly* 55, no. 3 (2003): 353–386.

Doyle, Laura. "The Flat, the Round, and Gertrude Stein: Race and the Shape of Modern(ist) History." *Modernism/modernity* 7, no. 2 (2000): 249–271.

Dray, Phillip. *At the Hands of Persons Unknown: The Lynching of Black America.* New York: Random House, 2002.

Durkheim, Émile. *On Suicide.* Translated by Robin Buss. New York: Penguin, 2006.

Dyer, Joyce. "Reading *The Awakening* with Toni Morrison." *Southern Literary Journal* 35, no. 1 (2002): 138–154.

Dyer, Richard. "Into the Light: The Whiteness of the South in *The Birth of a Nation.*" In *Dixie Debates: Perspectives on Southern Cultures,* edited by Richard King and Helen Taylor, 165–176. New York: New York University Press, 1996.

Dyer, Richard. *White: Essays on Race and Culture.* London: Routledge, 1997.

Dyer, Thomas G. *Theodore Roosevelt and the Idea of Race.* Baton Rouge: Louisiana State University, 1992.

Eakin, Paul John. "Henry James's 'Obscure Hurt': Can Autobiography Serve Biography?" *New Literary History* 19, no. 3 (1988): 675–692.

Edel, Leon. *Henry James: The Untried Years, 1843–1870.* New York: Avon, 1953.

Edel, Leon. "Portrait of Alice James." In *The Diary of Alice James,* edited by Leon Edel, 1–21. New York: Dodd, Mead & Co., 1934.

Edelman, Lee. *Bad Education: Why Queer Theory Teaches Us Nothing.* Durham, NC: Duke University Press, 2023.

Edelman, Lee. *No Future: Queer Theory and the Death Drive.* Durham, NC: Duke University Press, 2004.

Elfenbein, Anna Shannon. *Women on the Color Line: Evolving Stereotypes and the Writings of George Washington Cable, Grace King, and Kate Chopin.* Charlottesville: University of Virginia Press, 1989.

Eliot, T. S. *The Sacred Wood: Essays on Poetry and Criticism.* London: Methuen and Co., 1920.

Ellis, John. *Deterioration of the Puritan Stock and Its Causes.* New York: Published by the Author, 1884.

English, Daylanne K. *Unnatural Selections: Eugenics in American Modernism and the Harlem Renaissance.* Chapel Hill: University of North Carolina Press, 2004.

Esposito, Roberto. *Bios: Biopolitics and Philosophy.* Translated by Timothy Campbell. Minneapolis: University of Minnesota Press, 2008.

Esposito, Roberto. *Third Person: Politics of Life and Philosophy of the Impersonal.* Translated by Zakiya Hanafi. Malden, MA: Polity, 2012.

Ewell, Barbara C., and Pamela Glenn Menke. "*The Awakening* and the Great October Storm of 1893." *Southern Literary Journal* 42, no. 2 (2010): 1–11.

Farland, Maria. "Gertrude Stein's Brain Work." *American Literature* 76, no. 1 (2004): 117–148.

Feinstein, Amy. "Gertrude Stein, Alice Toklas, and Albert Barnes: Looking Like a Jew in *The Autobiography of Alice B. Toklas.*" *Shofar* 25, no. 3 (2007): 47–60.

Feinstein, Amy. *Gertrude Stein and the Making of Jewish Modernism.* Gainesville: University Press of Florida, 2020.

Felski, Rita. *Gender of Modernity.* Cambridge, MA: Harvard University Press, 1995.

230 BIBLIOGRAPHY

Ferguson, Roderick. *Aberrations in Black: Toward a Queer of Color Critique.* Minneapolis: University of Minnesota Press, 2004.

Fiedler, Brigitte. *Relative Races: Genealogies of Interracial Kinship in Nineteenth-Century America.* Durham, NC: Duke University Press, 2020.

Fleissner, Jennifer L. *Women, Compulsion, Modernity: The Moment of American Naturalism.* Chicago: University of Chicago Press, 2004.

Foucault, Michel. *The Birth of Biopolitics, Lectures at the Collège de France, 1978–1979.* Translated by Graham Burchell. New York: Picador, 2008.

Foucault, Michel. *The History of Sexuality.* Vol. 1, *An Introduction.* Translated by Robert Hurley. New York: Pantheon Books, 1978.

Foucault, Michel. "Passion According to Werner Schroeter." In *Foucault Live: Collected Interviews, 1961–1984,* translated by Lysa Hochroth and John Johnston, 313–321. South Pasadena, CA: Semiotext(e), 1996.

Foucault, Michel. *Security, Territory, Population: Lectures at the Collège de France, 1977–78.* New York: Picador, 2007.

Foucault, Michel. "The Simplest of Pleasures." In *Foucault Live: Collected Interviews, 1961–1984,* translated by Lysa Hochroth and John Johnston, 295–297. South Pasadena, CA: Semiotext(e), 1996.

Foucault, Michel. *"Society Must Be Defended": Lectures at the Collège de France, 1975–1976.* New York: Picador, 2003.

Foucault, Michel. "The Subject and Power." In *Power,* translated by Robert Hurley et al., 326–348. New York: New Press, 1997.

Freedman, Jonathan. "Coming Out of the Jewish Closet with Marcel Proust." In *Queer Theory and the Jewish Question,* edited by Daniel Boyarin, Daniel Itzkovitz, and Ann Pellegrini, 521–555. New York: Columbia University Press, 2003.

Freud, Sigmund. "Analysis of a Phobia in a Five-Year-Old Boy (1909)." In *The Standard Edition of the Complete Psychological Works of Sigmund Freud,* vol. 10, translated by James Strachey, 3–152. London: Hogarth, 1995.

Freud, Sigmund. *Beyond the Pleasure Principle.* Translated by James Strachey. New York: W. W. Norton and Company, 1989.

Freud, Sigmund. *The History of An Infantile Neurosis (1914).* In *The Standard Edition of the Complete Psychological Works of Sigmund Freud,* vol. 17, translated by James Strachey, 3–257. London: Hogarth, 1995.

Freud, Sigmund. *Three Essays on the Theory of Sexuality.* Translated by James Strachey. New York: Basic Books, 2000.

Freud, Sigmund. *Three Essays on The Theory of Sexuality (1905).* In *The Standard Edition of the Complete Psychological Works of Sigmund Freud,* vol. 7, translated by James Strachey, 125–248. London: Hogarth, 1995.

Freud, Sigmund. *Totem and Taboo: Resemblances between the Psychic Lives of Savages and Neurotics.* Translated by A. A. Brill. London: George Routledge and Sons, 1919.

Furer, Andrew J. "'Zone-Conquerors' and 'White Devils': The Contradictions of Race in the Works of Jack London." In *Rereading Jack London,* edited by Leonard Cassuto and Jeanne Campbell Reesman, 158–171. Stanford, CA: Stanford University Press, 1996.

Furui, Yoshiaki. "Lonely Individualism in *Moby-Dick.*" *Criticism* 62, no. 4 (2020): 599–623.

Furui, Yoshiaki. "'No One Is His Own Sire': Dead Letters and Kinship in Melville's *Pierre.*" Journal of the American Literature Society of Japan 8 (2010): 1–17.

Fusé, Toyomasa. "Suicide and Culture in Japan: A Study of Seppuku as an Institutionalized Form of Suicide." *Social Psychiatry* 15 (1980): 57–63.

Gallagher, Gary W., and Alan T. Nolan, eds. *The Myth of the Lost Cause and Civil War History.* Bloomington: Indiana University Press, 2000.

Gallup, Donald. "Appendix: The Making of The Making of Americans." In *Fernhurst, Q.E.D., and Other Early Writings,* by Gertrude Stein, 173–214. London: Peter Owen, 1972.

Gallup, Donald. "A Note on the Texts." In *Fernhurst, Q.E.D., and Other Early Writings,* by Gertrude Stein, vi–vii. London: Peter Owen, 1972,.

BIBLIOGRAPHY   231

Garber, Marjorie. *Dog Love*. New York: Touchstone, 1996.

Geertz, Clifford. "'From the Native's Point of View': On the Nature of Anthropological Understanding." *Bulletin of the American Academy of Arts and Sciences* 28, no. 1 (1974): 26–45.

Geller, Jay. "Freud, Blüher, and Secessio Inversa: Männerbünde, Homosexuality, and Freud's Theory of Cultural Formation." In *Queer Theory and the Jewish Question*, edited by Daniel Boyarin, Daniel Itzkovitz, and Ann Pellegrini, 90–120. New York: Columbia University Press, 2003.

Gibson, Mary. *Born to Crime: Cesare Lombroso and the Origins of Biological Criminology*. Westport, CT: Praeger, 2002.

Gilman, Charlotte Perkins. *Herland, The Yellow Wall-Paper, and Selected Writings*. New York: Penguin, 1999.

Gilman, Charlotte Perkins. *Women and Economics: A Study of the Economic Relation Between Men and Women as a Factor in Social Evolution*. Boston: Small, Maynard & Company, 1898.

Gilman, Sander. *Freud, Race, and Gender*. Princeton, NJ: Princeton University Press, 1993.

Gilman, Sander. *The Jew's Body*. New York: Routledge, 1991.

Gilroy, Paul. *The Black Atlantic: Modernity and Double-Consciousness*. New York: Verso, 1993.

Gleason, Philip. "The Melting Pot: Symbol of Fusion or Confusion?" *American Quarterly* 16, no. 1 (1964): 20–46.

Goldsby, Jacqueline. *A Spectacular Secret: Lynching in American Literature*. Chicago: University of Chicago Press, 2006.

Gordon, Colin. "Governmental Rationality: An Introduction." In *The Foucault Effect: Studies in Governmentality*, edited by Graham Burchell, Colin Gordon, and Peter Miller, 1–52. Chicago: University of Chicago Press, 1991.

Gordon, Linda. *The Moral Property of Women: A History of Birth Control Politics in America*. Champaign: University of Illinois Press, 2002.

Gossett, Thomas F. *Race: The History of an Idea in America*. New York: Oxford University Press, 1963. Reprinted 1997.

Graham, Wendy. *Henry James's Thwarted Love*. Stanford, CA: Stanford University Press, 1999.

Grant, Madison. *The Passing of the Great Race, Or the Racial Basis of European History*. New York: Charles Scribner's Sons, 1916.

"Great Scott! Doesn't the Judge Know That I'm Suffering from Alien Indigestion?" *Greenville Democrat* (Greenville, TN), May 2, 1923. 4.

Groos, Arthur. "Madame Butterfly: The Story." *Cambridge Opera Journal* 3, no. 2 (1991): 125–158.

Grossberg, Michael. *Governing the Hearth: Law and the Family in Nineteenth Century America*. Chapel Hill: University of North Carolina Press, 1988.

Gunning, Sandra. *Race, Rape, and Lynching: The Red Record of American Literature, 1890–1912*. Oxford: Oxford University Press, 1996.

Halperin, David M. *How to Do the History of Homosexuality*. Chicago: University of Chicago Press, 2002.

Halperin, John. "Henry James's Civil War." *Henry James Review* 17, no. 1 (1996): 22–29.

Haraway, Donna. "Teddy Bear Patriarchy: Taxidermy in the Garden of Eden, New York City, 1908–1936." *Social Text* 11 (1984–1985): 20–64.

Harris, Cheryl I. "Whiteness as Property." *Harvard Law Review* 106, no. 8 (1993): 1707–1791.

Harris, Trudier. *Exorcizing Blackness: Historical and Literary Lynching and Burning Rituals*. Bloomington: Indiana University Press, 1984.

Hartman, Saidiya. *Scenes of Subjection: Terror, Slavery, and Self-Making in Nineteenth-Century America*. Oxford: Oxford University Press, 1997.

Hayot, Eric. *The Hypothetical Mandarin: Sympathy, Modernity, and Chinese Pain*. Oxford: Oxford University Press, 2009.

Hemingway, Ernest. *A Moveable Feast: The Restored Edition*. Edited by Seán Hemingway. New York: Scribner, 2010.

Herring, Scott. "Eve Sedgwick's 'Other Materials.'" *Angelaki* 23, no. 1–2 (2018): 5–18.

232 BIBLIOGRAPHY

Herring, Scott. *Queering the Underworld: Slumming, Literature, and the Undoing of Lesbian and Gay History.* Chicago: University of Chicago Press, 2007.

Herring, Scott. "Willa Cather's Lost Boy: 'Paul's Case' and Bohemian Tramping." *Arizona Quarterly* 60, no. 2 (2004): 87–116.

Higham, John. *Strangers in the Land: Patterns of American Nativism, 1860–1925.* New Brunswick, NJ: Rutgers University Press, 1955.

Hill, Daniel Deils. *As Seen in Vogue: A Century of American Fashion in Advertising.* Lubbock: Texas Tech University Press, 2004.

Hillman, David. "Freud's Shylock." *American Imago* 70, no. 1 (2013): 1–50.

Hobhouse, Janet. *Everybody Who Was Anybody: A Biography of Gertrude Stein.* New York: Putnam, 1975.

Hocquenghem, Guy. *Homosexual Desire.* Translated by Daniella Dangoor. Durham, NC: Duke University Press, 1993.

Hoffman, Warren. *The Passing Game: Queering Jewish American Culture.* Syracuse, NY: Syracuse University Press, 2009.

Hoffmann, Tess and Charles Hoffmann. "Henry James and the Civil War." *New England Quarterly* 62, no. 4 (1989): 529–552.

Hofstadter, Richard. *Social Darwinism in American Thought.* Boston: Beacon Press, 1944.

Horn, David G. *The Criminal Body: Lombroso and the Anatomy of Deviance.* New York: Routledge, 2003.

Horne, Philip. "Henry James and 'the Forces of Violence': On the Track of 'Big Game' in 'The Jolly Corner.'" *Henry James Review* 27, no. 3 (2006): 234–247.

Horne, Philip. "'Poodle and Bull Moose': What Henry James, Theodore Roosevelt Felt about War, America, and Each Other." *Times Literary Supplement* 5802 (June 13, 2014): 13–15.

Horsman, Reginald. *Race and Manifest Destiny: The Origins of American Racial Anglo-Saxonism.* Cambridge, MA: Harvard University Press, 1981.

Hotchman, Barbara. "Reading Historically/Reading Selectively: *The Bostonians* in the *Century*, 1885–1886." *Henry James Review* 34, no. 3 (2013): 270–278.

Huang, Vivian L. *Surface Relations: Queer Forms of Asian American Inscrutability.* Durham, NC: Duke University Press, 2022.

Hurley, Natasha. *Circulating Queerness: Before the Gay and Lesbian Novel.* Minneapolis: University of Minnesota Press, 2018.

"The Increase in Suicide." *The Saint Paul Daily Globe* (Saint Paul, MN), August 4, 1895. 4.

"The Increase in Suicide." *Seymour Daily Republican* (Seymour, IN), April 11, 1910. 2.

"The Increase in Suicide." *The Word and Way: A Weekly Baptist Journal* (Kansas City, MO), May 19, 1904. 1.

"Increase of Suicide: Laurence Irwell Spoke of 'Racial Deterioration.'" *Detroit Free Press* (Detroit, MI), August 11, 1897. 2.

Iseman, Myre St. Walde. *Race Suicide.* New York: Cosmopolitan Press, 1912.

Jacobson, Matthew Frye. *Whiteness of a Different Color: European Immigrants and the Alchemy of Race.* Cambridge, MA: Harvard University Press, 1998.

James, Henry. *The American Scene.* London: Chapman and Hall, 1907.

James, Henry. "Anthony Trollope." *The Century Illustrated Monthly Magazine* (July 1883): 386–395.

James, Henry. *The Bostonians: Henry James, Novels 1881–1886.* Edited by William T. Stafford. New York: Library of America, 1985.

James, Henry. *The Complete Letters of Henry James.* Vol 1, *1884–1886.* Edited by Michael Anesko and Greg W. Zacharias. Lincoln: University of Nebraska Press, 2020.

James, Henry. *The Notebooks of Henry James.* Edited by F. O. Matthiessen and Kenneth B. Murdock. New York: Oxford University Press, 1947.

James, Henry. *Notes of a Son and Brother.* In *Notes of a Son and Brother and The Middle Years: A Critical Edition*, edited by Peter Collister, 5–406. Charlottesville: University of Virginia Press, 2011.

BIBLIOGRAPHY   233

James, Henry. *The Princess Casamassima.* New York: Penguin, 1987.

James, Henry. *The Princess Casamassima.* Vol. 2. London: Macmillan, 1921.

"Japanese Competition: The Protection American Labor Wants Is Restriction and Exclusion Laws Against the Cheaper Man." *Organized Labor* 1, no. 16 (1900): 1.

Jaros, Peter. "A Double Life: Personifying the Corporation from Dartmouth College to Poe." *Poe Studies* 47 (2014): 4–35.

Johnson, E. Patrick. *Sweet Tea: Black Gay Men of the South.* Chapel Hill: University of North Carolina Press, 2008.

Jung, Moon-Ho. *Coolies and Cane: Race, Labor, and Sugar in the Age of Emancipation.* Baltimore: Johns Hopkins University Press, 2006.

Kahan, Benjamin. *The Book of Minor Perverts: Sexology, Etiology, and the Emergence of Sexuality.* Chicago: University of Chicago Press, 2019.

Kahan, Benjamin. *Celibacies: American Modernism and Sexual Life.* Durham, NC: Duke University Press, 2013.

Kahan, Benjamin. *Sexual Aim and Its Misses.* Chicago: University of Chicago Press (forthcoming).

Kantorowicz, Ernst H. *The King's Two Bodies: A Study in Medieval Political Theology.* Princeton, NJ: Princeton University Press, 1957.

Kaplan, Amy. "Nation, Region, and Empire." In *Columbia History of the American Novel,* edited by Emory Elliot, 240–266. New York: Columbia University Press, 1991.

Katz, Jonathan Ned. *The Invention of Heterosexuality.* New York: Dutton, 1995.

Katz, Leon. "The First Making of *The Making of Americans*: A Study Based on Gertrude Stein's Notebooks and Early Versions of Her Novel." Unpublished dissertation, Columbia University, 1963.

Katz, Leon. Introduction to *Fernhurst, Q.E.D., and Other Early Writings,* by Gertrude Stein, ix–xlii. London: Peter Owen, 1972.

Katz, Leon. "Weininger and the Making of Americans." *Twentieth Century Literature* 24, no. 1 (1978): 8–26.

Kaufman, Eric P. *The Rise and Fall of Anglo-America.* Cambridge, MA: Harvard University Press, 2004.

Kelves, Daniel. *In the Name of Eugenics: Genetics and the Uses of Human Heredity.* New York: Knopf, 1985.

Kent, Kathryn R. *Making Girls into Women: American Women's Writing and the Rise of Lesbian Identity.* Durham, NC: Duke University Press, 2003.

Kermode, Frank. *The Sense of An Ending: Studies in the Theory of Fiction.* Oxford: Oxford University Press, 1967. Reprinted 2000.

Kessel, Sara Hirschfield. "Dainty Valerie Bergere: Talented Actress Talks Interestingly of Her Likes and Dislikes." *Buffalo Courier,* January 13, 1901. 2. New York.

Kiernan, James G. "Race and Insanity: The Negro Race." *Journal of Nervous and Mental Disease* 12, no. 3 (1885): 290–293.

Kingman, Russ. *A Pictorial Life of Jack London.* New York: Crown, 1979.

Kishi, Madoka. " 'The Ecstasy of the Martyr': Lesbianism, Sacrifice, and Morbidness in *The Bostonians.*" *Henry James Review* 37, no. 1 (2016): 100–116.

Kishi, Madoka. "Queering Immigration and the Social Body, 1875–1924." In *The Cambridge History of Queer American Literature,* edited by Benjamin Kahan, 89–109. Cambridge: Cambridge University Press, 2024.

Koretsky, Deanna P. *Death Rights: Romantic Suicide, Race, and the Bounds of Liberalism.* Albany: SUNY Press, 2021.

Krafft-Ebing, Richard von. *Psychopathia Sexualis: With Especial Reference to the Antipathic Sexual Instinct.* Translated by Franklin S. Klaf. New York: Arcade, 2011.

Kristeva, Julia. *Powers of Horror: An Essay on Abjection.* Translated by Leon S. Roudiez. New York: Columbia University Press, 1982.

Kushner, Howard. *Self-Destruction in the Promised Land: A Psychocultural Biology of American Suicide.* New Brunswick, NJ: Rutgers University Press, 1989.

234 BIBLIOGRAPHY

Labor, Earle. *Jack London: An American Life*. New York: Farrar, Straus and Giroux, 2013.

Laird, Holly A. "Between the (Disciplinary) Acts: Modernist Suicidology." *Modernism/modernity* 18, no. 3 (2011): 525–550.

Lani7. Twitter post, February 28, 2020. https://twitter.com/Lani_NG16.

Lanser, Susan S. " 'Queer to Queer': The Sapphic Body as Transgressive Text." In *Lewd and Notorious: Female Transgression in the Eighteenth Century*, edited by Katharine Kittredge, 21–46. Ann Arbor: University of Michigan Press, 2003.

Lazarus, Emma. "The New Colossus." In *The Poems of Emma Lazarus in Two Volumes*. Vol. 1, *Narrative, Lyric, and Dramatic*, 202–203. Boston: Houghton Mifflin, 1889.

LeBlanc, Elizabeth. "The Metaphorical Lesbian: Edna Pontellier in *The Awakening*." *Tulsa Studies in Women's Literature* 15, no. 2 (1996): 289–307.

Lemke, Thomas. "The Risks of Security: Liberalism, Biopolitics, and Fear." In *The Government of Life: Foucault, Biopolitics, and Neoliberalism*, edited by Vanessa Lemm and Miguel Vatter, 59–74. New York: Fordham University Press, 2014.

Leonard, Thomas C. *Illiberal Reformers: Race, Eugenics, and American Economics*. Princeton NJ: Princeton University Press, 2016.

Leonard, Thomas C. " 'More Merciful and Not Less Effective': Eugenics and American Economics in the Progressive Era." *History of Political Economy* 35, no. 4 (2003): 687–712.

Locke, John. *Second Treatise of Government*. Indianapolis, IN: Hackett, 1690. Reprinted 1980.

London, Jack. *The Call of the Wild*. In *Jack London: Novels and Stories*. New York: Library of America, 1982.

London, Jack. *Children of the Frost*. New York: Century, 1902.

London, Jack. *A Daughter of the Snows*. Philadelphia: J. B. Lippincott Company, 1902.

London, Jack. *John Barleycorn: Alcoholic Memoirs*. New York: Century, 1913.

London, Jack. *The Letters of Jack London*. Edited by Earle Labor et al. Stanford, CA: Stanford University Press, 1988.

London, Jack. *Martin Eden*. New York: Penguin, 1909. Reprinted 1993.

London, Jack. "The Other Animals." In *Revolution and Other Essays*, 235–266. New York: Macmillan, 1910.

London, Jack. *The Sea-Wolf*. In *Jack London: Novels and Stories*. New York: Library of America, 1982.

London, Jack. *Son of the Wolf: Tales of the Far North*. Boston: Houghton, Mifflin and Company, 1900.

London, Jack. *Stories of Boxing*. Edited by James Bankes. Dubuque, IA: William C. Brown, 1992.

London, Jack, and Anna Strunsky. *The Kempton-Wace Letters*. New York: Macmillan, 1903.

London, Joan. *Jack London and His Times: An Unconventional Biography*. New York: Book League of America, 1939.

Long, Alecia P. *The Great Southern Babylon: Sex, Race, and Respectability in New Orleans, 1865–1920*. Baton Rouge: Louisiana State University Press, 2004.

Long, John Luther. "Madame Butterfly." In *Madame Butterfly and A Japanese Nightingale: Two Orientalist Texts*, edited by Maureen Honey and Jean Lee Cole, 25–80. New Brunswick, NJ: Rutgers University Press, 2002.

"Lord Goring. . . ." *Vogue* (April 4, 1895): 213.

Loti, Pierre. *Madame Chrysanthème*. Translated by Laura Ensor. London: George Routledge and Sons, 1897.

Love, Eric T. L. *Race over Empire: Racism and U.S. Imperialism, 1865–1900*. Chapel Hill: University of North Carolina Press, 2004.

Love, Heather. *Feeling Backward: Loss and the Politics of Queer History*. Cambridge, MA: Harvard University Press, 2007.

Lovett, Laura L. *Conceiving the Future: Pronatalism, Reproduction, and the Family in the United States, 1890–1938*. Chapel Hill: University of North Carolina Press, 2007.

Lowe, Lisa. *Immigrant Acts: On Asian American Cultural Politics*. Durham, NC: Duke University Press, 1996.

BIBLIOGRAPHY 235

Lowe, Lisa. *The Intimacies of Four Continents.* Durham, NC: Duke University Press, 2015.

Lowell, Percival. *The Soul of the Far East.* New York: Macmillan, 1911.

Luibhéid, Eithne. *Entry Denied: Controlling Sexuality and the Border.* Minneapolis: University of Minnesota Press, 2002.

Lundblad, Michael. *The Birth of a Jungle: Animality in Progressive-Era U.S. Literature and Culture.* Oxford: Oxford University Press, 2013.

Lutts, Ralph H. *The Nature Fakers: Wildlife, Science and Sentiment.* Charlottesville: University Press of Virginia, 1990.

Lutz, Tom. *American Nervousness, 1903: An Anecdotal History.* Ithaca, NY: Cornell University Press, 1991.

Lydston, G. Frank. *Diseases of Society (The Vice and Crime Problem).* Philadelphia: J. B. Lippincott. 1906.

Lydston, G. Frank. *Sex Hygiene for the Male and What to Say to the Boy.* Chicago: Riverton Press, 1912.

Lye, Colleen. *America's Asia: Racial Form and American Literature, 1893–1945.* Princeton, NJ: Princeton University Press, 2005.

Maillard, Kevin Noble. "The Pocahontas Exception: The Exemption of American Indian Ancestry from Racial Purity Law." *Michigan Journal of Race and Law* 12, no. 3 (2007): 351–386.

Malinowska, Agnes. "From Atavistic Gutter-Wolves to Anglo-Saxon Wolf: Evolution and Technology in Jack London's Urban Industrial Modernity." In *The Oxford Handbook of Jack London,* edited by Jay Williams, 438–455. Oxford: Oxford University Press, 2017.

"Many Voices for Japanese Exclusion: Prominent Citizens Say that Coolies from the Mikado's Kingdom Are as Bad as Chinese Labor, and That Their Coming Should Be Checked by Law Before It Is Too Late." *The San Francisco Examiner* (San Francisco, CA), May 8, 1900. 7.

Marsh, Ian. *Suicide: Foucault, History and Truth.* Cambridge, MA: Cambridge University Press, 2010.

Martin, Joan. "Plaçage and the Louisiana Gens de Couleur Libre: How Race and Sex Defined the Lifestyles of Free Women of Color." In *Creole: The History and Legacy of Louisiana's Free People of Color,* edited by Sybil Kein, 57–70. Baton Rouge: Louisiana State University Press, 2000.

May, Elaine Tyler. *Barren in the Promised Land: Childless Americans and the Pursuit of Happiness.* Cambridge, MA: Harvard University Press, 1997.

Mbembe, Achille. *Critique of Black Reason.* Translated by Lauren Dubois. Durham, NC: Duke University Press, 2017.

Mbembe, Achille. "Necropolitics." Translated by Libby Meintjes. *Public Culture* 15, no. 1 (2003): 11–40.

McCallum, E. L. *Unmaking the Making of Americans: Toward an Aesthetic Ontology.* Albany: State University of New York Press, 2018.

McGuire, Hunter, and G. Frank Lydston. *Sexual Crimes among the Southern Negroes.* Louisville, KY: Renz and Henry, 1893.

McWhorter, Ladelle. "Enemy of the Species." In *Queer Ecology: Sex, Nature, Politics, Desire,* edited by Catriona Mortimer-Sandilands and Bruce Erickson, 73–101. Bloomington: Indiana University Press, 2010.

McWhorter, Ladelle. *Racism and Sexual Oppression in Anglo-America: A Genealogy.* Bloomington: Indiana University Press, 2009.

Meyer, Steven. *Irresistible Dictation: Gertrude Stein and the Correlation of Writing and Science.* Stanford, CA: Stanford University Press, 2001.

Michaels, Walter Benn. *Our America: Nativism, Modernism, and Pluralism.* Durham, NC: Duke University Press, 1995.

Micir, Melanie. *The Passion Projects: Modernist Women, Intimate Archives, Unfinished Lives.* Princeton, NJ: Princeton University Press, 2019.

Mieder, Wolfgang. "'The Only Good Indian Is a Dead Indian': History and Meaning of a Proverbial Stereotype." *Journal of American Folklore* 106, no. 419 (1993): 38–60.

236 BIBLIOGRAPHY

Miller, D. A. *The Novel and the Police*. Berkeley: University of California Press, 1989.

Miller, Matt. "Making of Americans: Whitman and Stein's Poetics of Inclusion." *Arizona Quarterly* 65, no. 3 (2009): 39–59.

Miller, Nathaniel. "'Felt, Not Seen Not Heard': Quentin Compson, Modernist Suicide, and Southern History." *Studies in the Novel* 37, no. 1 (2005): 37–49.

Morris, Edmund. *The Rise of Theodore Roosevelt*. New York: Modern Library, 1979.

Morrissey, Susan. *Suicide and the Body Politic in Imperial Russia*. Cambridge: Cambridge University Press, 2006.

Morrison, Toni. *Playing in The Dark: Whiteness and the Literary Imagination*. Cambridge, MA: Harvard University Press, 1992.

"Mr. Roosevelt's Creed." *New York Times*, October 19, 1884. 2.

Muñoz, José Esteban. *Cruising Utopia: The Then and There of Queer Futurity*. New York: New York University Press, 2009.

Murphy, Kevin. *Political Manhood: Red Bloods, Mollycoddles, and the Politics of Progressive Era Reform*. New York: Columbia University Press, 2009.

Ngai, Mae M. *Impossible Subjects: Illegal Aliens and the Making of Modern America*. Princeton, NJ: Princeton University Press, 2004.

Ngai, Sianne. *Our Aesthetic Categories: Zany, Cute, Interesting*. Cambridge, MA: Harvard University Press, 2012.

Ngai, Sianne. *Ugly Feelings*. Cambridge, MA: Harvard University Press, 2005.

Nietzsche, Friedrich. *Thus Spoke Zarathustra*. Translated by Thomas Common. New York: The Modern Library, 1917.

Nitobé, Inazo. *Bushido: The Soul of Japan, An Exposition of Japanese Thought*. New York: G. P. Putnam's Sons, 1907.

Nixon, Timothy K. "Gertrude Stein's Performance of Patriotism." *Studies in American Humor* 3, no. 24 (2011): 45–58.

Nordau, Max. *Degeneration*. Lincoln: University of Nebraska Press, 1993.

Nye, Robert A. *Crime, Madness and Politics in Modern France: The Medical Concept of National Decline*. Princeton, NJ: Princeton University Press, 1984.

Nye, Robert A. "Sociology and Degeneration: The Irony of Progress." In *Degeneration: The Dark Side of Progress*, edited by J. Edward Chamberlin and Sander L. Gilman, 49–71. New York: Columbia University Press, 1985.

O'Brien, James M. *Firsting and Lasting: Writing Indians Out of Existence in New England*. Minneapolis: University of Minnesota Press, 2010.

Oishi, Ricky. Twitter post, January 30, 2020. https://twitter.com/iromiud0211.

Okakura, Kakuzo. *The Book of Tea*. New York: G. P. Putnam's Sons, 1906.

Ordover, Nancy. *American Eugenics: Race, Queer Anatomy, and the Science of Nationalism*. Minneapolis: University of Minnesota Press, 2003.

Paris, Václav. *The Evolutions of Modernist Epic*. New York: Oxford University Press, 2021.

Park, Josephine Nock-Hee. *Apparitions of Asia: Modernist Form and Asian American Poetics*. Oxford: Oxford University Press, 2008.

Park, W. Anthony Sheppard. "Cinematic Realism, Reflexivity and the American 'Madame Butterfly' Narrative." *Cambridge Opera Journal* 17, no. 1 (2005): 59–93.

Pascoe, Peggy. *What Comes Naturally: Miscegenation Law and the Making of Race in America*. Oxford: Oxford University Press, 2010.

Patterson, Orlando. *Rituals of Blood: Consequences of Slavery in Two American Centuries*. New York: Basic Books, 1998.

Patterson, Orlando. *Slavery and Social Death: A Comparative Study*. Cambridge, MA: Harvard University Press, 1982.

Person, Leland. "In the Closet with Frederick Douglass: Reconstructing Masculinity in *The Bostonians*." *Henry James Review* 16, no. 3 (1995): 292–298.

Petty, Leslie. "The Political is Personal: The Feminist Lesson of Henry James's *The Bostonians*." *Women's Studies* 34 (2005): 377–403.

BIBLIOGRAPHY   237

Pick, Daniel. *Faces of Degeneration: A European Disorder, c. 1848–1918.* Cambridge: Cambridge University Press, 1989.

Pierce, Joseph M. (Cherokee Nation). "In Good Relations: Native Adoption, Kinstillations, and the Grounding of Memory." In *Queer Kinship: Race, Sex, Belonging, Form,*, edited by Teagan Bradway and Elizabeth Freeman, 95–118. Durham, NC: Duke University Press, 2022.

Poovey, Mary. *Making a Social Body: British Cultural Formation, 1830–1864.* Chicago: University of Chicago Press, 1995.

Pratt, Richard H. "The Advantages of Mingling Indians with Whites." In *Americanizing the American Indians: Writings by the "Friends of the Indian," 1880–1900,* edited by Francis Paul Prucha, 260–271. Cambridge, MA: Harvard University Press, 1973.

Preston, Carrie. *Learning to Kneel: Noh, Modernism, and Journeys in Teaching.* New York: Columbia University Press, 2016.

Puar, Jasbir. "Coda: The Cost of Getting Better: Suicide, Sensation, Switchpoints." *GLQ* 18, no. 1 (2012): 149–158.

Puar, Jasbir. *Terrorist Assemblages: Homonationalism in Queer Times.* Durham, NC: Duke University Press, 2007.

Quashie, Kevin. *Black Aliveness, or A Poetics of Being.* Durham, NC: Duke University Press, 2021.

"Racial Indigestion." *The Atlanta Constitution,* October 6, 1913. 13. Atlanta, GA.

Rahv, Phillip. Introduction to *The Bostonians,* by Henry James, v–ix. New York: Dial, 1945.

Rankine, Claudia. *Citizen: An American Lyric.* Minneapolis, MN: Graywolf Press, 2014.

Rastogi, Pallavi. *Postcolonial Disaster: Narrating Catastrophe in the Twenty-First Century.* Evanston, IL: Northwestern University Press, 2020.

Redding, Josephine. Editorial. *Vogue* (December 17, 1892).

Redding, Josephine. Editorial. *Vogue* (December 24, 1892).

Redding, Josephine. Editorial. *Vogue* (February 7, 1895).

Redding, Josephine. Editorial. *Vogue* (March 15, 1900).

Redding, Josephine. Editorial. *Vogue* (May 24, 1895).

Reed, Christopher. *Bachelor Japanists: Japanese Aesthetics and Western Masculinities.* New York: Columbia University Press, 2017.

Reesman, Jeanne Campbell. *Jack London's Racial Lives: A Critical Biography.* Athens: University of Georgia Press, 2009.

Régamey, Félix. "The Pink Notebook of Madame Chrysanthème." In *The Chrysanthème Papers: The Pink Notebook of Madame Chrysanthème and Other Documents of French Japonism,* 61–120. Translated and Edited by Christopher Reed. Honolulu: University of Hawai'i Press, 2010.

Rentoul, Robert Reid. *Race Culture; or, Race Suicide? (A Plea for the Unborn).* London: Walter Scott, 1906.

Rifkin, Mark. *When Did Indians Become Straight?: Kinship, the History of Sexuality, and Native Sovereignty.* New York: Oxford University Press, 2011.

Riis, Jacob A. *How the Other Half Lives: Studies Among the Tenements of New York.* New York: Dover, 1970.

Ripley, William Z. *The Races of Europe: A Sociological Study.* New York: D. Appleton and Company, 1899.

Roediger, David R. *Wages of Whiteness: Race and the Making of the American Working Class.* New York: Verso, 2007.

Roland, Gille. Twitter post, January 29, 2020. https://twitter.com/gilles_roland?lang = en.

Roosevelt, Theodore. "The Law of Civilization and Decay (Review)." In *American Ideals and Administration—Civil Service,* 347–369. Vol. 1 of *The Works of Theodore Roosevelt in Fourteen Volumes.* New York: G. P. Putnam's Sons, 1897.

Roosevelt, Theodore. *The Letters of Theodore Roosevelt.* Vol. 1, *The Years of Preparation, 1868–1898.* Edited by Elting E. Morison. Cambridge, MA: Harvard University Press, 1951.

238 BIBLIOGRAPHY

Roosevelt, Theodore. *The Letters of Theodore Roosevelt*. Vol. 2, *The Years of Preparation, 1898–1900*. Edited by Elting E. Morison. Cambridge, MA: Harvard University Press, 1951.

Roosevelt, Theodore. *The Letters of Theodore Roosevelt*. Vol. 6, *The Big Stick, 1907–1909*. Edited by Elting E. Morison. Cambridge, MA: Harvard University Press, 1952.

Roosevelt, Theodore. "Message." In *The Abridgement 1906: Containing the Annual Message of the United States to the Two Houses of Congress*, vol. 1, 7–59. Washington, D.C.: Government Printing Office, 1907.

Roosevelt, Theodore. "Nature-Fakers." In *Roosevelt's Writings: Selections from the Writings of Theodore Roosevelt*, edited by Maurice Garland Fulton, 258–267. New York: Macmillan, 1920.

Roosevelt, Theodore. "True Americanism." In *American Ideals and Other Essays, Social and Political*, edited by Theodore Roosevelt, 16–37. New York: G. P. Putnam's Sons, 1904.

Roosevelt, Theodore. "Twisted Eugenics." *Outlook* 106 (1914): 30–34.

Roosevelt, Theodore. *The Winning of the West: An Account of the Exploration and Settlement of Our Country from Alleghanies to the Pacific*. Vol. 1. New York: Current Literature Publishing Company, 1889. Reprinted 1905.

Roosevelt, Theodore. Prefatory Letter to *The Woman Who Toils: Being the Experiences of Two Gentlewomen*, by Mrs. John [Bessie] Van Vorst and Marie Van Vorst, vii–ix. New York: Doubleday, Page, and Company, 1903.

Ross, Edward A. "The Causes of Race Superiority." *Annals of the American Academy of Political and Social Science* 18, *America's Race Problems: Addresses at the Fifth Annual Meeting of the American Academy of Political and Social Science, April 12–13, 1901* (1901): 67–89.

Ross, Edward A. "Turning Towards Nirvana." *Arena* 4, no. 24 (1891): 737–744.

Ruddick, Lisa. *Reading Gertrude Stein: Body, Text, Gnosis*. Ithaca, NY: Cornell University Press, 1990.

Ryan, Susan M. "*The Bostonians* and the Civil War." *Henry James Review* 26, no. 3 (2005): 265–272.

Sahlins, Marshall. *What Kinship Is and Is Not*. Chicago: University of Chicago Press, 2013.

Sanger, Margaret. *Woman and the New Race*. New York: Eugenics Publishing Company, 1920.

Santner, Eric. *The Royal Remains: The People's Two Bodies and the Endgames of Sovereignty*. Chicago: University of Chicago Press, 2011.

Schmidt, Christopher. *The Poetics of Waste: Queer Excess in Stein, Ashbery, Schuyler, and Goldsmith*. New York: Palgrave, 2014.

Schneider, David. *A Critique of the Study of Kinship*. Ann Arbor: University of Michigan Press, 1984.

Schopenhauer, Arthur. *The World as Will and Representation*. Vols. 1–2. Cambridge: Cambridge University Press, 2010, 2018.

Schuller, Kyla. *The Biopolitics of Feeling: Race, Sex, and Science in the Nineteenth Century*. Durham, NC: Duke University Press, 2017.

Schuster, David G. *Neurasthenic Nation: America's Search for Health, Happiness, and Comfort, 1869–1920*. New Brunswick, NJ: Rutgers University Press, 2011.

Schuster, Joshua. *What Is Extinction?: A Natural and Cultural History of Last Animals*. New York: Fordham University Press, 2023.

Scott-Childress, Reynolds J. "Race, Nation, and the Rhetoric of Color: Locating Japan and China, 1870–1907." In *Race and the Production of Modern American Nationalism*, edited by Reynolds J. Scott-Childress, 3–20. New York: Routledge, 1999.

Sedgwick, Eve Kosofsky. *Epistemology of the Closet*. Berkeley: University of California Press, 1990.

Sedgwick, Eve Kosofsky. *Touching Feeling: Affect, Pedagogy, Performativity*. Durham, NC: Duke University Press, 2003.

Seidel, Kathryn Lee. "Art is an Unnatural Act: Mademoiselle Reisz in 'The Awakening.'" *Mississippi Quarterly* 46, no. 2 (1993): 199–214.

Seitler, Dana. *Atavistic Tendencies: The Culture of Science in American Modernity*. Minneapolis: University of Minnesota Press, 2008.

BIBLIOGRAPHY 239

Seitler, Dana. "Suicidal Tendencies: Notes toward a Queer Narratology." *GLQ* 25, no. 4 (2019): 599–616.

Seitler, Dana. "Willing to Die: Addiction and Other Ambivalence of Living." *Cultural Critique* 98 (Winter 2018): 1–21.

Seltzer, Mark. *Bodies and Machines.* New York: Routledge, 1992.

Shah, Nayan. *Contagious Divides: Epidemics and Race in San Francisco's Chinatown.* Berkeley: University of California Press, 2001.

Shaheen, Aaron. "Henry James's Southern Mode of Imagination: Men, Women, and the Image of the South in *The Bostonians.*" *Henry James Review* 24, no. 2 (2003): 180–192.

Shaker, Bonnie James. *Coloring Locals: Racial Formation in Kate Chopin's "Youth's Companion" Stories.* Iowa City: University of Iowa Press, 2002.

Sheppard, W. Anthony. "Cinematic Realism, Reflexivity and the American 'Madame Butterfly' Narrative." *Cambridge Opera Journal* 17, no. 1 (2005): 59–93.

Sherman, Richard B. "'The Last Stand': The Fight for Racial Integrity in Virginia in the 1920s." *The Journal of Southern History* 54, no. 1 (1988): 69–92.

Silber, Nina. *The Romance of Reunion: Northerners and the South, 1865–1900.* Chapel Hill: University of North Carolina Press, 1993.

Simmel, Georg. *On Women, Sexuality, and Love.* Translated by Guy Oaks. New Haven, CT: Yale University Press, 1984.

Smedley, Audrey, and Brian Smedley. *Race in North America: Origin and Evolution of a World View.* Boulder, CO: Westview, 2011.

Smith, Adam. *An Inquiry into the Nature and Causes of the Wealth of Nations.* Oxford: Clarendon Press, 1776. Reprinted 1979.

Solomon, Barbara Miller. *Ancestors and Immigrants: A Changing New England Tradition.* Chicago: University of Chicago Press, 1956.

Solomons, Leon M., and Gertrude Stein. "Normal Motor Automatism." *Psychological Review* 3 (1896): 492–512.

Somerville, Siobhan. *Queering the Color Line: Race and the Invention of Homosexuality in American Culture.* Durham, NC: Duke University Press, 2000.

Sontag, Susan. "Fascinating Fascism." In *Under the Sign of Saturn,* 73–108. New York: Vintage, 1981.

Spillers, Hortense J. "Mama's Baby, Papa's Maybe: An American Grammar Book." *Diacritics* 17, no. 2 (1987): 64–81.

Spiro, Jonathan. *Defending the Master Race: Conservation, Eugenics, and the Legacy of Madison Grant.* Burlington: University of Vermont, 2008.

Stange, Margit. *Personal Property: Wives, White Slaves, and the Market in Women.* Baltimore: Johns Hopkins University Press, 1998.

Stark, Jared. *A Death of One's Own: Literature, Law, and the Right to Die.* Evanston, IL: Northwestern University Press, 2018.

Stein, Gertrude. *The Autobiography of Alice B. Toklas.* New York: Modern Library, 1993.

Stein, Gertrude. *Baby Precious Always Shines: Selected Love Notes Between Gertrude Stein and Alice B. Toklas.* Edited by Kay Turner. New York: St. Martin's Press, 1999.

Stein, Gertrude. "Cultivated Motor Automatism: A Study of Character in Its Relation to Attention." *Psychological Review* 5 (1898): 295–306.

Stein, Gertrude. *Everybody's Autobiography.* London: Virago, 1937. Reprinted 1985.

Stein, Gertrude. *Fernhurst, Q.E.D., and Other Early Writings.* London: Peter Owen, 1972.

Stein, Gertrude. "The Making of Americans." In *Fernhurst, Q.E.D., and Other Early Writings,* 137–174. London: Peter Owen, 1972.

Stein, Gertrude. *The Making of Americans: Being a History of a Family's Progress.* Normal, IL: Dalkey Archive Press, 1995.

Stein, Gertrude. "The Modern Jew Who Has Given up the Faith of His Fathers Can Reasonably and Consistently Believe in Isolation (1896)." Edited by Amy Feinstein. *PMLA* 116, no. 2 (2001): 416–428.

240 BIBLIOGRAPHY

Stein, Gertrude. *The Notebooks of Gertrude Stein for The Making of Americans, 1903–1912.* Edited by Leon Katz. Orlando, FL: No publisher, 2021.

Stein, Gertrude. *Selected Writings of Gertrude Stein.* Edited by Carl Van Vechten. New York: Random House, 1946.

Stein, Gertrude. *Tender Buttons.* New York: Clair Marie, 1914.

Stein, Melissa N. *Measuring Manhood: Race and the Science of Masculinity, 1830–1934.* Minneapolis: University of Minnesota Press, 2015.

Stephens, Paul. "'Reading at It': Gertrude Stein, Information Overload, And the Makings Of Americanitis." *Twentieth Century Literature* 59, no. 1 (2013): 126–156.

Stevens, Hugh. *Henry James and Sexuality.* Cambridge: Cambridge University Press, 1998.

Stimpson, Catherine R. "Gertrice/Altrude: Stein, Toklas, and the Paradox of the Happy Marriage." In *Mothering the Mind: Twelve Studies of Writers and Their Silent Partners,* edited by Ruth Perry and Martine Watson Brownley, 122–139. New York: Holmes & Meier, 1984.

Stockton, Will. *Playing Dirty: Sexuality and Waste in Early Modern Comedy.* Minneapolis: University of Minnesota Press, 2011.

Stoddard, Charles Warren. *The Lepers of Molokai.* Notre Dame, IN: Ave Maria Press, 1885.

Stoddard, Lothrop. *The Rising Tide of Color Against White World-Supremacy.* New York: Charles Scribner's and Sons, 1920. Reprinted 1921.

Stokes, Mason. *The Color of Sex: Whiteness, Heterosexuality, and the Fictions of White Supremacy.* Durham, NC: Duke University Press, 2001.

Stokes, Melvin. *D. W. Griffith's "The Birth of a Nation": A History of "the Most Controversial Motion Picture of All Time."* Oxford: Oxford University Press, 2007.

Stoler, Ann Laura. *Race and the Education of Desire: Foucault's "History of Sexuality" and the Colonial Order of Things.* Durham, NC: Duke University Press, 1995.

Strahan, S. A. K. *Suicide and Insanity: A Physiological and Sociological Study.* London: S. Sonnenschein & Co., 1893.

Sunderland, Judith. Twitter post, February 3, 2020. https://twitter.com/sunderland_jude.

Susman, Warren. "'Personality' and the Making of Twentieth-Century Culture." In *Culture as History: The Transformation of American Society in the Twentieth Century,* 271–286. Washington, D.C.: Smithsonian Institute Press, 2003.

Swift, John N., and Gigen Mamoser. "'Out of the Realm of Superstition': Chesnutt's 'Dave's Neckliss' and the Curse of Ham." *American Literary Realism* 42, no. 1 (2009): 1–12.

Szuberla, Guy. "Zangwill's *The Melting Pot* Plays Chicago." *MELUS* 20, no. 3 (1995): 3–20.

Taylor, Melanie. "A Poetics of Difference: *The Making of Americans* and Unreadable Subjects." *NWSA Journal* 15, no. 3 (2004): 26–42.

Thompson, Warren. "Race Suicide in the United States" I–III. *Scientific Monthly* (1917): 258–269.

Ting, Jennifer. "Bachelor Society: Deviant Heterosexuality and Asian American Historiography." In *Privileging Positions: The Sites of Asian American Studies,* edited by Gary Y. Okihiro et al., 271–279. Pullman: Washington State University Press, 1995.

Tomes, Nancy. *Gospel of Germs: Men, Women, and the Microbe in American Life.* Cambridge, MA: Harvard University Press, 1998.

Tompkins, Kyla Wazana. *Racial Indigestion: Eating Bodies in the 19th Century.* New York: New York University Press, 2012.

"Topics of the Times." Editorial. *Woman's Exponent* (Salt Lake City, UT), September 15, 1886. 61.

Tregle, Joseph G., Jr. "Creoles and Americans." In *Creole New Orleans: Race and Americanization,* edited by Arnold R. Hirsch and Joseph Logsdon, 131–188. Baton Rouge: Louisiana State University Press, 1992.

Tuhkanen, Mikko. "Breeding (and) Reading: Lesbian Knowledge, Eugenic Discipline, and *The Children's Hour.*" *MFS* 48, no. 4 (2002): 1001–1040.

Turner, Frederick Jackson. "The Significance of the Frontier in American History." In *The Frontier in American History,* 1–38. New York: Henry Holt and Co., 1920.

BIBLIOGRAPHY 241

Turner, Kay. "This 'Very Beautiful Form of Literature': An Introduction to the Love Notes Between Gertrude Stein and Alice B. Toklas." In *Baby Precious Always Shines: Selected Love Notes Between Gertrude Stein and Alice B. Toklas*, edited by Kay Turner, 1–41. New York: St. Marin's Press, 1999.

Van Leer, David. "A World of Female Friendship: The Bostonians." In *Henry James and Homoerotic Desire*, edited by John R. Bradley, 93–109. New York: St. Martin's, 1999.

Varga, Donna. "Teddy's Bear and the Transfiguration of Savage Beasts into Innocent Children, 1890–1920." *Journal of American Culture* 32, no. 2 (2009): 98–113.

Veblen, Thorstein. *The Theory of the Leisure Class*. Oxford: Oxford University Press, 2009.

Vermette, David. *A Distinct Alien Race: The Untold Story of Franco-Americans*. Montréal, QC: Baraka Books, 2018.

"The Virginia 'Act to Preserve Racial Integrity' of 1924." In *Interracialism: Black-White Intermarriage in American History, Literature, and Law*, edited by Werner Sollors, 23. Oxford: Oxford University Press, 2000.

Wagner-Martin, Linda. *"Favored Strangers": Gertrude Stein and Her Family*. New Brunswick, NJ: Rutgers University Press, 1995.

Wald, Priscilla. *Constituting Americans: Cultural Anxiety and Narrative Form*. Durham, NC: Duke University Press, 1995.

Walker, Francis Amasa. "Immigration and Degradation." *Forum* 11 (1891): 634–644.

Warren, Calvin. *Ontological Terror: Blackness, Nihilism, and Emancipation*. Durham, NC: Duke University Press, 2018.

Weinbaum, Alys Eve. *Wayward Reproductions: Genealogies of Race and Nation in Transatlantic Modern Thought*. Durham, NC: Duke University Press, 2004.

Weininger, Otto. *Sex and Character*. New York: A. L. Burt, 1906.

Wells, Ida B. *On Lynchings*. Amherst, NY: Humanity Books, 2002.

Wendell, Barrett. *Barrett Wendell and His Letters*. Edited by Mark Antony DeWolfe Howe. Boston: Atlantic Monthly Press, 1924.

Werther–Jennie June ("Earl Lind"), Ralph. *The Female-Impersonators*. Edited by Alfred W. Herzog. New York: Medical Legal Journal, 1922.

Whalan, Mark. *American Culture in the 1910s*. Edinburgh: Edinburgh University Press, 2010.

Wiegman, Robyn. *American Anatomies*. Durham, NC: Duke University Press, 1995.

Wilde, Oscar. *The Picture of Dorian Gray*. New York: Penguin, 2000.

Wilderson, Frank B, III. *Red, White, Black: Cinema and the Structure of U.S. Antagonisms*. Durham, NC: Duke University Press, 2010.

Will, Barbara. *Gertrude Stein, Modernism, and the Problem of Genius*. Edinburgh: Edinburgh University Press, 2000.

Will, Barbara. "Gertrude Stein and Zionism." *MFS* 51, no. 2 (2005): 437–455.

Will, Barbara. "The Nervous Origin of the American West." *American Literature* 70, no. 2 (1998): 293–316.

Will, Barbara. *Unlikely Collaboration: Gertrude Stein, Bernard Faÿ, and the Vichy Dilemma*. New York: Columbia University Press, 2011.

Wilson, Sarah. *Melting-Pot Modernism*. Ithaca, NY: Cornell University Press, 2010.

Wilson, Woodrow. "Character of Democracy in the United States." In *An Old Master and Other Political Essays*, 90–140. New York: Charles Scribner's and Sons, 1893.

Wirt, William. *Sketches of the Life and Character of Patrick Henry*. Philadelphia: James Webster, 1818.

Woloch, Alex. *The One vs. the Many: Minor Characters and the Space of the Protagonist in the Novel*. Princeton, NJ: Princeton University Press, 2003.

"Worldwide Vigil for the Victims of the Atlanta Shooting." Hosted by KAC-Metro Atlanta, March 26, 2021. https://326vigil.org.

Yao, Xine. *Disaffected: The Cultural Politics of Unfeeling in Nineteenth-Century America*. Durham, NC: Duke University Press, 2021.

Yeazell, Ruth Bernard. Introduction to *The Death and Letters of Alice James*, 1–45. Berkeley: University of California Press, 1981.

242 BIBLIOGRAPHY

Young, Elliott. *Alien Nation: Chinese Migration in the Americas from the Coolie Through World War II.* Chapel Hill: University of North Carolina Press, 2014.

Young, Robert. *Colonial Desire: Hybridity in Theory, Culture, and Race.* New York: Routledge, 1995.

Zangwill, Israel. *The Melting-Pot: Drama in Four Acts.* New York: Macmillan, 1909.

Zolberg, Aristide. *A Nation by Design: Immigration Policy in the Fashioning of America.* Cambridge, MA: Harvard University Press, 2006.

Index

For the benefit of digital users, indexed terms that span two pages (e.g., 52–53) may, on occasion, appear on only one of those pages.

Abelove, Henry, 21–22, 204n.60
Abdur-Rahman, Aliyyah, 96
Act Prohibiting Importation of Slaves of 1807, 20
Adams, Henry, 45–46
Addams, Jane, 58
Alaska Game Bill of 1902, 111
Allen, Nathan, 46
American Scene, The (James, H.), 129, 131
anatomo-politics, 5, 8, 9–11, 32, 33–34, 76–77
  See also discipline and disciplinary power
Anglo-Saxons, 3–4, 24
  Boston Brahmins, 167
  Creoles and, 79–80
  The Making of Americans on, 137, 141
  in New England, 45–47, 198n.25
  Northland wilderness and, 111
  race suicide and, 46–47, 131
  Teutonism and, 103–5, 108–9, 110–11, 124–25
  See also old-stock Americans; native-born white Americans; whiteness
anti-Asian racism and violence, 162–64, 179–81, 193n.94, 219n.14
anti-Black racism and violence, 21, 23–24, 94–95, 96, 164–65
antisemitism, 135, 141–42, 152, 159–60
Arcimboldo, Giuseppe, 8
Arvidson, Heather, 166–67
Aryans, 30, 87, 105–6, 141–42, 163–64
  See also whiteness
Asianness and the Asiatic, 162–64, 165–67, 168–71
  Asian immigration and Asian immigrants, 15–17, 103, 129–30, 163–64, 165, 169–70, 179
  Asiatic impersonality, 166–67, 168, 169–70, 172–75, 176–78, 179–80
  See also anti-Asian racism and violence
assimilation, 130–31, 133–34, 136–37, 142–43, 147

assimilationist policies and violence, 102–3, 122–24, 126–27
atavism, 107–9, 118–19, 124–25
Auerbach, Jonathan, 112–13, 119–20
Awakening, The (Chopin), 64, 117
  biopower and biopolitics in, 76–78, 82–83, 84–86
  on consuming desire, 91
  Creoles in, 72–73, 78–80, 81–84, 91–92
  on eroticism and erotic economy of, 81–86, 91
  on freedom, 70–71, 72, 73–75, 76–77, 81–83, 92–93, 97
  laissez-faire and, 76–79, 82–83
  on liberal erotic economy, 72–73, 82
  liberalism and, 73, 81–83
  liberal subject and, 73–74, 82
  the New Woman and, 85, 92–93
  on property, 74, 81–82
  race suicide and, 69–70
  on slavery and freedom, 70–71, 72, 92–93, 97
  suicide in, 69, 72–73, 90, 91–92, 97
  Vogue and, 85–86
  on whiteness, 69–70, 79, 81–82

Bataille, Georges, 58
Bateman, Benjamin, 35–36
Beard, George, 48–50, 199n.40
becoming-animal, 121, 123–24, 125
Beistegui, Miguel de, 75
Belasco, David, 173, 176–77, 178
Bennett, Andrew, 35
Bergere, Valerie, 176–77, 178–79
Berlant, Lauren, 2, 159
biopolitical state, 11, 14, 29–30, 132, 172
biopolitical subjects, 35, 77–78, 82–83, 86, 164–65
biopolitics
  anatomo-politics and, 5, 8, 10–11, 33–34, 76–77
  COVID-19 pandemic and, 162

244 INDEX

biopolitics (*cont.*)
 eroticism and, 85–86
 of governmentality, 9–10, 32, 33–34, 35–36
 of population, 9–10, 27, 31–32, 33–34, 72–73,
  75–78, 82–83, 84–85, 128, 144–45, 155–
  56, 164
 race suicide and, 5–7, 13, 31
 racialization and, 27–28, 35–36
 replacement theory and, 160
 reproduction and, 19, 117–18
 securitization and, 14–15, 40
 sex and, 11, 28–29
 social body and, 11–12, 15, 31–32, 161–62
 sterilization and, 18
 of suicide, 6–8, 25
biopower
 death drive and, 30
 Foucault on, 2–3, 8, 12, 26, 30, 32, 75–76,
  192n.69
 race suicide and, 5–7
 sex, death and, 32, 33
 social body and, 7–8, 11–12, 29–30
 suicide and, 2–3, 6–7, 32
 two poles of, 5, 8
Birnbaum, Michele, 70
Blackness, 71–72, 97, 164–65, 166
 Black castration, 21, 25, 96
 Black deaths, 72–73, 95, 97
 Black flesh, 95–97
 Black male sexuality, 21
 Black phallus, 94–95
 Black women, enslaved, 71–72, 92–93
 See also anti-Black violence
Blaine, James, 41
Bloom, Harold, 150–51
body politic, 7–8, 11, 141–42
Bostonians, The (James, H.), 44–45
 on Anglo-Saxonism, 46–47
 on Civil War, 51–53
 ecstasy of martyrdom in, 57, 63–64, 122
 on eroticism and sacrifice, 57, 63–64
 feminism and female reformers in, 57–59,
  60–61, 63–64
 on lesbianism, 51, 200n.56
 neurasthenia and, 47, 51–52, 58
 on old-stock Americans, 45–46
 The Princess Casamassima and, 64–65
 race suicide and, 46–47
 on sacrificial death, 46–47, 51–53, 58, 63–64
 on wounded social body, 51
Bowlby, Rachel, 89–90
Boyarin, Daniel, 141–42, 152
Brandeis, Louis D., 74

Brigman, Ann, 53
Brown, Wendy, 56
Brown, William Wells, 92–94
Buck, Carrie, 18–19, 193n.88
Buck v. Bell (1927), 5–6, 18–19, 22–23
Burroughs, John, 99–100
Butler, Judith, 5–6

Call of the Wild, The (London), 99–100,
  118, 125
Cameron, Sharon, 166
Camus, Renaud, 159–60
Canaday, Margot, 142
Carter, Julian, 48–49
castration, 56–57, 152–54
Cather, Willa, 1–2, 5
Cecire, Natalia, 156–57
Century Illustrated Monthly Magazine, 44–
  45, 52–53
Chae Chan Ping v. United States (1889), 15–16
Chamberlain, Houston Steward, 105–6, 125–26
Chaney, William, 107–9, 114–15, 124–25
Chen, Mel Y., 165–66
Cheng, Anne Anlin, 166, 174, 177–78
Chesnutt, Charles, 95–97
Chinese Exclusion Act of 1882, 15–16, 129–30,
  163–64, 179–80
Chinese immigration and Chinese immigrants,
  163, 165
Chopin, Kate, 72–73, 81, 85–86
 "Désirée's Baby" by, 81, 85–86
 "An Egyptian Cigarette," 90
 "A Pair of Silk Stockings" by, 85–86
 in *Vogue,* 72–73, 85–86, 90
 See also Awakening, The (Chopin)
Civil War, U. S., 51–56, 57, 69–70
Clement, Tanya, 155
Cleveland, Grover, 41, 115–16
cloacal theory, 153–54, 218n.125
Clotel (Brown, W. W.), 92–94
Cohen, Ed, 15
Collier, Holt, 101–2
colonialism, 10–11, 112–13, 122–23
Connolly, Brian, 20
counter-conduct, 32
COVID-19 pandemic, 162
Creoles, 72–73, 78, 91–92, 203n.40
Cubberley, Ellwood, 16–17, 130

Damon, Mary, 135
Darwin, Charles, 89
Daughter of the Snows, A (London), 109–10, 112
Davenport, Charles B., 17

INDEX 245

"Dave's Neckliss" (Chesnutt), 95–97
Davidson, Arnold, 32
Dawes General Allotment Act in 1887, 115–16
Dean, Tim, 172–73, 221–22n.62
death drive, 6–8, 27, 28–31
death instinct, 27–29
*Declaration of the Rights of Man and of the
Citizen, The,* 11
degeneration and degeneration theory, 22–23,
25–27, 64–67, 107–8, 141–42, 152, 215n.68
Delany, Samuel, 157–58
Deleuze, Gilles, 121, 123–24, 125
Derrick, Scott, 106–7, 119–20
Derrida, Jacques, 30–31, 92
"Désirée's Baby" (Chopin), 81, 85–86
Deutscher, Penelope, 10–11
Dimock, Wai Chee, 74
discipline and disciplinary power, 5, 6, 8–11,
26–28, 32, 33–35, 73–75, 77–78, 82–
83, 96–97
See also anatomo-politics
Domínguez, Virginia R., 79–81
Doyle, Laura, 140–41
Durkheim, Émile, 5, 113–14
Dyer, Joyce, 70
Dyer, Thomas G., 80

Edelman, Lee, 6–7, 29–30, 197n.170
"Egyptian Cigarette, An" (Chopin), 90
Eliot, T. S., 166–67, 221–22n.62
Ellis, John, 47–48
Ellman, Maud, 166–67
Esposito, Robert, 30–31
Essays in Anglo-Saxon Law (Adams), 45–46
eugenics, 5–6, 15, 17–18, 21, 22–23
Ewell, Barbara C., 79–80

Feinstein, Amy, 135, 136–37
feminism, 50–51, 52–53, 57–59, 60–61, 63–64
Fiske, John, 80
Fleissner, Jennifer, 35, 73, 89–90, 144
Foucault, Michel
on biopolitics, 7–8, 15, 72–73
on biopower, 2–3, 8, 12, 26, 30, 32, 75–76,
192n.69
on freedom, 75–77
on genealogy of governmentality, 8–10,
190n.36
on homeostasis, 14–15
on psychoanalysis, 27–28
on sex and sexuality, 10–11, 32, 194–95n.112
on social body, 117
on suicide and sexuality, 33

on suicide as counter-conduct, 32–33
Frank, Leo, 135
French Revolution, 66, 67
Freud, Sigmund, 27–29, 114, 150–54, 218n.125
Fugitive Slave Act of 1850, 92–93

Galton, Francis, 17
Geary Act of 1892, 163–64
Geertz, Clifford, 165–66
gender, 42, 49, 145, 146
German Romanticism, 104–5
Gilder, Richard Watson, 44–45
Gilman, Charlotte Perkins, 86–88
Gilman, Sander, 27–28, 152, 215n.68
Goddard, Henry Herbert, 17
Graham, Wendy, 47–48, 50–51
Grant, Madison, 4–5, 13, 15, 17–18, 105–6,
109–10, 111, 124, 126, 159, 190n.24
Grant, Ulysses, 52–53
Great Replacement, the, 159–60, 197n.167
See also replacement theory
Guattari, Félix, 121, 123–24, 125

Hall, Prescott, 16–17
Haraway, Donna, 102
Harris, Cheryl, 71
Hartman, Saidiya, 96–97
Hayot, Eric, 164
Hemingway, Ernest, 133–34, 213n.36
Henry, Patrick, 94
heredity, 15
degeneration and, 65, 66
procreative logic of, 150–51
race and, 10–11, 19–20, 107, 110–11,
113, 115
suicide and, 25–27
Herko, Fred, 1
Herland (Gilman, C. P.), 87
Herring, Scott, 58, 217n.97
heteronormativity, 5, 23–24, 113, 115–16,
147, 150–51
heterosexuality, 19–20, 21–22, 23–24, 25, 43, 51,
53, 57–58, 89, 106–7, 141–42
Hitler, Adolf, 30
Hocquenghem, Guy, 142, 153
Holmes, Oliver Wendell, 18–19, 22–23, 167,
193n.88
homosexuality, 23–24, 32, 50–51, 53, 58, 119–
20, 141–43, 151–52, 194–95n.112
See also queerness
Horne, Philip, 42
Horsman, Reginald, 24, 104–5
Hwang, David Henry, 173

246 INDEX

immigrants
  Asian, 15–17, 103, 129–30, 163–64, 165, 169–70, 179
  assimilation of, 130–31, 134, 142
  Chinese, 163, 165
  James, H., on, 131–32, 147, 148–49, 160
  Jewish, 106, 116, 131–32, 135, 142, 160, 216n.72
  native-born white Americans and, 13, 125–26
  new immigrants (southern and eastern European immigrants), 4, 16–17, 103, 105, 107, 124, 125–26, 129, 159
  old-stock Americans and, 16–17, 46
  social body and, 148–49, 159
immigration
  Anglo-Saxonism and, 45–46
  eugenics and, 17–18
  Progressive Era, 15–16, 134–35
  race suicide and, 13, 15–17, 18, 129, 131, 138, 156
  restrictions, biologization of social body and, 13
Immigration Act of 1917, 17, 159
Immigration Act of 1924, 16–17, 159
impersonality, 166–67, 168, 169–71, 172–73, 221–22n.62
  Asiatic, 166–67, 168, 169–70, 172–74, 175, 176–78, 179–80
Indian Citizenship Act of 1924, 124
Ingalls, John J., 42
interspecies kinship, 102–3, 118–19, 120–21, 124–25
inversion theory, 151–52
involution, 125–27

James, Alice, 50–51
James, Henry
  The American Scene by, 129
  Civil War and, 53–56, 57
  on immigrants, 131–32, 147, 148–49, 160
  neurasthenia of, 49–50, 54
  Notes of a Son and Brother by, 54
  obscure hurt of, 56–57
  The Princess Casamassima by, 64–67
  Roosevelt on, 41–42, 43–45, 46–47, 99
  social body and, 56–57, 148–49
  See also Bostonians, The (James, H.)
James, William, 49–50, 136
Japanese Constitution, Article Nine of, 172
Jefferson, Thomas, 92–93
Jewishness, 131–32, 133–34, 141–42, 143–44, 150–54, 213n.36, 215n.68
  Jewish familialism, 137, 141, 215n.61

Jewish immigrants, 106, 116, 131–32, 135, 142, 160, 216n.72
  See also antisemitism
Jim Crow, 5–6, 70–71
John Barleycorn (London), 103
Johnson-Reed Act of 1924, 5–6, 124
June, Jennie, 23

Kahan, Benjamin, 15, 51, 63–64
Kant, Immanuel, 82–83
Kantorowicz, Ernst, 11
Katz, Jonathan Ned, 21–22
Katz, Leon, 132–33, 136, 138–39
Kempton-Wace Letters, The (London and Strunsky), 116–19, 120
Kent, Kathryn R., 149
Kermode, Frank, 161
kinship, 111
  interspecies, 102–3, 118–19, 120–21, 124–25
  totemic, 102–3, 112, 113, 114, 115, 120–21, 124–25
Kipling, Rudyard, 109
Krafft-Ebing, Richard von, 28–29
Kristeva, Julia, 131
Kroebe, Alfred, 122–23

laissez-faire economics and ethos, 72–73, 75–79, 82–83
Lanser, Susan, 142–43
Laughlin, Harry H., 17
Lazarus, Emma, 179
Lebrun, Robert, 74
Lemke, Thomas, 9–10
lesbianism, 50–51, 53, 58, 140–41, 200n.56
liberal erotic economy, 72–73, 82
liberal governmentality, 9–10, 11, 33–34, 72–73, 74–77
liberalism, 72–73, 81–83
liberal subject and liberal subjectivity, 34, 38–39, 73–74, 77–78, 82, 86, 91–92, 96–97, 161–62, 164
life instinct, 28
Lincoln, Abraham, 54
Locke, John, 74
Lodge, Henry Cabot, 44, 45–46
Lombroso, Cesare, 65
London, Jack, 39–40, 207n.2
  Alaska and, 108–11
  on Alaska Natives, 114–16, 119, 122, 123–25
  Burroughs and, 99–100
  The Call of the Wild by, 99–100, 118, 125
  Chaney and, 107–9, 114–15, 124–25
  A Daughter of the Snows by, 109–10, 112

on evolution, 125
on interspecies kinship, 102–3, 118–19, 120,
    121, 124–25
John Barleycorn by, 103
The Kempton-Wace Letters by Strunsky and,
    116–19, 120
on kinship in Alaska, 111
Martin Eden by, 98–99, 102–3, 109, 125–28
on nonhuman animals, 100, 102–3, 120–
    22, 124–25
on old-stock Americans, 103–4, 109–10
"The Other Animals" by, 100
on race, 102–4, 117–18, 124–25
Roosevelt and, 98, 99–100, 102–3, 125
The Sea-Wolf by, 106–7, 110
The Son of the Wolf by, 112–13
Teutonism and, 103, 112, 114–15, 117, 118–
    19, 122, 123–28
Long, John Luther, 173, 174–76, 178
Loti, Pierre, 173–74, 175
Love, Heather, 7, 33–34
Lowell, Percival, 167–68
Lukács, Georg, 33–34
Lundblad, Michael, 119–20
Lydston, G. Frank, 25–26, 130
Lye, Colleen, 162–63
lynching, 21, 94–95, 96

Madame Butterfly, fictional character and
    narratives of, 173–80
Madden, Bessie, 116
Making of Americans, The (Stein, G.)
    on Anglo-Saxons, 137, 141
    on assimilation, 133–34, 142–43, 147
    on biopolitical state, 132
    coprophilic aesthetics of, 133–34, 147–48
    denaturalization of procreative familialism
        and, 140
    on excretion and excrement, 133–34, 148,
        150–51, 158, 159
    fantasy of anal pregnancy and, 147
    on immigrants and immigration, 131–33, 134
    on Jewishness, 134, 141–42, 143–44
    populational imaginary and, 132, 144–
        45, 154
    queerness and homosexuality in, 136, 141–
        43, 147
    on race, 141
    on race, gender, and sexuality, 145, 146
    race suicide and, 133–34, 156–57, 158
    suicide in, 158
Marsh, Ian, 26–28
Marshall, Alfred, 89–90

Martin Eden (London), 98–99, 102–3,
    109, 125–28
maternalism, 86–88
Mbembe, Achille, 12, 191n.59, 192n.69
McCallum, E. L., 145–46
McWhorter, Ladelle, 21
Mendelian genetics, 15, 17, 18–20, 174–75
Michaels, Walter Benn, 34, 87, 89, 124
Miller, D. A., 33–34, 73–75, 77–78, 82
miscegenation, 20–21, 22, 89, 193n.94
Mitchell, Silas Weir, 49–50
modernism, 33–34, 87, 166–67
"Modern Jew Who Has Given up the Faith
    of His Fathers Can Reasonably and
    Consistently Believe in Isolation, The"
    (Stein, G.), 136–37
Morel, B. A., 22–23, 65
Morrison, Toni, 70
mugwumps, 41, 42, 43, 44–45
Muñoz, José Esteban, 1, 29
Murphy, Kevin, 42

Native Americans
    of Alaska, 112, 113–16, 119, 122, 123–25
    assimilationist policies and violence toward,
        102–3, 122–24, 126–27
    genocide of, 122–23, 126–27, 211n.116
    Indian Citizenship Act and, 124
    Progressive Era politics and, 115–
        16, 122–23
native-born white Americans, 3–4, 46, 107–9,
    117–18, 124, 129–30, 212n.129
    immigrants and, 13, 125–26
    Teutonism and, 106, 107, 125–26
    See also Anglo-Saxons; old-stock Americans
nativism, 4–5, 11, 103–4, 131, 163
naturalism, 33–35, 77–78, 144–45
Nazism, 30
necropolitics, 5–6, 12, 92–93, 111, 191n.59,
    192n.69
neurasthenia, 25–26, 47, 51–52, 54, 58, 64–65,
    106–8, 110–11, 114–15, 124–25
new immigrants, 4, 16–17, 103, 105, 107, 124,
    125–26, 129, 159
New Woman, the, 64, 72–73, 85, 92–93, 95
Ngai, Sianne, 177–78
Nietzsche, Friedrich, 56, 126–28
Nitobe Inazo, 170–71
nonhuman animals, 100, 102–3, 120–
    22, 124–25
Nordau, Max, 1, 65, 141–42
Norman Conquest, 104–5
Notes of a Son and Brother (James, H.), 54

248 INDEX

Okakura Kakuzo, 171
old-stock Americans, 4–5
    atavism and, 107
    The Bostonians on, 45–46
    immigrants and, 16–17, 46, 129–30, 131
    London and, 103–4, 109–10
    neurasthenia and, 48–49, 114–15
    race suicide and, 5–6, 13, 16–17, 18, 45–46,
        49, 107, 110–11, 168–69
    Teutonism and, 112, 124–25
    See also Anglo-Saxons; native-born white
        Americans
Orientalism, 166–71, 176
"Other Animals, The" (London), 100

Page Act of 1875, 5–6, 15–16, 163, 179–80,
    193n.94
"Pair of Silk Stockings, A" (Chopin), 85–86
Park, Josephine Nock-Hee, 166–67
"Paul's Case" (Cather), 1–2, 5
Peabody Loring, Katherine, 50
Person, Leland, 57–58
personhood, 34, 86, 156–57, 165–66, 168, 172–
    73, 174, 175–76, 177–78
Pick, Daniel, 65, 66
Pickford, Mary, 176, 222n.84
Pierce, Joseph M., 122–23
pleasure principle, 28
Plecker, Walter, 20–21
Plessy, Homer Adolph, 70–71, 115–16
Plessy v. Ferguson (1896), 19–20, 70–72, 81,
    94–95, 202n.10
Pratt, Richard Henry, 122–23, 211n.116
Prichard, James Cowles, 26–27
Princess Casamassima, The (James, H.), 64–67
procreative family and procreative familialism,
    115, 118–19, 120, 140
Progressive Era, 2, 3–5, 6–8, 11, 33
    anti-miscegenation legislation in, 20–21
    assimilationist policies, 102–3, 122–23
    citizenship and personhood, 166
    Creoles in, 79
    degeneration theory in, 22–23
    female reformers, 58
    heterosexual reproduction and racial
        reproduction in, 141
    immigration, 15–16, 134–35
    motherhood in, 86–87
    Native American politics, 115–16, 122–23
    nativism, 4–5, 11
    racial politics, 69–70, 102
    sex and gender in political landscape, 42
    state power and administrative state in, 75
    whiteness in, 24, 69–70, 80

psychiatry, 26–28
psychoanalysis, 27–28, 150–54
Pucccini, Giacomo, 173

Q.E.D (Stein, G.), 136–37
queerness, 136–37, 141, 147
    See also homosexuality

race, 79
    Asiatic, 163–64, 165–66, 168–69
    biologized, 6, 21, 22, 23–24
    gender and, 49, 145, 146
    genetic model of, 19–20
    heredity and, 107, 110–11, 113, 115
    heterosexuality and, 19–20, 21–22, 141
    Jewish, 136–37, 151–52
    London on, 102–4, 117–18, 124–25
    motherhood and, 86–87, 91–92
    of new immigrants, 130
    property and, 71–73, 87–88, 91, 94–95, 115–
        16, 117–18
    race suicide and, 5–6, 13–14, 26–27, 161–62
    reproduction and, 19–22, 70–73, 86–87, 91,
        113, 117–18, 141
    sexuality and, 6–7, 10–11, 19–24, 27, 28–29,
        145, 146, 194–95n.112
    totemic kinship and, 115
    white, 3–5, 13, 22–23, 39, 86–87, 110–11,
        118–19, 123–24
race suicide, 11, 33
    Anglo-Saxons and, 46–47, 131
    Asian exclusion and, 15–16
    Asiatic, 168–69
    The Awakening and, 69–70
    biopolitics and, 5–7, 13, 31
    biopower and, 5–7
    death drive and, 6–7, 27, 29–30
    eugenics and, 15
    heredity and, 26–27
    homosexuality and, 23
    immigration and, 13, 15–17, 18
    Japanese sensibility and, 172
    Jewish immigrants and, 131
    The Kempton-Wace Letters on, 117
    The Making of Americans and, 133–34, 156–
        57, 158
    the New Woman and, 64
    old-stock Americans and, 5–6, 13, 16–17, 18,
        45–46, 49, 168–69
    race and, 5–6, 13–14, 26–27, 161–62
    reproductive futurism and, 6–7
    Roosevelt on, 3–4, 13–14, 45, 46, 69, 125,
        189n.20, 193n.85
    Ross on, 4–5, 163–64, 168–69

sexuality and, 22, 27
social body and, 7–8, 11, 25–26, 27, 29, 31, 159–60
suicides in literature and, 5
Teutonism and, 106–7, 131
whiteness and, 4–5, 13–14, 49
racialization, 27–28, 35–36, 115–16, 164–66
racism, 111
scientific, 19–20, 105–6, 141–42, 221n.31
state, 14–15, 30
See also anti-Asian racism and violence; anti-Black racism and violence; antisemitism
Reconstruction, 20, 44–45, 46–47, 52–53
Redding, Josephine, 85, 87–89
replacement theory, 39, 159–60, 164, 197n.167
See also Great Replacement, the
reproduction
Asian immigrants and, 169–70
biopolitics and, 19, 117–18
etymology of, 19
excretion and, 149
heterosexual, 141
race and, 19–22, 70–73, 86–87, 91, 113, 117–18, 141
social body and, 18–19, 29
totemic kinship and, 113–14
reproductive futurism, 6–7, 29
Revolutionary Era, 92–94
Rifkin, Mark, 115
Riis, Jacob, 130, 134
Rikyu, Sen no, 171
Ripley, William Z., 16–17, 105–6, 107
Roediger, David R., 130
Roosevelt, Theodore, 49, 50–51, 193n.85
on American West, 49, 108–9
on Anglo-Saxons as "English speaking race," 80
Boone and Crockett Club of, 100–1, 111, 190n.24
as hunter, 100–2
on James, H., 41–42, 43–45, 46–47, 99
London and, 98, 99–100, 102–3, 125
on Nitobe, 170–71
on nonhuman animals, 100, 102
on race suicide, 3–4, 13–14, 45, 46, 69, 125, 189n.20, 193n.85
Ross, Edward A., 4–5, 15–16, 31, 163–64, 168–69, 219n.14
Ruddick, Lisa, 148

Santa Clara County v. Southern Pacific Railroad (1886), 166
Santner, Eric, 11–12
Saum Song Bo, 179

Schmidt, Christopher, 148
Schneider, David, 113
Schopenhauer, Arthur, 98–99
Schuller, Kyla, 10–11, 15
Schuster, David, 48–49
scientific racism, 19–20, 105–6, 141–42, 221n.31
Sea-Wolf, The (London), 106–7, 110
securitization, 8–10, 11–12, 14–15, 18, 40, 192n.69
Sedgwick, Eve Kosofsky, 39, 57, 146
Seitler, Dana, 35, 107
Seltzer, Mark, 34, 89, 144–45
seppuku, 170–71, 221n.50
settler colonialism, 112–13, 122–23
sexuality
anti-Black violence and, 94–95
biopolitics and, 11, 28–29
colonialism and, 10–11
death and, 27, 32, 33, 172–73
death instinct and, 28–29
Foucault on, 10–11, 32, 194–95n.112
heterosexuality, 19–20, 21–22, 23–24, 25, 43, 51, 53, 57–58, 89, 106–7, 141–42
homosexuality, 23–24, 32, 50–51, 53, 58, 119–20, 141–43, 151–52, 194–95n.112
neurasthenia and, 51–52, 107–8
of population, 18
queerness, 136–37, 141, 147
race and, 6–7, 10–11, 19–24, 27, 28–29, 145, 146, 194–95n.112
reality principle and, 28
reproduction and, 10–11
suicide and, 33
whiteness and, 94–95
Shah, Nayan, 163
Sheridan, Phillip, 126–27
Silber, Nina, 53
Simmel, Georg, 82–83
slavery, 20, 70–73, 81–82, 164–65
suicide and, 72–73, 92–94, 95, 96–97, 206n.91
Smith, Adam, 75
social body
animating and anthropomorphizing, 7–8, 18
assimilation and, 130–31
biologization of, immigration restrictions and, 13
biopolitics and, 11–12, 15, 31–32, 161–62
biopower and, 7–8, 11–12, 29–30
body politic and, 7–8, 11–12
Civil War and, 56
degeneration theory and, 25–26, 66–67
Foucault on, 117

250 INDEX

social body (*cont.*)
  heterosexuality and, 51, 53, 57–58
  immigrants and, 130–31, 148–49, 159
  individual body and, 25, 32, 48–49, 56, 57
  James, H., and, 56–57, 148–49
  The Making of Americans on, 148
  neurasthenia and, 48–49
  race and, 6
  race suicide and, 7–8, 11, 25–26, 27, 29,
    31, 159–60
  reproduction and, 18–19, 29
  sterilization and, 18–19
  suicide and, 6–7, 25–26, 29, 97
  white, 22, 29, 69
  wounded, *The Bostonians* on, 51
Solomon, Barbara, 46
Solomons, Leon, 144, 158
Son of the Wolf, The (London), 112–13
Sontag, Susan, 171
Spanish-American War, 80, 108–9
Spencer, Herbert, 126
Spillers, Hortense, 95–96
Spiro, Jonathan, 105–6, 111
state racism, 14–15, 30
Stein, Gertrude
  on assimilation, 133–34, 136–37
  on excretion and excrement, 149–51
  Freud and, 150–52, 153–54
  on Jewish familialism, 137, 141, 215n.61
  Jewishness and, 131–32, 133–34, 141, 143–
    44, 150–51, 213n.36
  "Modern Jew Who Has Given up the Faith
    of His Fathers Can Reasonably and
    Consistently Believe in Isolation, The" by,
    136–37
  Q.E.D by, 136–37
  queerness of, 136–37
  Tender Buttons by, 149
  Toklas and, 140–41, 143–44, 149–50, 154,
    158–59, 213n.36
  See also Making of Americans, The (Stein, G.)
Stein, Melissa, 21, 23, 194–95n.112
Steinlight, Emily, 33–34
sterilization, 18–19, 22, 193n.85
Stevens, Hugh, 51
stigmata, 56, 57–58
Stockton, Will, 147
Stoddard, Lothrop, 17, 80–81
Stoler, Ann, 10–11
Strahan, S. A. K., 26–27
Strunsky, Anna, 116–19, 120
suicide
  autoimmunity and, 30–32

  in *The Awakwning*, 69, 91–92
  biopolitics of, 6–8, 25
  biopower and, 2–3, 6–7, 32
  as counter-conduct, 32–33
  degeneracy and, 26–27
  freedom and, 94
  heredity and, 25–27
  involution and, 125–26
  in literature, 2, 3–4, 5, 7, 35
  of Madame Butterfly (fictional character),
    175–76, 178
  in *The Making of Americans,* 158
  in *Martin Eden,* 98–99, 102–3, 125–26, 128
  in *The Princess Casamassima,* 67–68
  in Progressive Era, 2, 3–5
  in Progressive Era literature, 34–35, 39–
    40, 92–93
  seppuku, 170–71, 221n.50
  sexuality and, 33
  slavery and, 72–73, 92–94, 95, 96–97,
    206n.91
  social body and, 6–7, 25–26, 29, 97
  See also race suicide

Taylor, Melanie, 146–47
Tender Buttons (Stein, G.), 149
Teutonism, 129–30, 134
  American, 124
  Anglo-Saxons and, 103–5, 108–9, 110–
    11, 124–25
  London and, 103, 112, 114–15, 117, 118–19,
    122, 123–28
  native-born white Americans and, 106,
    107, 125–26
  old-stock Americans and, 112, 124–25
  race suicide and, 106–7, 131
  whiteness and, 103, 122, 124–26
third-sex reformers, 42, 45, 46–47, 49, 51, 64, 67
Toklas, Alice B., 139, 140–41, 143–44, 149–50,
  154, 158–59, 213n.36
Tompkins, Kyla Wazana, 97
totemic kinship, 102–3, 112, 113, 114, 115, 120–
  21, 124–25
Tourgée, Albion, 71
Tregle, Joseph G., 79–80, 203n.40
Tuhkanen, Mikko, 83–84
Turner, Frederick Jackson, 108–9, 111–12, 149

Van Gennep, Arnold, 114
Varga, Donna, 101–2
Veblen, Thorstein, 86–87
Virginia's Racial Integrity Act of 1924, 20–21
Vogue, 72–73, 85–89, 90

INDEX 251

Wald, Priscilla, 134–35
Walker, Francis Amasa, 4
Ward, Robert DeCourcey, 18
Warren, Samuel D., 74
Weinbaum, Alys Eve, 19–20, 70–72, 81
Wendell, Barrett, 46
white blood, 71–72, 80–81
White Fang (London), 99–100
white men, 80–81, 179–80
whiteness
    The Awakening on, 69–70, 79, 81–82
    of Creoles, 79–82
    degeneration and, 22–23, 67
    heteronormativity and, 113, 115–16
    heterosexuality and, 24, 25
    in *Martin Eden,* 98–99
    miscegenation, anti-miscegenation laws and,
      20–21
    nation and, 13, 14–15
    native-born white Americans, 3–4, 13, 46,
      106, 107–9, 117–18, 124, 125–26, 129–30,
      212n.129
    in Progressive Era, 24, 69–70, 80
    as property, 71–73, 81–82, 86–87, 94–95
    race suicide and, 4–5, 13–14, 49
    racial categories of, 24–25

    sexuality and, 94–95
    of social body, 22, 29, 69
    totemic kinship and, 113
    whiteness studies, 25
    See also Anglo-Saxons; old-stock Americans;
      Teutonism
white supremacy and white supremacist
    violence, 4–6, 21, 39, 94–95, 103–
    4, 159–60
white women
    bodies of, 71–72
    motherhood and, 86–87
    performances as Madame
      Butterfly, 176–80
Wilderson, Frank, III, 164–65
Will, Barbara, 144
will to life, 98–99
Wilson, Sarah, 134
Wilson, Woodrow, 212n.129
Woloch, Alex, 132
Women and Economics (Gilman, C. P.), 86–87
wounded attachments, 56

Yeazell, Ruth Bernard, 49–50

Zangwill, Israel, 129–30, 136–37, 147